4 March 2021

To Robert
Happy Birthday!
Davide x

A Renaissance Marriage

A Renaissance Marriage

The Political and Personal Alliance of
Isabella d'Este and Francesco Gonzaga,
1490–1519

CAROLYN JAMES

OXFORD
UNIVERSITY PRESS

OXFORD

UNIVERSITY PRESS

Great Clarendon Street, Oxford, OX2 6DP,
United Kingdom

Oxford University Press is a department of the University of Oxford.
It furthers the University's objective of excellence in research, scholarship,
and education by publishing worldwide. Oxford is a registered trade mark of
Oxford University Press in the UK and in certain other countries

First Edition published in 2020

Impression: 1

Published in the United States of America by Oxford University Press
198 Madison Avenue, New York, NY 10016, United States of America

British Library Cataloguing in Publication Data

Data available

Library of Congress Control Number: 2019945421

ISBN 978–0–19–968121–1

DOI: 10.1093/oso/9780199681211.001.0001

Printed and bound by
CPI Group (UK) Ltd, Croydon, CR0 4YY

Acknowledgements

The research on which this book is based was begun during a year-long fellowship in 2001–2 at Villa I Tatti, the Harvard University Centre for Italian Renaissance Studies in Florence, then under the directorship of the late Walter Kaiser. A number of fellows became firm friends, especially Deanna Shemek, who was embarking on her own studies of Isabella d'Este that academic year, and whose marvellous English translations of a large selection of Isabella's letters, published in 2016, I have used extensively here. The library at I Tatti was a crucial resource and I wish to acknowledge the help of Michael Rocke, Kathy Bosi, and Ilaria della Monica. The fellowship permitted me to make frequent trips to the Archivio di Stato in Mantua, where I received unfailingly courteous and unstinting help from the former director, Daniela Ferrari, and her staff, including the current director, Luisa Onesta Tamassia. I also worked at the Archivio di Stato in Modena and Milan. I encountered friendly and very helpful archivists in both places. I have returned to these archives many times and to the Biblioteca Nazionale in Florence, helped by the award of an Australian Research Council Discovery Grant (2006–9), which permitted me to continue to gather new material and to develop what had become a very large project. The Cassamarca Foundation of Treviso also contributed to the completion of this book through its financial support of my appointment at Monash University. When I was not able to travel to Italy, the Louis Matheson Library at Monash University, especially its interlibrary loan department, has been central to my ability to gain access to secondary sources not held in Australia. Claudia de Salvo was indefatigable in tracking down books and articles that I needed.

I am most fortunate in having scholarly colleagues such as Molly Bourne, who shared her research on Francesco Gonzaga, and Deanna Shemek, whose knowledge of Isabella d'Este's life is formidable indeed. Both scholars read this book in draft and offered helpful suggestions for its improvement. I am grateful, too, to Sarah Cockram, whose monograph, *Isabella d'Este and Francesco Gonzaga: Power Sharing at the Italian Renaissance Court* (2013), has many themes in common with mine. Deanna Shemek, along with Anne MacNeil and Daniela Ferrari, direct the digital platform IDEA, Isabella d'Este's Archive, which makes available images of all the letters preserved in Isabella's *copialettere*, and explores her music-making and art patronage. See http://isabelladeste.web.unc.edu. This resource was still in development while I was researching the present book, but its riches will facilitate many new studies by other scholars.

I wish also to acknowledge the help of colleagues in Australia such as Barbara Caine, Clare Monagle, David Garrioch, Pauline Nestor, Diana Barnes, Constant Mews, and Kathleen Neal, with whom I collaborated on an Australian Research Council Discovery Grant, which investigated the history of women's letter-writing practices from the late medieval period to the twentieth century. That project has informed the present monograph from a methodological perspective. Adam Clulow read the entire manuscript of the book in draft and offered many valuable suggestions. Jessica O'Leary helped me with research assistance and has been a wonderful collaborator throughout her graduate studies at Monash University. Annamaria and Antonio Pagliaro provided advice about how to translate into English some of the more difficult passages in the letters of Francesco and Isabella and I am grateful for the friendship they have offered over many years, especially in the dark days of my husband Bill Kent's illness and premature death, when work on this book had to be largely set aside. Other scholars such as Alison Brown, Nerida Newbigin, Camilla Russell, and Glenda Sluga have all assisted my research in various ways.

My children James and Antonia Kent and my stepdaughter Margaret Kent have been important sources of support and I thank them for their forbearance in tolerating the many years of work that this book has entailed. I dedicate the book to them.

Contents

Illustrations   ix
Abbreviations   xi
Family Tree of the Este and Gonzaga Families   xvi

Introduction   1

1. Betrothal   11

2. Building a Spousal Relationship   27

3. The Crafting of Identity and the Division of Political Labour   52

4. Parallel Aspirations: First Fruits   73

5. Risk-Taking and Risk Management   92

6. Parenthood and Politics   113

7. Years of Crisis   134

8. A Mind of Her Own   159

Conclusion   185

Bibliography   189
Index   199

Illustrations

1. Francesco Gonzaga to Isabella d'Este, 11 March 1513, from Mantua, ASMn, AG, 2120, c. 36.   xiii

2. Isabella d'Este to Francesco Gonzaga, 13 March 1513, from Piacenza, ASMn, AG, 2120, cc. 116r–v.   xiv

Abbreviations

ASMo   Archivio di Stato, Modena
ASMn   Archivio di Stato, Mantua
AG   Archivio Gonzaga
b.   busta (box)
c.   carta (folio)

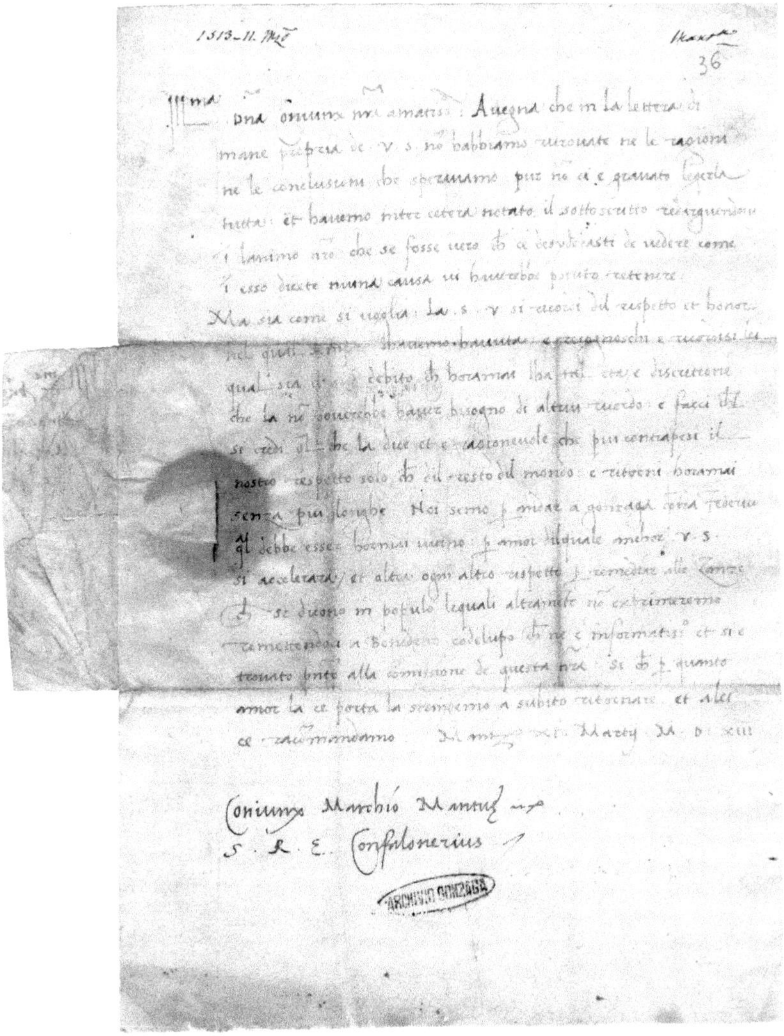

Figure 1. Francesco Gonzaga to Isabella d'Este, 11 March 1513, from Mantua, ASMn, AG, 2120, c. 36.

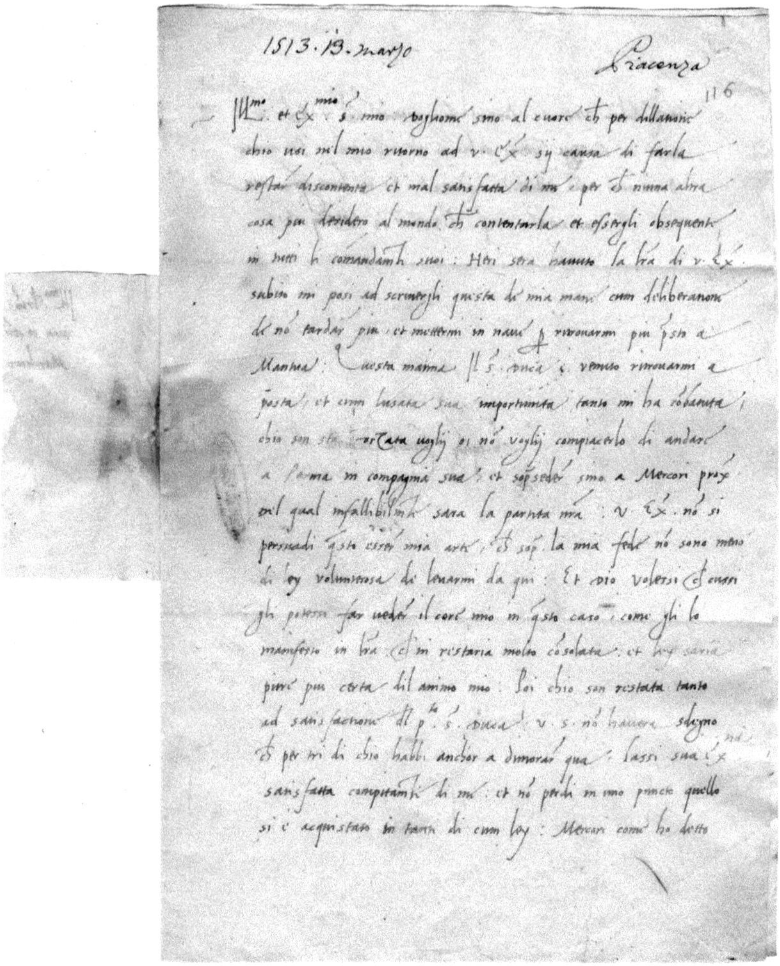

Figure 2. Isabella d'Este to Francesco Gonzaga, 13 March 1513, from Piacenza, ASMn, AG, 2120, cc. 116r–v.

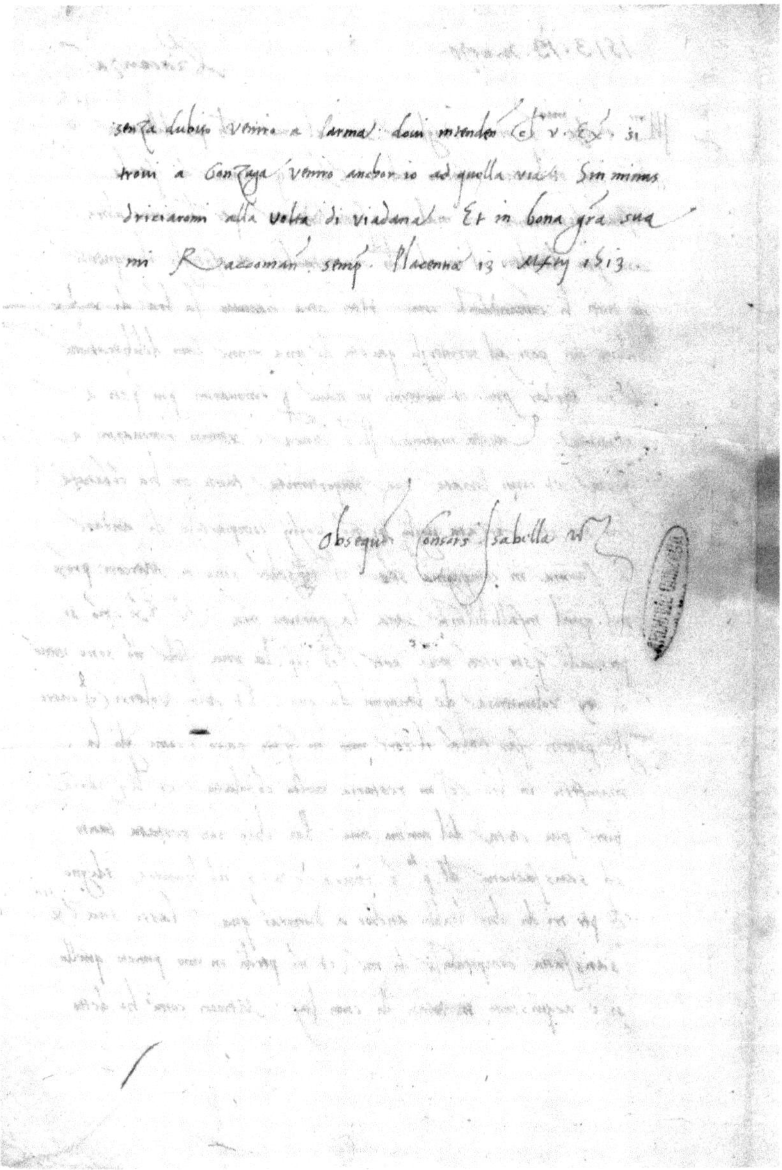

senza dubio venire a Parma dove intendo ... v. S. ... si
troni a Gonzaga venire ancora io ad quella ... Sin minus
drizarem nella volta di viadana. Et in bona gra sua
mi R...acomand semp. Piacenza 13 ...y 1513

obsequ... consors Isabella ...

Figure 2. Continued

Family Tree of the Este and Gonzaga Families

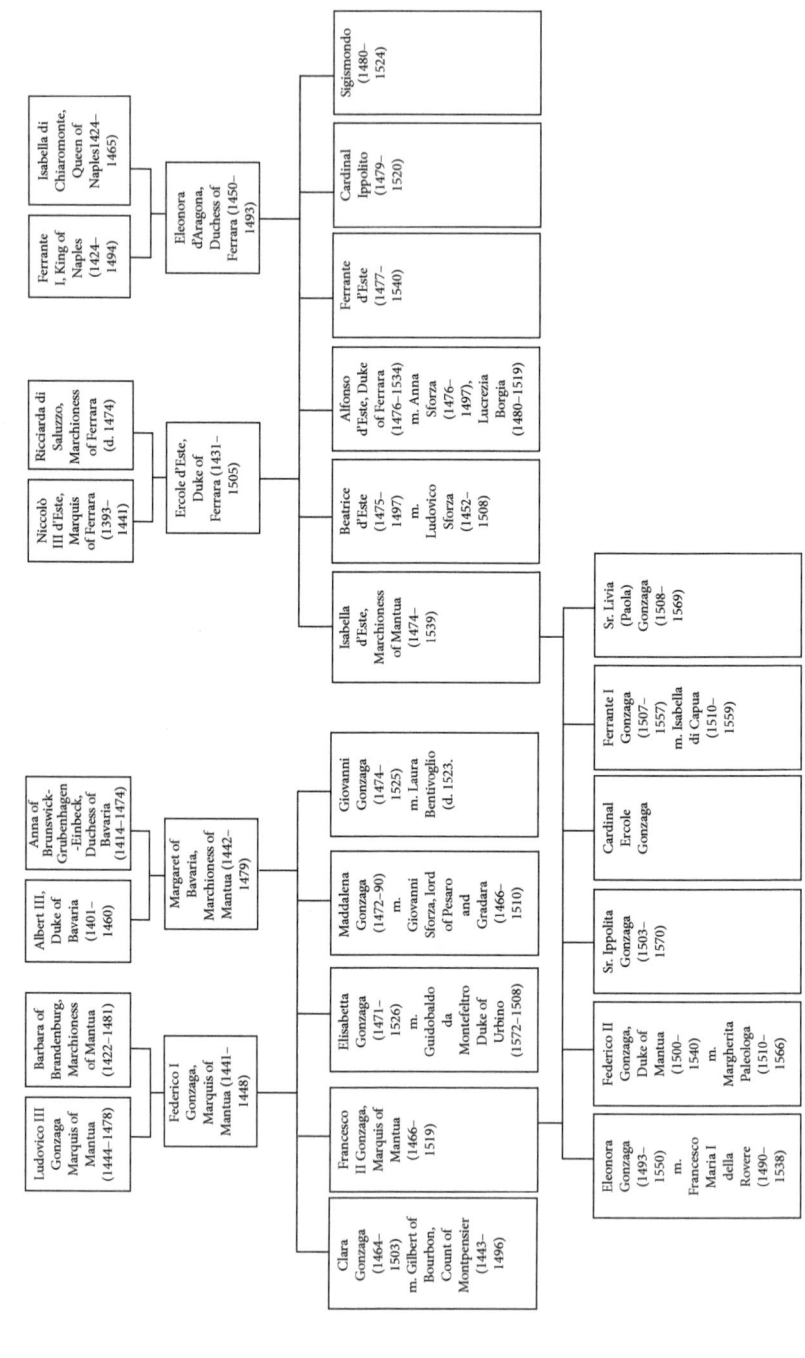

Introduction

In mid-October 1491, the marquis of the northern Italian city state of Mantua, Francesco Gonzaga, wrote from Pesaro to his wife, Isabella d'Este, while he was travelling in the Marches. He thanked her for receiving the Milanese ambassador during his absence and endorsed her intervention in a minor diplomatic dispute in the following terms: 'You have acted most prudently, nor could we have asked for anything better and thus we praise your every action; there is no need to say more about this matter because you have resolved it very well.'[1] The eldest child of the duke and duchess of Ferrara, Isabella was just seventeen when she received this praise and had been married for less than two years, but the message was testament to her husband's confidence that he could begin to leave the supervision of state affairs to her when he was temporarily away from Mantua. In the next two decades, as Francesco's regular sojourns at his country estates and visits to relatives in neighbouring courts were overtaken by periods of military service on near or distant battlefields, Isabella's work as her spouse's deputy became more complex and ever more crucial.

During the second half of the fifteenth century, overseeing the chancery and performing other administrative duties that could be promulgated discreetly within the enclosed space of the court had come to be seen as core duties of a prince's wife in the duchy of Ferrara and the marquisate of Mantua, as well as in other Italian city states ruled by local lords. In the southern kingdom of Naples, queens had long acted as regents. Such work could be defended on the grounds that it was merely an extension of the expectation that a married woman would oversee her husband's household, especially if he was called away from home by important business, urgent political developments, or was obliged to fight in a war. Isabella had been well educated to follow the example of her mother and grandmother, who both acted as regents, in the latter case for six consecutive years, while her husband, King Ferrante d'Aragona, subdued rebellious Neapolitan barons on the battlefield. Eleonora d'Aragona, duchess of Ferrara, regularly supported

---

[1] 'Vi seti governata prudentissimamente, né meglio haveressimo potuto desyderare, cossì vi laudamo de ogni operatione vostra, né diremovi altro circa questa parte, perché vui haveti satisfacto benissimo al bisogno.' Francesco Gonzaga to Isabella d'Este, 24 October 1491, from Pesaro, ASMn, AG, 2107, c. 69. Isabella's letter to her husband reporting on the meeting with the Milanese ambassador was written on 17 October 1491, from Mantua, ASMn, AG, 2107, c. 123. All translations are my own, unless otherwise indicated. I have provided the original Italian of quotes only when the source has not been published, or translated into English, by other scholars.

A Renaissance Marriage: The Political and Personal Alliance of Isabella d'Este and Francesco Gonzaga, 1490–1519.
Carolyn James, Oxford University Press (2020). © Carolyn James.
DOI: 10.1093/oso/9780199681211.001.0001

her spouse's regime by representing Ercole d'Este in day-to-day government and by mediating diplomatic relations between Ferrara and the kingdom of Naples, tasks for which she was carefully prepared during her girlhood. As a child, Francesco had witnessed the prominent political role of his German-born grandmother, Barbara of Brandenburg, and it is unsurprising that he embraced the opportunity for his own wife to serve as his political deputy in the same way that Barbara had helped Lodovico Gonzaga, the second marquis of Mantua.

Within the first decade of their marriage, which took place in early 1490, Francesco and Isabella went beyond the precedents established by their kin in previous generations. The catalyst for their more thorough-going and visible political collaboration was the challenges associated with the Italian Wars, which began in 1494, with the descent into the peninsula of the young king of France, Charles VIII, at the head of a large army. The Wars continued, with the involvement of a galaxy of other European protagonists, for the couple's entire marriage, lasting, indeed, until 1559, forty years after Francesco Gonzaga's death. Charles VIII's aim was to wrest the kingdom of Naples from its Aragonese rulers, to whom Isabella was related through her mother. The astonishing ease with which the king accomplished his mission profoundly shocked the Italian powers, while the formidable weaponry that the French army carried over the Alps and the utter ruthlessness of its battle-hardened mercenaries thoroughly intimidated the peninsula's inhabitants and whisked away the illusion that Italy's city states could remain in charge of their own destiny.

Although Charles VIII failed to maintain a hold over his conquest, the invasion marked only the beginning of successive attempts by the French crown to expand its territorial horizons by waging war on Italian soil. The ambitions of Louis XII and François I lay particularly in the north of Italy. The wealthy city state of Milan was an enticing prospective spoil, while the republic of Genoa, riven by political factions and so close to French territory, was an equally tantalizing quarry that had been long contested by the rulers of Milan and France. Mantua lay sandwiched between the duchy of Milan and its arch-rival, the republic of Venice. The two large states often took opposite sides in the conflicts associated with the Italian Wars and the frequent presence of large armies in the vicinity of Mantuan borders after the mid-1490s represented a serious threat to the stability and longevity of the Gonzaga regime.

Apart from the threats that came from foreign powers, opportunistic local players, such as the son of Pope Alexander VI, Cesare Borgia, were also a source of worry. In the first years of the sixteenth century Borgia, or Valentino as he was known in Italy, attempted to carve out a state for himself in central and northern Italy through military conquest. Francesco Gonzaga's sister Elisabetta and her husband, Guidobaldo da Montefeltro, duke of Urbino, were among a number of Gonzaga relatives driven into exile by Borgia. They, and the others who were turfed out of power by the pope's ambitious and notoriously violent son, remained adrift until the political fortunes of their enemy faded with the death of Alexander VI in 1503. The next papal incumbent, Julius II, proved just as problematic for lordly and oligarchical regimes which were technically papal feudatories, but had accumulated de facto autonomy in the late medieval centuries. As part of his campaign to reassert papal control over the Church's territorial possessions, Julius II ousted the Bentivoglio rulers of Bologna in 1506, and did so with the help of a reluctant Francesco Gonzaga, who, as the papal standard bearer, was obliged to collaborate with the pope in driving his own relatives into exile. Although Mantua was an imperial, rather than a papal feudatory, the fall of the Bentivoglio, whose hold on power had seemed so secure, served as an all-too-vivid reminder of what might lie in store for the marquisate.

Against all the odds, the Gonzaga hold over Mantua endured. In the first phase of the Italian Wars this survival was in large part due to nimble and coordinated diplomacy by Isabella and Francesco, who resorted to stalling for time and cultivating both allies and opponents to evade political dangers. In extreme circumstances, the marquis was prepared to argue that his wife pursued her own political goals, without his consent, if such a tactic was expedient. But, as we will see, that strategy proved to be something of a double-edged sword for Francesco. While it allowed him to deflect blame onto Isabella for his own lack of fidelity to allies, the excuse that he had no control over his spouse's diplomatic interventions damaged his reputation by undermining the projection of untrammelled husbandly and princely authority that were central aspects of his image-making as a potent and proud ruler.

Francesco's virile interpretation of masculinity was also fatally eroded by illness. In the last decade of his life, the marquis could no longer fight. He remained largely bedridden, within his urban palace of San Sebastiano, where he had moved in 1508 to secure greater privacy, after contracting the Great Pox. By 1513, it was no longer Isabella who acted as Francesco's deputy, but his personal secretary Tolomeo Spagnoli. Upset by her political eclipse and with few occasions for direct communication with her husband, Isabella decided to make use of the political expertise she had accumulated by spending Carnival 1513 in Milan, where she hoped to offer guidance to her young and inexperienced nephew, Massimiliano Sforza, the newly appointed duke of Milan. She also wanted to lobby the imperial and Spanish leaders of the anti-French coalition, known as the Holy League—who were at the Milanese court overseeing the transition from French rule to a restored Sforza regime after the defeat of Louis XII's forces—on behalf of her brother, the duke of Ferrara, who risked a papal takeover of his state.

Isabella's protracted absence from Mantua in the early months of 1513, and news of her high-profile diplomacy on behalf of natal relatives, tried Francesco's tolerance to breaking point. He wrote coldly to his wife on 11 March, accusing Isabella of having forgotten her marital duty and of tarnishing her reputation at

an age when she ought to have learned how to behave appropriately (Fig. 1).[2]
Deeply offended, Isabella replied to Francesco's letter, not with the acquiescence
he demanded, but with a forceful critique of their relationship:

> And do not think that even if you loved me as much as any person has ever loved
> another you could ever repay my loyalty. This is why Your Highness sometimes
> says that I am haughty, because knowing how much you owe me for this, and
> seeing that I am badly repaid, I sometimes change complexion and seem to be in
> effect what I am not.[3]

At almost forty, Isabella took the view that, having proved herself always loyal and
diligent in serving her husband's regime, she should not be ordered home as if she
were a recalcitrant child.

The angry epistolary exchanges between Francesco and Isabella in the late winter
of 1513 are in stark contrast to their amiable communications of October 1491.
The two sets of letters are indicative of the trajectory of the couple's relations, as
they evolved over time. While the union was in many ways a successful one, the
couple's voluminous correspondence reveals that their relationship was complicated and often volatile. As the following chapters will reveal, in the first years of
marriage, Isabella and Francesco found it hard to bond. Eventually, they established a satisfactory degree of mutual understanding and, perhaps, even personal
happiness, thanks to shared recreational interests and the pleasures of parenthood.
A burgeoning political collaboration also served to unite them more firmly before
the severe diplomatic quandaries and political crises they faced began to eat away
at the trust and cooperation they had so patiently built. A deterioration in their
rapport is heralded in correspondence of 1506, but their cross mutual reproaches
of March 1513 marked the lowest point in their marriage. Afterwards, there was
an uneasy truce punctuated by intermittent squabbles. Thus, in broad outline,
their lives together can be considered a drama in three acts, one that began with
an emotional and even physical stand-off, analysed in Chapters 1 and 2, achieved
gradual convergence, the focus of Chapters 3 to 6, and then unravelled in ways
that are examined briefly in Chapter 6 and at greater length in Chapters 7 and 8.[4]

While this is primarily a study of a political marriage as it was perceived and
negotiated by the couple themselves, it also takes into account how the relationship was viewed from the outside by contemporaries. Isabella and Francesco
exchanged thousands of letters with members of their family, with their personal
secretaries, and with an enormous number of other interlocutors. That evidence,

---

[2] Francesco Gonzaga to Isabella d'Este, 11 March 1513, from Mantua, ASMn, AG, 2120, c. 36.

[3] Isabella d'Este to Francesco Gonzaga, 12 March 1513, from Piacenza, Isabella d'Este, *Selected Letters*, ed. and trans. Deanna Shemek (Toronto: Iter Press, 2017), 361–2.

[4] The couple's political collaboration has been examined in recent years by Sarah D. P. Cockram. See her *Isabella d'Este and Francesco Gonzaga: Power Sharing at the Italian Renaissance Court* (Farnham: Ashgate, 2013).

together with the correspondence they wrote to each other, permits us to glimpse in unusual detail their individual characters and interests, their changing anxieties and hopes, and how they interacted with others in Italy and beyond. Their patronage of the arts, documented in written exchanges with painters, craftsmen, and agents, and in the artworks they commissioned, many of which are still extant, reveals how they wished to present themselves to others through visual and literary means.

The ways in which individuals experienced marriage has been very little examined in the context of premodern Europe. Scholars have focused almost entirely on matrimony as an institution, studying its legal, religious, economic, and social significance, rather than on its emotional and subjective dimensions.[5] It has been assumed until quite recently that evidence about the latter is almost entirely lacking, a conviction that is gradually being overturned as historians discover examples of marital correspondence that have survived within private family archives, or, as in the case of the Este-Gonzaga letters, in the chancery collections of Europe's early modern rulers.[6] In stark contrast to prescriptive sources, letters reveal the instability and incoherence of human behaviour in relation to gendered orthodoxies, under the pressure of external events and individual interpretations of what was appropriate at different stages of life and in particular social contexts.

The portrait of the couple presented in this book bears few similarities with that proposed by the late nineteenth-century archivist and antiquarian scholar, Alessandro Luzio, who characterized Isabella as a 'Machiavelli in skirts' yoked to an insensitive and unworthy husband, who was her inferior in every way.[7] While it is the case that the spouses did have rather dissimilar characters and sensibilities, the notion of a clear cut divide between their capacities and accomplishments is

---

[5] Trevor Dean and Kate J. P. Lowe, eds, *Marriage in Italy, 1300–1650* (Cambridge: Cambridge University Press, 1998); Michela De Giorgio, Christiane Klapisch-Zuber, and Marina Beer, eds, *Storia del matrimonio* (Rome; Bari: Laterza, 1996); Silvana Seidel Menchi, ed, *Marriage in Europe, 1400–1800* (Toronto: Toronto University Press, 2016); Silvana Seidel Menchi and Diego Quaglioni, eds, *Coniugi nemici: la separazione in Italia dal XII al XVIII secolo* (Bologna: Il Mulino, 2000); Silvana Seidel Menchi and Diego Quaglioni, eds, *Matrimoni in dubbio: unioni controverse e nozze clandestine in Italia dal XIV al XVIII secolo* (Bologna: Il Mulino, 2001); Silvana Seidel Menchi and Diego Quaglioni, eds, *Trasgressioni: seduzione, concubinato, adulterio, bigamia (14.–18. secolo)* (Bologna: Il Mulino, 2004); *I Tribunali del matrimonio (secoli XV–XVIII)* (Bologna: Il Mulino, 2006); Joanne Marie Ferraro, *Marriage Wars in Late Renaissance Venice* (Oxford: Oxford University Press, 2001); Thomas Kuehn, *Law, Family, and Women: Toward a Legal Anthropology of Renaissance Italy* (Chicago: University of Chicago Press, 1994); Thomas Kuehn, 'Marriage in the Archives: A Review Essay', *The Sixteenth Century Journal* 39.3 (2008): 731–6; Anthony Molho, *Marriage Alliance in Late Medieval Florence* (Cambridge, Mass.: Harvard University Press, 1994). For a new direction in approaches to Renaissance marriage, see Amyrose McCue Gill, '*Vera Amicizia*: Conjugal Friendship in the Italian Renaissance' (unpublished doctoral dissertation, University of California, Berkeley, 2008).

[6] Carolyn James, 'Marriage by Correspondence: Politics and Domesticity in the Letters of Isabella d'Este and Francesco Gonzaga, 1490–1519', *Renaissance Quarterly* 65.2 (2012): 321–52; Victoria Kirkham, 'Creative Partners: The Marriage of Laura Battiferra and Bartolomeo Ammannati', *Renaissance Quarterly* 55.2 (2002): 498–558; Barbara J. Harris, *English Aristocratic Women, 1450–1550: Marriage and Family, Property and Careers* (Oxford; New York: Oxford University Press, 2002).

[7] Alessandro Luzio, 'La reggenza d'Isabella d'Este durante la prigionia del marito (1509–1510)', *Archivio storico lombardo* 14 (1910): 5–104.

not supported by the record. In many ways, the two were well matched, having been educated to a similarly high standard and having grown up in a cognate cultural and political milieu. And yet their lives were very different. What follows reveals the profound significance of gender in determining the extent to which each individual's youthful aspirations were realized, or impeded, and how biology shaped their youth and then their experience of wedlock. The politically astute and discerning patron of the arts, so familiar to readers of the many popular biographies of Isabella, is certainly recognizable in the present interpretation, but we also glimpse a shy young woman, prone to melancholy, for whom sex and maternity were, at least initially, a huge psychological burden.[8] Isabella's depressive character, which she herself described as 'saturnine', was gradually submerged under the confident persona she cultivated as a mature woman.[9] But there are occasional hints of the hidden emotions of earlier days in confessional asides in her letters, which allow us to grasp the frustrations of womanhood, even in a privileged social context such as hers.

Unlike Isabella, Francesco was largely forgotten after his death, but his significance as an important cultural patron has been highlighted in recent times by Molly Bourne, who has studied the extensive archival material that documents the marquis's building projects and artistic commissions. This evidence shows that Francesco shared with his wife an educated appreciation of contemporary developments in architecture and the visual arts.[10] Although he was certainly as authoritarian and jealous of his lordly honour as any other Renaissance prince, Francesco emerges from the present study, not as Luzio portrayed him, but as a sometimes warm and often generous man, devoted to his children and certainly capable of sensitive thoughtfulness towards his wife.

As a youth, Francesco's imagination was fired by the prospect that he would be able to display his manhood through physical feats on the sports field and, ultimately, on the battlefield, where he would behave chivalrously and bravely. Those

---

[8] There is a very large literature on Isabella d'Este. The best biographies are Julia Cartwright, *Isabella d'Este, Marchioness of Mantua, 1474–1539. A Study of the Renaissance*, 2 vols (London: J. Murray, 1903); Daniela Pizzagalli, *La signora del Rinascimento. Vita e splendori di Isabella d'Este alla corte di Mantova* (Milan: Rizzoli, 2001) and Christina Shaw, *Isabella d'Este. A Renaissance Princess* (London: Routledge, 2019). For scholarship on her art patronage, see Francis Ames-Lewis, *Isabella and Leonardo: The Artistic Relationship between Isabella d'Este and Leonardo da Vinci* (New Haven, Conn.; London: Yale University Press, 2012); Stephen J. Campbell, *The Cabinet of Eros: Renaissance Mythological Painting and the Studiolo of Isabella d'Este* (New Haven, Conn.; London: Yale University Press, 2006); Clifford M. Brown, *Isabella d'Este in the Ducal Palace in Mantua: An Overview of Her Rooms in the Castello di San Giorgio and the Corte Vecchia* (Rome: Bulzoni, 2005); Clifford M. Brown, Anna Maria Lorenzoni, and Sally Hickson, eds, *'Per dare qualche splendore a la gloriosa città di Mantua': Documents for the Antiquarian Collection of Isabella d'Este* (Rome: Bulzoni, 2002); Clifford Brown with Anna Maria Lorenzoni, *Isabella d'Este and Lorenzo da Pavia: Documents for the History of Art and Culture in Renaissance Mantua* (Geneva: Librairie Droz, 1982). For Isabella's literary patronage, see Alessandro Luzio and Rodolfo Renier, *La coltura e le relazioni letterarie di Isabella d'Este Gonzaga*, ed. Simone Albonico (Milano: Sylvestre Bonnard, 2005).

[9] Isabella d'Este to Francesco Gonzaga, 16 June 1497, from Mantua, ASMn, AG, 2112, c. 86.

[10] Molly Bourne, *Francesco II Gonzaga: The Soldier-Prince as Patron* (Rome: Bulzoni Editore, 2008).

ambitions were projected in visual form in the frescoes that adorned his country residences, the sites of much of his diplomacy. Portraits of his favourite thorough-bred horses and hunting dogs communicated a hyper-masculine identity, while military themes advertised the dreams of a man who wished to become a great soldier-prince. The political and military realities that the foreign invasions ushered in highlighted the fanciful nature of Francesco's conceptions of glory and honour. Traditional military codes could not resist the force of ruthless, no-holds-barred warfare and the impact of new lethal technology, which made no distinction between humble foot soldiers and aristocratic commanders versed in the niceties of chivalrous fighting. But it was the impact of being infected by the Great Pox that most profoundly destroyed the athletic version of masculinity that Francesco cultivated as a young man.

Neither Isabella nor Francesco could escape the limitations and anxieties generated by contemporary interpretations of elite masculinity and femininity. But while the marchioness was aware of the constraints of her gender from girlhood, the marquis seems to have perceived the burdens of masculinity only when adversity undermined the physical basis of his former manly ebullience. Francesco's letters to his wife document the psychological impact of long-term illness on his self-image and his dogged attempts to preserve a convincing sol-dierly persona, despite the inroads the disease made on his ability to fight, or even to mount a horse. The to-and-fro of marital correspondence over almost three decades permits us to understand how the very different personalities of the spouses interacted with the social and political pressures to which they were each subject and to grasp some of the mechanisms which brought these two individuals together and what drove them apart. My goal in this book is not to judge either person, but rather to challenge the historical caricatures associated with the two protagonists by analysing aspects of the lived experience of a rela-tionship that began with the couple's betrothal in 1480 and ended with Francesco's death in 1519.

Negotiations of the marital hierarchy were rendered complex in the case of Isabella and Francesco by the fact that they stood on an equal footing in terms of education and political literacy. In a period when it was the norm for patrician women in the republics of Venice and Florence to be semi-literate, or even illiter-ate, aristocratic girls at the apex of Italy's princely societies, who were destined for princely or royal marriages, were often educated alongside their brothers, although, of course, boys were also rigorously inducted into the military arts through physically demanding forms of sport. Between the 1480s and the early years of the sixteenth century, the evident competence with which well-educated and politically experienced noblewomen performed their role as regents in Italy's principalities put pressure on orthodox notions of female inferiority. Indeed, the late medieval debate about women's moral and intellectual worth and their fitness for power, particularly lively in France during the early fifteenth century, was reinvigorated almost a century later in Ferrara, Mantua, Milan, and Urbino, stimulated by the unease that the increasing overt political and diplomatic roles of princely consorts began to provoke among conservatives in these states.[11]

Isabella followed her mother's example in encouraging male literary clients who wrote philosophical treatises and other works that justified, and even attempted to normalize, the prominent political and cultural roles that she and a select number of her relatives exercised. The marchioness looked particularly favourably on those willing to promote the idea that women like herself were capable of great deeds and even to suggest that the sexes were innately equal.[12] The small treatise, *De mulieribus*, written around 1500 by Mario Equicola, who became her secretary in 1519, explicitly suggested that women's supposed inferiority was merely the result of a lack of education, strict confinement to the domestic sphere, and men's determination to preserve their dominance. Equicola held up the marchioness as a living example of what women could achieve, if given the same training as men and opportunities to display their capacity for engagement in activities usually reserved for the male sex.[13] This idea, although well before its time, associated Isabella and her literary clients with thought-provoking new visions of elite womanhood, placing the Mantuan court at the forefront of intellectual debates on the subject. Isabella also took vigorous charge of a propaganda campaign promulgated in a range of artistic media, which presented her as a woman eminently capable of exercising political authority. Although, as we will see, Francesco was willing to concede that Isabella was remarkably intelligent and often sought her political advice, as they both grew older, he became anxious about her ambitions, fearing that his ability to bring her to heel was being eroded, as her self-confidence and public visibility as a political actor increased. It was primarily the marquis's concern to clip his wife's political wings, and his sporadic attempts to impose a heavy-handed husbandly authority over her, that sparked the major episodes of conflict between them.

The Marital Correspondence

Many of the letters that Isabella and Francesco wrote to each other are known to scholars. However, because they are dispersed over a very large number of

---

[11] Stephen Kolsky, *The Ghost of Boccaccio: Writings on Famous Women in Renaissance Italy* (Turnhout: Brepols, 2005).

[12] Carolyn James, 'In Praise of Women: Giovanni Sabadino degli Arienti's *Gynevera de le clare donne*', in *The Intellectual Dynamism of the High Middle Ages*, ed. Clare Monagle (Amsterdam: Amsterdam University Press, 2020); Carolyn James, 'Margherita Cantelmo and the Worth of Women in Renaissance Italy', in *Mirrors of Princesses: Virtue Ethics for Women 1250–1550*, ed. Karen Green and Constant Mews (Dordrecht: Springer, 2011), 145–63.

[13] Mario Equicola, *De mulieribus. Delle donne*, ed. Giuseppe Lucchesini and Pina Totaro (Pisa and Rome: Istituti editoriali e poligrafici internazionali, 2004); Kolsky, *The Ghost of Boccaccio*, 148–58.

files within the Gonzaga Archive, the correspondence has not been analysed systematically as a discreet collection. My first task in preparing for this book was to reconstitute the couple's exchanges, a complicated and time-consuming, but ultimately rewarding, endeavour which revealed not only that some three thousand of the letters they wrote to each other are extant, but that the marital correspondence is almost entirely intact, a remarkable state of affairs for the premodern centuries, and quite rare even in our own day. The extraordinary degree of preservation of the letters is largely due to chancery practices which ensured that the so-called *originali*—letters that were actually dispatched—were retrieved by the couple's secretaries once they had been read, and carried back to Mantua for filing, even though a copy almost always remained in the chancery registers of outgoing mail. In a large number of cases, particular letters exist in multiple versions, as an original, as a copy and, occasionally, as a minute, the last preserving evidence of how a letter evolved from a dictated draft to its final form.

Isabella and Francesco sometimes dispensed with the services of their secretaries and wrote in their own hands. However, according to conventional epistolary norms, it was incumbent on the person of lesser status to make the greater effort in the production of a letter. Therefore, as a woman, Isabella was supposed to show deference to her husband by regularly taking up the pen herself. But she did so strategically and quite rarely, writing in her own hand only when she wished to make a request of her husband, such as permission to travel, or to mollify him at times of marital conflict. She mostly dictated her letters and deployed acceptable apologies to explain her failure to write to Francesco in holograph. In a letter of 1494, for example, Isabella excused herself, perhaps somewhat self-mockingly, on the following grounds: 'I wanted to write in my own hand to Your Excellency but, having washed my hair today, I spent so much time drying it that the whole day passed.'[14] Although letters that Isabella wrote herself were not always recorded in copy books and were less likely to be returned to the chancery for filing, especially if she was travelling without a secretary, a close examination of Francesco's replies suggests that relatively few holograph letters have been lost. Isabella seems to have been almost as disciplined in her filing habits as her secretary.[15] The significance of holographs, as opposed to dictated letters, as well as the variations in registers of address, tone, and language have been the focus of much recent scholarship, including my own, and I have aimed to take account of the methodological insights provided by this work in the present study.[16]

---

[14] 'Io voleva scrivere de mia mano a Vostra Excellentia ma havendome hozi lavata la testa sono stata tanto a 'sugarla ch'el dì è passato.' Isabella d'Este to Francesco Gonzaga, 25 January 1494, from Mantua, ASMn, AG, b. 2109, c. 156.

[15] On the arrangement and content of the Gonzaga Archive, see Alessandro Luzio, ed, *L'Archivio Gonzaga di Mantova. La corrispondenza familiare, amministrativa e diplomatica dei Gonzaga*, vol. 2 (Verona: Mondadori, 1922).

[16] See, for example, Gary Schneider, *The Culture of Epistolarity: Vernacular Letters and Letter Writing in Early Modern England, 1500–1700* (Newark: University of Delaware Press, 2005); James

For a modern reader, the emotional import of the spouses' expressions of loyalty and affection, often couched in what appears to be an artificial rhetoric, is likely to be somewhat opaque. Isabella and Francesco never addressed each other familiarly in their letters. They always used their full titles and the polite form of pronouns and adhered to formal registers of language. Nonetheless, the correspondents had a good understanding of how subtly to manipulate formulaic phases to communicate shades of meaning. Although recovering how they understood and used the elaborate conventions of their epistolary milieu requires careful analysis, it is clear that, far from being emotionally disengaged—as Lawrence Stone suggested was the norm in early modern England among those who married for instrumental reasons—this late fifteenth-century Italian couple discussed a wide range of emotions, including disappointment and anger with each other, but also trust, affection, and tenderness towards their children.[17] Over time, the rhetorical tropes of love that appear so stilted in the early letters gradually accumulated greater warmth and animation, the evolution of a firmer emotional connection between the pair creating a more relaxed and intimate dialogue between them.

The historical specificity of how patriarchy was interpreted and put into practice in this early modern political and cultural context, as well as the ways in which social position and gender interacted to determine how a relationship would play out, emerge compellingly from the well-documented struggle by Isabella and Francesco to navigate a prudent path between tradition and innovation in their interpretation of the marital bond. Although the emotions documented in the couple's letters cannot always be taken at face value, analysed with due caution they provide a rare insight into the lives of two privileged aristocrats whose demeanour, behaviour, and relationships were constantly exposed to public scrutiny. The pair's agile improvisations in relation to masculine and feminine identities, and to the division of work, were usually prompted by the diplomatic dilemmas they faced. Inevitably such experiments prompted uncertainty and sometimes sharp discord, as they struggled to work out a modus vivendi in a perilous and rapidly changing political environment. In analysing how this marriage was inhabited emotionally, alongside how it operated politically, I aim to uncover the intricate intertwining of the private and public in a relationship that had to operate and succeed on both levels.

Daybell and Peter Hinds, eds, *Material Readings of Early Modern Culture: Texts and Social Practices, 1580–1730* (Basingstoke: Palgrave Macmillan, 2010); James Daybell, *The Material Letter in Early Modern England: Manuscript Letters and the Culture and Practices of Letter-Writing, 1512–1635* (Basingstoke: Palgrave Macmillan, 2012); James Daybell and Andrew Gordon, eds, *Cultures of Correspondence in Early Modern Britain* (Philadelphia: University of Pennsylvania Press, 2016); Carolyn James and Jessica O'Leary, 'Letter Writing and Emotions, 1100–1700', in *The Routledge History Handbook to Emotions in Europe, 1100–1700*, ed. Susan Broomhall and Andrew Lynch (Abingdon: Routledge, 2019), 256–68.

[17] Lawrence Stone, *The Family, Sex and Marriage in England 1500–1800* (London: Weidenfeld and Nicolson, 1977).

1

Betrothal

On Thursday, 25 May 1480, a delegation representing Federico Gonzaga, the marquis of Mantua, arrived at the neighbouring Este court in Ferrara. Its task was to ratify the betrothal of the duke of Ferrara's 6-year-old daughter, Isabella, to the 13-year-old Francesco Gonzaga, heir to the marquisate. Francesco Secco, the marquis's lieutenant, led the group of envoys and wrote of his first encounter with the future marchioness in a letter of 26 May. He explained to his master that Isabella was recuperating from an illness when the Mantuan delegation arrived and he and his entourage had therefore visited the child in her bedroom. After being presented with a letter and necklace from her betrothed, Isabella had responded graciously to the ambassadors and immediately tried on the gift, her precocious self-possession and ability to engage intelligently with her visitors seen by Secco as evidence of her suitability for the position she would assume in adulthood.[1]

Given his fiancée's confinement to bed, Francesco had remained at home, the only information available to him about his future spouse, a small, and now lost, portrait of her by the Ferrarese painter, Cosmè Tura.[2] A profile portrait of Francesco in early adolescence, by an unknown artist, presently owned by the National Gallery of Art in Washington, is likely to have been commissioned around this time as a reciprocal gesture.[3] The paintings functioned as a material reminder of the significant diplomatic gift that each family considered it conferred on the other through the union of their eldest children.

It was perhaps indicative of the confidence that their respective regimes were at last securely enough established that the Gonzaga and Este princes felt able to contemplate an alliance with each other, rather than pursue more ambitious connections, such as the German kinship ties sought by the Gonzaga in the previous two generations, or the royal Aragonese networks which Ercole d'Este's marriage in 1473 to Eleonora d'Aragona, daughter of the king of Naples, had secured. Beltramino Cusatro, the Mantuan lawyer who conducted the betrothal negotiations with Isabella's mother, assured her that Federico Gonzaga was bent on a local match, experience having taught him that Germans and other foreigners cared far more

---

[1] Francesco Secco's letters to the marquis are partially transcribed in Alessandro Luzio, *Isabella d'Este e Francesco Gonzaga promessi sposi* (Milan: L. F. Cogliati, 1908), 16–17.
[2] The portrait of Isabella is referred to in a letter of 17 April 1480, sent from Ferrara by the Mantuan ambassador, Beltramino Cusatro, to Federico Gonzaga, ASMn, AG, 1229, c. 120. See Luzio, *Promessi sposi*, 13.
[3] Bourne, *The Soldier-Prince*, 35.

A Renaissance Marriage: The Political and Personal Alliance of Isabella d'Este and Francesco Gonzaga, 1490–1519. Carolyn James, Oxford University Press (2020). © Carolyn James.
DOI: 10.1093/oso/9780199681211.001.0001

about the dowry than the bride.[4] Although this statement was doubtless a diplomatic ploy, there was perhaps an element of truth in the story. The unhappiness of the marquis's sister, Paula, after her marriage to Leonard, count of Gorizia, and protracted wrangles about the full payment of the dowry, may have convinced Federico it was better to look closer to home for a bride for his eldest son.[5]

Certainly, the Este and Gonzaga rulers could have expected to understand each other's political needs and viewpoints. The two dynasties had come to power in the late medieval centuries by means of similar strategies and via much the same route, although the rise of the Este had pre-dated that of the Gonzaga.[6] The papal fiefdom of Ferrara was already under Este control by 1264, with the imperial possessions of Modena and Reggio following in 1288 and 1289 respectively. However, it was not until the fifteenth century that the pope and the emperor legitimized this usurped power by recognizing the Este rulers as imperial and papal vassals in return for substantial feudal dues. Emperor Frederick III granted Borso d'Este the title of duke of Modena and Reggio in 1452, while Pope Paul II made him duke of Ferrara in 1471, just before his half-brother Ercole d'Este's succession that same year.[7]

Despite these advances, the autonomy of the Este regime remained circumscribed by interference from Ferrara's mighty neighbour, the Venetian republic. Citizens of Venice who lived in Ferrara enjoyed many privileges, including free access to the Po river and enviable other commercial concessions that were policed by a *visdomino*, a resident Venetian consul established in Ferrara as early as the twelfth century. This official had the power to prosecute those who infringed the Venetian monopoly on salt supplies from the marshes of Comacchio and generally acted as a spy, alerting Venice's government to commercial or political developments that might be damaging to its interests. To discourage further Venetian encroachments on their authority, the Este rulers maintained close diplomatic relations with the French crown.

Originally known as the Corradi, the Gonzaga adopted the name of their geographical base in the countryside south of Mantua, where they had accumulated vast areas of land before acquiring a large portfolio of properties in Mantua itself. Eventually the clan was able to challenge the Bonacolsi, hitherto the dominant family, and the Gonzaga quickly imposed their own authority over the city and its surrounding territories. Emperor Ludwig recognized this victory by ceding the imperial vicarage to Luigi Gonzaga in 1329. A quarter of a century later, Charles

---

[4] Luzio, *Promessi sposi*, 11–12.

[5] Isabella Lazzarini, 'Paola Gonzaga', in *Dizionario Biografico Italiano*, 57, 2001, http://www.trec-cani.it/enciclopedia/paola-gonzaga_%28Dizionario-Biografico%29.

[6] On the rise of the two political dynasties, see Trevor Dean, 'Ferrara and Mantua', in *The Italian Renaissance State*, ed. Andrea Gamberini and Isabella Lazzarini (Cambridge: Cambridge University Press, 2012), 112–31.

[7] Werner L. Gundersheimer, *Ferrara: The Style of a Renaissance Despotism* (Princeton, N.J.: Princeton University Press, 1973), 151–3; Antonio Frizzi, *Memorie per la storia di Ferrara*, vol. 4 (Ferrara: Abram Servadio, 1848), 20–1, 75–8, 156–8.

IV made Mantua an independent lordship, although it remained formally an imperial fiefdom in the sense that its rulers were expected to pay feudal dues and remain a faithful ally of the emperor. Gianfrancesco Gonzaga gained the hereditary title of marquis in 1433, after paying a large fee to Emperor Sigismund of Luxembourg, who visited Mantua for the ceremony of investiture, timed to coincide with the betrothal of his niece, Barbara of Brandenburg, to Gianfrancesco's son Lodovico. Thanks to their imperial connections, the Gonzaga rulers were able to play a significant role in contemporary politics throughout the second half of the fifteenth century.[8]

The cityscape of Mantua was substantially transformed as a result of a papal diet held there in 1459. The second marquis, Lodovico Gonzaga, made energetic preparations for this important event, but, despite his endeavours, visiting members of the Curia complained about the intolerable summer heat and the risk of falling victim to fevers, due to the abundance of stagnant water around the city. They dismissed Mantua as a place where 'nothing was to be heard except the frogs'.[9] These negative reactions prompted Lodovico to build new locks and embankments, so reducing the dangers that Mantua's watery environment posed to public health. Land was ceded to those who were willing to build fine houses that would contribute to the beauty of the city and the marquis himself embarked on an ambitious campaign of ecclesiastical patronage. He commissioned Leon Battista Alberti to design the new church of San Sebastiano and radically to make-over in a classicizing style the Benedictine church of Sant'Andrea in the centre of town. The ground-breaking architecture of these churches associated the Gonzaga with the power and prestige of ancient Rome, while the appointment in 1460 of Andrea Mantegna as court artist, one of the most innovative and classically literate painters of his day, also added to their reputation as patrons at the forefront of new cultural and artistic movements.[10]

The Este transformed Ferrara in similar ways. After wresting control of public works from communal committees, they used municipal funds for programmes of urban renewal and infrastructure improvements. Under Niccolò III d'Este, who ruled from 1393 until his death in 1441, major streets were paved and beautified

[8] Marina Romani, *Una città in forma di palazzo: potere signorile e forma urbana nella Mantova medievale e moderna* (Brescia: Ed. Centro di ricerche storiche e sociali Federico Odorici, 1995); Mario Vaini, *Dal comune alla signoria: Mantova dal 1200 al 1328* (Milano: Angeli, 1986), 275–83.

[9] Pius II, *Commentaries*, ed. and trans. Margaret Meserve and Marcello Simonetta, 2 vols (Cambridge, Mass.: Harvard University Press, 2003), 7.

[10] See Romani, *Una città in forma di palazzo*, 101–21, 137–50; Giovanni Rodella, 'L'ingegnere Giovanni da Padova ei principali interventi idraulici nel territorio gonzaghesco durante la seconda metà del Quattrocento', in *Il paesaggio mantovano nelle tracce materiali, nelle lettere e nelle arti*, vol. 3, ed. Eugenio Camerlenghi, Viviana Rebonato, and Sara Tammaccaro (Florence: L.S. Olschki, 2007), 159–78; Rodolfo Signorini, 'Paesaggio mantovano urbano e del contado nella cronaca di Andrea Stanziali/Vidali da Schivenoglia e non solo, fino al 1496', in *Il paesaggio mantovano*, 287–382; Isabella Lazzarini, 'I Gonzaga, la città, e territorio. Strutture dell'insediamento e potere signorile a Mantova fra Tre e Quattrocento', in *Il paesaggio mantovano*, 511–32.

with plantings of poplars, while flood mitigation projects, involving the Po and Reno rivers, were directed to controlling the regular inundations of low lying areas.[11] Heavily reliant for income on river traffic tolls, the regime continued to invest in and regulate the waterways, not least because the Ferrarese economy was otherwise almost entirely driven by agricultural revenues, with far less industrial or mercantile activity than in the bustling commercial centres of nearby Milan or Venice.[12] Religious institutions, particularly those in urban centres, were revitalized, the dominant family making sure, during that process, to concentrate ecclesiastical patronage in its own hands. The law and medical faculties of the university were strengthened in the hope that this improvement would facilitate recruitment of students from other parts of Italy and even from beyond the Alps, and so provide another means of stimulating the local economy. As well, a number of influential humanists were offered Este patronage, rendering the Ferrarese court an important scholarly centre.[13] Although it was not until Ercole d'Este's time that the architectural fabric of Ferrara was transformed in a major way, his creation in the 1490s of a rationally planned suburb to the north—the so-called Herculean Addition—was boldly innovative and much admired by contemporaries.[14]

Thus, Francesco and Isabella grew up in neighbouring courts that shared a rather similar history and culture. However, their parents did not assume that this common heritage would be enough to ensure the success of the union. They went to considerable lengths to foster familiarity between the child and youth during the pair's ten-year betrothal, in the hope that an early affection would be kindled and pave the way for the formation of a strong marital bond. They also sought to induct their new in-law into their own family, a process of acculturation and familiarization that proved particularly easy in the case of Francesco, since, by July 1484, shortly before his eighteenth birthday, he was an orphan.

A number of Ferrarese chronicles attest to Ercole d'Este's paternal mentoring of his future son-in-law, a role the duke no doubt hoped would give him the upper hand in the relationship. Isabella's preparation for marriage is less evident in the extant sources, although she makes several cameo appearances in ambassadorial correspondence, as well as in Francesco's letters of the early 1480s to his father. While he was able to shuttle back and forth between Mantua and Ferrara during the long prelude to his marriage, Isabella's gender and young age meant she visited her relatives in Mantua only rarely. But, when she did, her behaviour and character came under close scrutiny and thus we can know something of the interactions of the couple in the decade before their wedding.

---

[11] Frizzi, *Memorie*, 29.   [12] Gundersheimer, *Ferrara*, 82–3, 135–6, 276; Frizzi, *Memorie*, 33–7.
[13] Edmund Garratt Gardner, *Dukes and Poets in Ferrara* (New York: Haskell, 1904).
[14] Marco Folin, 'Gli Estensi e Ferrara nel quadro di un sistema politico composto, 1452–1598', in *Storia di Ferrara*, vol. 4 (Ferrara: Corbo, 2000), 22–76.

Preparations for Marriage

The earliest documented encounter of Francesco and Isabella is described in a letter of 26 June 1480, sent to Federico Gonzaga by the Mantuan ambassador to Ferrara, Bernardino Pusterla. The marquis had fallen ill earlier that month, prompting Isabella's mother, Eleonora d'Aragona, to travel to Mantua with her children and a large entourage, including Pusterla, to pay her respects to the sick man. After several days at the Gonzaga court, the Ferrarese visitors left, accompanied on the return journey by the adolescent Francesco. As the party travelled home along the Po River, the ambassador reported to the marquis that Francesco occasionally transferred from his small barge to the much larger state bucentaur occupied by Eleonora and her children.[15] During one of these times, Isabella was persuaded to join her betrothed on the upper deck. Under the watchful eye of her mother, who likely orchestrated the couple's public encounter, the young girl saluted Francesco in friendly fashion. The two kissed each other on the mouth, and then remained together until the cool wind prompted Isabella to retreat inside. Later, they sat together companionably at the open window of the vessel's main chamber, in a ritual rehearsal of their future union. However, according to the ambassador's account, things went awry when Isabella's 4-year-old brother, Alfonso, joined the pair and began to kiss Francesco very enthusiastically. The resulting hilarity among the company provoked Isabella into a tantrum. Her pride and strong sense of personal dignity, for which she later became so well known, seem to have been already on the ascendant. Isabella was only placated when a group of court musicians arrived by boat, providing an opportunity for those on board to dance. Afterwards, Francesco organized games for the younger children. The eight years that separated the betrothed pair constituted a significant age gap at this stage of their lives. The ambassador's letter reveals that Francesco soon availed himself of the chance to re-join the courtiers gathered outside on deck, preferring to regale the men with stories of sea battles, rather than to entertain a little girl who was so easily vexed.[16]

Upon arrival in Ferrara, Francesco himself wrote to his father about the first days in the city. We learn from a letter of 28 June 1480 that Ercole d'Este and a large contingent of his courtiers travelled three miles upstream to intercept the returning bucentaurs and, once the barges were moored, the duke led Francesco in procession

---

[15] A bucentaur (*bucintoro*) was an elaborately decorated vessel fitted out with several rooms, including sleeping accommodation. It had a sail and mast, but also oars. When going upstream, or in narrow parts of the river, it was drawn from a tow path by horses, or sometimes teams of men. On the Este bucentaurs, see Thomas Tuohy, *Herculean Ferrara: Ercole d'Este, 1471–1505, and the Invention of a Ducal Capital* (Cambridge; New York: Cambridge University Press, 1996), 154–60.

[16] 'Sopragionse lo Illustre Don Alfonso, qual cominciò a basare cussì frequentemente Don Francesco che tutti ne pigliorono solacio e festa excepto la Illustre Donna Isabella, la quale fece dimonstratione de havere per male tanti basi.' Bernardino Pusterla to Federico Gonzaga, 26 June 1480, from Figarolo, ASMn, AG, 1229, c. 109.

to the castle, with pipes and tambourines providing musical accompaniment. After he had eaten and rested, the youth was taken by Ercole to the Barco, the hunting park built by the duke in 1471 within the grounds of the villa of Belfiore, just outside the city walls to the north. There, Francesco was presented with a fine mount and two suitably aged courtiers to keep him company while he hunted. Ercole was attentive in other ways, accompanying his guest to Mass, so he might hear the ducal choir, exhibiting a new chapel dedicated to the Virgin Mary and proudly showing off other new building projects. But Francesco assured his father that he had also spent time with Isabella and had, on one occasion, played a game of 'ossi' with her, probably a form of the ancient children's game of jacks, or knucklebones.[17] It is likely that the youth had been instructed by the marquis to make sure he cultivated amicable relations with his future wife, as well as with her parents. Thus, he obeyed those paternal orders by occasionally condescending to play parlour games with Isabella, instead of the outdoor sports he loved.

The duchess also took an active role in welcoming Francesco into the Este family. She prepared rooms for him close to her own apartments in the castle and expected to visit him before he went to sleep and to kiss him goodnight, the death of the youth's mother in 1479 perhaps encouraging Eleonora to take on an explicitly maternal role.[18] The Gonzaga children had been forced to cope with Margarete Wittelsbach of Bavaria's sudden demise on their own, since Federico was away fighting at the time. Francesco communicated the sad news to his father in a letter which conveyed something of the intensity of his feelings:

> I am completely confused and lost. I am aware I have lost my mother who loved me with a perfect love and under whose care I could not fail to thrive. It seems to my sisters and brothers and to me that we are abandoned. We await the arrival of your Lordship with great desire.[19]

Evidence that the bond between Francesco and his mother was indeed close is suggested by an account of their relationship written by Margarete at the height of a very hot summer, two months before her death. She explained to her husband that both she and their eldest son were ill, their poor health exacerbated by the stifling heat within the Gonzaga castle, where it was impossible even to open the windows, because of the fetid smell of the moat, long unrefreshed by rain. Unable to sleep, she wanted to move to the airier and cooler villa of Porto, across the lake

---

[17]   Francesco Gonzaga to Federico Gonzaga, 28 June 1480, from Ferrara, ASMn, AG, 2104, c. 424.

[18]   Francesco Gonzaga to Federico Gonzaga, 4 July 1480, from Ferrara, ASMn, AG, 2104, c. 427. For another visit to Ferrara in September 1480, see ASMn AG, 2104, cc. 425 and 435.

[19]   'Io sto tutto confuso e smarito. Conosco haver perso mia madre, la quale me amava di perfettissimo amore e soto el governo de la quale non potevo stare se non molto bene. Pare a mie sorelle e fratelli et a me che siamo como abandonati. Aspetiamo con molto desiderio la venuta di Vostra Signoria.' Francesco Gonzaga to Federico Gonzaga, 19 October 1479, from Ferrara, ASMn, AG, 2104, c. 325.

that separated the city from the nearby countryside. Although she had suggested to Francesco that he move to the fortified Gonzaga residence of Goito, fifteen kilometres to the north of Mantua, for fear that harm might come to him in the undefended precincts of her suburban retreat, he had refused to be parted from her. Margarete had therefore permitted Francesco to accompany her to Porto, where, as she assured her husband, she was confident they would both recover.[20] The marchioness died soon afterwards.

It was perhaps a desire for distraction from the melancholic atmosphere at the Gonzaga court, following his mother's death, that prompted Francesco more frequently to seek recreation in Ferrara. Carnival was a particular attraction. In January 1481, for example, he slipped quietly into the city on the Feast of the Epiphany.[21] By the next day, with the encouragement of the duchess, he was already going about masked, in the company of a congenial group of young courtiers, who entertained themselves by pelting eggs at women unwise enough to venture forth onto the streets.[22] Francesco described the fun-filled days that followed in other letters to his father. He reported he had enjoyed a sled ride through the winter landscape with Isabella and her brother Alfonso and, later, he wrote of a snowball fight among the children that took place in the duchess's garden within the precincts of the castle. Even Eleonora and her ladies-in-waiting had briefly joined the battle, much to the horror of the duke, who arrived to see what all the noise was about, but quickly withdrew to avoid getting wet.[23] Francesco's sojourn ended with celebrations associated with the visit to Ferrara of his sister Clara, who was about to marry Count Gilbert Montpensier de Bourbon, whose ancestral seat was at Aigueperse in the Auvergne.[24] This match would later prove crucial to Francesco's ability to forge diplomatic connections in France, but his sister's marriage and departure from Italy must have been yet another wrench, since Clara, being two years older, had stepped into the emotional breach left by their mother's sudden death.

Francesco returned to Ferrara in late February 1481 and he was still there in May, after falling ill during the visit. During his recovery, he played cards with Isabella while resting in bed, this gentle recreation building on earlier efforts to create familiarity between the couple.[25] November 1481 saw Francesco in Este territory once more, for this was the hunting season. After exhausting supplies of game in the Barco, the men of the court decamped to the sea, where they fished

[20] Margarete of Bavaria to Federico Gonzaga, 9 August 1479, from Porto, ASMn, AG, b. 2104, c. 249. See also Margarete's letters of 13 and 20 August, cc. 251 and 252.
[21] Francesco Gonzaga to Federico Gonzaga, 6 January 1481, from Ferrara, ASMn, AG, 2104, c. 506.
[22] Francesco Gonzaga to Federico Gonzaga, 7 January 1481, from Ferrara, ASMn, AG, 2104, c. 507.
[23] Francesco Gonzaga to Federico Gonzaga, 8, 18, 21 January 1481, from Ferrara, ASMn, AG, 2104, cc. 510, 514, 516.
[24] Francesco Gonzaga to Federico Gonzaga, 24 and 29 January 1481, from Ferrara, ASMn, AG, 2104, cc. 517r–v and 519.
[25] Luzio, *Promessi sposi*, 19.

for eels in the wetlands of Comacchio and pursued boar and deer in the forests nearby.[26] Francesco found the masculine camaraderie of such pastimes very much to his liking and he availed himself of his Ferrarese relatives' hospitality with relish.

Federico Gonzaga was also keen to induct Isabella into his family, but given her age, delicate health, and the lack of a presiding female presence at the Mantuan court following the death of the marchioness, Eleonora d'Aragona was reluctant to allow long, or frequent, visits, for fear the child would not be adequately chaperoned. She finally permitted Isabella to spend Christmas 1481 in Mantua and to travel there in the care of Francesco and a party of eighty Ferrarese attendants. Wet weather delayed the departure from Ferrara, because the duchess refused to allow the child to leave in the rain, a stance that the marquis regarded as excessively protective and risked making his daughter-in-law 'too delicate', as he himself put it in a message sent via his ambassador. The diplomats had to smooth over this disagreement. Eleonora herself tactfully sent a message to Federico through his son that Isabella was full of enthusiasm for the visit. Francesco explained to his father in a letter of 10 November 1481 that the duchess felt it was necessary to be cautious, given that her daughter did not yet enjoy a robust constitution.[27] Towards the middle of December, Isabella finally set off for Mantua, but Eleonora's concerns about the bad weather were vindicated. Francesco informed his father in a letter of 14 December that they were making slow progress, since 'his consort' had not tolerated the erratic motion of the bucentaur, as it was laboriously pulled up stream in choppy water. The haulers on the tow-path had been forced to stop frequently to allow Isabella to recover.[28]

Once the journey was over, the visit proved a resounding success. The Mantuan ambassador to Ferrara reported that the duchess had received letters from Isabella describing the wonderful treatment she was being afforded at the Mantuan court. Eleonora relayed her appreciation of the warm reception, adding that she was only worried that the child would return reluctantly to Ferrara after being so indulged.[29] Years later, Francesco's brother Giovanni, Isabella's almost exact contemporary, provided a retrospective glimpse of her early interactions with the younger Gonzaga siblings in a letter to her of May 1513, sent from Milan. He recalled that, as children (and probably during this very visit), they had played together under a staircase and had cooked eggs in a silver bed warmer, establishing a friendship that, as he reminded Isabella, had stood the test of time.[30] Even though this fond recollection was in response to a bad-tempered complaint from

---

[26] Francesco Gonzaga to Federico Gonzaga, 2, 4, 9, 15, 26 November 1481, from Ferrara, ASMn, AG, 2104, cc. 569–76.

[27] Francesco Gonzaga to Federico Gonzaga, 10 November 1481, from Ferrara, ASMn, AG, 2104, c. 580 and Pietro Spagnoli to Federico Gonzaga, 11 and 13 December 1481, from Ferrara, ASMn, AG, 1229, cc. 169r–v and 172r–v.

[28] Francesco Gonzaga to Federico Gonzaga, 14 December 1481, from Figarolo, ASMn, AG, 2104, c. 583.

[29] Pietro Spagnoli to Federico Gonzaga, 22 December 1481, from Ferrara, ASMn, AG, 1229, c. 185.

[30] Giovanni Gonzaga to Isabella d'Este, 6 May 1513, from Milan, ASMn, AG, 1894, cc. 128r–130r (128r).

Isabella that Giovanni had failed to keep her adequately informed about news from the Milanese court, the relationship was usually amicable. The parity of age seems to have trumped the disparity of gender in this case, allowing the two to play together happily as 7-year-olds in a way that Isabella and Francesco could not.

It may also have during this early visit to Mantua that Isabella befriended Francesco's sister, Elisabetta Gonzaga, the future duchess of Urbino, who became a favourite companion and correspondent in later life. However, Isabella's first opportunity to acquaint herself with the family of her betrothed was short lived. At the end of December, there was another set of negotiations about how long the child should stay in Mantua: Eleonora wanted her to return immediately, while the Gonzaga pressed for a departure at the conclusion of Carnival.[31] The duchess had her way; Francesco and Isabella returned to Ferrara on 3 January to spend the Epiphany there, under her eagle eye.

The outbreak of the War of Ferrara on 30 April 1482, a conflict that followed escalating tensions between the Venetian republic and the duchy, put an end to such visits. Not only were the Este children swiftly removed southwards to the safety of Modena, relations between Ferrara and Mantua were somewhat strained by Federico Gonzaga's delay in coming to his ally's assistance, preoccupied as he was to safeguard his own territory from Venetian incursions.[32] He was also determined to wait until he received Milanese funds to pay the soldiers under his command.[33] Isabella was cared for in Modena by Luisa Strozzi, a Florentine widow who had left her natal city in 1434, along with her husband and father-in-law, Palla Strozzi, following the family's exile by the Medici.[34] With the guidance of her tutor Battista Guarino, Isabella composed a short, formal letter to Francesco, dated 22 May 1482, dutifully expressing her regret about being so far away.[35] In July, she succumbed again to the summer fevers that regularly afflicted her childhood and Eleonora rushed off to Modena to visit her.[36]

Meanwhile, Duke Ercole was withstanding the strain of the war poorly. As Venetian troops, led by the noted military captain, Roberto Sanseverino, penetrated his hunting park and skirmished at the very gates of the city in the final months of 1482, the duke retreated to bed, physically and psychologically prostrated, leaving his wife and her brother, Alfonso d'Aragona, the duke of Calabria, to turn the tide of a rapidly deteriorating situation. The Este children were brought

---

[31] Pietro Spagnoli to Federico Gonzaga, 31 December 1481, from Ferrara, ASMn, AG, 1229, c. 198r–199r.

[32] Ugo Caleffini, *Croniche: 1471–1494* (Ferrara: Deputazione Provinciale Ferrarese di Storia Patria, 2006), 33.

[33] Lorenzo de' Medici, *Lettere*, ed. Michael Mallett, vol. 7 (Firenze: Giunti-Barbèra, 1998), 6–7.

[34] Lisa Di Crescenzo, ' "Leaving Hell and Arriving in Paradise": Between Victimhood and Agency in the Exilic Experience of Luisa Donati Strozzi (1434–1510)', *Parergon* 34.2 (2017): 99–131.

[35] Luzio, 'Promessi Sposi', 21.

[36] Girolamo Ferrarini, *Memoriale estense: 1476–1489*, ed. Primo Griguolo (Rovigo: Minelliana, 2006), 147.

back to Ferrara at the beginning of February 1483 to visit their Neapolitan uncle.[37] The duke of Calabria's arrival in Lombardy with troop reinforcements was key to the conflict moving away from Ferrara to more distant battlefields. However, plague was rampant in the city throughout 1483 and 1484 and the deprivations associated with the ongoing war caused widespread famine and poverty, posing a serious political threat to the Este regime. The Peace of Bagnolo, signed on 7 August 1484, marked the end of a conflict that saw the duke entirely humiliated. Ercole d'Este gained nothing from the war. His Milanese and Neapolitan allies permitted Venice to retain the border territory of Polesine di Rovigo, a wetland area much prized for its abundance of game and other natural resources which had been occupied by Venetian troops during the fighting. All the special privileges enjoyed by Venetian citizens living in Ferrara and the long-standing taxes and monopolies imposed by Venice on its small neighbour, which so grated on the duke and his subjects, were reconfirmed.[38]

With an end of the disastrous war with Venice in view, Ercole attempted to resurrect his battered political fortunes through non-military means. He reactivated earlier policies centred on the ceremonialization of his person and lordship. Now, however, he co-opted Francesco into an ever more elaborate program of spectacle and conspicuous spending that promoted an image of princely magnificence. Fate assisted him. On 14 July 1484, just weeks before the War of Ferrara ended, Federico Gonzaga died. The 17-year-old Francesco thus became the fourth marquis of Mantua. On hearing the news, Ercole d'Este promptly left the encampment of the duke of Calabria and travelled to Mantua to comfort and offer advice to a young man who had lost both parents within half a decade.[39] It is likely that he was also concerned to make sure that the political transition would take place smoothly, with no attempts by the heir's paternal uncles to install themselves as regents. The death of his father marked the end of Francesco's descriptions of his sojourns at the Este court. However, a number of Ferrarese chroniclers recorded the visits to Ferrara of the new marquis of Mantua and observed the increasingly public nature of his interactions with the duke.

Male Bonding and the Crafting of Princely Identity

The Ferrarese official, Bernardino Zambotti, kept a diary from 1471 until 1504, now known in its published form as the *Diario ferrarese*. After studying law at the University of Ferrara, Bernardino had hoped to find employment at the Este

[37] Caleffini, *Croniche*, 501; Bernardino Zambotti, *Diario ferrarese dall'anno 1476 sino al 1504*, ed. Giuseppe Pardi, vol. 7, *Rerum Italicarum Scriptores*, XXIV (Modena: Zanichelli, 1934), 134.

[38] Lorenzo de' Medici, *Lettere*, ed. Mallett, vol. 7, 505–15.

[39] Zambotti, *Diario ferrarese*, 134 and 154; Ferrarini, *Memoriale*, 198–9.

court. However, he achieved only secondary positions as vicar of the podestà in nearby towns, postings that deprived him of the chance to observe at first hand many of the events he wanted to record.[40] He relied on his cousin, Zaccharia Zambotti, a doctor and well-favoured courtier, to provide him with an insider's view of what went on in the palaces and country residences of the Este family.[41] At times, this indirect access to information proved problematic. The chronicler mistakenly tells us, for example, that Isabella was with her mother and siblings on the podium of the Este palace's Great Hall during the ball that marked her betrothal in March 1480, rather than ill in bed. Bernardino's cousin appears to have neglected to mention Isabella's absence from the party. On the other hand, thanks to the doctor's eye for detail, Zambotti's account captures the splendour of the festivities much more convincingly than the austere reports of the diplomats who attended the occasion.[42]

Ugo Caleffini (born c.1439), was a recording notary for the ducal *spenditore*, or household paymaster, so knew a great deal about Este officeholders and court expenses. He also noted the betrothal of Isabella and Francesco in his chronicle. However, his informants about the celebrations in the palace were the confectioners responsible for creating the ninety magnificent sugar sculptures that were paraded before the guests during the banquet. While Zambotti tells us that these sculptures were of various animals and castles, elaborately decorated with the crests of the Gonzaga, Este, and their guests, Caleffini mentions only that they cost nine hundred *soldi* and were smashed up by the guests at the end of the evening, a comment that suggests he took a dim view of the duke's extravagance.[43] Certainly his critical attitude to Ercole d'Este is quite explicit in some of the other entries, a reflection perhaps of his disappointment about the decline in his employment fortunes, once Ercole came to power.

Yet another chronicler, Girolamo Ferrarini (born c.1457), whose memoire covers the years 1476–89, was a university friend of Bernardino Zambotti. He too was legally trained and, like Caleffini, became a ducal bureaucrat following his graduation, his first public office dating from June 1487. His diary ends in 1489, when he left Ferrara to take up a position in Mantua and then as an official in other northern towns.[44] Ferrarini says nothing at all about the betrothal in his *Memoriale*.

---

[40] Zambotti, *Diario ferrarese*, viii–ix.

[41] See, for example, Zambotti's reference to information provided by his cousin Zaccharia about Isabella's entrance into Mantua in 1490, *Diario ferrarese*, 214–15.

[42] Zambotti, *Diario ferrarese*, 76. Francesco Secco's letter describing the occasion is published in Luzio, *Promessi Sposi*, 16.

[43] Zambotti, *Diario ferrarese*, 76; Caleffini, *Croniche*, 33.

[44] Ferrarini, *Memoriale*, 18–19. On the Ferrarese chroniclers and their stances in regard to the Este dukes, see Marco Folin, 'Le cronache a Ferrara e negli stati Estensi (Secoli XV–XVI)', in *Storia di Ferrara*, vol. 4 (Ferrara: Corbo, 2000), 460–92; and Trevor Dean, 'Ferrarese Chroniclers and the Este State, 1490–1505', in *Phaethon's Children. The Este Court and Its Culture in Early Modern Ferrara*, ed. Deanna Shemek and Dennis Looney (Tempe, Ariz.: Arizona Centre for Medieval and Renaissance Studies, 2005), 169–87.

However, throughout the 1480s, all three of these chroniclers were attentive to the regular appearances of Francesco Gonzaga in their city, which suggests he was often visible in the streets, as well as at court. They wrote of the young man sympathetically, seemingly impressed by his extrovert personality and manly athleticism. When Francesco resumed his visits to Ferrara following the end of the war with Venice in August 1484, which came just weeks after the death of his father Federico, Zambotti and Ferrarini noted the change in the young man's lodgings. These were no longer in the castle, near the apartments of the duchess and her children, but rather in newly fitted-out rooms in the adjoining Este palace, close to where the duke resided. This change constituted a recognition of Francesco's new status as marquis of Mantua.[45] The chroniclers were also alert to the fact that, rather than young nobles of his own age, it was now almost always Duke Ercole who kept Francesco company, the two rulers regularly hunting, feasting, and gambling with their courtiers, either in Ferrara or Mantua, for weeks at a time. Ferrarini recorded that Francesco sometimes brought his younger siblings with him to Ferrara. They were relegated to the duchess's supervision.[46]

Ercole d'Este was regarded by contemporaries as moody and often withdrawn. The Mantuan ambassador to Ferrara, Giampaolo Arrivabene, noted in 1473 that the duke was a man of few words and, when he did speak, did so haltingly. He appeared to the ambassador to be 'saturnine in nature', in contemporary terms possessing humours that made him prone to melancholy.[47] Many years later, Isabella described herself in similar terms, when she requested that Francesco allow her to go to Brescia to watch a joust that would take place there in a few days. She argued that being saturnine, she needed diversion to prevent her from falling into listlessness.[48] Ercole seems to have recognized that melancholy was an undesirable trait in a prince and he took full advantage of Francesco's youthful exuberance to mask his own dour nature.

According to Caleffini, the young marquis of Mantua 'was much loved by the citizens of Ferrara.'[49] This comment appears in a journal entry of 24 April 1486, which describes the appearance of Francesco and his splendidly outfitted entourage during the parade that preceded the *Palio*, the main attraction of the spring festival held on the feast day of Saint George, the patron saint of Ferrara. The celebrations traditionally consisted of a series of races through the principal streets. The first and most prestigious event, a race of thoroughbred Barbary

[45] Zambotti, *Diario ferrarese*, 163; Ferrarini, *Memoriale*, 218.   [46] Ferrarini, *Memoriale*, 232.

[47] Luzio, 'Promessi sposi', 19.

[48] 'La Excellentia Vostra me ha priva de tutti quelli cum li quali pigliana qualche recreatione, per modo che quando stesse a questo modo, veneria insensata, essendo saturnina como sono....et però, intendendo che a Bressa se fa una giostra a li vinti de questo, la supplico se digni essere contenta ch'io gli vadi.' Isabella d'Este to Francesco Gonzaga, 16 June 1497, from Mantua, ASMn, AG, 2112, c. 86.

[49] Caleffini, *Croniche*, 671.

horses, was followed by a running of asses. Then there were footraces of Jewish men and of the city's prostitutes, the latter event eventually changed by a reform-minded Ercole to young girls from the country. The feast of Saint George had long been used by the Este rulers as an opportunity to impress both locals and the thousands of visitors who flocked into Ferrara for the occasion with displays of the regime's magnificence.[50] Ercole made sure that Francesco figured promin-ently in the pageantry. The Gonzaga stables boasted some of the finest bloodstock in all of Italy. Not surprisingly, one of the marquis's stallions took the prize in the major race that year, as indeed happened on many future occasions.[51]

In early January 1487, Caleffini reiterated in his chronicle that Francesco was very well regarded in Ferrara. This time, it was not the marquis's magnificent appearance among finely dressed courtiers that he praised, but the young prince's open-handedness: '[He] was much appreciated by the people of Ferrara because of his great liberality towards those who served him.'[52] Francesco's reputation for generosity had been established the previous year, when he presented his friend, Zaccharia Zambotti, with the expensive length of cloth, or *palio*, that he had won when his horse came first in a race held in the ducal hunting park. This gesture was recorded, not by Zambotti's chronicler cousin, but by Ferrarini, who wrote in his memoire that after the marquis gave the extravagant gift to Zaccharia, the *palio* was paraded through the city by the dwarf Diodato, the Este court jester, so spreading the news of Francesco's munificence and augmenting the favour with which he was viewed by the local population.[53]

Ercole's eldest son Alfonso was still a little too young to feature in his father's choreographed pageantry, but Francesco was a perfect filial figure. He was still amenable to direction, but sufficiently mature to take a central role in the jousts and tournaments that the duke staged in the city and at his country villas. Such events were central to the portrayal of the Este regime as possessing a long, illus-trious pedigree and their Francophile cultural aesthetic reminded the duke's sub-jects of Ferrara's links with France. The duke continued to present his relationship with Francesco as that of an indulgent father, as he had in the early 1480s, when he had regularly decreed an early start to Carnival, so the youth and his friends could take full advantage of the enjoyable period before the beginning of Lent. In 1487, Carnival began on 10 December, almost a month before the usual date.[54] Now the entertainments were no longer snowball battles with the students from the university, or pranks in the streets, but rather balls and great feasts hosted by some of the wealthiest courtiers in Ferrara, such as the Neapolitan exile,

---

[50] See Deanna Shemek, *Ladies Errant: Wayward Women and Social Order in Early Modern Italy* (Durham, N.C.: Duke University Press, 1998), 17–44, 194–207.

[51] Caleffini, *Croniche*, 671; Zambotti, *Diario ferrarese*, 164.   [52] Caleffini, *Croniche*, 681.

[53] Ferrarini, *Memoriale*, 232.   [54] Caleffini, *Croniche*, 681.

Sigismondo Cantelmo, and Giulio Tassoni, who became Francesco's intimate companions and jousting partners.[55]

Keen to match the fame of the Gonzaga as horse breeders, Ercole promoted his own court's ready access to a fine hunting reserve. The destruction wrought in the Barco by Venetian soldiers during the War of Ferrara was redressed by the duke in the mid-1480s with a major renovation of the park, which included the installation of a race course designed to entertain onlookers with its novel design. Instead of a conventional track, Ercole created a hippodrome, planted with hedges in the shape of a snail, so that the horses appeared and disappeared from the view of spectators, as the course curved sharply this way and that over a labyrinth of three miles.[56] The conspicuous pursuit of leisure was integral to a noble identity and the duke made Francesco the principal protagonist of spectacles that were designed to impress with their audacity, ingenuity, and splendour.

In the same period, Ercole initiated other innovative cultural projects that communicated his majesty without being reliant on masculine vigour. Francesco was required to be an admiring onlooker, rather than a lead participant, when the duke turned his attention to the staging of classical theatre, expanding on the apparatus of spectacle that his predecessor, Borso d'Este, had promoted with tableaux vivants, jousts in classical costumes, and processions with elaborate floats.[57] In January 1486, Francesco travelled to Ferrara to witness the duke's first production since ancient times of Plautus' comedy, *Menaechmi*, which was presented to a large audience in a newly built courtyard of the ducal palace.[58] No expense was spared on the staging, which included a backdrop of a fully rigged ship and sets of an urban piazza ringed by five wooden houses.[59] The costumes were overseen by the jurist and humanist scholar, Pellegrino Prisciano, who was an expert on ancient Roman theatre, while the text was translated into Italian by Isabella's tutor, Battista Guarini, also a renowned humanist.[60] At the conclusion of the play there was a spectacular display of fireworks, arranged on a Catherine wheel, or *girandola*.[61]

---

[55] Zambotti, *Diario ferrarese*, 198; Ferrarini, *Memoriale*, 217, 293.

[56] Ferrarini, *Memoriale*, 213, 241. Tuohy, *Herculean Ferrara*, 243–5. On the importance of the elite hunt as a means of achieving political legitimation and promoting a powerful masculine identity in the premodern centuries, see Thomas T. Allsen, *The Royal Hunt in Eurasian History* (Singapore: Institute of Southeast Asian Studies, 2013).

[57] Louise George Clubb, 'Staging Ferrara: State Theatre from Borso to Alfonso II', in *Phaethon's Children. The Este Court and Its Culture in Early Modern Ferrara*, ed. Deanna Shemek and Dennis Looney (Tempe, Ariz.: Arizona Centre for Medieval and Renaissance Studies, 2005), 345–62.

[58] See Giulia Torello-Hill, 'The Revival of Classical Roman Comedy in Renaissance Ferrara: From the Scriptorium to the Stage', in *Terence between Late Antiquity and the Age of Printing*, ed. Giulia Torello-Hill and Andrew Turner (Leiden; Boston: Brill, 2015), 219–35.

[59] Tuohy, *Herculean Ferrara*, 260.

[60] Caleffini, *Croniche*, 668; Ferrarini, *Memoriale*, 232.

[61] Zambotti claimed that ten thousand people watched the play; *Diario ferrarese*, 172. Ferrarini and Caleffini do not mention the exact number of onlookers, but describe a huge crowd of notables, both local and foreign, university scholars and teachers and citizens: Ferrarini, *Memoriale*, 232; Caleffini, *Croniche*, 668.

Following the widely acknowledged success of his initiative, Ercole put on two other plays in the following year. The first was by the contemporary writer Niccolò da Correggio. His *Cefalo* was staged during the wedding of the wealthy courtier Giulio Tassoni and Ippolita de' Contrari, also from one of the city's most elite families. Later in 1487, Plautus' *Amfitrione* was part of the entertainments during another marriage: that between Ercole's natural daughter, Lucrezia d'Este, and Annibale Bentivoglio, eldest son of Giovanni Bentivoglio, the leader of the Bolognese ruling oligarchy. Zambotti reported that in this production, as the court musicians played their instruments and the ducal choir sang 'perfectly', the heavens opened by means of elaborate stage machinery, revealing the god Jove. Following the conclusion of the play, the labours of Hercules were performed, to remind the audience of the duke's link with his ancient Roman namesake.[62] Lame in one foot since his early days as a soldier, the duke shored up his image as a potent political figure through ever more elaborate theatrical productions, something that Francesco was to do when illness compromised his own virile image towards the end of his life.[63]

Ercole's interpretation of princely magnificence was to have an enduring impact on Francesco, although the latter was already thoroughly attuned to the ways in which his father and grandfather had promoted themselves as learned and generous cultural patrons. The very cityscape of Mantua attested to his predecessors' use of classicizing architecture and the latest trends in the visual arts to promote themselves as wise and upright rulers, who deserved the power they wielded. But it was in Ferrara that Francesco learned exactly how to deploy civic and court festival and the rituals of hunting and jousting to impress his subjects, to attract allies, and to deter potential enemies from challenging his authority, by projecting a public image of majesty and assertive masculinity.

Francesco also observed the ways in which Eleonora d'Aragona compensated for her husband's political shortcomings, and occasionally fragile health, by stepping into the breach when he neglected state affairs, or fell ill. The duchess's role could hardly have seemed shocking to a young man who had been brought up in a court dominated by his powerful and politically astute grandmother, Barbara of Brandenburg. Certainly, Eleonora assumed it was appropriate for her to mentor Francesco politically in the period after his father's death. She wrote to him on 16 July 1484, addressing him as her son-in-law and brother, and urging him to embrace the prudence and wisdom of a mature man, despite his youth, and to observe the other virtues required by a lord. Above all, she recommended he be god fearing and impartially just. Although the duchess did not explicitly claim in her letter that these were qualities she herself strived to respect in governing on her husband's behalf, the confident tone of her instructions implies a right to offer

---

[62] Zambotti, *Diario ferrarese*, 178–80.   [63] See Chapter 8.

the fruits of her own political experience.[64] It is doubtful that Francesco thought much about Eleonora's advice at this point in his life. His deputy, Francesco Secco, who had served three generations of Gonzaga rulers as the regime's official lieutenant, largely took care of day-to-day administration, leaving the young bachelor to continue to enjoy long periods of manly leisure in the prelude to marriage and adult responsibilities. The honing of a strong body and the cultivation of a soldierly persona seem to have taken precedence over the mundane minutiae of government, since it was as a successful military commander that Francesco hoped to win the admiring accolades of his peers.

On 30 April 1489, Francesco exchanged rings with Isabella in a ceremony within the Este castle, this discreet family occasion noted only in passing in Caleffini's chronicle and not at all in the others.[65] Ferrarini was out of town at the time and unable to keep abreast of news, while Zambotti's attention was directed to his own family. His sister had died in childbirth the day before. However, it is likely that only those who resided at court would have been privy to this traditional nuptial ritual, perhaps brought forward because of the news, which had reached Ferrara six weeks before, that the marquis had signed a lucrative military contract with Venice.[66] Although this arrangement departed from a longstanding Gonzaga tradition to serve the duchy of Milan militarily, the contract satisfactorily launched Francesco onto a career trajectory to which he had aspired for his entire youth. In the prelude to the public wedding celebrations, scheduled to take place during Carnival 1490, Francesco made sure to present himself during a visit to Ferrara of November 1489, not as a youth revelling in Carnival pranks and May Day celebrations, as he had in the past, but at the head of an impressive squadron of men-at-arms. He thus proclaimed himself to be a fully fledged adult ready for matrimony and a soldier prince in the tradition of his male forebears.

[64] Eleonora d'Aragona to Francesco Gonzaga, 16 July 1484, from Ferrara, published in Luzio, *Promessi sposi*, 23–4.

[65] The ceremony took place on 30 April: Caleffini, *Croniche*, 738; Ferrarini, *Memoriale*, 322; Zambotti, *Diario ferrarese*, 206. On the ceremonies that made up the nuptial ritual, see Christiane Klapisch-Zuber, 'Zacharias, or the Ousted Father: Nuptial Rites in Tuscany between Giotto and the Council of Trent', in *Women, Family, and Ritual in Renaissance Italy*, trans. Lydia Cochrane (Chicago; London: University of Chicago Press, 1985), 178–212.

[66] Ferrarini, *Memoriale*, 313; Zambotti, *Diario ferrarese*, 211. The contract signed on 12 March awarded Francesco 30,000 ducats in peacetime and 40,000 in war for five years. Leonardo Mazzoldi, *Mantova: La storia, le lettere, le arti*, vol. 2 (Mantova: Istituto Carlo d'Arco per la storia di Mantova, 1961), 79.

2
Building a Spousal Relationship

After weeks of farewell parties hosted by wealthy courtiers and her own parents, Isabella set off on the journey to Mantua around midday on 12 February 1490. Dressed in a gown of gold brocade and mounted on a white horse, she was the focus of a splendid procession that made its way through the principal streets of Ferrara. A triumphal cart that conjured up the military victories of ancient Rome preceded her.[1] This sumptuously constructed vehicle was part of Isabella's dowry, valued in total at twenty-five thousand ducats. According to an ambassadorial report sent to Mantua several months before, the rest of the financial settlement consisted of seven thousand ducats in cash and a silver credenza worth two thousand ducats, as well as jewels, silks, brocades, and other luxuries, the smaller items packed into ten strongboxes and four *cassoni*, or marriage chests.[2] Studded with semi-precious stones and clad in gold leaf, eleven thousand sheets of which had been ordered from Venice, these four large coffers had been made by the court artist and goldsmith, Ercole de' Roberti. As they were carried through the streets, their richly decorated surfaces must have created a strong visual link with the similarly bejewelled figure of Isabella in her gold brocade dress, the young woman and her dowry boxes serving to advertise to the crowds that witnessed the procession the great wealth and magnificence of the house of Este.[3]

The bride's female relatives travelled behind her in four carriages, while the ambassadors of Hungary and Naples, representing Isabella's royal connections through her aunt, Queen Beatrice of Hungary, and her Aragonese kin in southern Italy, followed the women's vehicles on foot. The parade terminated at San Paolo on the Ferrarese tributary of the Po River, where a new state bucentaur, commissioned to take the main bridal party to Mantua, was moored. Everyone else boarded a flotilla of gaily decorated barges and other craft, leaving Ferrara 'widowed' as Caleffini put it, because no one of consequence remained at court.[4]

Francesco had spent Christmas 1489 in Ferrara, but, after the Epiphany, he had hastened home to spend the rest of January and the first weeks of February preparing to receive the bride and her relatives.[5] According to Bernardino Zambotti,

---

[1] Caleffini, *Croniche*, 750–1; Zambotti, *Diario ferrarese*, 213–14.
[2] Girolamo Stanga to Francesco Gonzaga, 16 November 1489, from Ferrara, ASMn, AG, 1231, cc. 665r–666v.
[3] Tuohy, *Herculean Ferrara*, 232.
[4] Caleffini, *Croniche*, 751; Zambotti, *Diario ferrarese*, 213–14.   [5] Caleffini, *Croniche*, 746.

A Renaissance Marriage: The Political and Personal Alliance of Isabella d'Este and Francesco Gonzaga, 1490–1519.
Carolyn James, Oxford University Press (2020). © Carolyn James.
DOI: 10.1093/oso/9780199681211.001.0001

who was again briefed by his cousin, after traveling by barge for two days, Isabella disembarked and rested overnight before setting off the next day for the last short stage of her journey. The marquis rode out of the city to meet the bridal party accompanied by a richly attired group of two hundred courtiers and ambassadors. The groom's entourage was escorted by several squadrons of soldiers, a reminder to onlookers of his recent appointment as a Venetian military captain. Isabella processed to the San Giorgio castle beneath a damask canopy carried by six Mantuan knights and was greeted along the way by a series of theatrical tableaux representing the celestial bodies, from which children dressed as angels emerged to recite poems in praise of her. The celebrations continued over the next days with feasting, dancing, and two elaborately staged jousts.[6]

In describing the events associated with the Este-Gonzaga wedding, Caleffini and Zambotti were influenced by a genre of ekphratic writing with its origins in classical antiquity, which aimed to preserve a record of the ephemeral splendours of such occasions.[7] For Italy's rulers, weddings were an opportunity to enhance their prestige, not only in the minds of the crowds that watched the events at first hand, but also in those who could be reached later through literary and visual media. Spurred on by the prospect of this large audience, the duke and the marquis spent so lavishly on the wedding that they had to impose new taxes and forced loans on the city's already hard-pressed citizens, risking an upsurge of popular discontent.[8] The two rulers' readiness to spend well beyond their means was indicative of the importance they placed on magnificence as a political instrument that would advertise their noble status and imply a degree of power that they certainly did not possess in reality.

The duke returned to Ferrara on 23 February. The duchess and Isabella's siblings followed three days later. Zambotti concluded that Francesco Gonzaga had overseen a wedding 'splendid and glorious in every way'. Caleffini merely commented that the duke and duchess had come back to Ferrara, having left their daughter with her husband.[9] Although he continued to note the visits of the marquis to Ferrara in the following year, thereafter Caleffini's interest declined, to be replaced by a focus on the newly married Alfonso d'Este, heir to the duchy. Isabella's youth and secluded existence within the Este palaces and villas meant that she rarely attracted the attention of the Ferrarese chroniclers; even during

    [6] Zambotti, *Diario ferrarese*, 214–15.
    [7] Examples of such stand-alone descriptions of other Este weddings are the *Hymeneo Bentivoglio* and the *Colloquium ad Ferrarium urbem*, both by the Bolognese writer Giovanni Sabadino degli Arienti. See *The Letters of Giovanni Sabadino Degli Arienti (1481–1510)*, ed. Carolyn James (Florence: L.S. Olschki; Perth: University of Western Australia, 2002), 19, 156–7.
    [8] For the enormous sums of money spent by the Este on Isabella's wedding, see Richard Brown, 'The Politics of Magnificence in Ferrara 1450–1505: A Study in the Socio-Political Implications of Renaissance Spectacle', unpublished PhD Dissertation, University of Edinburgh, 1982, 472–7.
    [9] Zambotti, *Diario ferrarese*, 215–16; Caleffini, *Croniche*, 753.

her wedding, she features in their accounts only as a magnificently dressed, distant figure on a white horse.

Yet it is at this moment that a new set of evidence comes to the fore, one that contrasts markedly with the glitter and pomp associated with the choreographed public events. The letters that Isabella sent to family members and friends in Ferrara in the aftermath of the Mantuan festivities reveal the trepidation, and even alienation, with which she approached married life. Although she had known her destiny for ten years and moved merely to a neighbouring state where, unlike many other dynastic spouses, she did not have to adapt to a new language, or to markedly different cultural norms, Isabella experienced the initial phase of marriage as a debilitating emotional shock. Francesco, on the other hand, took wedlock in his stride, maintaining many of his bachelor habits and spending long periods at his country estates, where he continued to devote himself to the manly pleasures of hunting boar and jousting.

The Establishment of Emotional and Physical Intimacy

The departure from Mantua of the last wedding guests, including her mother and sister, on 23 February 1490, plunged Isabella into melancholy. She attempted to alleviate a sense of isolation by writing immediately to her sister Beatrice, whose marriage to Lodovico Sforza, duke of Bari and defacto ruler of Milan, was still a year away. She begged Beatrice to represent her at their mother's nightly benediction, a ritual she could now only wistfully imagine from afar.[10] Isabella penned many other letters, but received little in return until early March, when a note from Diana di Cumani, one of Eleonora d'Aragona's ladies-in-waiting, lifted her spirits. It assured Isabella that everyone at the Ferrarese court missed her and that the duchess was so disconsolate about her elder daughter's absence that she could not bear to enter the empty bedroom.[11] Isabella hastened to respond to this news with grateful enthusiasm:

> Though we have always been certain of how tenderly she loves us, this was nonetheless the best news we could possibly have heard, for we will live content in this world to the degree that we know we are in her good graces. Though to us it is an agony to be torn from her, we won't expend many words to tell you so, because you know in some measure the passionate and incomparable love and honor we bear her. We will tell you just this: that when we see that evening has

---

[10] Isabella d'Este to Beatrice d'Este, 23 February 1490, from Marmirolo, in Isabella d'Este, *Selected Letters*, 25.

[11] Diana di Cumani to Isabella d'Este, 1 March 1490, from Ferrara, ASMn, AG, 1231, cc. 734r–v.

come and we cannot kiss her hand as is our custom, we become so ill-disposed that we can find no consolation.[12]

Writing to an older, sympathetic lady-in-waiting, whom she had known for many years, seems to have elicited an outpouring of bottled-up emotion. The references to the separation from her mother as an 'agony' and to her 'passionate and incomparable' filial love communicate Isabella's acute homesickness in the aftermath of the wedding. Although Francesco was hardly a stranger, thanks to his frequent visits to Ferrara throughout her childhood, Isabella's letters to Ferrara suggest she considered herself abandoned and in exile. The prospect of the consummation of the marriage was also possibly a source of anxiety, since this does not seem to have occurred while the guests were still in Mantua, except perhaps symbolically, through a ritual putting-to-bed ceremony.

In contrast to his wife's limited life experience, by the time he married, Francesco had already fathered at least one child and, at almost twenty-six, was likely to have been sexually active for a decade, or more. A baby girl, born in 1487 and named Margherita in honour of his mother, was entrusted to the care of his sister, Elisabetta Gonzaga, following the latter's marriage to Guidobaldo da Montefeltro, duke of Urbino. Only a few of Francesco's other illegitimate offspring are documented to the point that we know their names.[13] Casual sexual liaisons, and the children that sometimes came of them, were taken for granted by contemporaries as a prerogative of masculinity, especially in the case of a young prince.

Francesco's sexuality featured prominently in a posthumous biographical portrait by the physician, prelate, and humanist scholar, Paolo Giovio. In chapter five of the *Elogia virorum bellica virtute illustrium*, begun around 1520, a year after Francesco's death, Giovio praised the late marquis's 'splendid and unusual greatness of spirit', 'regal hospitality', outstanding stable of fine horses, and bawdy humour: 'Francesco was of a generous, open disposition, never a liar nor malicious; in his conversations, which were filled with double meanings, he ridiculed the modesty of women.'[14] Although Giovio conceded that Francesco's habit of 'changing women frequently' was responsible for his contracting the Great Pox, he wrote of this consequence sympathetically, as a scourge of the times, rather than as a punishment for promiscuity.[15]

---

[12] Isabella d'Este to Diana di Cumani, 4 March 1490, from Mantua, in Isabella d'Este, *Selected Letters*, 28.

[13] On Francesco's illegitimate children, see Bourne, *The Soldier-Prince*, 50, n. 79.

[14] Paolo Giovio, *Elogia virorum bellica virtute illustrium* (Basel: Pietro Perna (for Heinrich Petri), 1575), ch. 5, 234–6 (234). The English translations quoted here are from Molly Bourne, 'Mail Humour and Male Sociability: Sexual Innuendo in the Epistolary Domain of Francesco II Gonzaga', in *Erotic Cultures of Renaissance Italy*, ed. Sara F. Matthews-Grieco (Aldershot: Ashgate, 2010), 199–221.

[15] Giovio, *Elogia virorum bellica virtute illustrium*, 248.

Giovio's characterization is supported by earlier evidence associated with the marquis's male intimates, who knew they could please him by sharing details of their sexual exploits. The Gonzaga diplomat and courtier, Pandolfo Collenuccio, was permitted to address his master familiarly, an unusual privilege that indicated a particularly close bond between the two men. He wrote to Francesco on 12 March 1495 about an evening shared with three friends in a local brothel. The detailed account assumed that his correspondent knew both the male and female protagonists well and would take voyeuristic pleasure from the explicit description of their libidinous interactions. Francesco was in Venice at the time, marshalling troops and preparing to fight the French army, as it returned northwards after its defeat of the Aragonese monarchy in Naples. The timing of Collenuccio's letter was no accident: virile acts in the bordello would surely inspire similarly heroic deeds on the battlefield.[16]

Francesco's use of an erotic letter seal at another significant military moment further demonstrates this link. He closed up letters of 22 and 25 April 1507, addressed to Tolomeo Spagnoli, then his personal secretary and confidante, with a seal based on an ancient Roman *spintria*, a gaming or brothel token, depicting a copulating couple in a transgressive sexual position. Written in his own hand, Francesco's letter sent news of the successful reclaiming of Genoa by the French king, in whose service he was employed as a mercenary captain.[17] The pornographic image embossed on the red wax proclaimed victory even before the letter was opened: in the minds of his male contemporaries, sexual and military conquest were so closely intertwined that one might proclaim the other. Moreover, Francesco's courtiers assumed that when it came to assuaging his sexual appetite the marquis was not overly fussy about the means by which he might do so. In the autumn of 1506, when Francesco was encamped outside Bologna during papal military operations to expel the ruling Bentivoglio from the city, and no prostitutes were readily at hand, a young boy was procured for his gratification.[18] Here again, the relationship between soldierly victory and sexual dominance was seen by contemporaries as quite explicit.

Francesco's appreciation of scatological humour was also taken for granted within his circle at court and by male clients from elsewhere, such as the Bolognese priest and teacher of canon law, Floriano Dolfo, who wrote regularly to the marquis between 1493 and 1506, providing news and gossip that came his way in Bologna. When the priest learned that Isabella had given birth to the couple's first child, for example, he wrote consolingly to Francesco on 14 January 1494

---

[16] Bourne, 'Mail Humour and Male Sociability', 206–7. On the sexual culture of the Gonzaga court, see also Giancarlo Malacarne and Costantino Cipolla, eds, *El più soave et dolce et dilectevole et gratioso bochone: amore e sesso al tempo dei Gonzaga* (Milano: Angeli, 2006).

[17] Bourne, 'Mail Humour and Male Sociability', 205.

[18] Alessandro Luzio, 'Isabella d'Este di fronte a Giulio II negli ultimi tre anni del suo pontificato', *Archivio storico lombardo* 17 (1912): 245–334; 18 (1912), 55–144, 393–456 (see p. 254).

about the fact that he had fathered a girl, rather than the much-wanted heir. He joked that since a female baby was likely to be smaller than a male: 'you will have the advantage of deriving greater pleasure from your mutual embraces, since [your member] will not find such a large chamber that it would resemble a dried seed in a rattle, or a clapper in a bell.'[19] Francesco savoured this piece of male camaraderie, assuring Dolfo that he had ordered that the letter be read out to him twice.[20]

In another letter of 1494, this one undated, the same priest provided Francesco with a titillating literary anecdote modelled on Poggio Bracciolini's widely circulated epistle of 1416 to his friend and fellow Florentine, Niccolò Niccoli, which described the former's visit to the spa at Baden. The earlier humanist account of mixed bathing in a northern European context, a phenomenon unfamiliar to an Italian audience and therefore enjoyably shocking, was mildly voyeuristic. Dolfo's description of the licentious behaviour of the patrons of the thermal baths of Porretta, located in the Apennines above Bologna, was far more sexually explicit and tailored precisely to appeal to the marquis's lascivious tastes.[21]

Eventually, Isabella grew accustomed to her husband's crude sexual jokes and the aggressively masculine culture of his cronies. However, the road to what was probably a resigned tolerance was far from smooth. She seems to have been propelled into marriage armed with almost no information about sex, beyond vague instructions from her parents to do her duty promptly and cheerfully. Her sister Beatrice was equally ill prepared when she married Lodovico Sforza in January 1491.[22] In this case, the ensuing problems are vividly documented in letters between the Ferrarese ambassador to Milan, Giacomo Trotti, and the bride's father, Ercole d'Este.

Beatrice d'Este was fifteen when she married, the same age as Isabella had been when she wed Francesco, almost exactly a year before. Eleonora d'Aragona had firmly resisted attempts to hasten the wedding, on the grounds that her daughter was still too young, but the postponement was not sufficient to prevent a rocky start to the relationship. When the 40-year-old Lodovico attempted to consummate the union, following the elaborate wedding celebrations, he was rebuffed by

---

[19] Floriano Dolfo, *Lettere ai Gonzaga*, ed. Marzia Minutelli (Roma: Edizioni di Storia e Letteratura, 2002), 10–13.

[20] Francesco Gonzaga to Floriano Dolfo, 22 January 1494, from Goito, ASMn, AG, 2906, libro 149, c. 16v. I quote Molly Bourne's translation of this passage. See her 'Mail Humour and Male Sociability', 210.

[21] Dolfo, *Lettere ai Gonzaga*, 18–23.

[22] Ercole's instructions to Beatrice are referred to in a letter he sent to his daughter after hearing about her recalcitrant post nuptial behaviour . 'Et per conservatione del mutuo nostro amore, vi dicemo et comfortamo strettamente ad sapervi cum humanità et dextreza deportavi col prefato Illustrissimo Signore et esserli bona et obediente et sapervelo conservare, come però siamo certi che faceti et farete, et che non sapereste fare altramente per li ricordi che altre volte vi havemo dato.' Ercole d'Este to Beatrice d'Este, 30 January 1491, from Ferrara, ASMo, Carteggio principi esteri, minuti di lettere ducali a principi esteri, Milano, 1507, D22, c. 353.

his panic-stricken bride. Despite Lodovico's patient coaxing and the combined efforts of the girl's parents and the Ferrarese ambassador to persuade Beatrice to abandon her stubborn resistance, no progress had been achieved by 21 February 1491. Trotti reported to the duke of Ferrara that the exasperated groom had admitted that Beatrice was still embarrassed by any attempt to caress her and had feigned sleep when he had visited her bed chamber on the previous evening.[23] A little over two weeks later, Lodovico was able to hint to Trotti that sexual congress had at last been achieved, a message the ambassador conveyed promptly to the girl's worried parents.[24] Thereafter the relationship between Lodovico and Beatrice prospered. In January 1493, a healthy son was born, an outcome that saw a triumphant Beatrice able to bask in the favour of her husband and the warm approval of her Este relatives.

Isabella seems not to have rebelled so dramatically against the expectation that she would welcome her husband's sexual attentions, but there is a documented hint that the consummation of her marriage was traumatic enough for the memory to linger unpleasantly in her mind for decades. When her eldest daughter Eleonora wed the pope's nephew, Francesco Maria della Rovere, the marchioness sought reassurance from Alessandro Picenardi—a trusted courtier who, in December 1509, accompanied the bride to her new home in Urbino—that the first physical encounter between the couple had gone well. Picenardi's reply suggests that Isabella had confided in him about her own sexual initiation. She was worried that Eleonora's experience would be similarly negative.[25]

When exactly the union of Francesco and Isabella was sexually consummated, the ultimate ratification of the marital bond, is not revealed in the extant sources. It is likely to have occurred in the relative privacy of the rural palace of Marmirolo between late February and the first days of March 1490, when the couple were briefly together there following the exodus of guests from Mantua. In November 1489, Bernardino Ghisolfo, overseer of renovations at Marmirolo, had undertaken to work 'night and day' so that improvements to the main residence, then fifty years old, would be finished in time for the wedding. Ercole d'Este had agreed to be accommodated at this country palace to relieve the pressure on available rooms in Mantua and Francesco was eager to impress a father-in-law who took such an interest in building. Ghisolfo's letter reveals that the marquis was

---

[23] Giacomo Trotti to Ercole d'Este, 21 February 1491, from Milan, ASMo, Carteggio Ambasciatori, Milano, 6.

[24] Giacomo Trotti to Ercole d'Este, 13 March 1491, from Milan, ASMo, Carteggio Ambasciatori, Milano, 6. For a fuller discussion of the situation, see Carolyn James, 'What's Love Got to Do with It? Dynastic Politics and Motherhood in the Letters of Eleonora of Aragon and Her Daughters', *Women's History Review* 24.4 (2015): 528–47.

[25] Picenardi's letter to Isabella of 27 December 1509 is published in Alessandro Luzio and Rodolfo Renier, *Mantova e Urbino (1471–1539): Isabella d'Este ed Elisabetta Gonzaga nelle relazioni famigliari e nelle vicende politiche: narrazione storica documentata* (Torino: Roux, 1893), 193–5. He refers to the 'rottura', or rupture, Isabella had suffered.

concerned that the painters, Tondo de' Tondi and Gian Luca Liombeni, complete the decorations for one particular room which was to feature an image of a baby boy.[26] This was probably the marital suite to which Francesco brought his bride in late February 1490, the frescoed male child a symbol and talisman of the hoped-for fertility of the union. But it may have been an unpropitious beginning to their sexual couplings that created a degree of reserve between Isabella and her husband in the early phase of their marriage. An examination of the dispatch points of their correspondence in 1490 reveals that they were together very little that year. While it was assumed that princes and their consorts would inhabit separate apartments, have their own country villas, and spend most of their days and nights in the company of their respective courtiers or ladies-in-waiting, those in a position to observe the couple noted that the newlyweds spent more time apart than was usual.

Francesco was often in the country overseeing building renovations at Gonzaga and Marmirolo, and regularly travelled further afield, including five times to Ferrara, coinciding with Isabella briefly in late April. The marchioness stayed on in her natal court on that occasion for three weeks and returned there, without her husband, in July and November. For the rest of 1490, she was in Mantua, or its vicinity, frequently in the company of her sister-in-law, Elisabetta Gonzaga. From time to time, Francesco summoned Isabella by letter to join him at one of his country estates. On 31 May 1490, for example, he wrote that she was to come to the palace at Gonzaga, bringing as few attendants as possible, while on 22 July he asked her to meet him on the following evening at Marmirolo, again stipulating she should arrive with a minimal entourage. Francesco cited the shortage of accommodation as the reason for his request that his wife leave most of her companions behind in Mantua. However, it is likely he sought privacy, so he might overcome Isabella's reserve in a more intimate setting.[27]

When Isabella moved to Mantua in early 1490, Eleonora d'Aragona appointed two senior members of her own household to supervise the marchioness's younger ladies-in-waiting and to be the motherly figures to whom her daughter could turn for counsel. The women were also Eleonora's eyes and ears: her spies in effect.[28] Beatrice de' Contrari, from one of Ferrara's leading families, and a Neapolitan woman referred to simply as Collona—who had accompanied the duchess to Ferrara in 1473 and then served as Isabella's governess—made it their business to keep Eleonora informed about her daughter's behaviour. They also acted as

---

[26] Molly Bourne, *The Soldier-Prince*, 120–1. For a transcription of Bernardino Ghisolfo's letter to the marquis of 19 November 1489, see 310–11.

[27] Francesco Gonzaga to Isabella d'Este, 31 May and 1 June 1490, ASMn, AG, 2106, cc. 303 and 304; 22 and 23 July 1490, cc. 310 and 311.

[28] Catherine de Médicis similarly relied on senior members of the female entourage of Elizabeth de Valois to provide information about her daughter and Spanish court. See Susan Broomhall, "'My Daughter, My Dear": The Correspondence of Catherine de Médicis and Elisabeth de Valois', *Women's History Review* 24.4 (2015): 548–69 (551–2).

mediators between Francesco and his wife, smoothing the way for what they hoped would be the gradual establishment of conjugal love. Evidence of this role is preserved in the letters of Beatrice de' Contrari, most of which were dictated to Isabella's newly appointed secretary, Benedetto Capilupi. It appears that Beatrice could not write, or wrote poorly, a state of affairs that was far from unusual, even for a woman from a notable aristocratic background.

On 7 April 1490, Beatrice dictated a message to Capilupi which reported to Francesco on the reception of a letter that he had written to Isabella in his own hand, during his travels to Udine in the far north of Italy. The unusual gesture of writing in holograph had given his wife such pleasure, Beatrice assured the marquis, that Isabella had insisted on keeping the letter close to her heart, allowing no one to touch it, or even to look at it, except from a distance. Implying that a new husband should capitalize on such a warm display of wifely ardour, she urged a speedy return home: 'I pray you, come back soon!'[29] Francesco complied, but apparently saw no reason to delay resuming his travels. At the end of April, after having spent a week with Isabella in Ferrara, he set off from there on another journey, this time to Ravenna. Beatrice pursued him by mail once again, informing him that as his horse had disappeared from view, Isabella had lingered at the window of the Este palace and shed a tear or two at the prospect that she would not set eyes on her husband for some weeks.[30]

Later in 1490, in response to criticism that she had failed to send the marquis news that Isabella was ill, Beatrice explained in a letter of 4 August that not only had she lacked money to send a courier, she had heard that Francesco was himself unwell and had therefore not wanted to delay his convalescence with upsetting news. In any case, his anger was comforting, she assured him, since it was evidence that he missed his wife. Beatrice suggested that Francesco hurry home, on the grounds that Isabella could have no better doctor or medicine than him, 'because neither Collona, nor I, have the necessary means (*instrumenti*) to cure her.'[31] The sexual innuendo here heralded an approach that Beatrice was to use quite often. In early November, she again tried humour, appealing to Francesco to consider how she and Collona suffered, as they waited patiently, 'dead tired' and 'with cold feet', while Isabella prepared slowly for bed, sadly reflecting on the number of days that it had been since she had

[29] 'di continuo quella porta adosso, né ha volute ch' io habia gratia di poterla basare ... anzi, la tene stricta et cum rispecto, monstrandomila da longi ... Prego quella al venire presto.' Beatrice de' Contrari to Francesco Gonzaga, 7 April 1490, from Mantua, ASMn, AG, 2438, c. 412.
[30] Beatrice de' Contrari to Francesco Gonzaga, 30 April 1490, from Mantua, ASMn, AG, 1231, c. 873.
[31] 'Io existimi che non se ritrovi megliore medico né medicina de la Signoria Vostra, perché Collona né io non havemo li instrumenti necessarii.' Beatrice de' Contrari to Francesco Gonzaga, 4 August 1490, from Mantua, ASMn, AG, 2438, c. 413.

seen her husband.[32] Christmas saw Francesco once again in Ferrara, but not with his wife. Beatrice informed him that Isabella was tearful about his absence and needed comforting.[33] Throughout 1490, the marchioness's elderly retainer did her best to convince Francesco to minimize his absences from Mantua, but the jokes and anecdotes about a pitifully pining Isabella had little lasting effect.

Beatrice's lack of success in convincing Francesco of his wife's devotion is unsurprising given that he probably saw scarce evidence of it when Isabella was with him. However, Isabella was more forthcoming in writing, adhering in a letter of late April 1490 to a predictable, but elegantly crafted, script of how a new bride ought to write to her husband:

> I cannot help worrying, for I am unable to see you every day, and I recall how you said to me as you were leaving that you didn't feel very well. This was like a knife in my heart. I will not be glad until I have some word of Your Lordship. I pray you see fit to have me notified of your condition. You will excuse me if this letter is not written in my hand, for I am thoroughly disquieted by your departure.[34]

In his reply of 5 May, the marquis gently mocked Isabella's excuse for not writing in holograph, and there appears to be a note of irony in his response to her stylized expressions of love:

> By the grace of God, we are well, despite feeling rather desperately ill when we left. Trusting that you will also remain well, we urge you to be cheerful and to enjoy yourself until our return, which will be soon. We are not writing in our own hand, so as to avoid the toil, as indeed you have also done.[35]

Yet Francesco was equally conventional in his use of epistolary rhetoric. He referred to himself using the first person plural pronoun, as Isabella did in her letter to Diana di Cumani who, although clearly a friend and confidante, was a ducal servant and the marchioness's social inferior. In Francesco's case, the plural

---

[32] 'quando la debbe andare a lecto sta a numerare i giorni che la non ha veduto la Signoria Vostra et ne tene Collona et io a morire de somno et de freddo in pede. Però pregamo la Signoria Vostra, se l'ha chara la vita nostra, voglia retornare presto.' Beatrice de' Contrari to Francesco Gonzaga, 7 November 1490, from Mantua, ASMn, AG, 2438, c. 423.

[33] Beatrice de' Contrari to Francesco Gonzaga, 26 December 1490, from Mantua, ASMn, AG, 2438, c. 424.

[34] Isabella d'Este to Francesco Gonzaga, 30 April 1490, from Ferrara, in Isabella d'Este, *Selected Letters*, 32.

[35] 'Noy, per la Dio grazia, siamo sani, quantunche nel partirse fussimo alquanto disperati. El simile desyderamo sia sempre di Lei, così la comfortamo a vivere allegramente e tendere a darsi piacere insino a la ritornata nostra, che serrà presto. Né li scrivemo per hora de nostra mane per schivare faticha, come fa la Signoria Vostra anchor Lei.' Francesco Gonzaga to Isabella d'Este, 5 May 1490, from Ravenna, AGMn, AG, 2106, c. 302.

pronoun was a standard expression of the gendered hierarchy and of his princely status. His patronizing tone would not have been perceived as arrogance, but as an appropriate recognition of the patriarchal authority that he possessed in relation to his younger wife.

Isabella continued to write to Francesco in the same dutiful vein. When she was in Ferrara in November and December 1490, she assured him: 'I can take no pleasure here when I think about being so far from Your Lordship, whom I love more than my own life.'[36] In his reply, Francesco took his wife at her word and summoned her home to Mantua:

> Having understood from Your Ladyship's letters that because of our separation you cannot remain there in Ferrara with a quiet mind, which is as it should be given our immense reciprocal love, it seems to us that when you think you have been there for the amount of time that will satisfy the Illustrious Lord and Lady, our father and mother, the rest of the family and you yourself, having sought and obtained license from Their Excellencies, you ought to return home to satisfy once more our feelings and needs; thus with desire we await you.[37]

Isabella had an assured, if rather bland, arsenal of rhetoric with which to fulfil her wifely obligations to express marital love. She responded neutrally to the hint of sexual invitation here, thanking Francesco politely for his 'loving words' and assuring him 'I have no less desire to see you than you have me'.[38] But she remained in Ferrara for another week.

The marquis was willing enough to court Isabella, but his epistolary attempts to do so could be maladroit. During his own visit to Ferrara some months earlier to take advantage of the autumn hunting season, he apologized for not writing to Isabella on the grounds that he had not expected to stay so long. The hospitality of her parents and the innumerable pleasures he had experienced had made him forget everything else, including his duty to stay in touch with her. Apparently

---

[36] 'Adesso m'è parso fare el debito mio scrivere a la Signoria Vostra come non posso havere de alcuna cosa piacere quando penso essere lontana de la Signoria Vostra, la quale amo più che la vita propria.' Isabella d'Este to Francesco Gonzaga, 25 November 1490, from Ferrara, AGMn, AG, 2106, c. 412.

[37] 'Havendo compreso per le lettere de la Signoria Vostra che quella per la separatione nostra non pò stare lì a Ferrara cum l'animo quieto, che cussì debbe essere convenientissimo per lo immenso nostro amore reciproco, ni pare che quella, quando a Lei parà essere stata lì per quel tempo che la possi havere satisfacto a quelli Illustrissimi Signori, nostri padre et matre, et al resto, et a Lei stessa, havuta et impetrata bona licentia da le Loro Excellentie, ritorni a casa per satisfare anchora a lo animo et bisogni nostri, che cussì cum desyderio la aspectiamo.' Francesco Gonzaga to Isabella d'Este, 28 November 1490, from Marmirolo, AGMn, AG, 2106, c. 344.

[38] 'A la parte del ritorno mio a casa, ringratio la Excellentia Vostra de le amorevole parole che la me scrive. Et perché io non ho manco desiderio de vederla che l'habia Lei me, domane ritornata che sia da Belriguardo, dove vado hozi in cumpagnia de li Illustri Signori mei fratelli e sorella, serò cum la Excellentia de Madama et terminaremo el dì de la partita.' Isabella d'Este to Francesco Gonzaga, 2 December 1490, from Ferrara, AGMn, AG, 2106, c. 418.

unaware that this excuse was hardly tactful, Francesco promised to return home soon, after a night's stop at Gonzaga 'to see that building of ours, then we will come to your sweet lap'.[39]

The epistolary diplomacy in which the pair engaged in the early phase of their marriage—earnestly' correct on Isabella's side and benignly patronizing, with the occasional boorish slip on the other—was, nonetheless, an important first step in building a communicative channel that endured for their entire marriage. In these early days, the couple's dutiful expressions of affection were bolstered by gifts of seasonal and local produce, sent from the various country estates, or from Lake Garda, the marshlands of Comacchio, and the Adriatic Sea. Such gestures were not confined to married couples, of course, but were rather part of wider practices of gift-giving that included siblings, parents, and other relatives. Ultimately, gifts were seen by contemporaries as essential to the cultivation of loving relations at a personal and family level, but as intrinsic also to the conduct of diplomacy between states.[40] As representatives of a significant political alliance, Isabella and Francesco deployed gifts in both these senses.

Beatrice de' Contrari's dogged efforts throughout 1490 to encourage Francesco to spend more time with Isabella appear to have gone unnoticed by Eleonora d'Aragona, preoccupied as she was with the arrangements for the wedding of her younger daughter Beatrice. Her main concern in 1490 was with Isabella's health, but this worry was such a perennial one that it did not occur to the duchess to look beyond excessive fasting during Lent for an explanation of the fact that her Mantuan correspondents observed that Isabella had become rather too thin. In a letter of 11 April 1490, Eleonora merely enjoined Isabella to eat more heartily, so she would put on weight.[41] But when Isabella succumbed to fevers in the summer, as had happened often enough in previous years, Eleonora's concern escalated. She wrote regularly with instructions, especially concerning the consumption of too much fruit, particularly dangerous during illness, according to the medical wisdom of the day, when bodily humours were already out of joint.[42] Although Isabella reluctantly obeyed her mother, the illness lingered, prompting Eleonora to dispatch her own doctor, Francesco da Castello, whose merry sense of humour made him a favourite with the marchioness.[43] On 2 September, upon learning that Isabella was at last convalescing, Ercole d'Este agreed to lend her a singer

---

[39] 'prima capiteremo a Gonzaga per vedere quella nostra fabrica poi veniremo al dolce grembo suo.' Francesco Gonzaga to Isabella d'Este, 17 October 1490, from Ferrara, ASMn, AG, 2106, c. 339.

[40] On this theme, see Loek Luiten, 'Friends and Family, Fruit and Fish: The Gift in Quattrocento Farnese Cultural Politics', *Renaissance Studies* 33.3 (2019): 342–57.

[41] Eleonora d'Aragona to Isabella d'Este, 11 April 1490, from Ferrara, ASMn, AG, 1184, unnumbered folio.

[42] Eleonora d'Aragona to Isabella d'Este, 18 and 23 August 1490, from Ferrara, ASMn, AG, 1184, unnumbered folios.

[43] Eleonora d'Aragona to Isabella d'Este, 26 and 29 August 1490, from Ferrara, ASMn, AG, 1184, unnumbered folios.

from his court, to relieve the boredom of her long confinement to bed. He also sent his favourite tonic to speed her recovery.[44] The duchess was herself quite unwell that summer, which perhaps distracted her from realizing that something was seriously amiss with her daughter beyond a bout of ill-health.

Between November 1490 and February 1491, Isabella and her mother were frequently in each other's company. The marchioness travelled to Ferrara to join the Este party setting off for Milan to attend the wedding of Beatrice d'Este and Lodovico Sforza. Immediately afterwards mother and daughter returned to Ferrara together to celebrate yet another marriage; that between Alfonso d'Este, heir to the duchy, and Anna Sforza, Lodovico Sforza's niece. Francesco made a brief incognito appearance in Milan, but chose not to stay with his wife. The opportunity to spend so much time with her mother made the return to Mantua difficult for Isabella. Her low spirits were communicated to Eleonora in a letter of 24 February 1491. This holograph letter does not survive, but the duchess's reply of four days later summarizes part of its content. It refers to the 'sadness and vexation' that Isabella had admitted to feeling since the recent parting from her mother. The latter responded briskly, pointing out that, as a married woman, Isabella's emotional focus should now be her husband, not her family in Ferrara.[45] Yet there was also sympathy in her reply. The duchess was probably more relaxed than Beatrice de' Contrari about the time it might take for Isabella to bond with Francesco, having been subjected to a politically motivated marriage herself, but at the age of twenty-two, not fifteen. She permitted Isabella to return to Ferrara for an extended visit in the spring of 1491, and when Francesco questioned the length of the stay, Eleonora replied complacently that his impatience was a good sign that he was beginning to love his wife.[46]

However, by the summer of that year, the duchess was worried. She had learned that Isabella was still shy with Francesco and preferred to keep physically aloof from him. It is likely that Beatrice de' Contrari revealed the situation during one of her visits to Ferrara. Alarmed at the prospect that Isabella was unlikely to fall pregnant, given her reluctance to seek out her husband's company, Eleonora decided on a sterner approach. Having learned that Francesco was unwell and

[44] Ercole d'Este to Isabella d'Este, 2 September 1490, from Ferrara, ASMn, AG, 1184, unnumbered folio.

[45] 'Havemo havuto la vostra lettera de 24 del presente, per la quale ne faceti intendere quanto dolore et molestia sentiti quando ve partiti da noi.…Ma quando pensamo che partendosse da nui andati al Illustre Signor consorte et che non ce seti molto longi, ne stiamo consolati et lieti, come anche vui doveti stare.' Eleonora d'Aragona to Isabella d'Este, 28 February 1491, from Ferrara, ASMn, AG, 1185, c. 83.

[46] 'Ma ben ne piace summamente havere compreso per le lettere de Vostra Signoria il desiderio la ha de vedere sua mogliere et de conferire cum lei, parendoli mille anni che la non la vedesse, che è signo che Vostra Excellentia comenza a volerli bene.' Eleonora d'Aragona to Francesco Gonzaga, 23 May 1491, from Belriguardo, ASMn, AG, 1185, c. 117.

had retired to his residence at Marmirolo, she ordered Isabella to gather her courage and join him there:

> Knowing that you are likely to be bashful and will not presume to put yourself forward as would be appropriate, it seems necessary to us in this letter of ours to exhort and admonish you to go often to visit your lord consort during his illness and ask him how he had been and how he is now, and with loving words and a pleasant demeanour comfort and caress him, serving him with your own hands and doing what we did when the Illustrious Lord your father was ill, because you saw very well how we attended him constantly with our own hand; and acting thus you will increase his love and win our blessing.[47]

This letter was the first of four communications reiterating the same message. On 1 August, Eleonora accused Isabella of still acting too coldly during her husband's illness. After insisting again that personal nursing was required, she ended the letter on a threatening note: 'And thus we urge you not to be remiss, if you want us to be happy with you and your actions.'[48] Just over a week later, despite reassurances from her daughter that she was diligently caring for Francesco, Eleonora repeated her demand that Isabella put aside embarrassment and explicitly express concern and affection for her ill spouse.[49] Only on 17 August, with news that the marquis was on the road to recovery and that Isabella was visiting him regularly, did the duchess express her satisfaction: 'We greatly praise that you go every day to His Lordship, as you claim.'[50] The threat of a withdrawal of maternal approval proved to be a formidable weapon, since Isabella craved Eleonora's good opinion and was punctiliously obedient to her in a way she was to no one else.

It is likely that Isabella's visits to Francesco's sick bed did facilitate greater ease between the couple, as Eleonora had predicted. However, the duchess also

---

[47] 'Cognoscendo nui che voi pur soleti esser vergognosa et non arditi a canzare a farvi inanti, come se conveniria, ni pare per questa nostra exhortarvi et admonirvi che spesso andati a visitare il signor vostro consorte in questa sua indispositione, et che lo domandati come è stato, e come sta, et cum parole amorevole et bona ciera lo confortati et acarezati, servendolo de vostra mano et tenendo de li modi che nui tenivemo quando lo Illustrissimo Signor, vostro padre, era infermo, perché vui molto ben vedesti come gli attendevemo da ogni hora de nostra mano, et cussì facendo, redupplicareti lo amore et nui ve ne benediremo.' Eleonora d'Aragona to Isabella d'Este, 28 July 1491, from Belriguardo, ASMn, AG, b. 1185, c. 159.

[48] 'Et cussì vi stringemo ad non manchare se voleti che stiamo alegra di voi et de l'opere vostre.' Eleonora d'Aragona to Isabella d'Este, 1 August 1491, from Belriguardo, ASMn, AG, b. 1185, c. 163.

[49] 'bisogna che in questo caso faciati del virile et ve ricordiati come habiamo facto nui verso il vostro illustrissimo padre quando la Sua Celsitudine è stata infirma.' Eleonora d'Aragona to Isabella d'Este, 9 August 1491, from Ferrara, ASMn, AG, 1185, c. 171.

[50] 'grandemente laudiamo che ogni giorno andiati a Sua Signoria secundo ne significati.' Eleonora d'Aragona to Isabella d'Este, 17 August 1491, from Ferrara, ASMn, AG, 1185, c. 175.

decided that Isabella should be discouraged from so frequently returning to the familiar routines of her childhood and to the bosom of her natal family. In late January 1492, she denied her daughter's request to visit the Ferrarese court, stipulating firmly that, in future, she should only come if accompanied by Francesco.[51] Although there were times when Eleonora relaxed this rule, she remained adamant that Isabella should no longer perceive Ferrara as home. Thus, she began firmly to escalate the pressure on her daughter to fulfil her primary duty: to produce the male child who would secure the Gonzaga succession.

The Mysteries of Being with Child

In February 1492, almost exactly two years after Isabella married, gossip circulated in Ferrara that she was with child. The courtier Giovanni Maria Trotti wrote to the marchioness on 9 February asking her if the rumour was true.[52] It was not. Later that year, the news from Milan that her younger sister was expecting a baby fuelled renewed speculation at the Este and Gonzaga courts about when Isabella would fall pregnant. Although in poor health, Eleonora d'Aragona had hastened to Milan early in the new year to be with Beatrice when she gave birth. As she waited for the labour to progress, the duchess wrote to Isabella on 24 January 1493, recommending that she too should make every effort to become pregnant as soon as possible.[53] The next day Eleonora informed her elder daughter of the successful delivery of Beatrice's son. She added that the euphoria of producing an heir and surviving the birth quite unscathed had prompted the new mother to muse that having a baby was far easier than baking a cake in the middle of July. Eleonora assured Isabella that she agreed with Beatrice, having many times watched her pastry cooks sweating near the fire, as they mixed the batter and then constantly moved the baking dish on the hot coals, to prevent the cake from burning, a far from pleasant undertaking during the height of summer.[54]

Isabella seems not to have taken this maternal attempt to lighten her terror about the dangers of childbirth to heart. In fact, there was some suspicion, several months later, about her motives for taking a particularly zealous approach to Lenten fasting. Beatrice de' Contrari and Francesco exchanged letters on the subject and, having learned of her daughter's meagre diet, Eleonora sternly ordered

[51] Eleonora d'Aragona to Isabella d'Este, 31 January 1492, from Ferrara, ASMn, AG, 1185, c. 333.
[52] Giovanni Maria Trotti to Isabella d'Este, 9 February 1492, from Ferrara, ASMn, AG, 1232, c. 277.
[53] Eleonora d'Aragona to Isabella d'Este, 24 January 1493, from Milan, ASMn, AG, 1184, c. 530.
[54] Eleonora d'Aragona to Isabella d'Este, 25 January 1493, from Milan, ASMn, AG, 1184, c. 529.

her not to fast so strictly as to risk compromising her health.[55] Isabella replied to her mother's letters, promising to obey.[56]

While Isabella remained fearful of pregnancy, she and Francesco gradually established a more relaxed epistolary rapport, helped in no small part by shared interests, especially a mutual obsession with horse-racing. When the unofficial leader of the Florentine republic, Lorenzo de' Medici, orchestrated the victory of his own horse over the champion stallion sent from the Gonzaga stables in mid-1492, during the annual *Palio* held in Florence on the feast of San Giovanni, the couple commiserated with each other about the loss of the valuable prize and expressed outrage that Lorenzo's concern to win at all costs had prompted him to cheat.[57]

Isabella became ever more passionate about racing after Francesco presented her with several horses of her own. Safinato, a bay stallion, proved initially disappointing as a runner, coming last in the Mantuan *Palio* of 1491.[58] However, by the following year, he had won so many races that Francesco joked in a letter of 19 August that he was determined to take the horse back.[59] Isabella argued wittily in response that since her very person and soul and everything else she possessed were the property of her husband, he could not deprive her of the horse without depriving himself.[60] Sauro, given to Isabella by Francesco in 1492, also proved to be a winner.[61] Thus, in the early summer of 1493, when the marquis caught sight of a marvellous jenny that the king of Naples had sent to his granddaughter, he decided that Isabella was already well catered for in the equine department and threatened to take the gift for his own use. This was despite the fact that the king

[55] 'Illustrissimo Signor mio. Per obedire la Excellentia Vostra, da heri in qua non ho facto altro ch'a confortare et pregare la illustrissima madonna marchesana che la non volesse degiunare. Ma lei sempre stave più salda de non volere rompere el proposito suo, per modo che me fu forza dirli che lo scriveria a la Signoria Vostra. Lei, più cauta di me, comise a Benedetto che non me obedisse.' Beatrice de' Contrari to Francesco Gonzaga, 4 March 1493, ASMn, AG, 2443, c. 342. 'Volemo che poniati il degiunare da canto et che vi sforzati de mantenirvi, anci, accrescere de le carne…perché sentimo pur el vostro stare non essere bono.' Eleonora d'Aragona to Isabella d'Este, 1 March 1493, from Ferrara, ASMn, AG, 1184, c. 540. On 6 March Eleonora returned to the same theme (c. 543).

[56] 'per obedirla ho interlassato el digiuno cottidiano che havea principiato per mia devotione.' Isabella d'Este to Eleonora d'Aragona, 8 March 1493, from Mantua, ASMn, AG, 2991, libro 3, c. 15v.

[57] Francesco Gonzaga to Isabella d'Este, 28 June 1491, from Florence, ASMn, AG, b. 2107, c. 52 and Isabella d'Este to Francesco Gonzaga, 1 July 1491, from Porto, ASMn, AG, b. 2107, c. 158. On Lorenzo de' Medici's pursuit of horse-racing as a source of political prestige, see Michael Mallett, 'Horse-Racing and Politics in Lorenzo's Florence', in *Lorenzo the Magnificent. Culture and Politics*, ed. Michael Mallett and Nicholas Mann (London: The Warburg Institute University of London, 1966), 251–62.

[58] Isabella d'Este to Francesco Gonzaga, 29 June 1491, ASMn, AG, b. 2107, c. 155.

[59] Francesco Gonzaga to Isabella d'Este, 19 August 1492, from Gonzaga, ASMn, AG, b. 2108, cc. 48r–v.

[60] 'Ma non credo già che la me lo debba tuore, como la mottegia, cognoscendola signore de tal constantia et fede che la non disdiria mai quello che una volta havesse dicto, salvo se la non facesse conto de inganarse se stessa, perché, essendo el barbaro, la persona et anima mia de la Signoria Vostra, non poteria privarne me che la non se ne privasse prima Lei.' Isabella d'Este to Francesco Gonzaga, 1 September 1492, from Caiazzo, ASMn, AG, b. 2108, c. 199.

[61] Isabella d'Este to Francesco Gonzaga, 26 June 1492, from Mantua, ASMn, AG, b. 2108, c. 145.

had sent Francesco several fine horses as well. Isabella enlisted the help of her sister-in-law, Elisabetta Gonzaga, to resist any such move by her husband.[62] Their bantering exchanges about horses and racing suggest the couple had worked out ways to negotiate amicably with each other, in writing at least. Certainly, by 1493, we begin to see the emergence of the steely side to Isabella's character, as she stoutly defended what she considered her own property and entitlements.

In Francesco's defence, we must take into account that several months before the jenny arrived from Naples in early June 1493, he had himself given his wife another splendid horse, as well as a white parrot and a civet cat that he had ordered from Cairo.[63] All three gifts were part of a strategy of courtship which seems to have produced marvellously prompt results. On 4 March, Beatrice de' Contrari reported to the marquis on Isabella's pleasure in learning to master the magnificent new mount under the supervision of the court riding instructor. She assured Francesco that the marchioness had returned home after her lesson so pleased and proud that one would have thought she had been given a kingdom, rather than a horse. She opined that Isabella had become such a good horsewoman that if she and Francesco produced children they would be 'the best riders in the world'.[64]

Within weeks Isabella was pregnant, although she remained unwilling to concede that this might be the case for many months to come. Having learned from Francesco that Isabella was finally with child, Eleonora wrote joyfully to her elder daughter on 21 May 1493 advising her to be cautious about activities, such as horse-riding, that might now be risky.[65] Isabella responded dourly. She begged her mother to prevent the news from becoming public, since she was by no means sure that she was pregnant:

> If I had any sense that this was so, by my duty Your Ladyship would be the first to hear of it. So I pray you not to speak further of this, and if others should speak to you about it, say you know nothing, just as I know nothing.[66]

---

[62] Isabella d'Este to Francesco Gonzaga, 6 June 1493, from Mantua, ASMn, AG, b. 2991, libro 3, c. 65r.

[63] Beatrice de' Contrari to Isabella d'Este, 3 January 1493, from Mantua, ASMn, AG, 2443, c. 341. On the theme of exotic creatures as gifts, see Sarah D. P. Cockram, 'Interspecies Understanding: Exotic Animals and their Handlers at the Italian Renaissance Court', *Renaissance Studies* 31.2 (2017): 277–96.

[64] 'Apresso l'aviso come hozi la prefata madonna è montata sul Morelleto che gli ha donato la Signoria Vostra, et lo ha cavalcato sul Te. Poi è andata in volta per la terra, credo per fare la monstra de questo cavallo....è ritornata a casa cum tanta satisfactione che la non voria havere guadagnato uno reame...ha dimonstrato essere veramente moglier de Vostra Signoria come è manegiando cussì bene uno cavallo et credo che se havereti figlioli seranno li megliori cavalcatori del mondo.' Beatrice de' Contrari to Francesco Gonzaga, 4 March 1493, from Mantua, ASMn, AG, 2443, c. 342.

[65] Eleonora d'Aragona to Isabella d'Este, 21 May 1493, from Ferrara, ASMn, AG, 1185, c. 578.

[66] Isabella d'Este to Eleonora d'Aragona, 30 May 1493, from Porto, in Isabella d'Este, *Selected Letters*, 59.

Yet, at exactly the time that Eleonora wrote congratulating her daughter about the pregnancy, Isabella was in Venice, complaining in letters both to her husband and to her mother that she felt inexplicably tired. She put the weariness down to the strains of travel and the tedium of attending the long official functions mounted in her honour by the Venetian regime.[67] However, even after her return to Mantua, she admitted in letters of 28 May that she was 'completely exhausted'.[68] Her correspondents came to their own conclusions about her tiredness.

Convinced that Isabella was with child, Francesco had written benignly to her while she was in Venice, referring in a letter of 12 May to his 'singular and affectionate love'. He even enclosed a sonnet that he had commissioned from a court poet and copied out in his own hand.[69] A month later, he wrote to Lodovico Sforza, explaining that 'certain signs' had convinced him that his wife was pregnant and inviting the duke to be the godfather.[70] Isabella did not dare to criticize Francesco for telling her mother that she was expecting a baby. However, when she opened a letter from Milan, thinking it concerned routine political business, she discovered that her brother-in-law had also been informed. Most unhappy that there was now no way of containing the gossip that was sure to flourish, Isabella reproached Francesco for risking public humiliation, if it transpired she was not pregnant.[71] Following the trip to Venice, she sought refuge from the early summer heat and the curiosity of members of the court by retreating to her villa at nearby Porto. From there, she wrote gratefully to friends in Ferrara, such as Jacopo da Capua, whom she thanked for his sensitivity about the 'false rumours' of her pregnancy.[72]

By the beginning of July, Isabella must have been about twelve weeks pregnant, but still she denied it. Recent scholarship on early modern understandings of the female body gives credence to the possibility that a young woman in her first pregnancy might indeed be uncertain about whether she was with child, since

[67] Isabella d'Este to Francesco Gonzaga, 15 and 16 May 1493, from Venice. She wrote in a similar vein to her mother on 15 May 1493, ASMn, AG, 2991, libro 3, cc. 54r–v.

[68] 'me haverà per excusata se non gli scrivo de mia mane, perché veramente sono tutta stracha.' Isabella d'Este to Francesco Gonzaga, 28 May 1493, and Isabella d'Este to Eleonora d'Aragona on the same day, from Porto, ASMn, AG, 2991, libro 3, cc. 61r–v.

[69] 'La lettera de Vostra Signoria ne è stata tanto grato quanto quello depo [dopo] la sua partita da Mantua ne ha facto carestia, benché per el singulare et affectuoso amore che li portamo ne desyderamo le sue lettere ad noi sieno si rare....Ma per havere uno poeta apresso noi, che per essere di facundo ingegno, omne da lui servirisse qualche sonetto, de quali ne mandamo uno sotto scripto de nostra propria mano.' Francesco Gonzaga to Isabella d'Este, 12 May 1493, from Bocca di Ganda, ASMn, AG, 2108bis, c. 377.

[70] 'La illustrissima mia consorte se racommanda a la Excellentia Vostra et stassene a le volte cum certi signi, o siano alteratione de sorte che indicano pur gravedanza.' Francesco Gonzaga to Lodovico Sforza, 14 June 1493, from Mantua, ASMn, AG, 2108bis, c. 330.

[71] ''I seria però stato meglio de non acertarlo de la gravidenza mia, aciò che, non essendo poi vera, questa voce che va intorno non ne recevesse scorno.' Isabella d'Este to Francesco Gonzaga, 18 June 1493, from Porto, ASMn, AG, 2991, libro 3, cc. 67r–v.

[72] Isabella d'Este to Jacopo da Capua, 29 June 1493, from Porto, in Isabella d'Este, Selected Letters, 61.

ambiguities were intrinsic to understandings of the stages from conception to birth. The most reliable sign of pregnancy was usually regarded as the quickening, the beginning of foetal movement in the womb. It was recognized that this change usually occurred around the fourth month of pregnancy.[73] Contemporaries relied on the mother-to-be to report the quickening, but not everyone was keen to volunteer the information. Isabella's sister-in-law, Anna Sforza, for example, apologized to her uncle Lodovico Sforza in September 1497 for not informing him that she was pregnant on the grounds that, being a first-time mother, she was unaware of the sure signs and had no one to guide her. Only after the passing of six months was she confident enough to communicate the news that she was pregnant. Her uncle accepted this excuse as reasonable.[74] Sadly, that pregnancy ended with the death of mother and baby after a long and difficult birth.

Women were not necessarily expected to understand, or even note, changes in their bodies, if they were young and inexperienced. In a complex case that came to the attention of authorities in the mid-seventeenth century, the 13-year-old, recently married, Costanza Colonna, daughter of one of Rome's most powerful families, gave birth to an almost full-term baby that had died in utero. Until the very moment of birth, Costanza maintained she was a virgin and her husband, Francesco Sforza, impotent, a story authorities suspected was an attempt to escape from an unhappy marriage on the grounds that it was unconsummated.[75] When Giovanni Battista Castelli, a canon lawyer and Archbishop Borromeo's vicar general who was charged with investigating whether a crime had been committed, asked Costanza: 'Didn't your ladyship ever feel the creature in your body in all those months?' she replied 'I didn't think of it'.[76] As Renée Baernstein and John Christopoulos point out in their analysis of Costanza's situation, it is plausible that it was only in retrospect that a naïve young aristocrat recognized the physical indications of pregnancy. Those who attended the girl may well have interpreted the pains and fevers she reported, and the bodily changes they observed in her, as symptoms of an illness. On the other hand, it is also possible

---

[73] Susan Broomhall, '"Women's Little Secrets": Defining the Boundaries of Reproductive Knowledge in Sixteenth-Century France', *Social History of Medicine* 15.1 (2002): 1–15. Cathy McClive, 'The Hidden Truths of the Belly: The Uncertainties of Pregnancy in Early Modern Europe', *Social History of Medicine* 15.2 (2002): 209–27, 209–27 (212, 215–18). See also Patricia Crawford, *Blood, Bodies and Families in Early Modern England* (Harlow: Pearson/Longman, 2004), 79–112; Ulinka Rublack, 'Pregnancy, Childbirth and the Female Body in Early Modern Germany', *Past & Present* 150 (1996): 84–110.

[74] Gabriella Zuccolin, 'Gravidanza e parto nel Quattrocento', in *Beatrice d'Este, 1475–1497*, ed. Luisa Giordano (Pisa: ETS, 2008), 111–45 (136–7).

[75] On the sexual and other problems experienced by Costanza Colonna and Francesco Sforza, see P. Renée Baernstein and John Christopoulos, 'Interpreting the Body in Early Modern Italy: Pregnancy, Abortion and Adulthood', *Past & Present* 223.1 (2014): 41–75.

[76] As quoted in Baernstein and Christopoulos, 'Interpreting the Body in Early Modern Italy', 74.

that everyone colluded to help Costanza establish her lack of culpability for the baby's death.[77]

In Isabella's case, a plea of ignorance about the signs of pregnancy was surely less convincing than that of Anna Sforza, who could point to the demise, in 1493, of her mother-in-law, Eleonora d'Aragona, as the reason she had inadequate female guidance at the Ferrarese court. Beatrice de' Contrari was highly esteemed in Ferrara and Mantua as a healer and midwife. She kept Isabella under the closest surveillance and was convinced that the marchioness was pregnant as early as mid-May 1493, at what must have been about six weeks after conception.[78] However, the frequent and difficult pregnancies of her own daughter Ippolita often detained Beatrice in Ferrara. Mid-1493 was one of those occasions, which meant that she could not keep as close an eye as usual on the marchioness during this crucial time.

Frustrated by Isabella's continuing denials that she was pregnant, Eleonora wrote sternly to Isabella on 4 July informing her that the duke wished to know the truth. She demanded Isabella gain her husband's approval for a visit to Ferrara, so the situation could be clarified. If the pregnancy was confirmed, she could be taught how to use swaddling clothes and learn the other skills that would be necessary for a new mother to acquire. Eleonora insisted, however, that if Isabella was certain there was no baby on the way, she should stay at home.[79] Five days later, Isabella appeared in Ferrara, the prospect of seeing her natal family proving irresistible. It is also likely that she craved her mother's advice and support at a moment when the doubts she still clung to concerning a possible pregnancy must have been dissipating. On the very day of the marchioness's arrival in Ferrara, Eleonora wrote to her son-in-law assuring him that there was no doubt at all that Isabella was with child 'because every certain indication that it is possible to witness in a pregnant woman is apparent'.[80]

Isabella's secretary, Benedetto Capilupi, was among those who accompanied her to Ferrara. He wrote secretly to Francesco about the encounter between Isabella and her parents, as the marquis had ordered him to do. He also penned

---

[77] Baernstein and Christopoulos, 'Interpreting the Body in Early Modern Italy', 74–5.

[78] Isabella conveyed Beatrice's opinion to the duchess, but claimed it was incorrect. Isabella d'Este to Eleonora d'Aragona, 30 May 1493, from Porto, in Isabella d'Este, *Selected Letters*, 59.

[79] 'voressimo essere certa se siti gravida, perché essendo, potessimo far fare le fasse et altre cose vostre et che anche volevamo che venisti qua a piacere et per imparare de far fare epse cose...vi vederemo voluntieri se siti gravida. Ma se non siti gravida, non volemo che li veniati.' Eleonora d'Aragona to Isabella d'Este, 4 July 1493, from Ferrara, ASMn, AG, 1185, c. 599.

[80] 'gli significamo a suo contento come veramente la è gravida, et de questo Vostra Signoria non ni ha a fare alcuno dubio, perché gli vedono ogni signale et certeza che vedere se possi in dona gravida.' Eleonora d'Aragona to Francesco Gonzaga, 9 July 1493, from Ferrara, ASMn, AG, 1185, c. 603. Francesco had written to his mother-in-law the day before, expressing his confidence that Isabella was indeed pregnant, despite her continuing denials. He requested that the duchess make sure his wife did not overexert herself in Ferrara. Francesco Gonzaga to Eleonora d'Aragona, 8 July 1493, from Mantua, ASMn, AG, 2961, libro 1, c. 100.

letters for Beatrice de' Contrari and one for Collona on the same subject. These three employees, all of them in a position to know their mistress's most intimate secrets, sent detailed reports about Isabella's behaviour under intense interrogation by her mother, father, the court doctor and, finally, Beatrice de' Contrari herself, who left her sick daughter and came to court to examine the marchioness. The letters reveal the degree to which contemporaries in this elite context understood the phases of pregnancy and recognized that mothers and daughters might experience bearing children in a similar way.[81]

Knowing that Eleonora d'Aragona had already communicated with Francesco on 9 July, Capilupi wrote to the marquis with an update two days later. This letter, written in collaboration with Isabella's former governess Collona, described what transpired after the duchess proclaimed that her daughter was certainly pregnant. According to Capilupi, on the evening of 9 July, Eleonora questioned Isabella for three hours. It is probable that the secretary did not personally witness this interrogation, relying instead on Collona's account, since the women withdrew to the duchess's apartments. No doubt, Eleonora wished to establish whether quickening had occurred, so she would have a better idea of when the baby would be born. Isabella was forced to concede that perhaps it had: 'She confessed that she had already felt a certain thing beating within her body for many days, but did not know what it was.' According to Capilupi's letter, at that very moment, Francesco da Castello, the doctor who had treated Isabella in Mantua when she was ill in 1490, arrived with a message from the duke. Ercole wanted Isabella to confirm that she was expecting a child. Fearing an equivocal answer, Eleonora cut the doctor off in mid-sentence and hastily responded in the affirmative.[82]

The duchess knew her daughter well. Even on the following evening, when summoned to the duke's apartments and asked directly by her father if she was pregnant, Capilupi reported that Isabella 'rose from her seat and paid reverence to him, without saying yes or no'. But Ercole had his own battery of questions with which to establish the truth: 'He asked her whether she had experienced cravings and if her appetite had changed, or her stomach had been upset.' Isabella replied that she had felt none of these things and it was for this reason that she was so uncertain, 'seeming to feel unusually well'. For the duke, this answer was clinching evidence, since, as he explained to Isabella, her mother had experienced pregnancy in the same benign way. According to Capilupi, everyone in the room agreed that this was so and predicted the baby would be a boy.[83] He concluded

[81] On the theme of sexual knowledge see, Crawford, *Blood, Bodies and Families*, 54–78.

[82] 'Confessoè che già parechi dì havea sentito una certa cosa batterli el corpo, ma che la non sapeva ch'el fusse.' Benedetto Capilupi to Francesco Gonzaga, 11 July 1493, from Ferrara, ASMn, AG, 1232, cc. 644r-v.

[83] 'Heri sera andette poi a visitare Sua Excellentia, la quale disse queste parole. "Hor su, col nome de Dio, seti pur gravida?" Essa levòe da sedere et feceli reverentia, non respondendo sì né non. Dimandandoli se gli veniva voglia de alcuna cosa et se l'havea mutato el gusto né sentiva alcuna perturbatione de stomacho, la gli respose de non, et che per questo lei stava suspesa, parendoli stare

the letter with the news that Isabella's parents were very happy and had begun to order the things that would be necessary for the birth. He then begged the marquis not to write back, on the grounds that Isabella would be angry if she learned that he had secretly communicated with Francesco about the conversations with her parents.[84] In another letter of the same day, Capilupi passed on Eleonora's comment that Isabella was already as large as her sister Beatrice had been at the end of her pregnancy, the implication being that the baby was big and healthy and therefore surely a boy.[85] Collona, too, was optimistic, writing via Capilupi on 20 July that she could hardly wait to get back to Mantua to begin preparations for the birth.[86]

Isabella's stance in relation to her pregnancy was puzzling to her husband, her natal family, and to those who served her. As the marchioness's confidential secretary, Capilupi had to retain Isabella's trust, while maintaining excellent relations with the marquis, who claimed ultimate authority over his wife's entire household, something that would be contested by Isabella in later years, but to little avail. Just as Beatrice de' Contrari had risked Isabella's ire by informing Francesco so early that his wife was likely pregnant, on the grounds that he was the master and had to be told, Capilupi felt obliged to discharge his duty in the same diligent way. However, he tried to account for Isabella's behaviour in a sympathetic light. In an undated latter that must have been written around the middle of July 1493, the secretary explained to Francesco that:

> Every day I went about investigating whether she [Isabella] had confessed anything else, in order to report it to Your Lordship. These women here say they are convinced she feels it, but out of embarrassment, does not wish to say so.[87]

In the same message, Capilupi reported that Beatrice de' Contrari was due at court that very day. This was likely 21 July 1493, when she dictated a message to the marquis reporting on a thorough physical examination of Isabella. She assured Francesco that she had no doubt that the pregnancy was well advanced, even though Isabella was still recalcitrant, insisting that she would never concede

---

meglio che la facesse mai. "Non ve ne maravegliate" disse el signore suo patre, "perché la duchessa hebbe etiam lei cussì bona gravedenza". Ogniuno che gli era presente confirmò, pronosticando ch'el seria maschio et de questa opinione è tutta la corte e la cità.' Benedetto Capilupi to Francesco Gonzaga, 11 July 1493, from Ferrara, ASMn, AG, 1232, cc. 644r–v.

[84] 'Ma la supplico ben non me facia fare resposta alcuna, perché madonna mia non se cura anchora che alcuna certeza vadi intorno et lo haveria per male da me.' Benedetto Capilupi to Francesco Gonzaga, 11 July 1493, from Ferrara, ASMn, AG, 1232, cc. 644r–v.

[85] Benedetto Capilupi to Francesco Gonzaga, 11 July 1493, from Ferrara, ASMn, AG, 1232, c. 646.

[86] Collona to Francesco Gonzaga, 20 July, from Ferrara, ASMn, AG, 1232, c. 774.

[87] 'Ogni dì, sono andato investigando se doppo ha confessato altro, per renderne conto a la Signoria Vostra. Queste donne dicono che loro credino che la senta, ma che per vergogna non lo voglia dire.' Benedetto Capilupi to Francesco Gonzaga, from Ferrara, ASMn, AG, 2108bis, c. 429.

that she was with child until she could feel movements very frequently. Beatrice too attempted to justify Isabella's behaviour by explaining that quickening might not yet have happened, since it sometimes occurred as late as the beginning of the fifth month. In her view, Isabella was four months pregnant.[88]

The following day, having managed to secure privacy for a frank conversation with the marchioness, Beatrice dictated another letter to Francesco explaining that after persistent interrogation—and a reminder to Isabella that she had already admitted, even before leaving Mantua, that she had felt movements within her body—her young mistress had finally confessed that 'every day she felt stirrings, softly softly. But she did not want to say so, because it would immediately become public.' Like Capilupi, Beatrice asked the marquis to keep her letter confidential, since she feared a furious reaction from Isabella, if her secret briefings to Francesco came to light.[89] It is evident from these various comments that Isabella dreaded becoming the centre of interest as her pregnancy began to show and speculation escalated about the sex of the child. Her sister having already produced a boy, the expectation that she would do the same must have been a source of considerable anxiety.

Eleonora d'Aragona had suffered ill health for several years. Although only forty-three in 1493, that year the crises came more often and the recoveries were only partial. After Isabella left Ferrara on 8 August, the duchess continued to send reassuring messages to Mantua, aware that her daughter would become very fretful, once advancing pregnancy prevented any further visits to Ferrara. She also sent special foods to Isabella, dispensed advice about the dangers of horse-riding in the last months of pregnancy and mobilized her ladies-in-waiting to produce the exquisite linen that would be required by the grandchild she had so anxiously awaited and now secretly feared she might not know. Eleonora also commissioned a cradle, fit for a baby of royal Aragonese descent.[90] Between 19 and 28 September, despite fading strength, the duchess, or more likely her secretary, communicated by letter with Isabella daily to assure her that the doctors were optimistic they had the illness in hand.[91] The letters became less frequent in October; the last one, which accompanied a gift of fish, was sent on 16 October.[92] The duchess of Ferrara died that day. The news was kept secret from Isabella, for fear she would miscarry as a result of the shock. Before long, however, she became

---

[88] 'Io gli ho tochato el corpo, parme molto grosseto, ma non è maraveglia se la non sentesse già perché se sta molte volte in capo de li cinque mesi et al iudicio mio è solamente ne li quatro....Ben prego Vostra Signoria non voglia farne altra dimostratione.' Beatrice de' Contrari to Francesco Gonzaga, 21 July 1493, from Ferrara, ASMn, AG, 1232, c. 774.

[89] 'In fine me rispose che l'havea sentita e senteva ogni dì pian piano. Ma che la non lo voleva dire perché di subito seria publicata.' Beatrice de' Contrari to Francesco Gonzaga, 22 July 1493, from Ferrara, ASMn, AG, 1232, c. 715.

[90] Tuohy, *Herculean Ferrara*, 233.

[91] Eleonora d'Aragona to Isabella d'Este, from Ferrara, ASMn, AG, 1185, cc. 621–36.

[92] Eleonora d'Aragona to Isabella d'Este, from Ferrara, ASMn, AG, 1185, c. 648.

suspicious about the lack of correspondence from Ferrara and the upsetting truth was revealed.

Two and a half months later, on 31 December 1493, Isabella gave birth to a daughter, who was named Eleonora in memory of her recently deceased grand-mother. The magical properties of the several eagle stones, or aetites, given by well-wishers in the hope they would ease the labour, proved ineffective. Isabella admitted to a correspondent in Ferrara that she had delivered the baby with 'very great difficulty'.[93] Disappointed by the outcome of this first pregnancy, so publicly scrutinized and anticipated, and in deep mourning after her mother's death, Isabella put away the magnificent cradle sent by her parents as a gesture of faith that the baby would be a boy. Seen in the context of the early anxieties she experi-enced in relating to her husband sexually and the intense pressure to bear a son, Isabella's despondent response to the birth of a girl is hardly surprising and should not be seen as evidence of a lack of maternal feeling that many scholars have attributed to her.[94] Francesco took a different view of the birth of a girl. His wife was young and had proved she was fertile; there was plenty of time for an heir to arrive.

In March 1494, Isabella sought permission from Francesco to make a pilgrim-age to the Santa Casa at Loreto to fulfil a vow made during pregnancy, when she had prayed for a safe delivery. He agreed. A visit to the Virgin Mary's house, the site of the Annunciation, which was thought to have been carried by angels from Jerusalem to Croatia during the Crusades and then to Italy, was a pious project and a way for the marquis to reward and console his disappointed wife. After staying with her father and brothers in Ferrara for several weeks in mid-March 1494, Isabella set off for Ravenna, where she reported visiting the ancient sites of the city, before continuing to Rimini and then Loreto, where she briefly fulfilled her vow.[95] She travelled on to Gubbio to visit Elisabetta Gonzaga and Guidobaldo Montefeltro, detouring to Camerino and its surrounds, ruled by the Varano, before joining her Montefeltro in-laws at their other palace in Urbino. She described her travels to Francesco in great detail in a series of engaging letters.[96]

Soon after her departure from Mantua, Isabella wrote to Francesco explaining that she had made another promise while pregnant. She begged permission to make a detour before returning home, so she could visit the shrines at Assisi to

---

[93] One of the aetites had been sent by Niccolò Bendidio, her mother's long-time secretary. Isabella returned the stone on 2 February 1494. See ASMn, AG, 2991, libro 4, c. 23v. Isabella admitted the birth had been long and painful in a letter to the Ferrarese courtier, Bernadino de' Prosperi, who had asked to borrow the eagle stones for his wife, who was due to give birth. Isabella d'Este to Bernadino de' Prosperi, 2 February 1494, from Mantua, ASMn, AG, 2991, libro 4, c. 23v.

[94] See, for example, Pizzagalli, *La Signora del Rinascimento*, 87–8.

[95] Isabella d'Este to Francesco Gonzaga, 19 March 1494, from Ravenna, ASMn, AG, 2109, c. 191.

[96] Isabella d'Este to Francesco Gonzaga, 30 March–20 April 1494, from Gubbio and Urbino, ASMn, AG, 2109, cc. 191–211.

thank Saints Clare and Francis for protecting her during childbirth.[97] The marquis acceded to this request, on condition that Isabella hurried straight back to Mantua afterwards, a coda the marchioness chose to ignore.[98] She finally returned home in early May 1494, having extended her absence from the few weeks envisaged by Francesco, to almost two months, a pattern which was to become all too familiar to him in future years.

Isabella's itinerary to some extent matched Francesco's own travels in 1491. Her lyrical descriptions of the beauty of the countryside around Camerino and the keen interest she took in the architecture and decorative schemes of the palaces in which she lodged during her travels, communicated in regular letters to her husband, perhaps worked at this time to neutralize any annoyance he felt about the length of her absence, since these were interests they increasingly shared. Francesco was also well aware that Isabella's goodwill would be a crucial commodity in the months to come, since King Charles VIII's determination to oust the Aragonese monarch from Naples and claim the southern kingdom for himself was already dominating diplomatic correspondence. It was therefore likely he would have to take on the soldierly role for which he had long prepared, a prospect he looked forward to with enthusiasm.[99] The reluctance with which Isabella approached motherhood was nowhere in evidence when she embarked on her political apprenticeship. While Francesco aspired to win honour and fame on the battlefield, Isabella hoped to establish a reputation as a prudent and effective political actor in the tradition of her female forebears. The beginning of the Italian Wars in 1494 provided plentiful opportunities for Isabella to do so. She embraced a growing portfolio of administrative work with enthusiasm and diligence.

---

[97] Isabella d'Este to Francesco Gonzaga, 16 March 1494, from Ferrara, ASMn, AG, 2109, cc. 190r–v.

[98] Francesco Gonzaga to Isabella d'Este, 20 March 1494, from Marmirolo, ASMn, AG, 2109, c. 304.

[99] 'Haverite inteso le cose vanno per il tavolero, le quale sonno de sorte che se po' tenere per fermo la guerra et potria essere che presto se scopririano, come voi dovetti ben considerare, per il che seria necessaria la persona vostra a casa.' Francesco Gonzaga to Isabella d'Este, 14 March 1494, from Gonzaga, ASMn, AG, 2109, c. 309. On the likelihood of war, see also Isabella d'Este to Francesco Gonzaga, 25 January 1494, from Mantua, ASMn, AG, 2109, c. 156.

3

The Crafting of Identity and the Division of Political Labour

When Isabella arrived in Mantua in 1490, a precise memory of how previous incumbents had interpreted the role of marchioness had likely faded, Francesco's mother, Margarete of Bavaria, having died in 1479, and his grandmother, Barbara von Hohenzollern of Brandenburg, in 1481. While a number of elderly officials who had collaborated with Barbara in diplomatic and administrative matters may have remained within the chancery, it was probably the frescoes painted by Andrea Mantegna between 1465 and 1474 on the walls of the main audience room of the San Giorgio castle, now usually referred to as the *Camera degli sposi* and still largely intact today, which preserved the most vivid memory of her legacy. The group portrait of Lodovico Gonzaga (1412–78) and his German-born wife surrounded by their family and courtiers, on the north side of the chamber, constituted a celebration of the pair's dynastic achievements and of Barbara's importance as her husband's political mainstay.

The union of Francesco's grandparents had represented a spectacularly successful attempt by the Gonzaga to marry up, although securing such an important bride proved very expensive. Rather than receiving a rich dowry, the family had paid the huge sum of 50,000 florins to seal the alliance, in recognition of Barbara's superior ancestry and her family's imperial connections. The investment paid off handsomely. The Holy Roman Emperor, Sigismund of Luxemburg, granted the hereditary title of marquis to Francesco's great grandfather, Gianfrancesco, when Barbara and Lodovico were betrothed in 1433, and the marriage produced substantial other political advantages. The most important of these was the promotion, in 1461, of the couple's son, also called Francesco, to the cardinalate. This event elevated Gonzaga fortunes in the papal court and added greatly to the family's prestige.[1]

During her husband's military campaigns, Barbara oversaw government and became a notable political force, her bilingualism facilitating a central role in relations with Germany. Following Lodovico's death in 1478, Barbara supported her son, Federico, in the same way. His marriage to Margarete von Wittelsbach, sister of the duke of Bavaria, had continued the regime's northern connections. Letters

---

[1] Elisabeth Ward Swain, 'Strategia matrimoniale in casa Gonzaga: Il caso di Barbara e Ludovico', *Civiltà mantovana* 14 (1986): 1–14, ' "My Excellent and Most Singular Lord": Marriage in a Noble Family of Fifteenth-Century Italy', *Journal of Medieval and Renaissance Studies* 16 (1986): 171–95.

A Renaissance Marriage: The Political and Personal Alliance of Isabella d'Este and Francesco Gonzaga, 1490–1519.
Carolyn James, Oxford University Press (2020). © Carolyn James.
DOI: 10.1093/oso/9780199681211.001.0001

between Margarete and Federico show that the former was also well informed about foreign relations and, had she not died prematurely in October 1479, it is likely that Margarete would have taken on a much bigger political role in the aftermath of Barbara's death.[2]

Under Lodovico and then Federico Gonzaga, administrative and diplomatic matters were also coordinated by the regime's deputy, Francesco Secco, the envoy who travelled to Ferrara in May 1480 to ratify the betrothal of Isabella and Francesco. He had risen to prominence during the rule of Lodovico Gonzaga, who secured his lieutenant's on-going loyalty by marrying him to Caterina Gonzaga, an illegitimate daughter. Federico relied particularly heavily on Secco, since the marquis was estranged from his brothers, Gianfrancesco, lord of Bozzolo, Rodolfo, lord of Castiglione and Luzzara, and Lodovico, bishop of Mantua. Fearing an attempt by one or more of these brothers to assume power, if his precarious health carried him off to an early grave, as in fact transpired, Federico made arrangements for Secco to assume the regency, until Francesco reached his majority. In May 1485, the year after his father's death, Francesco went further, even agreeing that the regime's *luogotenente* should have the power to impose capital punishment, usually the sole prerogative of the head of state.[3] Thus, by the time Isabella became marchioness, Secco wielded a formidable degree of power.

As a child, Isabella was taught to sing, dance, and play various musical instruments, accomplishments expected of princely consorts, but her education went well beyond such traditional courtly skills. Although she did not master Latin, which she continued to try to improve in early adulthood, by the time she married, Isabella possessed a sophisticated degree of literacy and a confident grasp of the workings of government. Thus, the new marchioness was well equipped to take on a wide range of administrative work and to begin acting as a diplomatic bridge between her natal and marital kin. Isabella was sensitive, nonetheless, to the need to determine the type of political work that Francesco considered appropriate for her to perform. She was therefore tactful, but investigated the possibilities almost at once. In a letter of 7 April 1490, she explained to her husband that having noted an accumulation of petitions during his absence from the city, she had authorized the straightforward cases, after seeking advice from Secco. She also began to open incoming mail to see if there was anything else she could do to lighten Francesco's workload.[4]

---

[2] See, for example, letters written to Margarete in 1479 by the resident Mantuan ambassador in Milan, Zaccaria Saggi, in the months before her death, when Federico was away from Mantua fighting. These letters refer constantly to her coordination of political news and assume that she is fully apprised of diplomatic developments. Marcello Simonetta, ed., *Carteggio degli oratori mantovani alla corte sforzesca (1450–1500)*, vol. 11 (1478–79) (Roma: Ministero per i beni e le attività culturali, Direzione generale per gli archivi, 2001).

[3] Fermo d'Aragona Secco, 'Francesco Secco, i Gonzaga e Paolo Erba. Un capitolo inedito di storia Mantovana', *Archivio storico lombardo* 6 (1956): 210–61.

[4] See, for example, Isabella d'Este to Francesco Gonzaga, 29 May and 27 August 1490, from Mantua, ASMn, AG, 2106, cc. 365 and 387.

It was likely in response to her mother's direct encouragement that Isabella embarked on these initiatives. Several weeks after her return to Ferrara, following the conclusion of the wedding festivities in Mantua, Eleonora d'Aragona had written to her daughter instructing Isabella to behave circumspectly whenever the marquis was away, so that, through temperance, she would win his confidence and establish a reputation for wisdom beyond her years. The duchess continued in this educative vein, warmly approving the gifts that Isabella had distributed to members of the Gonzaga court on her arrival in Mantua, and reminding her that liberality to one's subjects was an important measure of those deemed fit to govern.[5] Both temperance and liberality were foremost among the princely virtues and traditionally regarded as beyond the intellectual and moral reach of a woman. Eleanora's advice implicitly critiqued that assumption by assuring her daughter that she should actively cultivate the qualities that would allow her to be an effective regent.

Like Lodovico and Federico Gonzaga, Ercole d'Este married a woman who outranked him socially. Eleonora became a powerful figure, not only by virtue of her royal blood and family connections, but also because she had been educated to assume political and diplomatic responsibilities and expected to do so. By 1478, the duke of Ferrara had begun to delegate many fiscal and administrative matters to his spouse and, once child-bearing duties came to an end by the close of that decade, Eleonora took on even more work in the chancery. Apart from the usual tasks of a princely consort, such as providing charity to the convents of the city and helping the poor and sick, the duchess frequently acted as regent, receiving petitioners, issuing edicts, dispensing justice, and entertaining dignitaries. Although wide ranging, the authority Eleonora wielded was not formally endorsed by legal mechanisms, as her mother Isabella di Chiaromonte's had been. As queen of Naples, Isabella had worked within an Aragonese tradition whereby the king's consort was formally recognized as her husband's political lieutenant.[6]

---

[5] 'confortamove a darve piacere honestamente et quando lo Illustre Signor, vostro consorte, non cè, haveti andare alquanto più retenuta; et quanto più libertà il vi dae, usarne mancho perché quanto più sareti temperata in questa vostra etade, tanto più sareti laudata et reputata per savia....Habiamo veduto la lista de li presenti haveti facto che ni haveti mandata et certo laudiamo che cussì habiate facto parendone essere officio de signori ad usare liberalitade verso li suoi subditi et familiari.' Eleonora d'Aragona to Isabella d'Este, from Ferrara, 12 March 1490, ASMn, AG, 1184, unfoliated.

[6] On Ercole's willingness to allow Eleonora to make decisions about routine administrative matters on his behalf, see his letters of 8, 9 March and of 4, 25, 31 May 1479, ASMo, Casa e stato, 67, cc. 26, 27, 45, 50, 52. These examples are typical of many similar letters. On Eleonora d'Aragona, see Luciano Chiappini, *Eleonora d'Aragona, prima duchessa di Ferrara* (Rovigo: S.T.E.R., 1956); Marco Folin, 'La corte della duchessa: Eleonora d'Aragona a Ferrara', in *Donne di potere nel Rinascimento*, ed. Letizia Arcangeli and Susanna Peyronel, 85 (Rome: Viella, 2008), 481–512; Enrica Guerra and Angela Giallongo, 'Eleonora d'Aragona e *I doveri del Principe* di Diomede Carafa', in *Donne di palazzo nelle corti Europee. Tracce e forme di potere dall'età moderna* (Milan: Edizioni Unicopli, 2005), 113–19; Jessica O'Leary, 'Politics, Pedagogy, and Praise: Three Literary Texts Dedicated to Eleonora d'Aragona, Duchess of Ferrara', *I Tatti Studies in the Italian Renaissance* 19.2 (2016): 285–307. Irma Schiappoli, 'Isabella di Chiaromonte, regina di Napoli', *Archivio storico italiano* 98 (1940): 109–24. See also the late fifteenth-century biography of Isabella di Chiaromonte in Giovanni Sabadino degli Arienti, *Gynevera de le clare donne*, ed. Corrado Ricci and Alberto Bacchi della Lega (Bologna: Gaetano Romagnoli, 1887).

Although Ercole was an indifferent soldier, he was often on the battlefield. The war with Venice in the early 1480s represented a serious political challenge and his wife's maintenance of order in Ferrara, while he was away fighting, was crucial. By 1484, Eleonora's oversight of state affairs had become routine. The contemporary chronicler, Ugo Caleffini, noted the development in his journal: 'In this period the duke of Ferrara worried little about government; rather his illustrious madam duchess ruled over and governed everything, as she had done in the past.'[7] Caleffini saw nothing wrong with this; indeed, he regarded Eleonora's attentive style of administration as an improvement on that of the duke, whom he portrayed as devoted to his own pleasures.

Eleonora attracted the attention of literary clients who hoped to gain her favour by writing works which argued that by virtue of her Aragonese lineage and prudent ways, she had all the prerequisites to govern well.[8] The duchess also presented herself in these terms. In the mid-1480s, she renovated her suite in the Torre Marchexana of the Castel Vecchio and added a balcony to the side of the tower to provide direct access between her bedchamber, private chapel, and study. The balcony overlooked the castle's moat—which was large enough for her eldest son Alfonso to sail around in a small boat when he was a child—while its back wall featured a painted view of the bay of Naples, crowded with sea-going craft of various dimensions.[9] The image of her natal city (perhaps based on the *Tavola Strozzi*, painted around 1472–3 for Ferrante d'Aragona and now in the Museo Nazionale di Capodimonte in Naples), reminded viewers of Eleonora's royal origins, an identity that was central to her authority. While the appearance of the duchess's study is largely unknown, it is likely that three panel paintings of illustrious ancient matrons: Portia, Lucretia, and the wife of Hasdrubal, executed by the court artist Ercole de' Roberti, were commissioned by Eleonora to decorate this room.[10]

Traditionally, female virtue was seen as passive. It was usually discussed in the context of a defensive protection of chastity through adherence to a strict domestic seclusion and the maintenance of a disciplined tongue. Eleonora d'Aragona is documented as having been a most eloquent speaker, assertive in the relationship with her husband and politically active.[11] Nonetheless, in the decorative schemes of her apartments, the duchess seems to have preferred to project a muted version

---

[7] Caleffini, *Croniche*, 640. See also similar reports of Eleonora's role as intermediary between the duke and his subjects in 1486 and 1487, at 666 and 683.

[8] O'Leary, 'Politics, Pedagogy and Praise'.

[9] Tuohy, *Herculean Ferrara*, 416–17 (document 21).

[10] For a discussion of the paintings, see Ruth Wilkins Sullivan, 'Three Ferrarese Panels on the Theme of "Death Rather than Dishonour" and the Neapolitan Connection', *Zeitschrift Für Kunstgeschichte* 57.4, (1994): 610–25; Margaret Ann Franklin, *Boccaccio's Heroines: Power and Virtue in Renaissance Society* (Aldershot: Ashgate, 2006), 131–48; Joseph Manca, *The Art of Ercole de' Roberti* (Cambridge: Cambridge University Press, 1992), 58–61, 133–9.

[11] Carolyn James, 'Florence and Ferrara: Dynastic Marriage and Politics', in *The Medici: Citizens and Masters*, ed. Robert Black and John E. Law (Florence: I Tatti Harvard Centre for Renaissance Studies, 2015), 365–78; O'Leary, 'Politics, Pedagogy and Praise'.

of her political qualities. Although the models of wifely constancy that appear in Ercole de' Roberti's paintings are certainly not timid in the face of peril, their decisiveness and fortitude are directed primarily to protecting the good name of their families and to securing their welfare. To her daughter, Eleonora was far more explicit about the precise political responsibilities of a princely spouse. She wrote them down in a letter of mid-April 1491:

> You well know that whoever has a husband and a state must also have many duties, keeping in mind that you also have to produce children, and it is necessary to look after them and conserve their possessions and the state, as well as to do those things which are necessary for your subjects and citizens, whenever it is required.[12]

The conventional expectation that a wife would oversee the household and look after the offspring she bore her husband is here widened considerably: Isabella had not only to produce and raise children, she was also obliged to ensure the welfare of her spouse's subjects. Eleonora had modelled this combination by giving birth to seven children in rapid succession in the early years of marriage, six of whom survived into adulthood, and then by operating authoritatively behind the scenes to ensure that the administrative bodies of government functioned smoothly.[13]

Isabella had already begun to tackle a much broader range of political work by the time she received her mother's letter of 15 April 1491, some government officials having recognized that the marchioness was an appropriate person to communicate with if her husband was unavailable. On 12 March, for example, she had reported to Francesco that the *podestà* of Viadana, a sensitive border area to the south-west, had arrived at court and sought an interview, because he was concerned about rising factional tensions in his jurisdiction between two prominent families. Her letter warned that although the warring parties had so far proved to be faithful subjects, there was a risk of unrest in a key area of the dominion.[14] The marquis, who was hunting at Gonzaga, responded immediately, instructing Isabella to keep the official in Mantua and assuring her he would hasten home to deal with the matter.[15] On 23 June, she reported to Francesco that she had granted audience to subjects who had requested an interview, so they would not have to

---

[12] 'Che ben sapeti che chi ha marito et stato bisogna che anche habi de le fatiche, reducendovi a memoria che anche havete ad haver de li figlioli et che bisogna attendere a mantenirli et conservarli la roba et stato et fare le cose che siano necessarie a li subditi et citadini suoi secundo accade.' Eleonora d'Aragona to Isabella d'Este, 15 April 1491, from Ferrara, ASMn, AG, 1185, c. 107.

[13] James, 'Florence and Ferrara'.

[14] 'poteria nascere qualche rugine e se ben loro sono fideli de Vostra Signoria, sentendo qualchuno che fussino malcontenti, se poteria fare de strani penserii.' Isabella d'Este to Francesco Gonzaga, 19 March 1491, from Mantua, ASMn, AG, 2107, cc. 99r–v.

[15] Francesco Gonzaga to Isabella d'Este, 20 March 1491, from Gonzaga, ASMn, AG, 2107, c. 23.

wait for his return, and had examined chancery correspondence, identifying urgent issues and ensuring that officials promptly punished those who broke the law.[16]

Francesco proved to be open to Isabella taking on this kind of administrative work. Indeed, in the postscript of a letter sent in June 1491 to his eldest sister Clara, countess of Montpensier, Francesco commented enthusiastically on his wife's eager appetite for political responsibilities.

> We have left the weight and governance of our state and dominion to our Illustrious Consort, knowing that we can well rely on her prudence and integrity, for even if she is still of tender age, she has shown great promise and ability in events of an important and honourable sort, and demonstrates in each of her actions a singular talent, so that we may with ease and great tranquility go wherever we wish without looking over our shoulder all the time, knowing that our consort is back at home, managing our government and our affairs.[17]

It was no coincidence that the political demise of the marquis's official deputy and uncle by marriage, who had served three generations of Gonzaga rulers, followed within months. On the surface, relations between Isabella and Francesco Secco had been cordial. However, as she grew more familiar with the workings of government, the extraordinary degree of power wielded by her husband's lieutenant became alarmingly evident.

Over the decades of his ascendancy, Secco had accumulated vast wealth and even boasted a small private army which kept a close guard on the approaches to his fortified estates at San Martino Gusnago and Bondanello. His attention to personal security was prompted by the fact he had acquired significant enemies, foremost among whom were Francesco's uncles, Rodolfo, Lodovico, and Gianfrancesco Gonzaga, who had been exiled by Secco on the grounds that they had been involved in failed plots to poison their brother Federico and then, in 1487, Francesco himself.[18] These relatives were frequently guests at the Este court in the early 1490s. They encountered their nephew Francesco there, eventually winning his trust and sowing doubt in his mind about the loyalty of his right-hand man. Although outwardly supportive of Secco, it is likely that Ercole d'Este collaborated in undermining him, knowing that this was now in Isabella's interests and therefore his own.[19] In May 1491, rumours reached the marquis from Ferrara that his personal chef, Bertolotto, as well as one of his secretaries, were

---

[16] Isabella d'Este to Francesco Gonzaga, 23 June 1491, from Porto, ASMn, AG, 2107, c. 152.

[17] Francesco Gonzaga to Clara Gonzaga, 20 June 1491, ASMn, AG, b. 2904, cc. 46r–47r. I quote here from the translation provided in Bourne, *The Soldier-Prince*, 37–8. On Clara Gonzaga, see Nicole Dupont-Pierrart, *Claire de Gonzague Comtesse de Bourbon-Montpensier (1464–1503), Une princesse italienne à la cour de France* (Lille: Septentrion, 2017).

[18] Secco d'Aragona, 'Francesco Secco', 215–16; Mazzoldi, *Mantova. La storia*, 84–90.

[19] On this point, and on the elimination of Secco more generally, see Cockram, *Isabella d'Este and Francesco Gonzaga*, 87–94.

secretly acting as Secco's spies.[20] Such whisperings about the deputy's purported treachery, combined with the realization that Isabella was not only a competent manager, but a trustworthy one, served as catalysts for Francesco's decision to rid himself of a tutelage that had become irksome, now that he was a mature married man.

Secco fled from Mantuan territory in September 1491, after he became convinced that his life was in imminent peril. He was condemned for treason in absentia.[21] Much to the Gonzaga couple's relief, the Venetian government accepted the situation, even though Secco had been the facilitator and guarantor of the alliance between Venice and Mantua and had been awarded a salary by the republic for his services as a military commander. That contract was now abruptly terminated. With no serious repercussions to cloud their victory, Isabella and Francesco took pleasure in confiscating Secco's lands and claiming the larger possessions he could not transport to Tuscany, where he sought refuge with his friend and supporter, Lorenzo de' Medici.

His deputy gone, Francesco still wished to be relieved of the tiresome aspects of everyday governance. He therefore encouraged Isabella to take on more of the work that Secco had routinely carried out, particularly as the new situation represented a satisfying reversal of roles: he was now the senior partner, with a young and seemingly pliable apprentice under his command. Isabella assured Francesco repeatedly in letters of this period that she would observe his instructions regarding administrative matters punctiliously. In doing so, she cautiously tested the boundaries of her delegated authority in a city that had not seen such a young woman stepping in as informal regent for many decades.[22]

Isabella strove to build consensus about her role as unofficial regent through visual and literary propaganda. Like her mother, she encouraged would-be literary clients, who presented the young marchioness with treatises and other works that took issue with the traditional assumption that women were innately unsuited for public responsibilities.[23] Isabella also commissioned paintings and collected artefacts that communicated her political and intellectual qualities. However, her artistic commissions were to be far more ambitious and complex than Eleonora's. The *grotta* and *studiolo* within her apartments eventually even rivalled the fame of the main reception room of the Gonzaga castle, the *Camera Picta* (*as it was then known*), where the frescoes painted decades before by

---

[20] Giuseppe Coniglio, 'La politica di Francesco Gonzaga nell'opera di un immigrato meridionale: Iacopo Probo d'Atri', *Archivio storico lombardo* 88 (1961): 131–67 (133).

[21] Mazzoldi, *Mantova. La storia*, 868–7; Secco d'Aragona, 'Francesco Secco', 219–30.

[22] For example, on 9 July 1491, she assured Francesco: 'me governarò secundo la instructione de Vostra Signoria', while, on 1 September, she wrote: 'Non ho voluto farne altra deliberatione finché non habia la voluntà de Vostra Excellentia, la quale obedirò in questo et in ogni altra cosa.' Isabella d'Este to Francesco Gonzaga, 9 July and 1 September 1491, from Mantua, ASMn, AG, 2107, cc. 163 and 180.

[23] On this theme, see James, 'In Praise of Women'; James, 'Margherita Cantelmo'; Kolsky, *The Ghost of Boccaccio*, 148–69.

Mantegna proclaimed the political efficacy of an earlier Gonzaga dynastic union. Francesco too used the visual arts to proclaim his aspirations and to promote knowledge of his qualities as a leader. Thus, we can understand some of the ways in which both he and Isabella defined themselves in the public imaginary and how the identities they projected evolved over time.

Virile Femininity

When Isabella arrived in Mantua in 1490, she and her ladies-in-waiting were accommodated on the first floor of the San Giorgio castle, directly above Francesco's apartment, the two levels connected by means of an intramural staircase. During Lodovico Gongaga's overhaul of the building in the 1460s, the mechanism for raising and lowering the drawbridge had been removed from the south-eastern tower, facilitating the creation of two small chambers on slightly different levels. The lower room in the Torretta di San Nicolò, referred to in contemporary documents as the 'secret room', was used by Lodovico and then his successor Federico I, as a treasury. The higher one, with a more elevated ceiling and plentiful light, became the men's study.[24] Between around 1483, when Federico Gonzaga created a new private retreat within the *Domus Nova*—a palace that was left unfinished because he died the next year—and Isabella's arrival seven years later, the rooms in the San Nicolò tower may have fallen into disuse. The marchioness was therefore able to incorporate her late father-in-law's former treasury and study into her own apartment, which provided access to the two tower rooms via a narrow stairway.[25]

When she first took over the rooms in 1490, Isabella merely added a number of storage cabinets and a decorative wall frieze featuring Gonzaga devices with an equine theme: the maize, trave, head plume, stirrups, and andiron. This choice reflected a dutiful identification with her husband's family and the famous Gonzaga horse stud, but it was also in keeping with her own passion for horseracing, discussed so often in correspondence with her husband around this time.[26] In July 1494, a new tiled pavement featuring Francesco's personal emblems—the blazing sun, the hawking glove, and the dog muzzle—was laid.[27] The tiles had been commissioned for the marquis's new bedchamber in his palace at Marmirolo, but, since too many were ordered, the left-overs were given to Isabella for her study, so she could replace the aging wooden floor riddled with mice nests.[28]

---

[24] Brown, *Isabella d'Este*, 43–4.   [25] Brown, *Isabella d'Este*, 43.
[26] Alessandro Luzio, ed., *I precettori di Isabella d'Este: appunti e documenti* (Ancona: Morelli, 1887), 17–18.
[27] Mariarosa Palvarini Gobio Casali, 'Ceramic Tiles for the Gonzaga', in *Splendours of the Gonzaga*, ed. David Chambers and Justine Martineau (London: Victoria & Albert Museum, 1981), 44–5, 173.
[28] See Bourne, *The Soldier-Prince*, 122–3; Palvarini Gobio Casali, 'Ceramic Tiles for the Gonzaga', 173.

As a child, Isabella had witnessed not only the development of her mother's *studiolo*, but also the one that Ercole d'Este built in 1479 in the Palazzo del Corte, situated above a garden loggia, which became a notable site for the conspicuous display of the owner's magnificence, as Isabella's was to become. The marchioness's travels in Umbria and the Marches in the early months of 1494, following the birth of her first child, provided opportunities to see other notable *studioli*. When she stayed with Elisabetta Gonzaga and Guidobaldo da Montefeltro at their palaces in Urbino and Gubbio, Isabella was able to examine at leisure the famous studies of Federico da Montefeltro, where the late duke's qualities as a scholar and warrior-prince, who possessed the entire range of cardinal virtues, were proclaimed in the decorative schemes.[29]

Plans for a makeover of her apartments are likely to have begun to take shape in the spring of 1495, during a month-long stay in Ferrara. On 1 May, Isabella wrote to her secretary in Mantua, asking for precise measurements of the *studiolo*, probably in order to discuss possibilities with her father.[30] She conceived the idea of adorning the room with a collection of allegorical paintings by a number of the best contemporary masters, whose work could be viewed and compared within the one space, an approach to the display of art works that had emerged in Florence among an elite group of male patrons, whom the marchioness wished to emulate.[31]

The five paintings that eventually adorned Isabella's *studiolo* in the tower of the San Giorgio castle—now all in the Louvre museum in Paris—were executed by Andrea Mantegna, Pietro Perugino, and Lorenzo Costa, over at least a decade and possibly almost two.[32] This long evolution was the result of the difficulties of finding painters who would agree to the marchioness's exacting requirements, as well as the distractions of the escalating administrative and diplomatic responsibilities that were Isabella's lot after the mid-1490s. The involvement of the Mantuan poet and humanist, Paride da Ceresara, as primary advisor in formulating the poetic inventions that shaped the iconography of several of the paintings is documented

---

[29] Luciano Cheles, *The Studiolo of Urbino: An Iconographic Investigation* (Wiesbaden: Ludwig Reichert, 1986), 21–3; Cecil H. Clough, 'Art as Power in the Decoration of the Study of an Italian Renaissance Prince: The Case of Federico da Montefeltro', *Artibus et Historiae* 16.31 (1995): 19–50; Dora Thornton, *The Scholar in His Study: Ownership and Experience in Renaissance Italy* (New Haven, Conn.: Yale University Press, 1997), 120–1.

[30] Isabella's letter to Benedetto Capilupi does not survive, but the secretary's reply, sent from Mantua on 2 May 1495 does. ASMn, AG, 2447, c. 283.

[31] See, for example, the diary entry from the 1470s of the wealthy Florentine merchant, Giovanni Rucellai, who lists the paintings, sculptures, and other works of art that he owned and displayed in his palace in Florence. Unusually, he provides the names of those who created the works and claims that they were the best masters working in Italy at the time. Giovanni di Pagolo Rucellai, *Zibaldone*, ed. Gabriella Battista (Florence: Sismel Edizioni del Galluzzo, 2013), 158.

[32] Campbell, *The Cabinet of Eros*, 280–301.

in a letter to him of 10 November 1504, in which Isabella commented on the difficulties of dealing with eccentric and tiresomely disobedient artists:

> It is difficult to say who has been the more frustrated by the delays, we who have not yet seen the completion of our study, or you, who is continually asked to invent new programs, which due to the contrariness of the painters are neither as promptly, nor as correctly, executed as we wish.[33]

The painters saw the situation somewhat differently, Perugino in particular finding the prescriptive nature of the commission not to his liking.

The precise meanings of the paintings by Mantegna, Costa, and Perugino were probably as debated in Isabella's own time as they are today, since she had no intention of commissioning works that were easy to decipher.[34] While unlearned viewers were likely to regard the images with a mixture of bafflement and awe, well-educated observers could be expected to reflect on the moral, philosophical, and historical significance of the literary fables represented in visual form. Mantegna was well known for his narrative inventiveness and antiquarian expertise and would certainly have understood what Isabella meant when she said she wanted paintings with a variety of elegant meanings in a classicizing vein.[35] Indeed, Mantegna's two paintings, *Mars and Venus* (sometimes referred to as the *Parnassus*), completed in mid-1497, and *Minerva Expelling the Vices* (also known as *Pallas and the Vices*), added to the study walls in 1502, set the benchmark for the others.[36] Pietro Perugino's *The Battle of Chastity and Lasciviousness* was completed in July 1505, after protracted negotiations with Isabella's agents in Florence about what he was to produce.[37] By then, Mantegna had embarked on a third picture, which he referred to as the *Comus* in a letter reporting on progress, but this work was still in a preliminary state when he died in 1506. The commission

[33] Isabella d'Este to Paride da Ceresara, 10 November 1504, ASMn, AG, 2994, libro 17, c. 46. For the original Italian, see document 66 in appendix II of Campbell, *The Cabinet of Eros*, 293–4.

[34] See for example, Egon Verheyen, *The Paintings in the Studiolo of Isabella d'Este at Mantua* (New York: New York University Press, 1971); Sylvie Béguin, *Le studiolo d'Isabelle d'Este, Catalogue* (Paris: Editions des musées nationaux, 1975); Gail A. Kallins, 'Mantegna's Minerva Overcoming the Vices Reconsidered', *Athanor* 12 (1994): 35–43; Phyllis W. Lehmann, 'The Sources and Meaning of Mantegna's Parnassus', in *Samothracian Reflections: Aspects of the Revival of the Antique*, ed. Phyllis W. Lehmann and Karl Lehmann (Princeton, N.J.: Princeton University Press, 1973), 57–178; and, most recently, Campbell, *The Cabinet of Eros*.

[35] This was how Isabella explained her requirements to Bellini in a letter of 28 June 1501. See Campbell, *The Cabinet of Eros*, 288.

[36] Brown, *Isabella d'Este*, 46; Lehmann, 'The Sources and Meaning of Mantegna's Parnassus', 165–6; Campbell, *The Cabinet of Eros*, 117–44 and 145–68; Verheyen, *The Paintings in the 'Studiolo' of Isabella d'Este*, 30–41, 117–44.

[37] Campbell, *The Cabinet of Eros*, 169–90; Verheyen, *The Paintings in the 'Studiolo' of Isabella d'Este*, 41–4.

was reassigned to Lorenzo Costa, who had already completed *Coronation of a Woman Poet*, on which he was working in 1505.[38]

In general terms, the five painted allegories emphasized the importance of fortitude, prudence, and self-discipline in defeating the vices, an interpretation that had obvious political resonances, once they were associated with the patron of the paintings. Under the protection of Isabella, devoted to the virtues and in possession of qualities associated with the goddess Minerva, harmony would preside in Mantua, permitting learning and creativity to flower unmolested. This message was consistent with Isabella's construction of herself as deserving of authority and capable of exercising it.

Of course, only a select audience would have gained admittance to the *studiolo*. Isabella therefore used other media to disseminate similarly politicized propaganda more broadly. Between May and September 1498, the medallist and sculptor, Gian Cristofano Romano (*c*.1465–1512) produced a finely wrought portrait medal of the marchioness in right profile, with her hair styled to evoke images of Roman empresses on antique coins. The reverse featured a winged female figure, usually assumed to be a personification of Peace, or Victory, taming a snake with a long wand. Sagittarius rides above her head and the motto BENEMERENTIUM ERGO (On account of high merits), invented by Isabella's humanist kinsman, Niccolò da Correggio, appears around the medal's edge.[39]

The inclusion of Sagittarius above the winged figure has long baffled scholars, since Isabella's birth sign was Taurus. However, it has been suggested that Sagittarius was her ascendant and, given that Jupiter was at home in that star, the reverse of the medal may be read as implying that by virtue of the powerful constellation under which she was born, Isabella possessed the capacity to rule wisely and would therefore facilitate social harmony and peace.[40] While the precise iconographical subtext of the reverse of Romano's portrait medal may have been elusive to contemporaries, those who were given one of the medals as a mark of the marchioness's esteem seem to have grasped the essential point. Apart from the political claims associated with Isabella's regal and classicizing profile, they noted that the medal communicated the marchioness's intelligence (*ingegno*), and her capacity to exercise political authority.[41]

As well as emulating imperial profiles on ancient Roman coins, the medal image was perhaps also inspired by a painted miniature of Eleonora d'Aragona on the opening folio of a manuscript dedicated to her. Entitled *Del modo di regere e*

[38]   Brown, *Isabella d'Este*, 46–8; Campbell, *The Cabinet of Eros*, 191–219; Verheyen, *The Paintings in the 'Studiolo' of Isabella d'Este*, 44–51.

[39]   Chambers and Martineau, *Splendours of the Gonzaga*, 160; Luke Syson and Dora Thornton, *Objects of Virtue: Art in Renaissance Italy* (Los Angeles, Calif.: J. Paul Getty Museum, 2001), 119–20.

[40]   Luke Syson, 'Reading Faces. Gian Cristofano Romano's Medal of Isabella d'Este', in *La corte di Mantova nell'età di Andrea Mantegna: 1450–1550*, ed. Cesare Mozzarelli, Roberto Oresko, and Roberto Venturi (Rome: Bulzoni, 1997), 281–94 (292).

[41]   Syson, 'Reading Faces', 288.

di regnare, the work was written by Antonio Cornazzano between 1476 and 1480.[42] The miniature, thought to have been painted by Cosmè Tura, depicts a determined young Eleonora in right profile, receiving the sceptre of power from a heavenly hand. The portrait thus reinforced the message of the text itself, which praised the duchess's capacity for justice, wisdom, prudence, and fortitude.[43] Since this manuscript was never published, few people would have been in a position to note the relationship between the medal portrait and the painting. However, Isabella may have appreciated the similarity of the images as a private tribute to her mother.

The large, half-length, portrait sketch of Isabella executed by Leonardo da Vinci in coloured chalks in 1499, now in the Louvre Museum, shares certain features in common with the medal created by Romano. The drawing would not have been disseminated as widely as the medal, but it was copied a number of times for presentation as a diplomatic gift. The marchioness's hands originally rested on a ledge, with the index finger of her right hand indicating a book, as an early copy of the portrait, held now in the Ashmolean Museum in Oxford, shows. The left side and bottom margins of the original were at some stage cropped— probably because those edges had become frayed over time as the image was copied and recopied—eliminating the book and truncating the subject's hands. In its original state, however, the association of Isabella with erudition and a love of literature, suggested by her finger indicating the book on the ledge at the base of the picture, would have been clear.[44]

Isabella was pleased by Leonardo's work and doggedly pursued him for a painted version of the portrait. He never obliged, perhaps because he was not particularly interested in the task, engaged as he was in experimenting with more radically new portrait formats. The ground-breaking images of Ginevra de'Benci, painted between 1474 and 1476, and of the duke of Milan's mistress, Cecilia Gallerani, executed around 1490 and particularly notable for its serpentine pose, are indicative of Leonardo's reconceptualization of the genre.[45] Isabella was curious about the latter painting and, in April 1498, asked Gallerani to send it from Milan to Mantua by courier, so she could compare the style of the work with several portraits by Giovanni Bellini.[46]

Leonardo wanted his portraits to capture what he called 'the motions of the mind', and he strived to achieve this goal through subtle gradations of light and shade on

---

[42]   The manuscript is now in the Pierpont Morgan Library, MS M.731.

[43]   On Cornazzano's text, see O'Leary, 'Politics, Pedagogy and Praise', 285–307.

[44]   Francis Ames-Lewis, *Isabella and Leonardo: The Artistic Relationship between Isabella d'Este and Leonardo da Vinci* (New Haven, Conn.; London: Yale University Press, 2012), 116–61; Chambers and Martineau, *Splendours of the Gonzaga*, 159–60.

[45]   John Pope-Hennessy, *The Portrait in the Renaissance* (London: Phaidon, 1966), 101–5.

[46]   Isabella's letter to Gallerani and the latter's replies are transcribed and translated into English in Ames-Lewis, *Isabella and Leonardo*, 223–5.

an entire face.[47] Although Isabella was certainly open to new representational developments, Leonardo represented her in right profile, perhaps because the marchioness insisted that the chalk drawing follow the general format of the Romano medal, at least in relation to her face. The rest of her body faces the viewer, as if Isabella has turned her gaze momentarily away, a pose that gives the figure a fascinating dynamism. Leonardo produced a very fine work, although the Louvre original is so badly damaged that it is difficult to recover the subtle texturing and delicate colouring that the artist achieved, using a French technique that he probably learned at the Sforza court.[48] Isabella seems to have appreciated the sophisticated finesse of the portrait and approved of her representation as a woman of dignity and intellect.

The desire to project herself as unusually erudite also found expression in the marchioness's collecting practices, as they evolved from a focus on carved gems and small precious objects to a broader range of artefacts, including marble and bronze sculptures and ancient architectural fragments. Isabella initially envisaged her *grotta* and *studiolo* as repositories for her books and personal valuables, a conception in keeping with the precedents established by Eleonora d'Aragona and also by her relative, Ippolita Sforza, in their studies. Thus, in September 1491, she ordered a large number of books from Venice, predominantly chivalric romances in the vernacular, a genre of writing she particularly enjoyed.[49] Over time, she also acquired works of Roman and Greek literature, ordering deluxe printed editions of the classics from Aldus Manutius' press in Venice, and books continued to have a prominent place in her study.[50] However, by the time the first of Mantegna's paintings was installed in the *studiolo*, Isabella was determined to acquire a significant collection of antiquities, including sculptures, hard stone vases, medals, coins, and gems, which would be displayed alongside contemporary works. By doing so, she intended to stimulate debate about, and evoke appreciation of, the striking comparisons she had orchestrated. Stepping into the highly competitive and prestigious arena of collecting antiquities, hitherto entirely male territory, was a bold initiative by Isabella, designed to set her apart from other women and to promote her reputation as at the forefront of cultural developments.[51]

---

[47] Pope-Hennesssy, *The Portrait in the Renaissance*, 101.

[48] Ames-Lewis, *Isabella and Leonardo*, 119–25.

[49] For Isabella's letter of 24 September 1494 to Giorgio Brognolo, the Mantuan ambassador in Venice, see Luzio and Renier, *La coltura e le relazioni letterarie*, 7–8.

[50] Luzio and Renier, *La coltura e le relazioni letterarie*, 9–25. Letters of July 1501 reveal that Isabella was negotiating with her agent in Venice, Lorenzo da Pavia, to acquire good quality vellum for a deluxe printed edition of Virgil's works and with Alfonso Trotti in Ferrara, so she could have the works of the recently deceased poet and humanist, Niccolò Lelio Cosmico, copied. She explained to Alfonso: 'To embellish our *studiolo*, we are taking care to have the works of every modern author, whether Latin or vernacular'. See Isabella d'Este, *Selected Letters*, 166–7. See also the letter of 16 May 1505 to Aldus Manutius in which Isabella orders a complete set of small format editions in Latin, at 258–9.

[51] Rose Marie San Juan, 'The Court Lady's Dilemma: Isabella d'Este and Art Collecting in the Renaissance', *The Oxford Art Journal* 14 (1991): 67–78.

About the time the last paintings were installed in the *studiolo*, the marchioness embarked on a refurbishment of the *grotta*, so as to better house her growing collection of ancient and contemporary artefacts, books, and manuscripts, as well as the finely crafted musical instruments she had commissioned, many of which she played expertly.[52] She installed cabinets and covered up the vaulted ceiling, frescoed with signs of the zodiac, with a gilded and elaborately carved wooden lining, made between 1506 and 1507 by the marquetry specialists, Antonio and Paolo Mola.[53] The new ceiling featured Isabella's own devices of the lottery tickets, suggestive of fortune and its mastery, and the musical pause, a bar of music containing only rests and repeats, signifying silence, a reference perhaps, as Stephen Campbell suggests, to the owner's prudent discretion or, in musical terms, to the passing of time.[54] These early personal devices, or *imprese*, were to be joined by others, equally tantalizing in their openness to many interpretations, but all indicative of the marchioness's desire to suggest that she possessed an exceptional degree of emotional and mental equilibrium.

Isabella's significance as a collector has been the subject of an enormous amount of scholarship and it is beyond the scope of this chapter to discuss the many ancient and contemporary artefacts that she acquired between the late 1490s and her husband's death in 1519, when she moved her apartments from the San Giorgio castle to the ground floor of the adjoining *Corte Vecchia* palace.[55] The self-conscious linking of the old and new became a notable feature of the way Isabella stored and displayed artefacts in the *grotta*. For example, she paired a gold version of the portrait medal of her by Romano—presented in a magnificent enamel frame studded with diamonds and precious stones (now in the Kunsthistorisches Museum in Vienna)—with a lost, but well-documented, large antique cameo of Augustus and Livia, the Roman couple also in profile. This juxtaposition indicated to observers that Isabella wished to associate herself, not only with the prestige of owning a rare, ancient cameo, but also with its ancient imperial resonances.

Similarly, a *Sleeping Cupid* attributed at the time to the ancient Greek sculptor, Praxiteles of Athens, was placed on one side of the *grotta*'s only window, while Michelangelo's interpretation of exactly the same theme, conceived as an exercise to deceive contemporaries into believing that the work was ancient, was situated on the other. Both these sculptures, one ancient and the other contemporary, were obtained with difficulty and, in the case of Michelangelo's *Cupid*, with a degree of ruthlessness. Isabella finally acquired the 'Praxiteles' sculpture from the

---

[52] William F. Prizer, 'Isabella d'Este and Lorenzo da Pavia, "Master Instrument-Maker"', *Early Music History* 2 (1982): 87–127.

[53] Bourne, *The Soldier-Prince*, 276.   [54] Campbell, *The Cabinet of Eros*, 75–7.

[55] For a comprehensive bibliography on this theme and the documents relating to Isabella's acquisitions for her *grotta* and *studiolo*, see Brown et al., *Per dare qualche splendore*.

Bonatto family, after negotiations that lasted from 1498 to 1505.[56] Michelangelo's work initially belonged to her brother-in-law, Guidobaldo da Montefeltro, but was appropriated by Cesare Borgia when he invaded Urbino in June 1502. Isabella enjoyed cordial relations with the pope's son and asked for the sculpture as a gift, a request to which Borgia acceded.[57] When Guidobaldo regained the duchy, and attempted to reclaim the work, Isabella refused to return it, on the grounds that she had sought and obtained his blessing before requesting the *Cupid* from Borgia and had thereby saved the piece from ending up in enemy hands.[58]

Thus, by hook and by crook, she gained some outstanding pieces. Despite limited financial means and a series of frustrating delays, by the time Isabella declared the *grotta* finished in April 1508, the privilege of gaining admittance to her steadily growing collection of precious artefacts and to the adjoining *studiolo* was increasingly seen as a mark of favour to distinguished visitors.[59] Those who entered the marchioness's apartment encountered a multi-media presentation of her learning and cultural sophistication, the smallness of the spaces rendering the experience all the more dazzling. Thus, while Isabella could not compete with the large building programmes and extensive decorative programs of her husband and father, she achieved prominence as a patron by exploring new avenues of self-promotion, through collecting antiquities at a time when this was an activity confined to men and by commissioning arcane mythological paintings which marked her out as a woman of rare intellect and taste, who possessed the full range of political attributes, including magnificence.

The Warrior-Prince

Francesco's obsessions with hunting, fine horses, and hounds, as well as the desires he harboured in relation to establishing himself as one of Italy's foremost generals, dominated the iconography of paintings he commissioned in the 1480s. Unlike Ercole d'Este, who prioritized the upgrading of his urban palace when he first came to power, Francesco preferred to put his stamp on the Gonzaga rural properties, especially Marmirolo, ten kilometres to the north of Mantua, and his favourite residence, Gonzaga, thirty kilometres to the south. He built new palaces at both estates to supplement the accommodation already available, so as to

---

[56] Brown et al., *Per dare qualche splendore*, 160–72. Bourne, *The Soldier-Prince*, 208.

[57] Brown et al., *Per dare qualche splendore*, 156–7.

[58] Brown et al., *Per dare qualche splendore*, 177–80. Isabella's justification for keeping the Cupid is set out in a letter of 29 December 1503 to Giovan Lucido Cattaneo. See Isabella d'Este, *Selected Letters*, 242–3. Bourne, *The Soldier-Prince*, 208.

[59] A summary of the visits to Isabella's rooms and collection during her lifetime and beyond is provided in Brown et al., *Per dare qualche splendore*, 25–8.

entertain important diplomatic visitors through the hunting of game and other physical sports. Neither of these architectural complexes survive but, as Molly Bourne discovered, the projects are well documented in archival evidence.[60]

One of Francesco's early projects at Marmirolo was a series of paintings representing *The Triumphs of Alexander the Great*, the subject matter likely inspired by the fact that he shared a birthday with the ancient Greek ruler. The new palace that Francesco built at Gonzaga also had a pictorial cycle of triumphs, but here the allusions were literary, since they probably represented *The Triumphs of Petrarch*. However, military themes were strongly evident in the Room of the Victories at Gonzaga which celebrated the soldierly exploits of his grandfather, Lodovico II Gonzaga.[61]

These themes were consistent with Francesco's youthful interests, but, in the early 1490s, he also began to commission frescoes with more tantalizingly sophisticated themes that were indicative of a desire to be seen as knowledgeable about, and in contact with, a world far beyond Mantua. He ordered large murals of eight important cities for his new palace at Gonzaga, each image framed by fictive architecture in a classicizing style.[62] Teofilo Collenuccio, the son of the prominent courtier, Pandolfo Collenuccio, was placed in charge of overseeing the project. The fresco cycle was to consist of accurate portraits of Constantinople, Rome, Naples, Florence, Venice, Cairo, Genoa, and either Paris or Jerusalem. The marquis's conception was perhaps influenced by what he had heard about a series of city views painted by Bernardino Pintoricchio between 1484 and 1487 at the Villa Belvedere in Rome.[63]

Girolamo Corradi, an artist known for his expertise in copying maps, and Polidoro, whose responsibility it was to add animals, people, and other enlivening details to the paintings, began work on the cycle in 1493.[64] It proved far from easy to find images of the eight cities that were sufficiently reliable and detailed enough to satisfy the marquis's requirements, since this was a pictorial genre that was only beginning to gain traction. Views of Constantinople, Rome, Florence, and Venice were eventually obtained and the frescoes depicting these cities were satisfactorily completed. After a protracted search for an accurate model, Cairo was added to the walls in April 1494. This fresco became a particular source of interest, since the appearance of Cairo was a mystery to most contemporaries. When exactly Genoa was painted is not documented, but several years were to elapse before it joined the other views and Francesco was still looking for an image of Paris in 1497.[65] He may never have found one. Even so, by the end of April 1494, the marquis was

[60] Bourne, *The Soldier-Prince.*   [61] Bourne, *The Soldier-Prince*, 125–6, 147.

[62] Molly Bourne, 'Francesco II Gonzaga and Maps as Palace Decoration in Renaissance Mantua', *Imago Mundi* 51 (1999): 51–82.

[63] Bourne, *The Soldier-Prince*, 231.   [64] Bourne, *The Soldier-Prince*, 230.

[65] Bourne, *The Soldier-Prince*, 238–40.

so convinced of the success of the Room of the Cities as an expression of his princely magnificence that he commissioned Battista Spagnoli, a noted Carmelite poet and intellectual, to provide verses 'in praise and acclamation of our room' that could be inscribed into the coffered ceiling, so that the memory of the room's creator would be preserved in perpetuity. Leaving nothing to chance, he instructed his secretary Antimaco to tell Spagnoli 'to see that they are sumptuous, and that they suitably express the goodness that the prince deserves'.[66]

Francesco undertook a similarly novel decorative scheme at Marmirolo, again under the attentive supervision of Teofilo Collenuccio. This time the program involved cartographical murals—two of them earthly and one celestial. The Room of the Planisphere, is likely to have been decorated with images of the planets, while the Room of the World Map, executed by Francesco Mantegna and his assistants in 1494, probably included a representation of the known world, based on Ptolomy's *Geography*, which was in the marquis's library. The adjacent Greek Room depicted five locations in the eastern Mediterranean, namely Constantinople, Adrianopole and Vlorë, the straits of the Bosphorus, and Rhodes. Each image had an accompanying label and Latin inscription, the spelling carefully researched by Collenuccio, who again consulted Ptolemy's text.[67] The frescoes in these rooms made explicit references to the marquis's familiarity with the geographical details of the Ottoman Empire. The walls also featured a Turkish banquet and a portrait of Casim Bey, the ambassador of the Ottoman sultan Bâyezîd II (ruled 1481–1512), who visited Mantua and Marmirolo in mid-1493.[68] In conjunction with images in the Room of the Maps, which showed Turkish women making their way to the baths and men heading for the mosque, the frescoes spoke of Francesco's knowledge of Islamic religious culture and of Turkish social customs.

By the time he married, Francesco was on excellent terms with the sultan. He sent at least one envoy to the Ottoman court most years between 1491 and 1500 and, thereafter, a little less frequently.[69] The sultan's stables in Constantinople and elsewhere were stocked with fine equine breeds, but were particularly renowned for a light, robust animal with hard hooves that could run fast over long distances, making it ideal for the *Palio* races held in Italy's urban centres.[70] These Turkish

[66] Francesco Gonzaga to Antimaco, 29 April 1494, from Mantua, ASMn, AG, 2906, libro 151, c. 3v. transcribed and translated in Bourne, *The Soldier-Prince*, 231, 357.

[67] Bourne, *The Soldier-Prince*, 125.

[68] Bourne, *The Soldier-Prince*, 125; and Molly Bourne, 'The Turban'd Turk in Renaissance Mantua: Francesco II Gonzaga's Interest in Ottoman Fashion', in *Mantova e il Rinascimento italiano. Studi in onore di David S. Chambers*, ed. Philippa Jackson and Guido Rebecchini (Mantua: Sometti, 2011), 53–64.

[69] Antonia Gatward Cevizli, 'More Than a Messenger: Embodied Expertise in Mantuan Envoys to the Ottomans in the 1490s', *Mediterranean Studies* 22.2: (2014), 166–89.

[70] Elizabeth Tobey, 'The Palio Horse in Renaissance and Early Modern Italy', in *The Culture of the Horse*, ed. Karen Raber and Treva Tucker (Houndsmills, Basingstoke, and New York: Palgrave Macmillan, 2005), 63–90.

horses were therefore much sought after by members of the Italian political elite, including by Francesco. However, while it may have been the desire for excellent horses that prompted the marquis to cultivate Bâyezîd II in the first instance, recent scholarship has discovered there were other layers to the relationship.[71]

Despite the fact that the marquis was the ruler of a tiny, landlocked state, with seemingly little to offer the sovereign of a mighty empire, Bâyezîd II responded warmly to Francesco's diplomatic overtures, recognizing that he might be able to provide information about Prince Cem, the sultan's younger half-brother, who was a papal captive between 1489 and 1495, when he fell into the hands of the French. Keeping track of Cem's whereabouts was essential to Bâyezîd II, who worried that his brother might be a possible rival for the throne, if he ever escaped from Europe. Although the sultan made several attempts to have Cem killed, the prince died, probably from natural causes, in February 1495. Bâyezîd II then wanted the body repatriated, purportedly to ensure it received an Islamic burial, but probably also to have evidence of his half-brother's demise. He hoped the marquis would assist him.[72]

The sultan also feared that he would face an invasion from Charles VIII from across the sea, if the French king conquered Naples and gained access to the southern Italian coast. Thus, he was keen to obtain Italian-bred mules suitable for warfare and some of the latest military technology being manufactured in northern Italy, particularly armour made from hardened steel and produced in a way that enabled it to be forged into curved shapes. Italian armour was much more effective in protecting the breast, back, and stomach of fighters than Ottoman mail shirts. Although there was a papal ban on providing military equipment to enemies of the Christian faith, Francesco sent the sultan, and several top Ottoman officials, stomach and throat armour, as well as mail sleeves. He also dispatched Bernardino Messaglia, who was in charge of the Mantuan armoury and came from a famous Milanese family of master armourers, to deliver the goods and perhaps to take measurements for commissions that required more precise fitting.[73] The other Gonzaga envoy sent to collect horses in the early 1490s, Alessio Beccaguto, was a noted military engineer. It is likely that he secretly supplied the

---

[71] See Gatward Cevizli, 'More Than a Messenger' and her more recent essay, 'Portraits, Turbans and Cuirasses: Material Culture between Mantua and the Ottomans in the 1490s', in *Global Gifts: The Material Culture of Diplomacy in Early Modern Europe*, ed. Zoltán Biedermann, Anne Gerritsen, and Giorgio Riello (Cambridge: Cambridge University Press, 2017), 34–55. For a broader perspective on contacts between the Italian courts and the Islamic world, see Isabella Lazzarini, 'Écrire à l'autre. Contacts, réseaux et codes de communication entre les cours italiennes, Byzance et le monde musulman aux XIVe et XVe Siècles', in *La correspondance entre souverains. Approches croisées entre l'Orient musulman, l'Occident latin et Byzance (XIIIe–Début XVIe s.)*, ed. Denise Aigle and Stéphane Péquignot (Turnhout: Brepols, 2013), 165–94.

[72] Gatward Cevizli, 'More Than a Messenger', 167–8.

[73] Gatward Cevizli, 'More Than a Messenger', 169–75.

sultan with information about the latest designs in Italian fortifications, which now had to resist cannons of considerable firepower.[74]

The willingness of Francesco to provide illicit military supplies and intelligence to an enemy of Christendom speaks volumes, not only about his obsession with making his stables the finest in Europe, but also a desire to establish himself as a crucial diplomatic conduit to the Ottoman elite. The visits to Constantinople of Bernardino Messaglia and Alessio Beccaguto paved the way for a state visit to Mantua by the sultan's ambassador, Casim Bey, also a military expert, who used his visit to gather information about new martial hardware and defences being developed in the Italian peninsula.[75]

Isabella was in Ferrara during the ambassador's visit in mid-1493. She had been summoned by her mother to establish whether she was pregnant and, as we have seen in Chapter 2, Francesco was keen to have certainty on that score. He therefore requested that his sister Elisabetta come to Mantua from Urbino to help him welcome both the Turkish ambassador and the papal envoy, whose visits coincided. It was thus Isabella's rooms, and those of her retinue, in the San Giorgio castle which were redecorated from floor to ceiling with carpets and rich tapestries in preparation for Casim Bey's arrival.[76] During a week-long stay in Mantua and its environs, the ambassador was entertained lavishly and took part in a grand hunt at Marmirolo.[77]

Even before Casim Bey's visit, Francesco seems to have been interested in Ottoman styles of dress. In February 1492, for example, he had sought to have a turban sent from Venice, perhaps to wear during Carnival. The request left his Venetian agent, Giorgio Brognolo, perplexed at first, since the word *turbante* was unfamiliar to him, the noun not yet having entered Italian. Yet turbaned Turks would have been ubiquitous in Venice, so when the marquis explained he was referring to a head dress, the item was sent without delay. In 1493, again during Carnival, Francesco ordered ten more turbans, this time made from cloth bought in Viadana, a subject town within Gonzaga territory.[78] The marquis may have wished to present his courtiers, as well as himself, in Turkish costume, in preparation for Casim Bey's visit.

Francesco was already noted for his distinctive beard, styled to recall that worn in ancient times by the emperor Hadrian. Andrea Mantegna's *Madonna delle Vittoria*—painted to commemorate the marquis's role in the military encounter

---

[74] Gatward Cevizli, 'More Than a Messenger', 175–8.

[75] Bourne, *The Soldier-Prince*, 52. Isabella congratulated her husband on the beauty and quality of the horses sent by the sultan in a letter of 3 February 1493, ASMn, AG, 2961, libro 1, c. 21r.

[76] See letters from Federico de Casalimaggiori and Matteo Sacchetti (Antimaco) to Isabella d'Este of 16 and 19 July 1493, in Pietro Ferrato, *Il marchesato di Mantova e l'impero Ottomano alla fine del secolo 15: documenti inediti tratti dall'archivio storico dei Gonzaga* (Mantova: Stabilimento tipografico Mondovi, 1876), 2–3.

[77] Bourne, *The Soldier-Prince*, 340.   [78] Bourne, 'The Turban'd Turk', 60.

in July 1495 between the Italian League's forces and Charles VIII's army at Fornovo in northern Italy—shows a splendidly armoured Francesco with his signature moustache and short beard, manicured to coincide with the length of his bobbed hair. The terracotta bust by the sculptor and medallist Gian Cristoforo Romano, now in the Museo della Città in Mantua, also depicts Francesco with the same facial hair, as do all the extant medals and coins bearing his adult image. In his *Istoria di Mantova*, Mario Equicola claimed that the marquis of Mantua was the first Italian lord to maintain a permanent beard: 'Francesco revived an ancient fashion in such a way that in our own day he has had innumerable imitators.'[79] By the early sixteenth century, as many portraits attest, including that of Baldassare Castiglione by Titian, the beard had become very fashionable among the Italian political elite.[80]

In occasional combination with a turban, Francesco's beard encouraged the revival of the epithet 'il Turco', associated with his grandfather, Lodovico Gonzaga, who had also imported Turkish horses.[81] As Francesco acknowledged in a letter to Bâyezîd II of 24 July, the sultan's deigning to include him 'among those he cherished' was known to 'all Italy'. As a ruler of a minor state, the marquis referred to himself in correspondence with Bâyezîd II as a 'servant and slave'.[82] Yet, Francesco's attempts to learn Turkish, and his efforts to draw attention to his controversial relationship with the sultan through sartorial display and the frescoed images of Turkish themes on the walls of his palaces, suggests that he saw the connection with Constantinople as an important means to secure an even grander role in European politics than his ancestors had enjoyed.[83]

Given these lofty aspirations, it is unsurprising that the marquis was eager for Isabella to oversee his affairs at home, while he sought glory on the battlefield and attempted to enlarge his tiny dominion through territorial conquest. As this chapter has shown, he made sure to alert contemporaries to his intentions through the iconography of his artistic commissions. Isabella did the same, although the challenge for her was to overcome conventional prejudices that threw doubt on a woman's capacity to govern. Read together, the couple's programmes of cultural patronage could be seen as entirely complementary, each contributing to Mantua's reputation as well governed and a creative milieu. Eventually, as we will see, a spirit

---

[79] 'Il primo de gli imperadori, che notrisse la barba fu Traino. Francesco ritornò l'uso tralasciato in modo, che a' nostri giorni ha hauuto infiniti imitatori.' Mario Equicola, *Dell'istoria di Mantova libri cinque*, ed. Benedetto Osanna (Mantua: Francesco Osanna, 1607, reprinted Bologna: Forni, 1968), 207.

[80] Douglas Biow, 'The Beard in Sixteenth-Century Italy', in *The Body in Early Modern Italy*, ed. Julia L. Hairston and Walter Stephens (Baltimore: Johns Hopkins Press, 2010), 176–94, 347–9.

[81] Léon-Gabriel Pélissier, 'La Politique du marquis de Mantoue pendant la lutte de Louis XII et de Ludovic Sforza (1498–1500)', *Annales de la Faculté des lettres de Bordeaux*, 1 (1892): 35–120 (106).

[82] Francesco Gonzaga to Bâyezîd II, 24 July 1493, in Ferrato, *Il marchesato*, 2–3.

[83] Hans-Joachim Kissling, 'Francesco II Gonzaga ed il Sultano Bâyezîd II', *Archivio storico italiano*, 125 (1967): 34–68 (40).

of competition emerged between the pair in relation to their political and cultural self-fashioning, but their administrative and diplomatic collaborations in the 1490s so resembled the precedents established in Mantua and Ferrara by their parents and grandparents that the marquis took it for granted that this was how things should be.

4

Parallel Aspirations

First Fruits

The network of strategic marriages contracted by the Este and Gonzaga in the second half of the fifteenth century meant that Isabella and Francesco were closely related to the rulers of Milan, Ferrara, and Urbino, to the dominant family in Bologna, to the Aragonese monarchy in Naples, to Bourbon relatives of the French king, and to several German political dynasties. In the diplomatic scene that emerged in the early 1490s, these competing connections proved to be both a blessing and a curse. News of Charles VIII's preparations to reclaim the kingdom of Naples for the French crown—a project that was based on inheritance rights stretching back to the king's Anjou ancestors—began to be taken seriously by the Italian powers in early 1494. It was already well known, however, that Lodovico Sforza, the de facto ruler of Milan, had entered into a formal alliance with Charles VIII in January 1492, hoping, by doing so, to eliminate the interference in his affairs of the Neapolitan relatives of Isabella d'Aragona, who was married to his nephew, Gian Galeazzo Sforza. The Aragonese were intent on ensuring that the duchy of Milan passed from uncle to nephew, once the latter reached his majority. Lodovico was determined that would not happen.[1]

In this complex scenario, Isabella Este's desire to stretch her wings beyond routine chancery administration intensified. In mid-January 1495, she gained her husband's approval to travel to Milan to be with her sister, when Beatrice gave birth to a second child. On 4 February, the duchess produced another son, an outcome that gave Isabella renewed cause for envy. Francesco assumed his wife would return promptly to Mantua after the baby was baptized. However, within days of the birth, Sforza requested that the marchioness be permitted to remain at his court until the end of Carnival. The duke wrote in his own hand and in the most persuasive terms, making it impossible for Francesco to refuse, much as he desired to do so. He suspected his wife of engineering the situation and reproached her obliquely in a letter of 8 February.[2]

---

[1] Michael Mallett, 'Personalities and Pressures: Italian Involvement in the French Invasion of 1494', in *The French Descent into Renaissance Italy*, ed. David Abulafia (Aldershot: Ashgate, 1995), 151–63.
[2] Francesco Gonzaga to Isabella d'Este, 8 February 1495, from Mantua, ASMn, AG, 2110, c. 166.

A Renaissance Marriage: The Political and Personal Alliance of Isabella d'Este and Francesco Gonzaga, 1490–1519.
Carolyn James, Oxford University Press (2020). © Carolyn James.
DOI: 10.1093/oso/9780199681211.001.0001

Isabella was unrepentant. She was convinced that she could achieve significant political rewards for her husband at the Milanese court. Even before her sister's baby arrived, the marchioness was apparently in full diplomatic flight, charming the Venetian ambassador to Milan so well that he remained 'her slave'. This information was provided to the marquis by Benedetto Capilupi, who gushed in a letter of 28 January 1495 that if Francesco had been a fly on the wall when his wife received the ambassador, he would have been amazed by her prudent and appropriate words. The secretary assured his correspondent that Isabella had also impressed the duke, bringing great honour to herself and to her husband.[3] There can be little doubt that the marchioness was behind her secretary's glowing reference, designed to secure Francesco's blessing, so she could advocate for him at a moment that saw the constellation of Italian alliances in rapid flux.

After visiting her father and brothers in Ferrara and then her Gonzaga relatives in Umbria between early March and mid-May 1494, Isabella had spent the rest of that year at home, keeping an attentive eye on things in the city, while her husband travelled from one country residence to another, hunting and overseeing building works at his estates. It seems she grew restive in the provincial atmosphere of Mantua and embraced the excuse of her sister's confinement to spend time in the more stimulating court of Milan. Within a month of arriving there, Isabella wrote jokingly to Antonio Maria de Collis, a Mantuan courtier with whom she was on familiar terms, accusing him of having 'little wit, less brain and ample ignorance' for so foolishly encouraging a prompt return to Mantua.

> You know that there is no place where we reside with more pleasure and status than we do here, thanks to the great favor we are shown by this most illustrious lord duke of Milan, the greatest lord in the world. He thinks of nothing but amusing and entertaining us in every way possible.... So you really are insane to write us to return home, for since we have been here we haven't had a care in the world. What's more, you can be sure that we have no intention of leaving here until after the arrival of the emperor, who is expected in three or four months.[4]

The day before, Isabella had written in very different terms to her sister-in-law, Clara Gonzaga—who was staying in Mantua to be closer to her husband, Gilbert de Montpensier, leader of the French army's expedition to claim the kingdom of Naples—assuring her that she would prefer to be at home, rather than in Milan.[5]

---

[3] Benedetto Capilupi to Francesco Gonzaga, 28 January 1495, from Milan, ASMn, AG, 1630, c. 419. Published in Antonella Grati and Arturo Pacini, eds, *Carteggio degli oratori mantovani alla corte sforzesca (1450–1500)*, vol. 15 (1495–98) (Rome: Ministero per i beni e le attività culturali, Direzione generale per gli archivi, 2003), 86–7.

[4] Isabella d'Este to Antonio Maria de Collis, 20 February 1495, from Milan, in Isabella d'Este, *Selected Letters*, 68–9.

[5] Isabella d'Este to Clara Gonzaga, 19 February 1495, from Milan, in Isabella d'Este, *Selected Letters*, 68.

That this statement was a polite lie is suggested by the fact that although Isabella did not succeed in remaining at the Milanese court for three or four months, as she had assured de Collis she intended to do, she did stay for eight weeks. She left Milan in the second week of March 1495, but soon set off again, this time for Ferrara, where she remained for a month from late April. These long absences tested Francesco's patience. Indeed, the first signs of potentially serious tensions are documented in the pair's correspondence of the mid-1490s. However, as this chapter will show, the threat of conflict between them was quickly neutralized by external events, especially by Francesco's first opportunity to take to the battlefield and his surprising success in convincing contemporaries that he was a capable and courageous military commander.

Diplomatic Quandaries

While Isabella was travelling in Umbria in April 1494, Francesco had welcomed a large French ambassadorial delegation, headed by Stuart d'Aubigny, who was intent on persuading the marquis to allow Charles VIII's invading army to traverse Mantuan territory on its way south. Isabella's maternal grandfather, Ferrante d'Aragona, had died in January of that year. It was therefore the new king, Alfonso d'Aragona, who sent emissaries to Mantua in the hope that Francesco would side with his Neapolitan kin against the French.[6] As war looked increasingly inevitable, the duke of Ferrara was cautiously non-committal, although his Francophile leanings were taken for granted.[7] Venice also declared neutrality, not wanting to be drawn into a conflict on Italian soil while it was engaged in resisting Ottoman encroachment on its maritime territories. His Venetian military contract obliged Francesco to follow suit. He therefore informed republican authorities of the diplomatic approaches of both the French and the Neapolitans, while endeavouring to remain on good terms with both parties, a ploy that had worked well in the past to protect the Mantuan state from being claimed by stronger powers.[8]

During the summer of 1494, the Neapolitan navy attempted to attack Genoa from the sea, so as to prevent the French from landing heavy weaponry there. By September, the southerners had lost the maritime battle, as well as the tenuous foothold established by their infantry at Rapallo. After learning of these first defeats, the marquis admitted to Isabella that he had congratulated Lodovico Sforza on the French-Milanese victories 'against his conscience'. He insisted that she too put aside personal regret about the fate of their Aragonese relatives and

[6] Mazzoldi, *Mantova. La storia*, vol. 2, 97–8.
[7] Joël Blanchard, 'Political and Cultural Implications of Secret Diplomacy: Commynes and Ferrara in the Light of Unpublished Documents', in *The French Descent*, ed. Abulafia, 231–47.
[8] Mazzoldi, *Mantova. La storia*, 100.

write to her sister Beatrice in the same pragmatic spirit.[9] Francesco sought insurance in other directions as well, remaining in epistolary contact with his sister Clara until she arrived in Mantua in late November 1494, as well as with her French husband, the commander of the invading army.[10] Clara remained in Mantua or its environs until 1497, sustaining keen suspicions in Venice about the marquis's ultimate loyalties.

Gian Galeazzo Sforza died, possibly in suspicious circumstances, in October 1494, thereby permitting his uncle to assume the title of duke of Milan and to discard the role of regent. The primary reason for Lodovico Sforza's support of the French expedition thus evaporated. Given the formidable size of the invading army and the unforeseen power of its weaponry, Lodovico realized that his power to control the unfolding political scenario was almost negligible. He worried that his own state might be vulnerable to attack by the French army and therefore secretly sought to change sides, deciding to resist, rather than help, Charles VIII. Isabella perceived the new diplomatic climate in Milan as a golden opportunity, since her husband's military contract with the Venetian regime was due for renewal. Within weeks of her arrival in Milan in January 1495, she was actively seeking a better deal for Francesco with her Sforza brother-in-law.

Rather than attempting to persuade Francesco directly to seek a Milanese contract, Isabella instructed Capilupi to prepare the ground. In a letter to the marquis of 4 February, the secretary pointed out that there would inevitably be tensions associated with the forthcoming alliance between the rival states, Milan and Venice, so the moment was right for Francesco to offer his allegiance to the highest bidder.

> The friends that your Lordship has here say that this is the year that you must know how to sell your merchandise, because in the time of your predecessors, there was never such a fine opportunity.[11]

Two weeks later, the marchioness took up the issue herself, urgently enjoining Francesco to pretend he was ill and so avoid any agreement with Venetian authorities, until she could secure a better contract for him with the duke of Milan.[12] Isabella wrote confidentially on the same day to Gerolamo Stanga, a Mantuan

---

[9] 'avisandove che se bene scrivemo alegrandose de questa rotta che l'ha data alla gente 'ragonese che 'l facimo contra consientia nostra, come possite comprendere.' Francesco Gonzaga to Isabella d'Este, 15 September 1494, from Venice, ASMn, AG, 2109, c. 419.

[10] Francesco Gonzaga to Isabella d'Este, 5 November 1494, from Marmirolo, ASMn, AG, 2109, c. 365. On the behaviour of the French forces in northern Italy, see Paolo Margaroli, '"Traitres Lombardi": The Expedition of Charles VIII in the Lombard Sources up to the Mid-Sixteenth Century', in The French Descent, ed. Abulafia, 371–89.

[11] Benedetto Capilupi to Francesco Gonzaga, 4 February 1495, from Milan, in Grati and Pacini, eds, Carteggio degli oratori mantovani, vol. 15, 94–6.

[12] 'Io la conforto et prego ad non andare a Venetia, se la dovesse ben fingirsi amalata, aspectando prima de intendere qualche fondamento de la pratica mia.' Isabella d'Este to Francesco Gonzaga, 19 February 1495, from Milan, ASMn, AG, 2110, cc. 22r–v.

diplomat with whom she enjoyed warm relations, asking him to work with Rodolfo Gonzaga to make sure that Francesco did not go to Venice before she could conclude negotiations in Milan.[13]

However, on 23 February 1495, while Isabella was still busily engaged in talks with the duke, the marquis renewed his contract with Venice for another five years, agreeing to an annual salary of 44,000 gold ducats. He explained firmly to Isabella that his honour precluded a change of allegiance and that was the end of the matter.[14] Although the Venetian republic refused to grant Francesco the position of captain general, on the grounds that he had no experience of leading an army and had never even been on a battlefield, Francesco decided to accept the less prestigious title of governor general, confident that he would at least be paid, something that was far from assured in any pact with Milan.[15]

Francesco no doubt felt vindicated five days later, when Isabella informed him that Gilbert de Montpensier and his army had marched unopposed into Naples on 22 February. She reported Sforza's shock at the lack of resistance encountered by the French, describing the duke as 'more dead than alive' after hearing how easily Charles VIII's mission had been accomplished.[16] There were celebrations at the Milanese court to mark the expulsion of the Aragonese monarch from Naples, but Isabella admitted that there was little appetite for the festivities and people in Milan only pretended to be happy.[17] She reflected on the harsh lessons to be learned from the shocking capitulation in Naples:

> This case must serve as an example to all the lords and potentates of the world to take more account of their subjects' hearts than of fortresses, treasure, and men-at-arms, since the discontent of subjects prompts a worse war than any enemy to be found beyond city walls.[18]

Isabella took the political fall of her Aragonese relatives to heart in her own future administrative practices, although it may also have been her mother's habit of granting regular audiences to those who sought to bring grievances to her

---

[13] Isabella d'Este to Gerolamo Stanga, 19 February 1495, from Milan, in Grati and Pacini, eds, *Carteggio degli oratori mantovani*, vol. 15, 110.

[14] 'ad noi, non sta bene, né possiamo cum honore parlarne più.' Francesco Gonzaga to Isabella d'Este, 25 February 1495, from Mantua, ASMn, AG, 2110, c. 173.

[15] Mazzoldi, *Mantova. La storia*, 100–1.

[16] 'el Signor duca è rimasto più morto cha vivo, perché non existimava che cussì presto dovesse essere destructo.' Isabella d'Este to Francesco Gonzaga, 27 February 1495, from Milan, ASMn, AG, 2110, c. 52.

[17] 'Hozi s'è facto processione per fingere allegreza et cussì continuaremo le feste et balli benché poca voglia se ne habia.' Isabella d'Este to Francesco Gonzaga, 1 March 1495, from Milan, ASMn, AG, 2110, c. 49.

[18] 'Questo caso debbe essere exemplo a tutti li signori et potentie del mondo de fare più extima de li cuori di subditi che de forteze, thesoro et gente d'arme, perché la mala contenteza de li subditi fanno pegiore guerra cha l'inimico che se trova a la compagna.' Isabella d'Este to Francesco Gonzaga, last day of February 1495, from Milan, ASMn, AG, 2110, c. 51.

attention that inspired her to do the same. As we will see, following her return to Mantua later that year, Isabella remained closely attuned to the mood of the city, to pre-empt problems that could so easily proliferate once her husband was fighting beyond state borders. She was acutely aware of the dangers of being perceived as too inexperienced to secure the well-being of Mantua's population, or, as a foreigner, not sufficiently invested in local issues.

The marquis's reluctance to seek a Milanese military commission was likely based as much on a visceral dislike of Lodovico Sforza, as a concern to maintain his pledge to Venice. Francesco's competitive attitude to his Sforza brother-in-law had emerged publicly in 1491, during the duke's marriage to Beatrice d'Este. Francesco had initially apologized to Lodovico for his inability to attend the wedding, on the grounds it would be too risky to leave Mantua, given that his wife could not stand in for him, and that many other relatives would also be at the Milanese court. This was an entirely acceptable excuse. Even the father of the bride remained in Ferrara for the same reason. However, the prospect of partici-pating in the jousts that were to be part of the festivities proved too enticing. Francesco travelled to Milan in disguise and lodged secretly at the house of the Venetian ambassador. Despite these precautions, his presence in the city was almost immediately common knowledge at the Milanese court.

As Eleonora d'Aragona recognized, so blatantly advertising loyalty to Venice in the duke's own capital was a diplomatic blunder of the first order. She wrote con-cernedly to her husband, explaining that as soon as Lodovico had learned that Francesco was in Milan, he had offered accommodation and to pay all the marquis's expenses, as their relationship as brothers-in-law required.[19] When Francesco surreptitiously visited his mother-in-law in her lodgings within the Sforza castle, still under the illusion he could preserve his incognito status, Eleonora attempted to persuade him to join Isabella immediately. Others advised Francesco to transfer from the residence of the Venetian ambassador to the nearby house of the count of Caiazzo, where Isabella could also discreetly move. His presence at the wedding would be thus regularized and the problematic dip-lomatic situation smoothed over.[20] Although Francesco ignored both suggestions, in another effort to be conciliatory, Lodovico invited his brother-in-law to the castle for a formal visit. When the marquis failed to appear, the duke made enquiries about his whereabouts, discovering that instead of keeping the appoint-ment, Francesco had dallied in the piazza in front of the Sforza castle to watch a group of jousters. He had then gone off to the house of an arms dealer, his mind apparently more occupied by thoughts of the forthcoming tournament and the

---

[19] Eleonora d'Aragona to Ercole d'Este, 23 and 25 January 1495, from Milan, ASMo, Casa e stato, 132, cc. 42r–v; c. 47.

[20] Eleonora d'Aragona to Ercole d'Este, 23 January 1495, from Milan, ASMo, Casa e stato, 132, cc. 43r–v.

need to stock up on equipment than by concerns about diplomatic niceties.[21] It is unlikely that Francesco simply forgot about Lodovico's invitation, which he probably perceived as a summons by a man who tended to treat him as a vassal. By refusing to acknowledge the duke's message, Francesco expressed his defiance and princely independence. However, this proud stance was somewhat undermined by a lacklustre performance in the tournament held on 26 January. Thus, the trip to Milan proved misguided. Not only did he fail to impress peers with his physical prowess, he suggested to the plethora of ambassadors and other influential people gathered in Milan for the wedding that he lacked prudence and political perspicacity.

Sforza bided his time before taking revenge for the snub he had suffered. In May 1494, Milanese spies intercepted a letter from Charles VIII, which thanked the marquis for having welcomed the French ambassador d'Aubigny and his party so warmly when they had visited Mantua a few weeks earlier. The duke of Milan promptly sent that letter to the Venetian authorities, in the hope that the evidence of direct communication from the king of France would embarrass Francesco and render his loyalty to Venice suspect.[22] Sforza also tacitly encouraged destructive incursions into Mantuan territory by Milanese mercenaries. In a letter of 16 May 1494, Francesco angrily complained to the duke that he was surely aware that his soldiers had stolen animals belonging to Mantuan subjects and had cut the bridges near the mouth of the river Oglio, a tributary of the Po, acts which the marquis interpreted as deliberate provocations by his brother-in-law.[23]

Given this history of recrimination and vendetta, Isabella's attempts in early 1495 to persuade her husband to seek patronage from Lodovico in the form of a military commission were doomed to failure. Nonetheless, Francesco was well aware that his wife enjoyed good relations with the duke and was keen to profit from their friendship. Thus, when she visited Milan in 1495, Francesco instructed Isabella to pursue a number of judicial causes on his behalf.[24] He also hoped she would be able to convince Lodovico to grant his brother, Giovanni Gonzaga, a military commission, an enterprise Isabella tackled energetically, but without immediate success.[25] In requiring his wife to confine herself to lobbying for such

[21] Eleonora d'Aragona to Ercole d'Este, 25 January 1495, from Milan, ASMo, Casa e stato, 132, c. 46. Ercole d'Este replied to Eleonora from Ferrara on 26 January, promising to keep the matter of Francesco's imprudent behaviour a secret. ASMo, Casa e stato, 132, cc. 50r–v.

[22] Mazzoldi, *Mantova. La storia*, 98.

[23] Francesco Gonzaga to Lodovico Sforza, 16 May 1494, from Mantua, ASMn, AG, 2961, libro 3, c. 12v. Mazzoldi, *Mantova. La storia*, 98–9.

[24] Francesco's many letters to Isabella requesting her intervention on behalf of his clients are in ASMn, AG, 2110, cc. 159, 161, 163, 169, 175, 178. On 3 March 1495, he requested that Isabella investigate the possibilities of a Milanese contract for his brother Giovanni. Francesco Gonzaga to Isabella d'Este 3 March 1495, from Mantua, ASMn, AG, 2110, c. 176.

[25] The duke eventually accepted Giovanni Gonzaga into his service in May 1495. See Coniglio, 'La politica di Francesco Gonzaga', 148.

favours, Francesco sent a clear message that he expected her to resist striking out on her own in interstate relations.

On 31 March 1495, a coalition consisting of Milan, Venice, Mantua, Florence, the kingdom of Spain, the kingdom of Naples, and the Holy Roman Empire resolved to attack Charles VIII's army as it marched back up the Italian peninsula towards France. The hastily formed alliance was prompted by the high degree of alarm about the unforeseen and spectacular French successes in the previous months. Francesco was nominated leader of the League's forces, despite continuing Venetian doubts about his competence in such a role. He therefore began to make preparations for the forthcoming campaign, which included having to raise a large amount of cash for immediate military expenses. Money was also urgently needed to fund the on-going campaign to secure a cardinal's hat for his brother, Sigismondo. When Francesco was summoned to Venice, Isabella was visiting her family in Ferrara. The marquis pondered how best to recall his wife, while preserving her good will, since he needed to pawn her jewels, something he knew would be sure to annoy her.

Rather than simply ordering Isabella to return home immediately, Francesco attempted to take a subtler approach. Having received an aggrieved letter from her concerning the Mantuan stable master's failure to permit her horses to run in the annual Ferrarese *Palio*, the marquis replied genially to his wife, assuring her that he had severely disciplined the man and she was free to do as she saw fit with her own horses.[26] Capilupi also wrote to Isabella about the incident the same day, corroborating that the stable master was in disgrace. The secretary had remained in Mantua during Isabella's trip to Ferrara, a decision he now bemoaned since he found himself bearing the brunt of the marquis's growing impatience. He warned Isabella that if she wished to be 'a dear wife' she should return immediately.[27]

But Francesco was still determined to be patient. He dispatched Capilupi to Ferrara with a gift for Isabella. The secretary reported promptly on her response:

> My Illustrious Lord, having arrived here, I presented to my Illustrious Lady the medals you entrusted me with, which were received very warmly. She says that she will look after them carefully and thanks you very much for deigning to send them to her. After greeting her in your name, faithfully and dextrously I repeated all the loving and cordial words that you told me to say concerning your desire that she return.[28]

[26] Francesco Gonzaga to Isabella d'Este, 4 May 1495, from Mantua, ASMn, AG, 2110, c. 185.

[27] Benedetto Capilupi to Isabella d'Este, 4 May 1495, from Mantua, ASMn, AG, 2447, cc. 284r–v.

[28] 'Illustrissimo Signor mio. Gionto che fui qui, presentai a la mia Illustrissima Madonna le medaglie che me dette Vostra Excellentia, quale gli furono molto chare. Dice che ne farrà bona conserva, ringraciandola pur assai che la se sia dignata mandargele. Doppo le salute, rese in nome de Vostra Signoria fidelmente et cum dextreza, gli feci intendere tutte le amorevole et cordiale parole che la me disse cussì circa el desyderio del ritorno suo.' Benedetto Capilupi to Francesco Gonzaga, 9 May 1495, from Ferrara, ASMn, AG, 2447, cc. 163r–v.

He concluded the letter to Francesco on a reassuring note, explaining that a multitude of words from a mere servant would be outweighed by a single command from a husband, since the marital bond required instant and absolute obedience from a wife.[29] It soon became apparent, however, that immediate compliance would not be forthcoming. The marquis was therefore obliged to resort to more direct pressure, urging Isabella in a letter of 11 May to leave Ferrara at once:

> It seems to us time that you came home, especially given we have to go to Milan and there is nobody here to attend to our affairs, as has already been relayed to you.... Therefore, it is utterly necessary for you urgently to prepare to return home.[30]

Isabella replied on 12 May in her own hand, not to this letter of command from her husband, but to Capilupi's earlier communication. Her convoluted and wheedling prose suggest an awareness of the need to placate her husband, but also a determination to remain in Ferrara:

> My Illustrious Lord, having understood from Benedetto Your Lordship's desire that I return to Mantua before you go to Milan, but given you will have to leave at once and that my presence in Mantua is not particularly consequential, I beg you to allow me to remain here until you get back, when I too will immediately return, and, while I assure Your Lordship that there is no place I stay more willingly than with Your Lordship, since this is impossible because of your departure, I beg that I be permitted to stay here, because Your Lordship's absence from Mantua means I will remain there with little pleasure.[31]

Francesco was forced to go to Milan without having secured his wife's return home.

---

[29] 'Ma como anche dissi a Vostra Celsitudine, non gli bisogna mezo alcuno, perché Lei, cum una sua parola sola, la poterà sempre governare a suo modo, perché ad uno minimo cigno de Vostra Signoria darrà più credito ch'a centomilia parole de' servitori, ricircando cussì el vinculo matrimoniale.' Benedetto Capilupi to Francesco Gonzaga, 9 May 1495, from Ferrara, ASMn, AG, 2447, cc. 163r–v.

[30] 'Ad noi pareria tempo che ve ne dovesti tornare a casa, et maxime andando noi a Milano, che qua non resta alcuno che habia cura de le cose nostre, come per il simile ve havemo facto dire.... Siché per ogni respecto ve deve movere ad retornare ad casa cum celerità.' Francesco Gonzaga to Isabella d'Este, 11 May 1495, from Mantua, ASMn, AG, 2110, c. 188.

[31] 'Illustrissimo Signor mio, havendo inteso da Benedeto el desiderio che haveria la Signoria Vostra ch'io retornasse a Mantoa nanti che l'andasse a Milano, ma havendo Lei a partirse presto, e non essendo la persona mia de più importancia a Mantoa de quello sia, la prego sia contenta che resti qui fin tanto sia tornata, che poi subito io anche tornarò, certificando la Signoria Vostra che non sto in loco più volentiera come facio apresso la Signoria Vostra. Ma non potendo, per la partita sua, la prego voglia che resti qui, perché, non essendo a Mantoa la Signoria Vostra, gli starrà con pocho piacere.' Isabella d'Este to Francesco Gonzaga, 12 May 1495, from Ferrara, ASMn, AG, 2110, c. 27.

From there, he wrote to Isabella neutrally, reporting only his warm reception at court the previous day and the safe receipt of the jewels she had reluctantly sent for pawning. However, a hint that he was angry about his wife's refusal to obey the command to hasten home is suggested by the abrupt refusal in the closing sentence to contemplate Isabella's request to bring three young Ferrarese girls back to Mantua to become ladies-in-waiting.[32] A letter from Benedetto Capilupi of 16 June, sent to the marquis after he had again left Mantua, this time to begin marshalling troops in the Veneto, documents continuing tensions between the spouses. Isabella had returned from Ferrara by then, but there seems to have been a public falling out between the couple in the prelude to Francesco's second departure, which upset the marchioness to the point that she became ill.

> I found her in bed with something of a fever, caused by the displeasure inflicted by Your Excellency's departure, because, after you spoke to her in the presence of those gentlemen of the court, she continued to cry day and night. Today she has recovered and is without a fever, as you will learn from a letter from [the doctor] Master Matteo.[33]

While the marquis's increasing reliance on Isabella as his political deputy gave her greater leverage in attempting to strike a balance between obeying husbandly orders and getting her own way, it would seem that it was she who inevitably paid the greater emotional price for the battle of wills that ensued.

Once Francesco was busily engaged in military preparations, his anger faded, helped, no doubt, by the fact that he was able proudly to report on 19 June that his appointment as governor general of the League's army had been announced formally before an assembly of allied forces. He listed the 'worthy men of great experience' he had chosen to lead the Venetian squadrons as they marched in formation towards the Taro valley.[34] This strategic position in the Apennines, some sixty kilometres from Parma and at the intersection of Emilia Romagna, Tuscany, and Liguria, was where the encounter with the French was expected to take place.

---

[32] 'Alla parte de quelle putte quale ve voreste menare cum voi, ve respondemo che noi non se ne contentamo che ne menate alcuna et però ve confortamo ad lassarle stare tutte.' Francesco Gonzaga to Isabella d'Este, 17 May 1495, from Milan, ASMn, AG, 2110, c. 190.

[33] 'L'ho ritrovata in lecto cum un poco de febre, causata da la displicentia presa de la partita de Vostra Excellentia, perché doppo che la gli parlò in presentia de quelli zentilhomini, sempre pianse quello dì et la nocte. Hozi è stata bene et senza febre, come meglio intenderà per la lettera de maestro Mattheo.' Benedetto Capilupi to Francesco Gonzaga, 16 June 1495, from Mantua, ASMn, AG, 2447, c. 286.

[34] 'gli significamo como havemo partito questo felice exercito in quatro colonelli, como per l'alligata lista intenderà, et havemo facto tri merescalchi, cioè il conte Ioan Francesco da Gambara, el conte Alovisio Avogadro et messer Marcho da Martinengho, homini degni et de grande experientia.' Francesco Gonzaga to Isabella d'Este, 19 June 1495, from Senago, ASMn, AG, 2110bis, c. 437.

By 1 July, the League's army was encamped at Giarolo, a fortified town north of Fornovo. From there, Francesco sent his uncle, Rodolfo Gonzaga, and the renowned mercenary captain, Giovanfrancesco Sanseverino, on a reconnaissance mission to determine from which direction the adversary might come. No sooner had the men returned to camp after assessing the lie of the land, than news reached the marquis that a party of enemy soldiers was in the vicinity, sent ahead to seek out a suitable base for the main army. According to the Venetian chronicler, Marino Sanudo, the French scouts consisted of 500 light horse and 1,500 infantrymen.[35] Francesco launched a surprise attack on this advance force and, heavily outnumbered, the French retreated in disarray. Sanudo recorded that thirty of their number were killed and twelve taken prisoner, the League's generals commandeering much welcome booty and a large ransom for the release of a wounded French nobleman.[36]

Francesco wrote triumphantly to Isabella on 2 July about the demoralizing effect of this victory on his opponents: 'the enemy is so intimidated by us that it is an incredible thing, and rightly so, recognizing us as the most powerful and largest army that this age has seen for a long time and perhaps ever'. He concluded the letter with a reflection on his astonishing ability even to forego breakfast, if the cry to take up arms rang out at first light.[37] Despite his naïveté regarding the austerities of soldiering, Sanudo noted in his chronicle that Francesco lacked neither courage nor bloodlust, attesting that the marquis undertook to kiss on the mouth and reward with ten ducats the first soldier who bought him an enemy head on a lance, a promise he was soon obliged to fulfil.[38]

The battle of Fornovo, which took place on 6 July, proved extremely bloody. The terrain on which the two armies met was treacherous, the river Taro having breached its banks after heavy rain, turning the whole valley into a quagmire peppered with river stones. Sanudo wrote in shocked terms about the heavy death toll on both sides, a consequence of the style of warfare promulgated by the battle-hardened northerners. The Italians were largely unfamiliar with fighting that gave no quarter, but were forced to adapt quickly and to give as good as they got.

---

[35] Marino Sanudo, *La spedizione di Carlo VIII in Italia*, ed. Rinaldo Fulin (Venezia: Marco Visentini, 1883), 450.

[36] Sanudo, *La spedizione di Carlo VIII*, 450. See also the account of this encounter by Francesco Gonzaga's secretary, Iacopo Probo d'Atri, in Carlo Visconti, ed., 'Croniche del Marchese di Mantova', *Archivio storico lombardo* 6 (1879): 37–68, 333–56, 500–13 (46–8).

[37] 'Non è seguito altro se non che li inimici essere tanto intimoriti de noi, che è cosa incredibile, et meritamente, retrovandose noi il più potente et magno exercito che gran tempo fa et forse mai ad questa età fosse visto.' 'Doe volte se siamo messo da tavola questa mattina et ne siamo levati, che se è gridato "arme arme", ma non ve potriamo dire quanto voluntiera et cum quanta tollerantia duramo queste fatighe.' Francesco Gonzaga to Isabella d'Este, Valley of the Taro, 2 July 1495, ASMn, AG, 2961, libro 4, cc. 20v–21r.

[38] Sanudo, *La spedizione di Carlo VIII*, 450.

No lives were spared, everyone being dispatched at sword point, as much on our side as on that of the French. No prisoners were taken, unlike in Italian wars, but rather the French shouted: 'No quarter! No quarter!' Ours: 'To the death! To the death!' So, it was a very cruel battle and the earth flowed with much blood.[39]

Francesco's letter to Isabella of the following day also described the encounter of the two armies as 'most cruel'. He expressed sadness about the deaths of Rodolfo Gonzaga, Giovanni Maria Gonzaga, and a number of other nobles from his squadron. However, his main reaction was anger. Although the death toll in enemy ranks had also been heavy, he explained that a decisive victory had eluded his side because of the disobedience and greed of the Albanian light horsemen, who had left off fighting too early in order to plunder the enemy's baggage trains.

The French diplomat, Philippe de Commynes, narrated a similar story in his memoire. According to his account, the French placed the most capable and well-equipped men in the vanguard of their nine-thousand-strong force, leaving the main corps and rear guard strung out along the valley and vulnerable to attack from behind. Part of the Italian army, including Francesco Gonzaga's squadrons, crossed the river and attacked the rear guard at the narrowest point of the pass. The poorly defended baggage train, which consisted of six thousand pack animals carrying a fabulous array of booty, proved too tempting a diversion for the Greek and Albanian stradiots employed by Venice, with the result that the League's initial advantage was lost.[40] Although Francesco alluded briefly to having acquitted himself well in the battle and referred to the capture of two very important generals from the French side, the tone of his letter to Isabella of 7 July is sombre.[41]

Charles VIII and most of his army managed to break through the Taro valley to safety with fewer casualties than the League's forces sustained. Nonetheless, the king's precipitous flight northwards and his flattering overtures to Francesco Gonzaga through his representative Commynes, following the main engagement, did much to convince even the sceptical Venetians that the marquis had been the hero of the day.[42] Francesco too began to see the events of 6 July in a rosier light.

---

[39] 'Non si sparagnava la vita l'uno l'altro, ma tutti per el fil di la spada erano mandati sì da nostri quam da franzesi. Non si faceva presoni, come in le guerre de Italia, ma franzesi cridavano: A la gorgia! A la gorgia! Nostri: A la morte! A la morte! Sì che era crudelissima battaja et assà sangue coreva la terra.' Sanudo, *La spedizione di Carlo VIII*, 477. The term 'a la gorgia' was an allusion to Plato's *Gorgias*, and was associated with a continental style of warfare which gave no quarter. Cecil H. Clough, 'The Romagna Campaign of 1494: A Significant Military Encounter', in *The French Descent*, ed. Abulafia, 191–215.

[40] Philippe de Commynes, *The Memoirs of Philippe de Commynes*, ed. Samuel Kinser, 2 vols (Columbia, S.C.: University of South Carolina Press, 1969–73), vol. 2, 526–32.

[41] Francesco Gonzaga to Isabella d'Este, 7 July 1495, from the Taro valley, ASMn, AG, 2961, libro 4, c. 26r, published in Bourne, *The Soldier-Prince*, 366 and also in Alessandro Luzio and Rodolfo Renier, *Francesco Gonzaga alla battaglia di Fornovo (1495)* (Mantova: Adalberto Sartori, 1976), 12–13. On the battle, see also Galeazzo Nosari, 'Una Leggenda Metropolitana: Francesco II a Fornovo', *Civiltà Mantovana* 101.3 (1995): 91–5.

[42] Kinser, ed, *The Memoirs of Philippe de Commynes*, 538.

By the time he wrote to his sister Elisabetta on 16 July, the deep regret he had felt about the deaths of his uncle Rodolfo and childhood friend, Giovanni Maria Gonzaga, had been overtaken by a triumphalist conviction of his own pivotal role in securing what he referred to as 'the liberation and liberty of Italy'. He hinted that he expected soon to be richly rewarded for his decisive contribution to the defeat of the French invaders.[43]

Francesco's optimism proved well founded. On 23 July, the Venetian government nominated him captain general of their forces and awarded him an annual salary of two thousand ducats. Isabella was also acknowledged with a gift of a thousand ducats. Francesco reported this happy outcome to his wife in a letter of 27 July, sent from Casallogiano where he and his troops had moved eight days before to lay siege to Novara, a Milanese possession which had been occupied in June by the duke of Orléans, the future king of France, Louis XII.[44] There he received the baton and standard of his new position. The long siege, which lasted until 21 September, showed Francesco a boring, but no less brutal, side of war, as he and his allies cut off the town's water supplies, starved its citizens into submission, and maintained nightly vigils, fully armed and on horseback, to catch anyone who tried to escape through the city gates under cover of darkness. He marvelled at his stoicism in enduring such tiring work, but also requested that Isabella send a pack of cards, so he might while away the tedious days of waiting for the authorities in Novara to concede defeat and open the city gates.[45]

Growing self-satisfaction about his military performance and gratification at the accolades of the Venetian regime clouded Francesco's political instincts to the point that he persuaded himself that he could afford to accept an invitation from King Charles VIII to visit him at Vercelli. Although he sought and received Venetian permission, the ambiguity of the response from republican officials should have warned the marquis that he was venturing into risky diplomatic territory. On 21 September, as the terms of a truce were being worked out with the duke of Orléans and the siege of Novara drew to an end, Francesco wrote to Isabella asking her to send by express courier his two finest outfits and 'a variety of perfumes', so he might be suitably bathed and attired for a royal audience.[46]

---

[43] Francesco Gonzaga to Elisabetta Gonzaga, 16 July 1495, from San Giorgio (Pavia), ASMn, AG, 2961, libro 4, c. 35r, published in Luzio and Renier, *Francesco Gonzaga alla battaglia di Fornovo*, 14.

[44] Francesco Gonzaga to Isabella d'Este, 27 July 1495, from Casallogiano, ASMn, AG, 2110, c. 403.

[45] 'Noi stamo sani et maravigliamose noi medesimi como possiamo resistere ad tante fatighe, in le quale, per Dio gratia, ognhora se sentimo più gagliardi perché le faciamo voluntiera.' Francesco Gonzaga to Isabella d'Este, 26 August 1495, from Casallogiano, ASMn, AG, 2110, c. 391. See also letters of 28 August and 7 September 1495, from Casallogiano, ASMn, AG, 2110, cc. 394 and 403. On the ruthlessness of such sieges and the bloody sacks that followed, see Stephen Bowd, *Renaissance Mass Murder: Civilians and Soldiers during the Italian Wars* (Oxford: Oxford University Press, 2018).

[46] 'Et perché potria essere che andarissimo ad fare reverentia alla Christianissima Mayestà, ve piacia subito volando mandarme li dui nostri tavardi belli, et le due cappe belle, et li dui zupponi d'oro tirato, et qualche bella camisa lavorata, et profumi de più sorte, et questo cum ogni celerità, perché il tempo è breve, mandandole in dui valisoni grandi, o in qualche altro modo, che non se habiano

On 6 October, he described the honourable reception given him by the French king, who showed Francesco his most beautiful horses and insisted he choose two of them as a gift.[47] The marquis reciprocated several days later, sending Charles VIII an equivalent number of superb stallions from the Gonzaga stables.[48]

This highly visible exchange of compliments compounded Venetian annoyance with Francesco's unauthorized involvement in negotiating the terms of the treaty, signed on 9 October. The Peace of Vercelli, promulgated by the duke of Milan and the French king's ambassadors, was finalized without consulting the Venetians, or the Spanish, who objected strongly to Sforza's agreement to allow the French to use the port of Genoa to supply their forces still in Naples. In consenting to facilitate a swap of important prisoners—the so-called Bastard of Bourbon, captured at Fornovo and held in comfort in Mantua, for Fregosino Fregoso, a Genoese who had fought on the League's side—Francesco allowed himself to be drawn into the Milanese-French negotiations. The Venetians expected that their captain general would report by letter on a daily basis. When this did not occur, the Mantuan ambassador to Venice, Giorgio Brognolo, was summoned to account for his master's arrogant behaviour. The resident envoy wrote immediately to Francesco, alerting him to the fact that the Venetian regime was displeased that he had allowed himself to be manipulated by the duke of Milan into neglecting his duty to consult Venetian authorities before agreeing to any of the terms of the peace treaty.[49] With the end of the crisis precipitated by the French victory in Naples, the temporary alliance between Milan and Venice was in rapid decline.

Francesco's failure to present himself to Charles VIII as the republic's representative, rather than in his own right as ruler of Mantua, undermined the already shaky trust with which he was viewed in Venice. Encouraged by his sister Clara, Francesco continued actively to court the French, his correspondence with the king offering Lodovico Sforza further opportunities to intercept the exchanges and send them on to Venice. While determining which alliance would protect his regime most effectively was difficult in the diplomatic chaos of the mid-1490s, Francesco's impatient craving for recognition on the wider European political stage prompted him to underestimate the risks associated with neglecting his contractual obligations to his employer and republican neighbour.

---

casone de guastarse, facendo de nocte et giorno vengano volando, senza perdimento alcuno de tempo.' Francesco Gonzaga to Isabella d'Este, 21 September 1495, from Novara, ASMn, AG, 2110bis, c. 409.

[47] Francesco Gonzaga to Isabella d'Este, 6 October 1495, from Novara, ASMn, AG, 2110bis, cc. 417r–v.

[48] Francesco Gonzaga to Isabella d'Este, 10 October 1495, from near Cremona, ASMn, AG, 2110bis, c. 422.

[49] Giorgio Brognolo to Francesco Gonzaga, 7 October 1495, ASMn, AG, 1435, as cited in Mazzoldi, *Mantova. La storia*, 139, n. 137.

The Challenges of Regency

With Francesco beyond Mantuan borders in the second half of 1495 and the perception in the city that he had his mind only on military logistics, Isabella's role as his deputy became far more apparent and, therefore, controversial. There were some who took the opportunity to express their disgruntlement about issues that had long been festering, but were now at a critical point due to the depleted state of treasury coffers. The celebrations of the marquis's wedding and the improvements to his country palaces had been very costly, as had a lavish review of his troops in 1492, which had required stabling for a thousand horses. Less than three years later, the huge expenses associated with the preparations for war created another revenue crisis. By the time the marquis set off to fight, salaries of chancery bureaucrats and many other Gonzaga employees were badly in arrears. Yet Francesco hounded his tax collectors for more money, so he could meet the large outlays of cash required in the encampment throughout the second half of 1495.[50] This was a very challenging political environment for Isabella to manage.

The problems were not long in coming. On 30 June 1495, Isabella assured Francesco that a report sent to him concerning unrest in the city was unfounded, the lie motivated by maliciousness on the part of his informer. It was true, she admitted, that a certain Iacomo da li Organi had spread a rumour that there was no bread to be had at the market. However, this troublemaker had only just been arrested. News of his incarceration had not been made public, so whoever had written to the marquis could not have known of the incident. Isabella reassured her husband that all was well:

Your Lordship should not worry and attend only to the military enterprise, because, with the advice of these magnificent gentlemen and officials, I will govern matters of state here in such a way that you will neither be troubled, nor damaged, and everything will be done for the good of the subjects. And when something is said or written about disorder, and you have not been advised of it by me, assume as a matter of principle that it is a lie, because, since I allow not only officials, but any subject, to have the opportunity to be able to speak to me whenever they want to, nothing can happen without it being anticipated before any disorder follows.[51]

---

[50] See, for example, Francesco Gonzaga to the magistrates of the exchequer, 10 July 1495, from the League's encampment, ASMn, AG, 2961, libro 4, c. 28v and his order to Antonio de Roberto to send the tax income for the preceding three months, 12 July 1495, from San Giorgio (Pavia), ASMn, AG, 2961, libro 4, c. 29v.

[51] 'La Signoria Vostra stia pur cum l'animo quieto et attendi solamente a l'impresa militare, ché le cose qua dil stato, cum consilio de questi magnifici zentilhomini et officiali, governarò per forma che la non haverà molestia né danno et tutto se farrà cum beneficio de li subditi. Et quando gli fusse dicto o scripto de desordine, et non habia aviso da me, metti per una maxima che la sia bosia, perché dando io adito non solum a li officiali, ma a tutti li subditi de potermi parlare ogni volta che vogliono, non

It seems, though, that there were, in fact, food shortages, caused, no doubt, by the lucrative opportunities for merchants to supply the League's troops, instead of Mantua's citizens. As Isabella was forced to admit in a letter of 5 July, placards lamenting the situation had been found that morning, attached overnight to the walls around the city's piazzas. Worried that he would hear an exaggerated version of the difficulties she faced, Isabella explained to Francesco that she had lifted the ceiling on the price of grain several days before to encourage supplies to come out of stockpiles. Although the initial increase in the cost of bread likely provoked the anonymous criticism, she assured him that the large quantities of grain that were now flooding the local market had already begun to drive prices down. She concluded her letter with more reassurance: 'As I wrote to Your Lordship in my other letters, things are governed with so much consultation with men of integrity that no one can justly lament or criticize [my] orders.'[52]

Yet there were also serious issues to deal with in the provinces. The salaries of guards responsible for patrolling the south-east Mantuan border at Ostiglia and other nearby settlements had been left unpaid. Worried about the possible repercussions for the security of the borders if Gonzaga employees were unable to feed their families adequately, Isabella ordered Antonio Donato, an official at Ostiglia, to send the guards twenty sacks of grain from supplies at the Gonzaga estate there. As Isabella reported to Francesco in mid-July, despite repeated requests, Donato ignored her, disdaining to obey a woman.

> He went off to Gonzaga, showing his utter contempt for the poor guards and for me, a situation that has given me no little molestation, considering the necessity of the poor men, stationed as they are in that place, and the little respect that he shows for my [authority] since, after all, he must obey me in much more important matters than this, given it is Your Excellency's intention that he and your other officials and subjects obey me.[53]

---

può occorrere cosa a che non sia proveduto nanti che desordine segui.' Isabella d'Este to Francesco Gonzaga, 30 June 1495, from Mantua, ASMn, AG, 2110, cc. 69r–70r.

[52] 'Come per altre mie ho scripto a Vostra Excellentia, le cose se governano cum tal consulta de homini integri che alcuno non può iustamente dolersi, né biasmare li ordini.' Isabella d'Este to Francesco Gonzaga, 5 July 1495, from Mantua, ASMn, AG, 2110, c. 76.

[53] 'se n'è andato a Gonzaga, cum delegiare li poveri provisionati et me insieme, cosa che a me ha dato non picol molestia, consyderato la necessità de li poveri homini constituti nel loco dove stanno et più la poca stima ch'el si fa di facti mei; che pur el doveria in molto maior cosa de questa obedirmi, essendo cossì intentione de la Excellentia Vostra che lui e li altri officiali et subditi de quella me obediscano.' Isabella d'Este to Francesco Gonzaga, 15 July 1495, from Mantua, ASMn, AG, 2110, c. 83. Several weeks later, Isabella discovered that it was not only the guards at Ostiglia who had not been paid. Those at the gates of the city and at many other strategic places in the state had not received their salaries, prompting her to urge Francesco to authorize the release of grain to them as well. Isabella d'Este to Francesco Gonzaga, 19 August 1495, from Mantua, ASMn, AG, 2110, c. 125.

Isabella therefore ordered that the grain be taken from the outmanoeuvred Donato's own supplies and then carefully accounted for her decision to Francesco. Once Donato apologized for his disobedience, Isabella restored what she had had taken from him and requested her husband forget the matter.[54] In this way, she asserted her authority, but avoided making a dangerous enemy. However, other problems proliferated.

On 29 July, Isabella conceded that criticism of her was still rampant in the city, not only on account of her gender, but also because anyone from Ferrara was perceived as sympathetic to the French. A 'foreign' woman in charge of state affairs was inevitably regarded as suspect and blamed for the poverty and suffering associated with the war. Isabella seems to have taken such prejudices for granted. As she explained to Francesco, she had not informed him about the situation, since it was impossible to establish exactly who was responsible for spreading the negative comments about her. But, at Francesco's insistence, she agreed to have read out in various parts of the city a letter from him assuring the Mantuan population that the marchioness had his full confidence.[55] These public proclamations, combined with Isabella's level-headed response to the challenges to her authority, contributed to the dying down of civic unrest. Given that much of the anxiety in the city was about the high price of basic commodities and the proximity of a large foreign army, the retreat northwards of the soldiers, away from Mantuan territory, also helped to restore calm.

In the immediate aftermath of the battle of Fornovo, Isabella orchestrated elaborate celebrations of her husband's role as the self-styled saviour of Italy. She authorized displays of fireworks and ordered that the bells of all the churches in Mantua be rung continuously. Two bronze portrait medals showing Francesco in profile and dressed in armour, with an inscription that referred to his restoration of the liberty of Italy, were quickly commissioned. Once he was pronounced captain general of the League's forces by the Venetian regime, a silver coin was also struck. It carried an image of the marquis on a charging steed and in splendid military dress, with his new title inscribed below. The reverse of the medal depicted Mantua's famous relic, a precious phial of the blood of Christ.[56] Such numismatic images could circulate widely, conveying the message of the marquis's success to the local population, but also abroad.

---

[54] 'Hora, essendosi esso Antonio Donato recognosciuto del mancamento suo et havendomi diman-dato perdono, gli ho facilmente remesso ogni iniuria, cossì prego la Excellentia Vostra che anchora Lei per amore mio gli vogli perdonare.' Isabella d'Este to Francesco, 20 July 1495, from Mantua, ASMn, AG, 2110, c. 106.

[55] 'Questi dì de mi et de tutti li Ferraresi se parlava molto sinistramente et cose de mala sorte, ma perché erano nel populazo, né se haveria potuto cavare l'origine, me ne son passata senza dimonstra-tione alcuna. Tuttavia, per satisfare a Vostra Excellentia, ho facto legere publicamente in più loci la lettera che me scrive de Zoanne Michele et maestro Iacomo aciò che ognuno intenda che sono in gratia sua.' Isabella d'Este to Francesco Gonzaga, 29 July 1495, from Mantua, ASMn, AG, 2110, c. 98.

[56] Bourne, *The Soldier-Prince*, 71.

In October, the court painter Francesco Bonsignori was dispatched to Fornovo to prepare sketches of the landscape, so he might more convincingly depict the battle in a fresco cycle destined for the palace at Gonzaga, where Francesco often entertained important guests.[57] Andrea Mantegna began work on the *Madonna della Vittoria*, a large altarpiece now in the Louvre Museum, depicting Francesco kneeling in pious gratitude beneath an enthroned Virgin and child, the pair surrounded by saints. The painting was to decorate a new votive church in the city dedicated to the marquis's victory at Fornovo.[58] Another commemorative commission, probably an altar for the chapel of Santa Maria dei Voti in Mantua's cathedral of San Pietro, was also set in train, although this project was never to be completed, due to a shortage of funds.[59]

News of the events at Fornovo even reached Constantinople remarkably quickly, thanks to Francesco's dispatch of an envoy to inform the sultan of his triumph. On 16 August 1495, Casim Bey, Bayezid II's ambassador, wrote to Francesco, summarizing the report that the Mantuan envoy had delivered to the Ottoman court:

> that Your Lordship, having battled with the king of France, with the help of God and your own valour, defeated him and killed many French noblemen and many, many other worthy men, so that he fled with his remaining army, and Your Lordship, in the first great battle, almost captured him.[60]

In this passage, Casim Bey regurgitated the essential elements of the marquis's propaganda campaign, one that was disseminated in every media available to him.

When Francesco returned to Mantua in November 1495, his military fortunes seemed to be dramatically on the ascendant. Isabella too could claim to have done an excellent job in maintaining order within the city and countryside at a critical time. Although, in the early 1490s she had occasionally annoyed Francesco by prolonging her absences from Mantua, when he wanted her back in the city, and by venturing beyond his instructions in diplomatic interactions with Milan, the opportunity for each of them to take on challenges in line with their respective aspirations kept the pair firmly united. The marquis's reluctance to acknowledge the limits of his autonomy in relation to the far more powerful states of Milan and Venice might be seen as characteristic of a young man eager to prove his masculinity and to proclaim his princely power. Yet this reckless tendency did not abate with greater maturity, something that Isabella struggled to redress. In August

---

[57] Bourne, *The Soldier-Prince*, 71.

[58] Ronald W. Lightbown, *Mantegna: With a Complete Catalogue of Paintings, Drawings, and Prints* (Berkeley: University of California Press, 1986), 177–84 and Bourne, *The Soldier-Prince*, 72–86.

[59] Bourne, *The Soldier-Prince*, 86–99.

[60] Cassim Bey to Francesco Gonzaga, 16 August 1495, from Constantinople, published in Ferrato, *Il Marchesato*, 6–7.

1495, she had made the first of many appeals to her husband to avoid a foolhardy impulsiveness in his approach to warfare:

> It upsets me very much that you always put your person in so much danger, so
> I beg and supplicate that you take great care to protect your life and don't expose
> yourself to every dangerous enterprise, because your office and duty is perfectly
> well satisfied when you govern and command others.[61]

Amid such worries, the restlessness that Isabella had begun to feel by late 1494 and that manifested itself in a desire to escape from dull political chores in the chancery subsided. Greater responsibilities at the helm of government and the uncertainties of war held out the promise of an ever-larger sphere of political action and the marchioness embraced her duties energetically. With the prospect of further military duty ahead, Francesco endorsed his wife's readiness to extend her role as regent. Thus, the mid-1490s saw the pair well satisfied with their respective roles.

---

[61] 'non me piace già che la se metti sempre a tanto periculo de la persona sua como la fa, però la prego e supplico voglia havere grande advertentia a conservarsela et non se exponere ad ogni impresa periculosa, perché molto bene satisfare al officio et debito suo quando la governa et commanda a li altri.' Isabella d'Este to Francesco Gonzaga, 26 August 1495, from Mantua, ASMn, AG, 2110, c. 128.

5

Risk-Taking and Risk Management

One of Francesco's most ubiquitous emblems, a crucible containing gold bars that resist the flames of a fire beneath it, accompanied by the motto 'Domine, probasti me et cognovisti me' (Lord you have examined me and you have known me), proclaimed him as a man of steadfast loyalty and integrity. This flaming crucible eventually adorned two of the ceilings of the San Sebastiano palace in Mantua, appeared on the reverse of some of the coins that bore his profile, and featured on the bronze bust of the marquis by Gian Cristoforo Romano.[1] Another personal symbol, an armoured gauntlet, which decorated an anteroom of the palace of Marmirolo, also associated Francesco with the virtue of fidelity.[2] Yet, late 1497, around the time he began to associate himself with the crucible surrounded by flames, coincided with the marquis's dismissal as Venice's captain-general, for what was seen as insufficient loyalty and an insulting refusal to consult Venetian authorities before making decisions. The republic regarded the marquis as entirely subject to its authority in his military role as captain-general, but, as a ruler in his own right, Francesco could not be seen to be docilely obedient to a state run by a mercantile elite. Conflict was an inevitable consequence of this failure to reconcile mutual expectations.

The vulnerability of Mantua to attack from both foreign and local powers in the first decades of the Italian Wars also meant that prevarication, temporizing, and swift changes of allegiance, seen by contemporaries as intrinsically female vices, were the political order of the day. It was perhaps an awareness of this gendered association that irked Francesco as he was forced to abandon youthful notions of honourable behaviour in relation to allies, for the sake of political survival. To compensate for his failure to adhere to one set of manly attributes, Francesco was frequently overly assertive in other ways. During his military deployments, he bad-mouthed enemies well known to be vindictive, publicly vented frustration about the inadequacies of his allies, and refused to take precautions to ensure his food was not poisoned. Such reckless behaviour horrified Isabella, but the marquis saw it as a means to communicate his courage and potency.

---

[1] See the illustrations in Bourne, *The Soldier-Prince*, 604, 615, 647.
[2] Bourne, *The Soldier-Prince*, 127.

A Renaissance Marriage: The Political and Personal Alliance of Isabella d'Este and Francesco Gonzaga, 1490–1519.
Carolyn James, Oxford University Press (2020). © Carolyn James.
DOI: 10.1093/oso/9780199681211.001.0001

Isabella's political style was as much shaped by her gender as Francesco's was by his. While imperious and harshly punitive to those who displeased her, this side of her character usually only came into play in relation to her servants, ladies-in-waiting, and, occasionally, court bureaucrats. In a diplomatic setting, Isabella kept her emotions strictly in check, a quality emphasized in the iconography of the paintings she commissioned for her study in these years. She thought strategically about the long-term implications of policy decisions and was wily rather than aggressive, if only because, as a woman, she was used to navigating the constraints that came with the delegated nature of her authority.

The marchioness's caution was a useful foil for her erratic husband and the benefits of the couple's political collaboration were particularly evident in the decade between the battle of Fornovo and the death of Ercole d'Este in January 1505. The bond between Mantua and Ferrara remained strong, both states facing the same powerful foes. Francesco adapted his alliances according to the prevailing political winds, entertaining multiple diplomatic strategies until he could determine where his interests lay. The duke of Ferrara was equally pragmatic. By sharing intelligence, and through a combination of luck and nimble diplomacy, the two ruling dynasties, united through Isabella, avoided the fate of a number of their less fortunate relatives. As Isabella and Francesco witnessed their brother-in-law, Lodovico Sforza, driven out of Milan by the French in 1499 and Francesco's sister Elisabetta and her husband, Guidobaldo da Montefeltro, humiliated by Cesare Borgia and forced to flee Urbino in 1502, there was room for satisfaction that their regime had survived, when so many others had not. Although they sometimes disagreed about how to tackle political problems, their alliance remained firmly intact.

Prudence: A Womanly Virtue?

After his success during the battle of Fornovo and appointment as captain-general of the Venetian forces, Francesco was required to take a lead role in the Italian League's campaign to eliminate the last pockets of French occupation in the kingdom of Naples. Isabella therefore again prepared to oversee government on her husband's behalf. This time, however, the task was more daunting, due to the uncertainties of epistolary communication over such a long distance, the open-ended timeframe of the League's southern expedition, and her husband's renewed exposure to the dangers of war. Isabella was also some months into a second pregnancy and was frequently unwell, although few people, apart from her husband, knew why. Even Beatrice de' Contrari was kept in the dark. She wrote concernedly to Isabella on 11 February 1496 about persistent rumours circulating at the Este court that the marchioness and her husband had not slept together, even once, while they were together in Ferrara that January. Beatrice had also heard from her contacts in Mantua that the marquis was still not speaking to his wife.[3] While the first part of the rumour was likely true, because of the couple's renunciation of sex once Isabella realized she was pregnant, their letters to each other suggest they were on good terms. Beatrice's letter is indicative of the intense public scrutiny to which the pair's relationship was subject and the ways in which court gossip might combine truth with fiction, by escalating from a simple observation to an elaborate edifice built on rumour and wild speculation.

Soon after Francesco set off for Venice to begin marshalling troops and making other preparations for the forthcoming battle in the south, Isabella's wrote to him expressing her anxieties:

> The last time Your Excellency left for the field I was displeased, but I took comfort both because you were not going so far away and because soon word of your activities returned to me almost daily. But now I don't know where to find comfort, considering the distance and the danger of the place where you are going; and it seems Your Lordship has been gone not one day but a thousand. Think now what lies ahead for me.[4]

It was not only Francesco's physical safety that Isabella worried about. Given the problems she had initially faced in establishing her authority when her husband had last headed off to war, she was aware that the Mantuan population was likely to be even more ill at ease, once the marquis was too far away to oversee her decisions regarding day-to-day government. Isabella therefore issued a precautionary edict which banned the carrying of weapons in the city, explaining to Francesco on 27 February that she had done so to ensure that public order was maintained at a sensitive time.[5]

Isabella's preoccupations were well founded, since she faced an almost immediate, if minor, challenge after her husband's departure. When the rector of the hospital in Mantua suddenly died, Isabella wrote to Francesco on 2 March proposing a certain Gasparo da la Fera as a suitable replacement. After gaining her husband's approval for the candidate, Isabella attempted to organize the appointment, only to find that the hospital board was reluctant to cooperate, wanting written confirmation from the marquis before it would act. She admitted to Francesco that she was hesitant to impose her will on the board, for fear there

---

[3] 'seria desiderosa intendere de suo ben stare per quanto intendo Zecheto ha havuto a dire qua ch'el Illustrissimo Signor marchese non ha mai dormito con Vostra Excellentia né gli parla da poi che la ritornò de qui; ne ho hauta non poca passione.' Beatrice de' Contrari to Isabella d'Este, 11 February 1496, from Ferrara, ASMn, AG, 1234, c. 386.

[4] Isabella d'Este to Francesco Gonzaga, 24 February 1496, from Mantua, in Isabella d'Este, *Selected Letters*, 82.

[5] Isabella d'Este to Francesco Gonzaga, 27 February 1496, from Mantua, ASMn, AG, 2992, libro 6, c. 32r.

would be even greater resistance. In response he wrote back teasingly, expressing his utter surprise at her timidity; he had always assumed that she 'was a lady not to be brooked'.[6] The marquis certainly had good reason to know this side of his wife's character. Yet, despite the joke at her expense, he was sympathetic to Isabella's situation and made sure to bolster her confidence by fulsomely praising her prudence and foresight in regular letters.

In external relations, Isabella was more adventurous. Lodovico Sforza had continued to encourage her desire to become the major go-between in diplomatic interactions between Milan and Mantua, imagining, no doubt, that he could bend such a young woman to his will. While she did act as the duke's advocate and was seduced for a while by his purported willingness to take her seriously as a mediator, Isabella proved not to be as malleable as her brother-in-law expected. While relations between the two remained friendly, the limitations of that amity emerged in March 1496, while Francesco was making his way south with his troops. Sforza suddenly issued an edict, forbidding shepherds at Fossa Caprara and other small settlements on the Po River from grazing their animals on land that was technically Milanese territory, but had long been used by Mantuan communities situated near the border. Isabella dispatched an experienced Gonzaga envoy to Milan to negotiate a resolution to the issue and, having informed Francesco of her action, received a grateful letter from him, sent on 3 April, from a village near Caserta.

There is no need to say anything other than to commend you for having sent Donato de' Preti to Milan and for all the other provisions you have made, which were appropriate and entirely prudent and circumspect and all I hoped of you. We would be pleased to learn how things develop, although it has become apparent to us just how soon the illustrious lord duke has forgotten our interests and the reverence and loyalty we have given him and all we have done to his benefit.[7]

---

[6] Isabella d'Este to Francesco Gonzaga, 11 March 1496, from Mantua, ASMn, AG, 2992, libro 6, c. 50v. Francesco responded the next day: 'Noi non possimo fare che non se maravigliamo alquanto che Vostra Signoria non habii facto mettere per rectore de l'hospitale messer Gasparo da la Fera, secondo noi gli scrissimo, et che siate restata per parole de' presidenti ad exequire l'ordine nostro, che è stato contra la speranza havevamo in Lei, che ne persuadevamo che fosti madonna da doverse fare obedire, et maxime havendoglilo, come è dicto, scripto noi.' Francesco Gonzaga to Isabella d'Este, 12 March 1496, from Fano, ASMn, AG, 2111, c. 34. For Isabella's letters of 19 March on the issue see ASMn, AG, 2111, c. 224.

[7] 'non accade dire altro se non commendarve de l'havere mandato a Milano Donato de li Preti et de tute le altre previsione haveti facte, le quale sono state conveniente et piene de ogni prudentia et circumspectione et como speravamo da voi. Haverimo piacere ne faciati intendere il successo de la cosa, se bene ne pare comprendere che molto presto lo Illustrissimo Signor duca de Milano se sii domenticato de li facti nostri, de la reverentia et servitù gli portamo et di quello havemo facto in suo beneficio.' Francesco Gonzaga to Isabella d'Este, 3 April 1496, from San Germano, ASMn, AG, 2111, cc. 49r–v.

Isabella also intervened herself. On 14 April 1496, she appealed to the duke to give due weight to the advantages of her status as an intermediary in Milanese-Mantuan relations when he considered her request to withdraw the edict: 'the good opinion that you have always had of me, has given me greater authority and credit with my lord [husband]'.[8] While Lodovico gave ground slightly in response, promising to revisit the question when his advisory council met in two weeks, he insisted that Isabella forbid Mantuan shepherds from using the pasture in the meantime. The marchioness replied promptly that she had no authority to issue such an order 'without the licence and the express permission of my lord, who quite rightly could complain about me, my role being merely to conserve his possessions in the state they were in when he left Mantua and not to alter them in any way'.[9] She argued that Lodovico should at least wait until her husband returned to Mantua before implementing the edict, on the grounds that convention dictated that even the humblest soldier could rest assured that his possessions and economic interests would be safeguarded while he was fighting away from home.[10]

When these carefully calibrated appeals, couched first in personal terms, then on the basis of her own limited political capacity for manoeuvre, and finally with reference to what was generally regarded as acceptable behaviour in times of war, failed to change the duke's mind, Isabella resorted to lobbying the Venetian government to intervene. A letter of 19 June 1496 to the Mantuan ambassador in Venice, Giorgio Brognolo, suggests the matter dragged on for months.[11] Isabella showed, nonetheless, that she could negotiate as competently as any of the male envoys who represented the marquis. Like these men, she relied on personal charm, rational argument, persistence, and emotional control to get her way and was careful to represent herself as the obedient representative of the head of state.[12] Even if she failed in this instance, Isabella continued to be an effective conduit to Sforza.

---

[8] 'Ho etiam cognosciuto che lo amore suo, e lo bono conto l'ha sempre tenuto de mi, m' ha dato qualche più autorità e credito cum esso signor mio.' Isabella d'Este to Lodovico Sforza, 14 April 1496, from Mantua, ASMn, AG, 2992, libro 6, n. 307, cc. 89r–90r.

[9] 'Dico ch'io non ardiria mandare alcuna persona a Vostra Excellentia per questo effecto senza licentia et expressa commissione del signor mio, quale meritamente se poteria dolere di me, essendo l'officio mio solamente de conservare le cose sue nel stato che erano quando partì da Mantua et non de alterarle in alcun modo.' Isabella d'Este to Lodovico Sforza, 27 April 1496, from Mantua, ASMn, AG, 2992, libro 6, n. 335, cc. 100r–101r.

[10] 'Et questo posso io testificare, perché l'ho concesso a molti de quelli che militano cum esso signor mio et lo medesmo se observa per li altri signori.' Isabella d'Este to Lodovico Sforza, from Mantua, 27 April 1496, from Mantua, ASMn, AG, 2992, libro 6, n. 335, cc. 100r–101r.

[11] Isabella d'Este to Giorgio Brognolo, 18 June 1496, from Mantua, ASMn, AG, 2992, libro 7, n. 113, cc. 43v–44r.

[12] On the overlap between qualities required in an ambassador and those recommended to women in near contemporary treatises, see Tracy Adams, 'Married Noblewomen as Diplomats: Affective Diplomacy', in *Gender and Emotions in Medieval and Early Modern Europe: Destroying Order, Structuring Disorder*, ed. Susan Broomhall (Farnham: Ashgate, 2015), 51–65.

She also tried out her diplomatic skills in relation to the republic of Venice. The marchioness proved to be more aware than her husband of the need not to antagonize such a powerful neighbour, especially while Francesco was serving its government in a generously remunerated military capacity. Thus, when an ambassador of the king of France requested a safe conduct to travel through Mantuan territory to reach Milan in late May 1496, and the marquis was too far away to be consulted quickly, Isabella discussed the issue with her husband's brother, the protonotary, Sigismondo Gonzaga, and a number of politically experienced members of the court, before denying the request. In a letter reporting on the decision, she explained to Francesco that granting a safe passage to a representative of an enemy power would be sure to anger the Venetian authorities. But she reassured him that she had sent her secretary, Benedetto Capilupi, known for his persuasiveness, to explain the difficulties to the French ambassador and so avoid offence in that direction as well.[13]

Francesco's approach to diplomatic relations with Venice was far less defensive. As in the autumn of 1495, when he became involved in establishing the terms of the truce with Charles VIII, the marquis failed to recognize the perils of assuming too great a degree of autonomy in the wheeling and dealing that took place at the conclusion of the League's victorious campaign of 1496 which ended the French occupation of Naples. Without consulting Venetian authorities, Francesco released Paolo Vitelli, a hostage taken during the battle of Atella. He did so to engineer the freedom of his brother-in-law, Duke Guidobaldo da Montefeltro, who had been taken prisoner by the Orsini at Soriano. The marquis also rendered assistance to another brother-in-law. Count Gilbert de Montpensier had been appointed viceroy of Naples by the king and was responsible for the occupying forces which Charles VIII left behind when he returned to France. In July 1496, during the battle by the Aragonese to retake the southern kingdom, Gilbert was captured at Atella, and then held in the mosquito-infested environs of Pozzuoli. Francesco sent his personal physician in an effort to save the life of his sister's husband. However, Gilbert's state of health continued to deteriorate and he died in November 1496, before he could be repatriated to France.[14] While Francesco's assistance to relatives might have been forgivable, his offer of hospitality to the Venetian mercenary captain Gorlino, who had fallen into disfavour with his employers, was seen as a needless provocation that could not be overlooked.[15] Complaints about the marquis's failure to respect Venetian sensibilities mounted within the republic's councils.

---

[13] Isabella d'Este to Francesco Gonzaga, 5 June 1496, from Mantua, ASMn, AG, 2992, libro 7, n. 78, cc. 30v–31v.

[14] Francesco received regular information about the declining health of Gilbert de Montpensier from his ambassador Jacopo d'Atri. See ASMn, AG, b. 807, cc. 262–6.

[15] Grati and Pacini, eds, *Carteggio degli oratori Mantovani*, vol. 15, 21.

In late August 1496, himself suffering from malarial fevers and perhaps typhoid, and physically reduced to the point that, as he joked in a letter to Isabella, he had to use the last notch on his belt to keep his breeches from falling down, Francesco gained the permission of the king of Naples to set off for home.[16] He reached Ancona on 9 October, reported to Venice in late November and then retired to his country estates, seeking to recover physically and mentally from the deprivations of the campaign. He also wanted to resume the building projects at Marmirolo and Gonzaga that had stalled during his absence. Isabella continued her stewardship of government in Mantua, husband and wife communicating continually through letters and oral messages conveyed by their secretaries.

However, the Mantuan ambassador to Milan reported worriedly in mid-February 1497 that rumours of Francesco's Francophile sympathies, so apparent in the aftermath of the battle of Fornovo, continued to circulate in Lombardy and the Veneto. Francesco did nothing to contradict the gossip.[17] Indeed, he did the opposite by having the widowed Clara Gonzaga escorted back to France in April by Pietro Gentile da Camerino, a man perceived as responsible for conducting negotiations with Charles VIII over a French military commission for the marquis. This was a possibility that Clara had been actively advocating with the king in an effort to reconcile her natal and marital loyalties. The capture and imprisonment in Milan of Agostino da Carignano, a friar that torture soon revealed to be a Mantuan secret agent, sent to France to work out the detailed terms of such an engagement, further compromised Francesco's reputation in Venice. As a consequence, his well-paid and prestigious military contract was abruptly cancelled by the republic in July 1497.[18]

In response to this blow, Isabella and her secretary worked hard to persuade Lodovico Sforza to appoint Francesco to a position equivalent to the Venetian one. However, rumours that an agreement between the marquis and the king of France was close to being finalized proliferated, muddying the diplomatic waters in Milan as well.[19] Isabella received an angry letter from the duke on 18 November 1497, ordering her to write immediately to Francesco in her own hand insisting he stop secret negotiations with the French. The peremptory command could have left the marchioness in little doubt about the limits of Lodovico's friendship.

---

[16] Isabella acknowledged this news on 3 September. Isabella d'Este to Francesco Gonzaga, 3 September 1496, from Marmirolo, ASMn, AG, 2111, cc. 315r–v.

[17] Ghivizano de' Ghivizani to Francesco Gonzaga, 17 February 1497, from Milan, in Grati and Pacini, eds, *Carteggio degli oratori mantovani*, vol. 15, 144–7.

[18] Alessandro Luzio and Rodolfo Renier, 'Delle relazioni di Isabella d'Este Gonzaga con Ludovico e Beatrice Sforza', *Archivio storico lombardo* 17 (1890): 74–119, 346–99, 619–74 (see in particular 647).

[19] Donato de' Preti to Francesco Gonzaga, 23 June and 21 October 1497, from Milan, in Grati and Pacini, eds, *Carteggio degli oratori mantovani*, vol. 15, 171–2 and 189–93.

Not averse to a little blackmail, the duke of Milan also made it clear to Isabella that he had already reported the marquis's double dealing to her father.[20]

Although Francesco dispatched his brother Giovanni to Milan to patch things up there, he also sent Gian Giacomo Trivulzio, one of Charles VIII's most important military commanders, an expensive gift of six hunting falcons.[21] While that initial gesture had been approved by Sforza, the friendly correspondence that ensued between Trivulzio and Gonzaga was intercepted by Lombard authorities. Benedetto Capilupi was in Milan endeavouring to secure a satisfactory contract for the marquis and bore the full brunt of Sforza's fury.[22] The secretary attempted to alert Francesco to the need for far greater discretion in his dealings with the French. To make the advice more palatable, Capilupi deflected responsibility for it onto 'certain friends of your lordship' who 'have suggested to me that it would be wise if you desisted from this practice [giving such gifts], even if was authorized [by the duke]'.[23]

Several months later, Girolamo Redini, an Augustinian friar often deployed by Francesco for delicate diplomatic missions in Rome, was far franker about his master's political shortcomings. He had been sent to the papal court to advance the campaign for a cardinal's hat for the marquis's brother, Sigismondo Gonzaga. In a letter to Isabella of 22 April 1498, Redini outlined the difficulties he faced. 'Here', he claimed, 'one hears both the good and evil of the whole world'.[24] He assured her that while she was respected in Rome, the marquis was widely distrusted because of malicious rumours promulgated there by his own men. However, the friar's critique suggests that he did not regard Francesco as entirely innocent of responsibility for his bad reputation and wished to alert Isabella to the consequences of her husband's garrulousness under the influence of drink.

I am not surprised in the least that the Venetians sacked him. I am not surprised that his brother is not a cardinal. I am not surprised that he is ridiculed and that he is said to lack stability and a brain.... It is necessary for him to be wiser and to show that he is intelligent and not mad, as they have wished to depict him and

---

[20] Lodovico Sforza to Isabella d'Este, 18 November 1497, from Milan, in Luzio and Renier, 'Delle relazioni di Isabella d'Este Gonzaga', 649–50.

[21] Benedetto Capilupi to Isabella d'Este, 25 November 1497, from Milan, in Grati and Pacini, eds, *Carteggio degli oratori mantovani*, vol. 15, 216–18.

[22] Benedetto Capilupi to Francesco Gonzaga, 7 January 1498, from Milan, in Grati and Pacini, eds, *Carteggio degli oratori mantovani*, vol. 15, 251–2.

[23] Benedetto Capilupi to Francesco Gonzaga, 1 January 1498, from Milan, in Grati and Pacini, eds, *Carteggio degli oratori mantovani*, vol. 15, 241–2.

[24] 'qui se intende tutto el ben e el male dil mondo.' Girolamo Redini to Isabella d'Este, 22 April 1498, from Rome, ASMn, AG, 852, cc. 430r–431r.

that he knows how to be discreet and that it is false, and merely scoundrels lying through their teeth, that wine makes every secret spill from his mouth.[25]

As a cleric, whose office was to preach, Redini could be far blunter than a secretary.

The friar also delivered a stern homily directly to Francesco. In a letter of 20 April, he admonished the marquis: 'to abandon your beasts and attend to honourable things', assuring him: 'you could be the first man of Italy, if you desired. This is your moment.' Redini knew his master well. Francesco was indeed attending to his animals: he was at Gonzaga, taking advantage of the abundant spring game. 'For the love of God', the friar wrote, 'look out for traitors. For the entire journey, I have had to mend the mischief that your own people have wrought, including those you trust.'[26] A week later, Redini returned to his theme: 'Here, one hears as much about your affairs, as in Mantua itself. In fact, it is much worse because of the many lies and slanders that are promulgated and believed perhaps by more people than would be the case there.'[27] He begged Francesco to exercise greater discretion in his choice of confidantes, since 'these are frightening times and whoever does not think so has little sense'. He also advised the marquis to trust only Isabella, on the grounds she was utterly loyal and her advice sound: 'she knows everyone and is aware of each person's leanings and attitudes.'[28] Permitting himself a brief priestly reflection on the virtues of marriage, Redini commended the marchioness to Francesco's husbandly ministrations:

I therefore beg your illustrious lordship that you offer her good companionship and keep her content, as I know you do, because, in truth, besides being useful to your body and soul, this will bring you great honour and the approval of all Italy and whoever says otherwise are traitors and outright miscreants.[29]

---

[25] 'Non mi maraviglio zià che lui da Venetiani sia casso. Non mi maraviglio ch'el fratel suo non sii cardinal. Non mi maraviglio che sii delezato e ditto che non ha né stabilità né cervello.... Pur bisogna che etiam lui sii savio e monstri che l'ha inzegno e ch'el non è matto, como che l'hanno volute dipinzere, e ch'el sapia tenere in se qualche tratto, e che falso è, e se mentino li ribaldi per la gola, quando dicono ch'el vino gli chazi tutti li secreti fuor di buocha.' Girolamo Redini to Isabella d'Este, 22 April 1498, from Rome, ASMn, AG, 852, XI, c. 436. This letter is partially transcribed in Cockram, *Isabella d'Este and Francesco Gonzaga*, 203–4.

[26] 'lassati le bestie e atendeti a le cose honorevole. Voi sieti el primo homo de Italia se voi voleti. Adesso è el tempo vostro.... Vostra Signoria Illustrissima, per l'amor de Dio, si guardi da traditori; per tutto el viazo ho havuto da fare a saldare le piage che vi fanno li vostri, e di chi vi sieti fidati.' Girolamo Redini to Francesco Gonzaga, 20 April 1498, from Rome, ASMn, AG, 852, cc. 430r–431r.

[27] 'Qui tanto s'intende li fatti vostri quanto a Mantua. Anci pezo, ché molte bosie et poltronie sono ditte qua e credute forsi da molti che non sarianno credute là.' Girolamo Redini to Francesco Gonzaga, 27 April 1498, from Rome, ASMn, AG, 852, cc. 437r–439r.

[28] 'Questi sono tempi da temere e chi non teme ha puocha consideration.... Sapiati che sua signoria ce conosce tutti, e scia a qual canto et passio ciaschun penda.' Girolamo Redini to Francesco Gonzaga, 27 April 1498, from Rome, ASMn, AG, 852, cc. 437r–439r.

[29] 'Prego etiam, Vostra Illustrissima Signoria, che gli facia bona compagnia et tengala contenta, como scio che fate, perché, in verità, ultra ch'el vi sia utile al corpo e a l'anima, questo vi è grandissimo honore e fati a piacere a tuta Italia, e chi altro vi persuade sono traditori e ribaldi expressi.' Girolamo Redini to Francesco Gonzaga, 27 April 1498, from Rome, ASMn, AG, 852, cc. 437r–439r.

Companionship could not have figured very large in a period that saw Isabella almost always in Mantua, apart from a sojourn in Ferrara from mid-July to early October 1497, and Francesco residing in one country palace after another, with only brief appearances in the city. Nonetheless, the couple's letters, full of family news, political updates, and the systematic exchange of diplomatic correspondence, suggest their relations were harmonious in the late 1490s, even if Isabella had to work hard to redress her husband's dangerous tendency to indulge in braggadocio with his male peers.

Although Francesco insisted on maintaining control of administrative appointments and judicial appeals, he was appreciative of Isabella's quick response to criminal acts in the city and her efforts to resolve border conflicts before they escalated, such as the one that emerged near Correggio in the spring of 1499. Again, it involved a struggle over the grazing of sheep on disputed pasture. Francesco granted his wife authority to negotiate with the local authorities and fulsomely praised her successful intervention: 'Your Ladyship should do as you see fit, in this case and every other, since we will always approve your every action, knowing you to be prudent and wise thanks to your experience and intelligence.'[30] He was also happy to consult Isabella about foreign policy in this period, recognizing that he needed her help.[31]

Double Diplomacy

The death of Charles VIII on 7 April 1498 and the ascension to the throne of Louis XII came as a shock to the Italian powers, especially to the duke of Milan. The duchy that Lodovico Sforza had schemed so ruthlessly to acquire and hoped to pass on to the legitimate sons that he had sired in middle age was contested by the new French king, who declared a dynastic right to the state of Milan, on the basis of descent from his grandmother, Valentina Visconti. As Louis XII manoeuvred to isolate the duchy's incumbent ruler, Francesco's first instinct was to support his Sforza brother-in-law, perhaps calculating that he would now have vastly more bargaining power to secure the high-level Milanese military command he craved and considered his due. However, the duke of Milan was resolutely determined to engage Galeazzo Sanseverino, a very experienced soldier and staunch ally, to whom he had given his illegitimate daughter Bianca in marriage, to lead the Milanese forces against the French. Francesco would have to be content with the

---

[30] 'La Signoria Vostra et in questo caso, et in ogni altro, faccia quel che li piace, che sempre approbaremo ogni sua actione, cognoscendola per experiencia e de ingegno, prudente e savia.' Francesco Gonzaga to Isabella d'Este, 11 April 1499, from Gonzaga, ASMn, AG, 2113, c. 17.

[31] See, for example, letters of July 1497 and of June 1499. Francesco Gonzaga to Isabella d'Este, ASMn, AG, 2112, cc. 21–30 and 2113, cc. 29, 30, 34, 35. On Isabella's work with Gonzaga diplomats in Milan, see Cockram, *Isabella d'Este and Francesco Gonzaga*, 114–21.

role of captain general of Milan's ally, Maximilian I, Holy Roman Emperor-elect and technically the marquis's feudal overlord.

Isabella and her father were co-opted by the duke of Milan to persuade Francesco to accept this less enticing commission. The marchioness took the view that it was more important to secure a satisfactory salary, than the most prestigious military position, which could come later. She wrote urgently to that effect in her own hand, apologizing to Francesco for her poor calligraphy on the grounds that she was writing in a great hurry in the privacy of her *grotta*.[32] However, Francesco was well aware that Maximilian lacked money. The prospect of a regular salary from that direction was therefore poor.

Although Isabella continued to be confident that the duke of Milan would not forsake his Mantuan relatives, a letter to her of late May 1498 from Benedetto Capilupi shows Lodovico Sforza's crafty machinations at work. The secretary reported a conversation in which the duke declared that, while he could be sure that Isabella agreed with him that the Venetians were the natural enemies of lordly regimes such as theirs, Francesco had been slow to perceive where his true interests lay.[33] This comment, which complimented Isabella on her political perspicuity and dug slyly at Francesco, was in response to the news that Mantua's resident ambassador in Venice had just been recalled by the marquis, paving the way for a closer relationship with Milan. Francesco arrived at the Milanese court a day later. Despite the two rulers' personal animosities, the pact between them was celebrated publicly with mutual expressions of love. A month later, Isabella oversaw the lavish preparations for a three-day visit to Mantua by her brother-in-law and a large Milanese entourage, the huge cost of entertaining so many people forcing her to borrow seven hundred ducats in Bologna in order to mount a sufficiently honourable reception.[34]

But matters moved frustratingly slowly. To counter Francesco's growing discontent, the duke offered him the position of grand quartermaster of the Milanese forces. Under pressure from Ercole d'Este to persuade Francesco to be satisfied with this concession, Isabella wrote to her husband about the offer on 12 July 1498. She was frank about her father's view, but was careful not to take his side, expressing support instead for Francesco's stance, which was to hold out for a better deal:

> To obey my lord father, I send you his letter and the examples [of the privileges associated with the title] so you understand everything, but I do not wish to obey him by persuading your lordship to accept it, it seeming to me that your resolution to wait is much better.[35]

---

[32] Isabella d'Este to Francesco Gonzaga, 9 May 1498, in Luzio and Renier, 'Delle relazioni di Isabella d'Este Gonzaga', 654.

[33] Benedetto Capilupi to Isabelle d'Este, 27 May 1498, from the Abbey of Chiaravalle, in Grati and Pacini, eds, *Carteggio degli oratori mantovani*, vol. 15, 321–3.

[34] Luzio and Renier, 'Delle relazioni di Isabella d'Este Gonzaga', 657–8.

[35] 'Per obedire el signor mio patre, gli mando essa lettera et exempli aciò che la intenda el tutto, ma non voglio già obedirlo in comfortare Vostra Signoria ad acceptarla, parendome molto megliore la

Although the marquis signed a military agreement with the duke of Milan in late 1498, he was soon distancing himself from the alliance, alarmed by the news that a formal pact between Louis XII and the republic of Venice had been signed on 9 February. With the assistance of his sister Clara, who enjoyed excellent relations with the king, Francesco courted Louis and sought reconciliation with Venice, while keeping the door open to Lodovico Sforza and the Holy Roman Emperor. But, when French troops under the command of Gian Giacomo Trivulzio crossed the Alps in August, the marquis was careful not to help his Milanese brother-in-law, realizing the duke was almost certainly a doomed man.

After the fall of Alessandria and the advance of the French army towards Milan, Lodovico Sforza fled the duchy and sought refuge in Germany with the emperor. Trivulzio and his troops entered Milan on 2 September and those holding out in the fortress were forced to concede defeat two weeks later. Francesco sent messengers to congratulate Louis XII, who was already on his way to Italy to claim his prize. Clara insisted by letter that her brother should pay homage to the king and, on 2 October 1499, Francesco travelled to Pavia, where Louis was preparing for a triumphant march into Milan.[36] Thanks to the countess's high standing at the royal court, the French king immediately noticed Francesco. He invited the marquis to join a hawking expedition and then to demonstrate his riding skills during a display of northern European and Italian styles of horsemanship. Francesco reported to Isabella that Louis had also taken him aside and the two had walked arm-in-arm through the cloisters of the Certosa of Pavia, while the king recounted biographical anecdotes, especially his involvement in various battles and his experience of a period of imprisonment.[37] When Louis processed into Milan, Francesco was part of the victory parade, as was his father-in-law, Ercole d'Este.[38]

Following this grand event, Francesco presented the king with several magnificent falcons. The men watched the birds fly, before setting off together to see the sights of the city, Louis holding the marquis by the hand in a sign of particular esteem.[39] Several days later, Francesco reported to Isabella that he had been presented with the Order of St Michael and hoped that great benefits would soon flow from his friendship with the French monarch.[40] Beneath this confident veneer, however, Francesco was worried by the alliance between the republic of Venice and the French, since rumours continued to circulate that the two intended to divide the small princely states of northern Italy between them. The

---

resolutione che l'ha preso de expectare el termine.' Isabella d'Este to Francesco Gonzaga, 12 July 1498, from Mantua, ASMn, AG, 2111, c. 286.

[36] Dupont-Pierrart, *Claire de Gonzague*, 224.
[37] Francesco Gonzaga to Isabella d'Este, 3 and 4 October 1499, from Pavia, ASMn, AG, 2113, cc. 60r–v, 62r–64r.
[38] Grati and Pacini, eds, *Carteggio degli oratori mantovani*, vol. 15, 29–30.
[39] Francesco Gonzaga to Isabella d'Este, 7 October 1499, from Pavia, ASMn, AG, 2113, cc. 66r–69r.
[40] Francesco Gonzaga to Isabella d'Este, 10 October 1499, from Pavia, ASMn, AG, 2113, c. 74.

Ferrarese ambassador confirmed that such an outcome was likely in a letter to Ercole d'Este of 22 April 1500, news that was promptly sent to Mantua.[41]

There were serious political threats from another direction as well. In 1498, to ingratiate himself with Pope Alexander VI, Louis XII had made the pope's son, Cesare Borgia, the duke of Valence. The king then supported Borgia's marriage, in May 1499, to Charlotte d'Albret, sister of the king of Navarre.[42] The duke of Valence, who became known in Italy as Valentino, was thus among those who rode into Milan with Louis XII, his friendship with the king paving the way for his forthcoming military campaign to create a state for himself in north and central Italy.[43] While an imperial, rather than a papal, fiefdom, Mantua was nonetheless vulnerable to an opportunistic attempt by Borgia to add it to the list of states he wished to conquer. Cultivating the French king was therefore a crucial defence strategy.

Isabella's prominent role in relations with Milan, made all the more evident by the frequent use of Capilupi as an envoy, made her a suspect figure in the eyes of the French and their Venetian allies. On 16 October 1499, while her husband was still in Milan paying court to the king, she therefore took steps to redress this situation. She wrote to Donato de' Preti, the Mantuan resident ambassador in Venice, asking him to contact Accurse Maynier, the French representative there, and explain to him that her former attachment to Lodovico Sforza was at an end. The letter to de' Preti was clearly meant to be shown to Louis XII's ambassador. It was true, Isabella wrote, that she had felt affection for her brother-in-law. However, once he had begun to treat her husband badly, those warm feelings had cooled, to be entirely replaced by the Francophile loyalties she now shared with her spouse:

> Now, we are most decidedly French [in our sympathies], due to the attention and honours bestowed by His Majesty on our consort; and when Your Lordship arrives here you will know that, if in the past we were well disposed towards you, now we are even more so and completely dressed in lilies.[44]

In his reply of 2 November 1499, sent from Venice, Maynier purported to be convinced of the marchioness's change of heart.[45]

As the new century opened, Francesco continued to hedge his bets, on the one hand instructing Jamet de Nesson, his ambassador to France, to pass on intelligence about the preparations of Lodovico Sforza to retake Milan and, on the other, pledging loyalty to the emperor-elect, with whom Sforza had taken refuge.

[41] Dupont-Pierrart, *Claire de Gonzague*, 229.

[42] Grati and Pacini, eds, *Carteggio degli oratori mantovani*, vol. 15, 317, n. 1.

[43] Michael Mallett and Christine Shaw, *The Italian Wars*, 49.

[44] Isabella d'Este to Donato de' Preti, 16 October 1499, from Mantua, published in Alessandro Luzio, *Isabella d'Este e i Borgia* (Milano: Casa Editrice L. F. Cogliati, 1915), 47.

[45] Luzio, *Isabella d'Este e i Borgia*, 47.

The marquis sent his brother Giovanni and one hundred mounted archers to assist Sforza's attempt to regain his duchy in February 1500. This minimal level of support did nothing to change the outcome of events. The former duke of Milan was captured at Novara in April 1500, and handed over to the French, remaining Louis XII's prisoner until his death at Loches in 1508.[46]

Frustrated by her brother's oscillating loyalties and ambiguous behaviour, Clara Gonzaga had to work even harder to persuade Louis XII not to consider the marquis completely unreliable. She implored Francesco in a letter of 21 November 1500 to avoid undermining her diplomatic efforts on his behalf: 'I beg you please to remain constant in your good intentions and devotion towards this most holy lord king, who is a god on earth and a wise man who keeps his promises.'[47] The constancy that Clara advocated was impossible in the circumstances. As the nearby states of Fano, Pesaro, Rimini, Cesena, Forlì, Faenza, and Imola fell to Cesare Borgia in 1501 and 1502, Francesco and Isabella could only look on in horror, afraid that Mantua would share a similar destiny. In a letter of 23 April 1501, which included a description of the battle over Faenza, ruled until then by Astorre Manfredi, Francesco commented to his wife that he was sending the account, since he knew she would 'take pleasure in seeing evidence that the honour and *virtù* of Italians are not as dead and buried as some barbarians claim.'[48]

Many of the displaced rulers, including the lord of Pesaro, Giovanni Sforza, who had been married to Francesco's sister Maddalena before she died in child-birth in 1490, sought refuge in Mantua, their cordial reception attracting the baleful attention of the Borgia pope and his son. On 1 May, Ercole d'Este wrote urgently to his daughter and son-in-law, warning them not to show sympathy for Valentino's victims.[49] The duke of Ferrara was busy protecting his own state by negotiating a marriage between his heir Alfonso and the pope's daughter, Lucrezia Borgia, a match that was perceived by many, including Isabella, as dishonourable to the Este family. The wedding took place in Rome in December 1501, to be followed in the early days of the new year by a lavish ceremony in Ferrara, which Isabella somewhat grudgingly attended. She described the spectacular celebra-tions to her husband in a series of detailed letters, which chronicle Ercole's efforts to use the occasion to promote his dynastic prestige by mounting impressive,

---

[46] Michael Mallett and Christine Shaw, *The Italian Wars, 1494–1559: War, State and Society in Early Modern Europe* (Harlow, UK; New York: Pearson, 2012), 42–53.

[47] Clara Gonzaga to Francesco Gonzaga, 21 November 1500, ASMn, AG, 2114, c. 229. See Léon Gabriel Pélissier, 'La politique du Marquis de Mantoue pendant la lutte de Louis XII et de Ludovic Sforza (1498–1500)', *Annales de la Faculté des lettres de Bordeaux* 14 (1892): 35–120. For several of Clara's most important letters to Francesco Gonzaga, see Léon Gabriel Pélissier, *Louis XII et Lodovic Sforza (8 avril 1498–23 juillet 1500)* (Paris: Librairie Thorn et Fils, 1896), 90–5.

[48] 'aciò che la pigli piacere vedendo che l'honore e la virtù de' Italiani non è cossì morta e sepulta come dicono alcuni barbari.' Francesco Gonzaga to Isabella d'Este, 23 April 1501, from Revere, ASMn, AG, 2114bis, c. 257.

[49] Luzio, *Isabella d'Este e i Borgia*, 66.

although in Isabella's view, excessively long, productions of classical theatre and various forms of pageantry.[50] Francesco remained in Mantua to make sure the bride's brother did not take advantage of his absence to attack the city.

In June 1502, Cesare Borgia seized the duchy of Urbino, forcing its ruler Guidobaldo da Montefeltro to flee for his life to Mantua, where his wife, Elisabetta Gonzaga, happened to be visiting her brother and sister-in-law. They joined other relatives, similarly ousted from power by Borgia. In mid-July, Francesco travelled to Asti to intercede for these refugees with Louis XII, who had returned to his new Milanese acquisition. Almost at once, an emissary of Cesare Borgia, the apostolic protonotary, Francesco Trocio, appeared in Mantua. Isabella warned her husband that she feared he had been sent by Duke Valentino to gather intelligence about the strength of their loyalty.[51] Although negotiations were then underway regarding the betrothal of their eldest son to Borgia's baby daughter, the marchioness was well aware that this alliance would not prevent reprisal, if the duke gained the impression that they were not reliable allies.[52]

Isabella's response to the arrival of Trocio has been analysed by several scholars, who have shown the extent to which she was steeped in the techniques of counter-espionage.[53] On 15 July 1502, she wrote urgently to her husband, asking him to send her a letter that could be shown to Borgia's envoy as proof of their strong support for his master. Francesco's reply of 18 July duly complied. He wrote of his friendly feelings for Valentino, and his support for the idea of betrothing their eldest children. However, he also mentioned Louis XII's cordial reception of Guidobaldo da Montefeltro and justified his lobbying on behalf of his brother-in-law at the French court on the grounds of family duty.[54] Isabella judged this letter to be insufficiently reassuring and composed another, dictating it to a secretary in the usual way and making sure the letter appeared to have travelled from Asti. She explained herself in a letter to her husband of 20 July.

[50] Isabella d'Este to Francesco Gonzaga, 31 January to 11 February 1501, from Ferrara, ASMn, AG, 2114bis, cc. 314–25.

[51] Isabella d'Este to Francesco Gonzaga, 15 July 1502, from Mantua, ASMn, AG, 2115, cc. 148r–v.

[52] Francesco refers to the negotiations regarding the betrothal, largely conducted by Isabella, in letters of exactly this time. See Francesco Gonzaga to Isabella d'Este, 18 July 1502, from Asti, ASMn, AG, 2115, cc. 61r–62v and 64–5. Isabella d'Este to Francesco Gonzaga, 15 July 1502, from Mantua, ASMn, AG, 2115, cc. 148r–151v.

[53] Sarah D. P. Cockram, 'Epistolary Masks: Self-Presentation and Dissimulation in the Letters of Isabella d'Este', *Italian Studies* 64.1 (2009): 20–37; Deanna Shemek, 'Mendacious Missives: Isabella d'Este's Epistolary Theater', in *Writing Relations: American Scholars in Italian Archives*, ed. Deanna Shemek and Michael Wyatt (Florence: L.S. Olschki, 2008), 71–86: Luzio and Renier, *Mantova e Urbino*, 138–40.

[54] Negotiations for a betrothal between the 2-year-old Federico Gonzaga and Cesare Borgia's baby daughter are mentioned in a letter of 23 December 1502 from Isabella to Francesco Malatesta, the Mantuan ambassador in Florence. See Isabella d'Este, *Selected Letters*, 212–13.

Your Lordship's letter containing certain parts which did not seem to me appropriate to show to Duke Valentino's man, I had a special letter written and expanded it somewhat ... and I send a copy to Your Excellency in order that you may be completely informed.[55]

Trocio left Mantua on 22 July, seemingly appeased. Seen in the context of the evolution of her political partnership with Francesco, Isabella's actions in the face of this crisis reveal her taking a bolder and more autonomous role in addressing such perilous situations, a stance that the marquis now encouraged.

However, Isabella could hardly allow herself a sigh of relief after Trocio's departure before she learned that her husband had publicly insulted Borgia, calling him a bastard and the son of a priest in the presence of King Louis XII. She also became aware that Francesco was careless about the risk of poison at the French court in Milan, eating companionably with his staff, including the grooms and pages, and having no one to oversee the tasting of his food. Given the possibility of retribution from the pope's son, once he learned of Francesco's insults, such complacent behaviour struck her as unthinkable.[56] Borgia was known to be vindictive, even before he assassinated some of his closest lieutenants, whom he suspected of treachery, later that year at Senigallia. On 23 July, Isabella urged Francesco to be more attentive to his safety. In a detachable postscript, she wrote in her own hand: 'My lord, do not mock this letter of mine, or say that women are cowards and are always afraid, because their malice is much greater than my fear and your courage.'[57] Here she shows herself aware of the contemporary dynamics of masculinity which, in her husband's case, encouraged him to disdain what she considered a sensible level of caution. Francesco replied appreciatively, but nonchalantly, to his wife, contenting himself with a joke about her recent acquisition of Michelangelo's *Cupid*, which Isabella had described as having 'no equal', even if it was modern, rather than ancient. He quipped good-humouredly that on his return home he hoped to have the monopoly on the kisses of their little son, while she was busy kissing the *Cupid*.[58]

After travelling around the former Sforza state with the French court until mid-October 1502, Francesco was obliged to continue to demonstrate his fealty

---

[55] Isabella d'Este to Francesco Gonzaga, 20 July 1502, from Mantua, ASMn, AG, 2115, cc. 155r–156r. See Cockram, *Isabella d'Este and Francesco Gonzaga*, 141 (Cockram's translation). Isabella's fake letter is transcribed in the appendix at 210. See also, Shemek, 'Mendacious Missives', 75–8.

[56] Luzio, *Isabella d'Este e i Borgia*, 110–11.

[57] Isabella d'Este to Francesco Gonzaga, 23 July 1502, from Mantua, ASMn, AG, 2115, cc. 160r–v. See Cockram, *Isabella d'Este and Francesco Gonzaga*, 141 (Cockram's translation). Isabella's letter is transcribed at 211–12.

[58] Isabella d'Este to Francesco Gonzaga, 22 July 1502, from Mantua, ASMn, AG, Autografi Volta 1, fascicolo 103, and Francesco Gonzaga to Isabella d'Este, 29 July 1502, from Milan, ASMn, AG, 2115, cc. 69r–70r. Both letters are partially transcribed in Brown et al., *Per dare qualche splendore*, 158–9.

by following the king as the court moved from Milan to Turin and then on to Lyon, Lapalisse, Blois, and Romorantin. From Lyon, Francesco wrote to Isabella describing the arduous crossing of the Alps: 'we passed such rugged mountains and rocky terrain that we truly believe we will not have to perform any other penance for the sins we have committed up till now.'[59] The marquis returned to Mantua in February 1503 but, within months, Isabella had to reassume her role as regent. Francesco's appointment as lieutenant-general of the French forces, who were to contest Spanish control of the kingdom of Naples, meant he had to spend July in Parma organizing the campaign and then to set off for the south. However, the death of Alexander VI and the election of a new pope stalled the army's progress. The marquis spent September at Isola degli Orsini, in the vicinity of Rome, fighting just a few localized battles. While he reported to Isabella on 16 September that he was feeling so well that he was often troubled by sexual desire for her, two weeks later he complained that his stomach was giving him such pain that he was struggling to cope with a rapid physical decline. Polluted water and the unhygienic conditions of the camp had undermined Francesco's health. He begged his wife to make sure that the local Dominican tertiary, Osanna Andreasi, revered for her mystical relationship with Christ and ability to predict the future, prayed urgently for his recovery.[60]

Given the marquis's history of changing sides, he was viewed with suspicion by his allies. In this period, communicating by letter was more than usually fraught with insecurity because of the heightened risk of interception by spies. The French kept the marquis's correspondence under the closest surveillance, something that Isabella realized in early October 1503, when she warned Francesco that eleven of her letters to him had gone unanswered. She explained that a bundle of letters from him and many other people had just arrived in Mantua from Milan, almost all of them opened.

> When I first saw them all wet, I thought that they had come open in your postal service through a combination of accident and water. But then when I read a letter from Niccolò Scaldamazza that had been forwarded to me by Mazzo, I understood that they had been sent by the Parma post as far as Milan and, falling into the hands of Monsignore Gran Maître [Charles d'Amboise], they were

---

[59] 'habiamo passato tale asperrime montagne e rupe che veramente credemo noi non ci bisogni fare altra penitentia de nostri peccati commissi insino al dì hodierno.' Francesco Gonzaga to Isabella d'Este, 27 October 1502, from Lyon, ASMn, AG, 2115, c. 45.

[60] 'Di la persona stamo bene tanto che spesso desyderamo la Signoria Vostre per haverne gran bisogno, essendo spesso stimulati de la carne; supportaremo finché Dio ni farà gratia de essere seco.' Francesco Gonzaga to Isabella d'Este, 16 September 1503, from Isola degli Orsini in Lazio, ASMn, AG, 2911, libro 179, cc. 79r–v. 'Partemo questa matina da Valmontone più debile che ne sentissimo mai in vita nostra per passione di stomacho.' Francesco Gonzaga to Isabella d'Este, 2 October 1503, from Valmontone in Lazio, ASMn, AG, 2115bis, cc. 271–2. On Osanna Andreasi, see Bourne, *The Soldier-Prince*, 253–70.

opened and then returned to Niccolò with the explanation that this was done to see if there was anything in them for their purposes.[61]

Two of the letters, written on 19 and 22 September, had certainly been tampered with. Another of 22 September arrived intact, its small size seemingly too insignificant to attract attention. However, one of the intercepted letters, that of 19 September, contained frank comments by Francesco about the bad behaviour of French troops towards the local population and the resulting widespread hatred of the foreigners.[62] Although alarmed about the regrettable breach of security, Isabella assured her husband that she had not given any public sign of her displeasure about the interception of mail addressed to her, for fear that news of any such reaction would reach French authorities in Milan and make the situation worse. She was also careful not to criticize Francesco, advising him to do as he saw fit in response to the information she sent, but suggesting that, in the future, he should use a cipher for such highly confidential commentary.[63]

The marquis had himself begun to entertain the possibility that his letters to Isabella were being diverted, since he commented on 17 September that he had received few replies from her. Yet, in that very letter, he frankly expressed his frustration about the poorly organized campaign and the inadequacies of the other leaders.

> We have never seen a more chaotic, or more disordered, thing than this army; nor do we know how it is possible to hope for any honour, since between the leaders there is very little love and less intelligence; between the French and Italian troops there is only hatred, the French fearful and lost, the Italians lacking in diligence, it seeming to them that the French cause is none of their business, each as disobedient as the other. There is neither order in this camp, nor proper government.[64]

Isabella did not mention this indiscreet outburst when she wrote to Francesco on 1 October, probably because his letter of 17 September had not yet arrived. It did

---

[61] Isabella d'Este to Francesco Gonzaga, 1 October 1503, from Mantua, in Isabella d'Este, *Selected Letters*, 228–9.

[62] 'Li disordini di questi francesi li fanno odiare a tutti li habitatori de questo paese e già non li vogliono dar victualie, siché siamo come affamati, si assassinano in ogni loco.' Francesco Gonzaga to Isabella d'Este, 19 September 1503, from Isola degli Orsini, ASMn, AG, 2911, libro 179, cc. 89v–90r.

[63] 'Né seria male che la facesse notare una ziffera et per el primo di nostri cavallarii che la expedirà mandami lo exemplo, aciò che occurrendoni cosa da respecto, la se potesse usare per più cautela.' Isabella d'Este to Francesco Gonzaga, 1 October 1503, from Mantua, ASMn, AG, 2115bis, cc. 384r–385r.

[64] 'mai vedessimo la più incomposita, né più disordinata cosa di questo exercito, né sapemo come se ne possi sperare honor alcuno: prima fra questi capi è pochissimo amor e pocha intelligentia; fra la gente francese et italiane oculto odio, li francesi impauriti e persi, li italiani pochi diligenti, parendoli che per francesi non sia di lor facto il debito conto, l'uno e l'altro disobedienti. Ordine non gli è in questo campo, né forma de governo.' Francesco Gonzaga to Isabella d'Este, 17 September 1503, from Isola degli Orsini, ASMn, AG, 2115bis, cc. 250r–251r.

get to Mantua eventually, although the letter's substantial size and large seal likely attracted the attention of those charged with keeping the mail passing through Lombardy under surveillance. On 5 October, Isabella returned to the theme of excessive risk-taking, advising Francesco not to rush into battle before adequate reinforcements arrived, since such impetuousness would neither help the king, nor bring him honour:

> I mention this, not because I am unaware that it is not a woman's task to speak of military matters, or because I consider Your Excellency imprudent, but because it is incumbent on me not to wish to see you endanger your person, or your honour, knowing that you are just as intrepid as you are prudent.[65]

The marquis was actually in little danger from death in battle. He was also probably entirely unconcerned about the French learning of his criticisms, since he was already planning to quit the campaign in disgust. Although the troops under his command won a few minor victories in towns south of Rome, once he became ill, the prospect of the comforts of Mantua seemed to have loomed ever larger in Francesco's imagination.

Indeed, in a second letter of 17 October, he wrote to Isabella tenderly, expressing gratitude for a package of linen and silk clothing that she had sent and assuring her of his love: 'Few things are as dear to us as you are and nothing at all is more [dear] than you.'[66] Isabella was in the last phase of another pregnancy and her husband's feelings were especially benign. Not only had his wife governed ably and obediently on his behalf, exercising autonomy only in response to emergencies and to excellent effect, she continued to do her biological duty very satisfactorily. Having learned that Francesco's health had deteriorated in the insalubrious conditions of the Roman countryside and that he had sought permission from Louis XII to return home, Isabella responded to her husband with equal warmth, writing on 17 November:

> The news of your illness, which must be serious given that it is necessary to quit the camp and head for home, has upset me greatly, since I know the greatness of your spirit and inclination to fight means it must be a matter of extreme necessity. I await your Excellency with great desire, so as to see you and serve you during your indisposition.[67]

[65] 'Questa parte toccho, non perché non sappia ch'el non sia officio di donna il parlare de arme et che non conosca Vostra Excellentia prudente, ma perché a me toccha a non volerla vedere in periculo, né de la persona, né del honore, conoscendo che in Lei non è mancho animo che prudentia.' Isabella d'Este to Francesco Gonzaga, 5 October 1503, from Mantua, ASMn, AG, 2115bis, cc. 386r–387r.

[66] 'havemo recuvute tutte le altre robbe di lino, d'oro e di seta che la ni scrive mandarci, cose tutte ne le quale non estimamo tanto che siano preciose quanto che vengono da la Signoria Vostra, ché poche cose havemo chare come Lei e niuna più di Lei.' Francesco Gonzaga to Isabella d'Este, 17 October 1503, from Arci in Lazio, ASMn, AG, 2115bis, c. 279.

[67] 'me hanno adducto dispiacere grandissimo intendendo il male che gli è sopragiunto, il quale non può essere picolo essendo necessitato levarsi de campo et redursi a casa, che per la grandeza de l'animo

Although she gave birth to another girl in November 1503, Francesco could afford to be gracious, given that the all-important male heir had been born three years before. He joked in a letter of 23 November 1503, sent while he was journeying slowly northwards, that although he had hoped for a 'little soldier', he was grateful the delivery had been unproblematic, 'because your life and person is more important than any number of children that you could ever give birth to'.[68] Isabella comforted herself in the face of yet another disappointing outcome with the comment: 'It suffices that Federico is well and that he is so beautiful and prosperous that he could count for two sons'.[69]

The couple were reunited a little before Christmas. Meanwhile, the French campaign continued to deteriorate. In early November, Louis XII's army, led by Francesco's replacement, the marquis of Saluzzo, encountered the main body of Spanish forces at the Garigliano river, about sixty kilometres north of Naples. The antagonists remained bogged down on either side of the river for some six weeks, amid almost continual rain that made the movement of artillery and horses impossible. With resources stretched and the French infantry left unpaid, discipline broke down. Under a highly competent commander, Gonzalvo Fernández de Córdoba, known as 'el gran Capitán', the Spanish forces decisively won the day. On 27 December, they suddenly crossed the Garigliano and attacked the French, provoking panic and a retreat towards the coastal town of Gaeta, which fell to the Spanish soon afterwards.[70] Through a well-timed withdrawal from the war, Francesco avoided the derision to which the defeated French captains were subjected as they retreated northwards through Rome. On 31 January 1504, the king signed the Armistice of Lyon, thereby conceding defeat. Francesco remained mostly at his country estates that year, devoting himself to the outdoor activities he so enjoyed and to regaining his physical vigour. He visited Ferrara twice and reported to Isabella in mid-1504 on the decline of her father. Ercole d'Este died towards the end of January 1505, bringing to an end the mentoring role he had played in the life of his son-in-law, now a man approaching forty.

suo et inclinatione al guerregiare scio ch'el non può essere se non per extrema necessità. Io expecto Vostra Excellentia cum summo desiderio per poterla vedere et servire in questa sua indispositione.' Isabella d'Este to Francesco Gonzaga, 17 November 1503, from Mantua, ASMn, AG, 2115bis, cc. 418r–v.

[68] 'La nova che tanto expectavimo de intendere il facile e felice parto di Vostra Signoria heri ni venne cum grandissimo nostro contento, benché speravimo che la ni dovesse fare uno soldadello, ma poi che l'è stata una soreciola....Ma mettendo da canto il mottegiare, ni alegramo e contentamo summamente che Vostra Signoria sii bene scaricata cum sua salute, perché la vita e persona sua ni è più grata cha quanti figlioli la ni potesse parturire.' Francesco Gonzaga to Isabella d'Este, 23 November 1503, from Sermoneta, ASMn, AG, 2115bis, cc. 313r–314r.

[69] Isabella d'Este to Francesco Gonzaga, 13 November 1503, from Mantua, in Isabella d'Este, *Selected Letters*, 239–40.

[70] On the failure of the French campaign, see Atis Antonovics, 'Hommes de guerre et gens de finance: The Inquest on the French Defeat in Naples 1503–4', in *Italy and the European Powers. The Impact of War, 1500–1530*, ed. Christine Shaw (Leiden: Brill, 2006), 26–32.

In the years immediately preceding Duke Ercole's demise, Francesco relied more and more on his wife, whose oversight of the administrative apparatus of government and diligent diplomacy proved to be crucial ingredients of his ability to retain power, despite being so often on distant battlefields. While he asserted his princely honour and masculine prowess through military exploits and bold diplomatic gambles, Isabella took the view that the vagaries of fortune could be turned to good account through risk management. Francesco associated himself with the attributes of Mars, the god of war, Isabella with Minerva, the goddess portrayed in the paintings adorning her apartments as battling the vices with an arsenal of virtues traditionally associated with wise government. But Isabella was careful to maintain a subdued public profile, so her political interventions did not provoke undue controversy. This careful balancing of roles, and the promise of dynastic continuity that came with the rapid increase in the couple's progeny after 1500, contributed to the perception that the Gonzaga-Este marriage was a successful partnership in personal, as well as political, terms. As parenthood and mutual devotion to their children papered over some of the differences of sensibility that had sometimes divided them in the early years of marriage, the couple themselves could justifiably come to a similar conclusion.

6

Parenthood and Politics

On 17 May 1500, her twenty-sixth birthday, Isabella gave birth to a son. The beautiful cradle, sent by her parents in 1493, could at last be unpacked to receive the long-awaited Gonzaga heir. Francesco's relaxed attitude about the female gender of the first two children, the second of whom lived only a few months, had likely evaporated long before the tenth anniversary of the couple's marriage and it may have been worry about the outcome of this crucial pregnancy that prompted him to remain in Mantua in the prelude to the birth. Afterwards, he stayed in the city until late July, a break to his usual habits that might be explained by a concern to make sure that Federico, a name given in honour of the newborn's paternal grandfather, was well cared for in the first dangerous months of life. The baby's robust health and pleasing development seem to have had a profound impact on the couple's hitherto desultory fertility. Their more frequent cohabitation, stimulated by the mutual delight they took in their son, resulted in the birth of five more children, two of them boys, in the following eight years. The succession was thus secured with a comfortable margin and the tradition among ruling dynasties whereby a second son would be educated to assume a high-profile position in the Church's clerical hierarchy and a third trained for a military career could be perpetuated into another generation.[1]

Wet-nurses, governesses, and tutors played major roles in nurturing and raising Federico and the other children, but they remained under the closest scrutiny of Isabella and to a lesser, but still important, extent of Francesco. The couple's descriptions of the quotidian pleasures of parenthood and their epistolary discussions about the education of their sons and daughters provide an unusually vivid entrée into how childhood was perceived and catered for in this elite context, the evidence at dramatic odds with a now largely discredited scholarship which suggested that premodern parents remained emotionally aloof from babies and young children for fear that they would die, or because offspring left the paternal hearth very young.[2] Francesco and Isabella were certainly fearful that Mantua's

---

[1] On this theme, see Monica Ferrari, Isabella Lazzarini, and Frederico Piseri, *Autografie dell'età minore. Lettere di tre dinastie italiane tra Quattrocento e Cinquecento* (Rome: Viella, 2016), 58.

[2] On the trajectory of the history of childhood in premodern Europe, see Joanne Marie Ferraro, 'Childhood in Medieval and Early Modern Times', in *The Routledge History of Childhood in the Western World*, ed. Paula S. Fass (Abingdon: Routledge, 2013), 61–77; and Margaret L. King, 'Concepts of Childhood: What We Know and Where We Might Go', *Renaissance Quarterly* 60.2 (2007): 371–407.

A Renaissance Marriage: The Political and Personal Alliance of Isabella d'Este and Francesco Gonzaga, 1490–1519.
Carolyn James, Oxford University Press (2020). © Carolyn James.
DOI: 10.1093/oso/9780199681211.001.0001

marshy surrounds would pose a risk to their children's health and their offspring were frequently sick from malarial fevers and other common ailments, but their worries on this score did not prevent the parents from lavishing attention and love on their burgeoning family. Indeed, the pleasure they took in Federico's babyhood, documented in dozens of letters elaborating on his winsome ways, welded the pair together firmly during the boy's early years. He represented the biological success of their union and was the embodiment of their dynastic hopes for the future.

Yet, in the very month of Federico's birth, Francesco was so worried about Louis XII's territorial ambitions in northern Italy, following Lodovico Sforza's failed attempt to regain the duchy of Milan, that he mobilized over twenty thousand troops to defend his borders, having learned in late April that both Ferrara and Mantua were being discussed as possible compensations to Venice, if the republic agreed to cede Cremona to the French king in exchange. The birth of an heir powerfully focused the efforts of Isabella and Francesco to defend the state Federico would eventually inherit, at a time when the dangers posed by opposing armies in the immediate vicinity of Mantua continued to escalate. While their children indubitably created a stronger bond between the couple, even that source of emotional strength was eventually tested by the political uncertainties they faced in the early years of the sixteenth century.

Once Francesco resumed his regular visits to Gonzaga, Goito, and Revere in the late summer of 1500, the flow of correspondence between the couple again gathered pace, the exchanges containing not only the usual political news and administrative updates, but now also details about the milestones of Federico's babyhood. The two wrote good-humouredly about their efforts to outdo the other in winning their little son's affections. In late October, for example, after learning of the pleasure Isabella derived from contemplating the perfect beauty of their 5-month-old's nude body, Francesco responded that jealousy of that experience would speed his return to Mantua.[3] But Isabella endeavoured to inflame her husband's envy even further by writing in the following terms:

> Concerning what Your Excellency wrote in response to the pleasure and consolation I took in seeing our son nude, in truth it is even more than Your Lordship has understood, since, as he grows so beautifully and pleasingly, he gives me ever greater satisfaction, as well as to everyone else who sees him.[4]

---

[3] Francesco Gonzaga to Isabella d'Este, 21 October 1500, from Goito, ASMn, AG, 2114, c. 67.

[4] 'Circa la parte che me scrive la Excellentia Vostra del piacere et solazo che io me pilio de vedere et godere el filiolo nostro nudino, l'è vero anchor più che non ha inteso la Signoria Vostra, perhò che esso col suo ben crescere bello e piacevole me ne da causa a me et ad ogniuno ch'el vede.' Isabella d'Este to Francesco Gonzaga, 22 October 1500, from Mantua, ASMn, AG, 2114, c. 157.

The letter galvanized the marquis into hastening back to the city to see how his son had grown, but he took satisfaction in turning the tables on Isabella, several months later, when she visited her brothers in Ferrara. He wrote triumphantly that not only had her absence prompted the baby to transfer his love from mother to father, it was he who had witnessed the first attempts of their son to talk:

> We have compassion for Your Ladyship, considering how strange it must seem not seeing our big baby all the time, as you usually do and as I am doing. But so that you will not worry, we advise you that he is more beautiful, bigger, and livelier that ever; and although he doesn't yet know how to form any words, nonetheless with a continual babble he shows signs of wanting to speak early; and what pleases me most is that since Your Ladyship's departure from Mantua for Ferrara he has not showed as many signs of love for you, as for us when we merely leave his room.[5]

The despatch points of Francesco's correspondence indicate that once his wife returned home, he set off again to keep a wary eye on his borders. However, he returned often enough to Mantua for Federico to expect to see him in Isabella's bedroom in the San Giorgio castle, as she reported to her husband on 21 April 1501: 'Our little son and I are just fine. In the mornings when he is brought to my bed, he goes all around looking to see if he will find Your Lordship!'[6] The fond mother wrote again the next day, assuring her husband that she had given Federico not only the four kisses that he had asked her to deliver, but so many more that the child had grown restive under her affectionate assault. She added: 'at every mention of Your Excellency's name, he turns to look for you and with his little hand summons you often.'[7] The civic celebrations on the feast of San Giorgio provided yet another excuse to describe Federico's baby talk and enthusiasm for his father: 'He is here on the terrace with me, and as he sees people coming and going from St. George, with his little hand and his mouth he calls, "Pa!" and with many clownish antics he keeps me entertained.'[8]

---

[5] 'Havemo compassione a la Signoria Vostra consyderando quanto li debbe parere strano il non vedere ogni hora il nostro puttone come la soleva fare, e come faciamo noi. Ma aciò che la ne stii cum lo animo quieto, la avisamo come l'è più bello, più grosso e più gagliardo che mai; et anchor ch'el non sappia formar parola, non dimeno cum uno continuo garrulare fa segno di volere parlare presto; e quel che più ni piace è che di la partita di la Signoria Vostra da Mantua a Ferrara, el non ha facto segno di tanto amor, quanto il fa se noi si partemo solamente di la sua camera.' Francesco Gonzaga to Isabella d'Este, 1 February 1501, from Mantua, ASMn, AG, 2114bis, c. 243.

[6] Isabella d'Este to Francesco Gonzaga, 21 April 1501, from Mantua, in Isabella d'Este, *Selected Letters*, 160.

[7] 'ad ogni parola dove è nominata Vostra Excellentia, se volta a guardarla se 'l la vede, et cum la sua manina la chiama spesso.' Isabella d'Este to Francesco Gonzaga, 22 April 1501, from Mantua, ASMn, AG, 2114bis, c. 334.

[8] Isabella d'Este to Francesco Gonzaga, 23 April 1501, from Mantua, in Isabella d'Este, *Selected Letters*, 160.

At the end of July, after Federico was diagnosed as suffering from an infestation of worms, a problem mentioned frequently in relation to all the Gonzaga children, Isabella dispatched a doctor to brief Francesco about the baby's recovery, entrusting him with a letter which assured the absent father that Federico had not forgotten his Pa: 'I asked the baby if he wanted me to commend him to Your Lordship. He replied immediately, "Yeth, yeth!"'[9] A week later, she sent news that their son had taken his first steps:

> The news I have to offer Your Excellency is that today our little boy started to walk on his own. He took four steps without being held, though he was carefully watched. He and we were as pleased as one can say, though since he moved with a bit of a wobble it seemed he was playing the drunk. And then when I asked him if he wanted to be commended to Your Lordship, he answered, 'Yeth, Pa!'[10]

Isabella's attempts to mimic Federico's baby talk and the descriptions of his rapid and gratifying development were designed to sustain Francesco's keen interest in the boy and perhaps to draw her husband away from the bacchanalian pleasures of his country retreats. The strategy seems to have worked. Upon receiving the letter, the marquis rushed home to witness the toddler's amusingly wobbly gait for himself.

In mid-December 1501, Francesco and his 18-month-old son began to communicate by letter. Having heard from his secretary, Tolomeo Spagnoli, that Federico had stoutly defended his absent Pa's honour, Francesco sent the child the plumpest duck that his falcons had killed that day at the Goito estate.[11] In return, he received a thank-you letter in the voice of Federico, playfully choreographed by Isabella's secretary for the father's amusement: 'If now when I am so little I take the side of Your Excellency, against the illustrious lady, my mother, think what I will do when I am big and aim to follow the paternal example.'[12] Isabella's

---

[9] The Italian reads 'rispose subito, "Ci! Ci"', an attempt by Isabella to capture the baby's lisping rendition of 'sì'. Isabella d'Este to Francesco Gonzaga, 29 July 1501, from Mantua, in Isabella d'Este, *Selected Letters*, 167. On this and other examples of Isabella's rendering of Federico's baby talk in letters to Francesco, see Deanna Shemek, "'Ci Ci" and "Pa Pa": Script, Mimicry, and Mediation in Isabella d'Este's Letters', *Rinascimento* 43 (2003): 75–91.

[10] Isabella d'Este to Francesco Gonzaga, 7 August 1501, from Mantua, in Isabella d'Este, *Selected Letters*, 169. Francesco responded with pleasure from Sacchetta the following day. ASMn, AG, 2114bis, c. 272.

[11] 'Tolomeo, nostro secretario, in nome di la Illustrissima Madonna, tua madre, ni ha referto, cum quanto animo tu defendi l'honore nostro ove bisogna, cosa che molto ni è piaciuta, e per la quale meriti che noi anchor ne ricordamo di te. Unde, havendo hogi uno de nostri falconi facto una bella volata, e morta una anedra grassa, te la mandamo a donare in segno di amor, la quale goderai insieme cum tua matre prefata, a la quale donarai li fasiani che ti mandamo in nome nostro et la salutarai infinite volte et basarai.' Francesco Gonzaga to Federico Gonzaga, 17 December 1501, from Goito, ASMn, AG, 2114bis, c. 305.

[12] 'Se adesso che son cossì picolo tengo la rasone de la Excellentia Vostra cum la Illustrissima Madonna mia matre, pensi quello ch'io farò quando serò grande e che vorò imitare le vestigie

collusion in this episode is made clear by her own communication of two days later, acknowledging a gift of twelve pheasants that Francesco had also sent for her table:

> When Capilupi asked our baby boy if he wanted him to write Your Excellency anything from him, he replied with certain words in his own language. Then, looking at [Capilupi], he kissed the trunk in which he had been placed, in such a way that we could see he meant that he commended himself to you and kissed Your Lordship's hand. Which I do too![13]

We witness here the way in which the couple expressed affection for each other through loving anecdotes about the child they had created.

That those tender feelings may have translated into a more relaxed sexual rapport is suggested indirectly in a letter exchange of mid-1502. After discovering an unusually shaped mushroom in his brother Giovanni's garden at Revere, Francesco packaged it up and sent it to Isabella in Mantua. In an accompanying note, he joked that since the strange fungus resembled another fruit that their sister-in-law was very familiar with, it should be presented to her.[14] Isabella replied the next day in the same spirit, reporting on Laura Bentivoglio's good-natured response:

> Judging by the fruit that Your Lordship sent me, it seems that the Lord Giovanni is little favoured by nature, it having produced in small form, not only the things pertaining to his person, but even those in his garden.... And Milady Laura, his wife, to whom I sent it, says that although it is very small, nevertheless she will conserve it among the dearest things she has.[15]

Such sexual jokes were much appreciated by Francesco, as we saw in Chapter 2. The mushroom incident was a mild example of the pranks that the marquis and his courtiers so enjoyed, but that he felt confident that his wife would collude in teasing Laura about her husband's small penis suggests that Isabella had by

---

paterne.' Federico Gonzaga to Francesco Gonzaga, 18 December 1501, from Mantua, ASMn, AG, 2114bis, c. 310.

[13] Isabella d'Este to Francesco Gonzaga, 7 August 1501, from Mantua, in Isabella d'Este, *Selected Letters*, 171–2.

[14] Francesco Gonzaga to Isabella d'Este, 5 June 1502, from Revere, ASMn, AG, 2115, c. 29.

[15] 'Per la monstra del fructo che me ha mandata Vostra Signoria, mi pare ch' el Signor Zoanne habi poca gratia cum la natura, producendo in picola forma non solum le cose de la persona sua, ma anchora del giardino. Et Madonna Laura, sua moglie, a chi l'ho mandata dice che se ben è molto picola, non di meno la conservarà ne la più chara cosa che l'habi.' Isabella d'Este to Francesco Gonzaga, 6 June 1502, from Mantua, ASMn, AG, 2115, c. 130.

then reconciled herself to Francesco's recreational tastes and was prepared to reciprocate in kind.

The pair's relationships with their daughters are less visible in the documentary record, although there are glimpses of Eleonora's babyhood in letters where Isabella reported to Francesco on their eldest child's weaning and recovery from various bouts of illness.[16] Capilupi's correspondence is also an occasional source of information. In the weeks following the birth of the couple's sickly second child on 13 July 1496, Francesco wrote to Eleonora from southern Italy, while on campaign. That letter does not survive, but we learn from Capilupi's response of 3 September that the marquis had joked to his daughter that she was probably jealous of the new baby and secretly wanted to kill her. The secretary explained to Francesco that he had encountered Eleonora playing in the garden of the Gonzaga castle, under the supervision of her governess Paula and Beatrice de' Contrari. When she caught sight of him, the child had excitedly asked if she could dictate a reply to her father's letter. She wanted to protest that she had no wish to kill the baby and to report that her little sister was far from well and had a very ugly face. Capilupi described what happened next: 'and so I was forced to write there in the garden and it was charming to see her make a great effort to dictate some words and certainly the letter was all her own composition; then with her little hand, guided by me, she signed her name.' He added that Eleonora was bursting with excitement about her father's return and looking forward to the presents that he had promised to bring home for her at the conclusion of the war.[17]

Eleonora's affection for her father is also documented in another of Capilupi's letters to Francesco, written ten days later, in which he described the 2-year-old's delighted recognition of her Pa's portrait in newly completed frescoes at Marmirolo,

---

[16] In a letter of 20 March 1498, for example, Isabella reported: 'Qua non c'è cosa di nova digna de le orechie sue se non che, doppo la partita de Vostra Excellentia, la Elionora, nostra figliola, ha patito uno poco de febre causata da freddore, ma adesso la febre l'ha lassata et va se ne per camera et sta bene da uno poco de tosse in fora.' Isabella d'Este to Francesco Gonzaga, 20 March 1498, from Mantua, ASMn, AG, 2112, c. 250. For reports on Eleonora's weaning, see letters to Francesco of 4 and 12 April 1496, ASMn, AG, 2111, cc. 231r–232r and 233r–v.

[17] 'la voleva che respondesse a la Signoria Vostra et cossì me fu forza scrivere lì in l'orto, et era una zentileza a vederla affanarse a dirmi qualche parola; è certo che la lettera fu tutta sua sententia. Poi cum la sua manina, aiutata da me, fece la sottoscriptione.... la dice che la gli porterà de belle cose.... Et del presto ritorno de Vostra Excellentia non può stare de allegreza in li panni.' Benedetto Capilupi to Francesco Gonzaga, 3 September 1496, from Mantua, ASMn, AG, 2449, cc. 291r–v. The letter written by the secretary and signed by Eleonora is in ASMn, AG, 2111, c. 441. Such epistolary ventriloquism was the first step in the young child's training to dictate and write letters, something that would consume many hours of her adulthood. On the teaching of children to dictate and write letters in the Italian courts, see Monica Ferrari, 'Lettere di principi bambini del Quattrocento lombardo', *Mélanges de l'école française de Rome* 109.1 (1997): 339–54; and Monica Ferrari, '"Per non manchare in tuto del debito mio": L'educazione dei bambini Sforza nel Quattrocento', in *I bambini di una volta. Problemi di metodo. Studi per Egle Becchi*, vol. 3, Storia dell'educazione (Milan: Franco Angeli, 2006), 15–40. The marquis was similarly solicitous after the birth of Federico, sending Eleonora some toy figurines made from dough, perhaps to redress the child's sense that her brother had stolen all the attention that she had previously monopolized. See Isabella d'Este to Francesco Gonzaga, 23 November 1500, from Mantua, in Isabella d'Este, *Selected Letters*, 154.

which depicted the marquis surrounded by his courtiers.[18] Isabella had left the gravely ill Margherita in the care of Beatrice de' Contrari and Violante de' Preti, the second of whom had looked after the previous generation of Gonzaga children. Both women were well versed in looking after sick babies. The marchioness retreated with Eleonora to the country, perhaps in resigned recognition that the infant would not live. She wrote to Francesco on 23 September, sorrowfully informing him that their little girl had died after a long struggle and had flown to heaven that very night.[19]

Capilupi's testimony that Eleonora was already attempting, even before her third birthday, to master aspects of letter-writing, so she could communicate with her father, suggests that formal lessons were not far in the future. Isabella's education had begun when she was about four and it is likely that she ensured that Eleonora's studies were initiated similarly promptly.[20] By the age of eight, Eleonora had her own tutor, a detail revealed in a letter of April 1502 from Isabella to the lord of Carpi, Alberto Pio of Sabaudia. Eleonora's teacher, Sigismondo Golfo della Pergola, had apparently travelled to Carpi to settle some of his affairs, but had not confined his absence to the three-day leave he had been granted. Isabella therefore sought Pio's help in securing the teacher's immediate return to Mantua:

If these delays are your responsibility and are not really due to Sigismondo, we ask that out of respect for us you expedite him quickly and give him such satisfaction that he will no longer have reason to ask us for leave for this purpose. Your Lordship knows how significant it is to lose time for learning. Given Eleonora's age, and the convenience of this mild weather, we would take this as a great favor from Your Lordship, to whom we offer ourselves always.[21]

While this letter reveals Isabella's concern that Eleonora's education not be interrupted, another, sent four years later, shows that she was also exercised by her daughter's emotional well-being. Eleonora and her sisters had been sent away from Mantua in the summer of 1506, because of outbreaks of plague in the city. Isabella wrote to Francesco in early October, explaining that she wished to replace the steward who was looking after the girls, since, although he was a well-intentioned and worthy young gentleman, he was, in her view, 'very cold, of little presence and not sufficiently experienced' to provide appropriate company to

[18] Benedetto Capilupi to Francesco Gonzaga, 13 September 1496, from Venafro near Campobasso. ASMn, AG, 2450, c. 168. See Molly Bourne, *The Soldier-Prince*, 122, n. 61.

[19] Isabella d'Este to Francesco Gonzaga, 23 September 1496, from Marmirolo, in Isabella d'Este, *Selected Letters*, 102.

[20] On Isabella's education, see Luzio, 'Isabella d'Este e Francesco Gonzaga', 21; and Luzio, *I precettori di Isabella d'Este*, 11–17. An early letter to her father Ercole d'Este, probably dictated when she was about four, is in ASMo, Casa e stato, 133, unfoliated and undated. See Isabella d'Este, *Selected Letters*, 23.

[21] Isabella d'Este to Alberto Pio di Sabaudia, 21 April 1502, from Mantua, in Isabella d'Este, *Selected Letters*, 193–4.

children who had been without their parents for some time.[22] Only Eleonora is mentioned by name; her sisters—Livia, almost five, and Ippolita two years younger—are referred to only as 'le altre putte'. At nearly thirteen, Eleonora is likely to have felt her isolation more acutely than her siblings and Isabella may well have identified with her eldest daughter, since, pregnant once more, she herself had endured a boring summer at the villa of Sacchetta, declaring its sedate country routines entirely contrary to her nature.[23] Having finally obtained Francesco's permission to return to Mantua, Isabella's thoughts turned to her similarly marooned daughter.

The prospect of Eleonora becoming the future duchess of Urbino was already being discussed in 1503 and, two years later, she was formally betrothed to Francesco Maria della Rovere, nephew of both Pope Julius II and of the childless Duke Guidobaldo da Montefeltro, who nominated the boy heir to the duchy.[24] By the age of nine, Eleonora was not only studying under a new teacher—the humanist schoolmaster, Francesco Vigilio—but also acquiring the social skills she would need as the spouse of a princely ruler. A letter to Francesco of 21 November 1502 suggests that Isabella regarded Eleonora as too timid. She explained to her husband that she had attempted to redress their daughter's bashfulness by extending the visit to the Gonzaga court of the youngest daughter of their Gonzaga relative, Antonia del Balzo of Gazzuolo, 'so she can teach Eleonora a bit of her daring'.[25] The girl kept Eleonora company during the latter's long recuperation from an illness.

Whether the influence of her more extrovert playmate rubbed off on Eleonora we do not learn, but, once fully recovered, she was sent off to acquire greater poise and confidence by dining with prominent Mantuan courtiers at their city palaces.[26] Eventually, Eleonora seems to have developed too much independence for her mother's liking. In July 1506, Isabella reproved her daughter for poaching one of her footmen, and ordering shirts for him, without seeking permission.[27] Eleonora replied forthrightly to her mother's accusatory letter, explaining that the footman

---

[22] 'Nel tempo che la Elionora cum li altri nostri figlioli è stata fora senza noi, intendo che hanno patito molti incommodi per non esserli apresso persona sufficiente, perchè Salattino che fa l'officio del sescalco è molto freddo, di poca presentia et manco experientia, anchora ch'el sii giovene da bene et bono, quanto dire se possa, come scia Vostra Excellentia.' Isabella d'Este to Francesco Gonzaga, 12 October 1506, from Mantua, ASMn, AG, 2116, c. 267.

[23] 'voria ridurmi a Mantua, non potendo hormai più durare in questa fastidiosa stantia di villa, contraria in tutto alla natura mia.' Isabella d'Este to Francesco Gonzaga, 31 August 1506, from Sacchetta, ASMn, AG, 2116, c. 242.

[24] On the betrothal, see Isabella d'Este to Giovanna della Rovere, 29 April 1505, from Mantua, in Isabella d'Este, *Selected Letters*, 257–8.

[25] Isabella d'Este to Francesco Gonzaga, 21 November 1502, from Mantua, in Isabella d'Este, *Selected Letters*, 205–7.

[26] Isabella d'Este to Francesco Gonzaga, 2 December 1502, from Mantua, in Isabella d'Este, *Selected Letters*, 211–12.

[27] Isabella d'Este to Eleonora Gonzaga, 9 July 1506, from Mantua, in Isabella d'Este, *Selected Letters*, 269–70.

Oliviero had manipulated her, pretending he had nowhere to stay and had, in effect, ordered the shirts himself, without her knowledge.[28] Whether innocent of her mother's charge, or not, Eleonora's articulate epistolary rebuttal suggests she was already a young person to be reckoned with, as Isabella herself was at the same age.

Although Federico shared the tutors of his sisters, his future destiny as marquis of Mantua required careful preparation in other respects. Even when he was a toddler, Isabella and Francesco scrutinized their son keenly, looking for signs that he was innately suited to take on his father's mantle. On 2 December 1502, for example, Isabella informed Francesco, who was in France at that time, following the peregrinations of the royal court, that their son had now been completely weaned and a governess chosen to take over from the wet nurse. She then described a test she had set the child to gauge his possession of the princely virtue of liberality, revealing along the way that Federico was already learning to gamble, a perennial feature of court life and certainly a leisure activity to which both his parents were addicted.

> After I had finished the letter in my own hand, he wanted to dine with me, and he behaved in the most charming way in the world. Then when he was set down to play at dice with ten ducats in front of him, I purposely had someone knock at the door of the room and say that there was a poor man who was asking for charity. At this, on his own and without anyone's prompting him to do so, he immediately took one ducat and had it given [to the beggar] saying, in his own words, 'Tell him to pray to God for me, and also for my Pa'.[29]

The far-fetched suggestion that Federico was aware of his status as heir to the marquisate and able to behave accordingly at the age of two and a half was implied in another of Isabella's letters of the same period. This time, she foregrounded her son's impressive dignity during the civic ceremonies that marked the beginning of the year. As was customary, the merchants of the city had expressed their homage to the regime by presenting Isabella, as her husband's representative, with a finely made sword. The marchioness had presided over the gift-giving with Federico at her side. She reported to Francesco that their son had risen to the occasion with exceptional aplomb: 'After accepting it and thanking them in your Excellency's name, I handed it to Federico who, all by himself and without any reminders from anyone, said these exact words: "many thanks, we will save it for our Lord Pa."'[30]

---

28 Eleonora Gonzaga to Isabella d'Este, 11 July 1506, from Mantua, ASMn, AG, 2116, c. 321.
29 Isabella d'Este to Francesco Gonzaga, 2 December 1502, from Mantua, in Isabella d'Este, *Selected Letters*, 211–12.
30 Isabella d'Este to Francesco Gonzaga, 3 January 1503, from Mantua, in Isabella d'Este, *Selected Letters*, 213.

Yet Isabella also occasionally mocked such exaggerated narratives of Federico's precocious behaviour. In November 1503, for example, in an attempt to distract Francesco from the deprivations and discomforts of the battlefield, she regaled him with an account of the amorous exploits of their son:

> Federico is in love with Antonio da Bologna's daughter! His head is so turned that he keeps to no road or path. He caresses her with abandon, gives her necklaces as gifts, and favors her in other ways. I make sure that he is well chaperoned, but since he is who he is, everyone is his accomplice.... Your Excellency may be able at this point, with a letter or by some other means, to mediate and remind him that while his father is on the battlefield, it is not appropriate for a son to pursue love.[31]

The anecdote fell entirely flat at first. As Francesco admitted, he thought Isabella was referring to Federico, his meat steward, and had become furious at such impudence and impropriety in a servant. Then, after rereading the letter, he had burst into laughter and sent a reply that mimicked Isabella's mock serious tone:

> Concerning this matter, it seems to us that Your Ladyship shouldn't be upset, given that such a love is laudable in a lad, especially one who is the sole male among so many females born every day and, because of them, having the household full of girls, concerning whom we firmly believe that he will not use such tact and modesty that we used and because you say everyone is indulgent Your Ladyship should know that I have to be the good one, who will never overlook anything to indulge and please him.[32]

Isabella had recently given birth to Livia Giulia, so Federico now had three sisters and indeed inhabited an environment almost entirely dominated by females.

Although Francesco was prepared to joke about the gender imbalance in his household, in the same letter of 23 November 1503, he registered his disapproval of Isabella's decision to take Federico with her to see a performance of *Il Formicone*, a comedy based on Apuleius' *The Golden Ass*, by a writer who called himself

---

[31] Isabella d'Este to Francesco Gonzaga, 7 November 1503, from Mantua, in Isabella d'Este, *Selected Letters*, 235–6.

[32] 'Ma di ciò non ni pare che Vostra Signoria si debbi dolere, essendo acto laudabile in uno garzone uno tal amore, maxime havendo ad esser solo maschio fra tante femine che ogni dì nascono, et per esse havendo ad esser tutta la casa piena de doncelle, circa le quale credemo ben ch' el non usarà quel reguardo e modestia che havemo usata noi e perché la dice che ogniuno gli è tercio, sappia la Signoria Vostra che noi havemo ad essere il bono, che non lassaremo mai cosa a fare per compiacerlo e contentarlo.' Francesco Gonzaga to Isabella d'Este, 23 November 1503, from Sermoneta in Lazio, ASMn, AG, 2115bis, cc. 313r–v.

Publio Filippo Mantovano. The play was directed by Francesco Vigilio and performed by his students.[33]

> Nor was there any call for Your Ladyship to allow Maestro Vigilio to attract him through comedies, so that he becomes his disciple, since we wish that he learns little literature and that little from others, on the grounds he [Vigilio] was an enemy of Maestro Pietro and our partisans; and already we are thinking about taking [Federico] with us when we leave the city, so he will become a proper man.[34]

Francesco refers here to Vigilio's predecessor as schoolmaster, the grammarian Pietro Marcheselli da Viadana, who had died in mid-1502. Isabella had awarded Vigilio the dead man's house, so allowing him to take over the school. Competitors for the much-desired position had complained stridently to the absent marquis about his wife's decision, hence Francesco's championing of his own clients and resentment of Vigilio. Francesco was also fearful that his son would become too bookish, if Federico's education was left entirely to Isabella. Having noted that the pastoral environment of Gonzaga encouraged the child to be more physically active and agile, in the spring of 1503, he ordered that Federico be sent to him there. But once the boy arrived, Francesco wrote reassuringly to Isabella that he had adhered to age-appropriate activities by showing their son the pregnant mares and explaining to him that they all had little barbary foals inside.[35]

Encouraged by the indications that his heir had inherited the paternal love of outdoor pursuits and thoroughbred animals, Francesco summoned Federico more often. In June 1504, Isabella was obliged to accede to her husband's order to send the 4-year-old to him, but she wrote anxiously about the dangers associated with such a young child being outside in the elements and away from her supervision.

---

[33] Luzio and Renier, *La coltura*, 59–60.

[34] 'Nè bisogna che la Signoria Vostra lo lassi atthraere a Maestro Francesco cum comedie, perché l'habbia ad esser suo discipulo, ché noi volemo che l'impari poche littere e quelle poche da altri cha da lui, per essere stato emulo di Maestro Pietro e di la parte nostra, e già pensamo de cominciarlo a condure cum noi fora aciò ch'el doventi da bene.' Francesco Gonzaga to Isabella d'Este, 23 November 1503, from Sermoneta in Lazio, ASMn, AG, 2115bis, 313r–v. On Vigilio's appointment as grammar master following the death of Pietro Marcheselli da Viadana, see Luzio and Renier, *La coltura*, 58–60.

[35] 'Federico monstra pur la sanità sua in ogni cosa, maxime nel correre e saltare, che è qualche cosa più di quello ch'el sole far a Mantua, e forsi ch'el li pare di esser un pocho più alargato e libero. . . . Ma il suo peculiar dilecto è de li cavalli e noi havemo havuto il modo di satiarlo, perché ultra quelli poletri che tenemo qua in la stalla, li havemo facta la monstra de tutte le barbare che hano li barbarini dreto.' Francesco Gonzaga to Isabella d'Este, 26 April 1503, from Gonzaga, ASMn, AG, 2115bis, c. 211.

But since the baby boy's body has suffered again from diarrhea, more likely due to the winds that have governed these days than to anything else, I think it appropriate (not because I think Your Lordship will be insufficiently vigilant, but moved by the overabundant love I bear him) that I lovingly remind you to keep him out of the wind and away from animal droppings, and to forbid him to undress down to his shirt or to ride horseback too much, especially in the evening right after dinner, all of which things the doctors condemn as extremely harmful to him.[36]

Federico travelled to the Gonzaga estate at Revere with a small entourage that included Benedetto Capilupi. Soon after the party's arrival, a letter in the secretary's hand, purporting to have been dictated by the child, was dispatched to reassure Isabella that all was well. While the content was hardly likely to dispel motherly worries about Federico's physical safety, the secretary's desire to entertain the marchioness is evident in the droll description of her son's initiation into hunting. Presented in the first person, the letter narrates Federico's virile encounter with a cockerel. After vanquishing the bird with his miniature bow and arrow, he had presented it in triumph to his governess, who cooked it for his supper. On the following day, he progressed to a larger quarry. The pursuit of a goose by the small hunter is presented in epic terms: 'And in the end, I wounded and conquered it; and because perhaps Your Ladyship won't believe it, I am sending it to you as a gift. I didn't want to finish it off, so that you could have it fresh and it will be good to eat tomorrow.' A postscript provided the mock-tragic denouement: 'During the writing of the letter, the goose died.'[37]

Isabella is not likely to have believed that Federico dictated this account word-for-word. However, almost a year earlier, the secretary had assured Francesco in a postscript that this was precisely how the five lines of a letter from Federico thanking his father for the song birds he had sent for the boy's supper had been produced.[38] These two examples demonstrate Capilupi's sensitivity to the different dynamic in the relationship of each parent with their son. The letters written by Capilupi to Francesco in Federico's voice eschew jokes, aiming instead to communicate the child's earnest affection for his father. From 1503, Federico's letters, written in collaboration with Capilupi and signed 'El puton del pa' [From Pa's big boy] became routine. Full of enthusiastic details of visits to the palace stables, or those on the Te island on the outskirts of Mantua, the letters were both a

---

[36] Isabella d'Este to Francesco Gonzaga, 11 June 1504, from Mantua, in Isabella d'Este, *Selected Letters*, 250–1.

[37] 'Et al fin l'ho ferito e conquistato, e perché forsi Vostra Signoria non lo crederia, ge lo mando a donare. Non l'ho voluto finire di amaciare, aciò che la lo possi haver fresco e bono domatina da mangiare.' The postscript reads: 'Scrivendosi la littera, l'ocho è morto.' Federico Gonzaga to Isabella d'Este, 14 June 1504, from Revere, ASMn, AG, 2116, c. 87.

[38] 'Queste sono state parole proprie del Signor Federico.' This is Capilupo's postscript in a dictated letter from Federico Gonzaga to Francesco Gonzaga, 11 June 1503, ASMn, AG, 2115bis, c. 437.

pedagogical tool, teaching the child to master essential epistolary skills, and a means of preserving the emotional connection with a man so frequently away from his family. Francesco sent gifts of marzipan and other special treats to Federico, as he had done in the early years of Eleonora's childhood.

By the age of six, Federico was regularly at one or other of the Gonzaga country estates, from where he reported to his father on the horses kept there and dispatched gifts of produce, following customs that were generations old.[39] Killing game, taking a keen interest in the Gonzaga equine breeding programme and engaging in vigorous exercise were exactly what Francesco had in mind for his son to prepare him for the military role that he himself placed such store by. However, Isabella also had her way, since Francesco Vigilio became the boy's tutor. In 1506, Eleonora and Federico together wrote to their father in support of their teacher, after Vigilio was accused of counterfeiting money.[40] The marquis had, by then, changed his mind about the schoolmaster, since, at the end of that year, he ordered Vigilio to organize a production of the same comedy to which Isabella had taken Federico in 1503. *Il Formicone* was staged in the Palazzo della Ragione in Mantua to entertain two visiting cardinals.[41]

Francesco was perhaps also reassured that Federico showed sufficient proclivity for manly outdoor pursuits as not to be turned into a milksop by too much study. At the age of eight, the boy's enthusiasm for school was far less keen than his tutor expected. In July 1508, Vigilio informed Isabella that, although her son had memorized many passages from Ovid and was practising others to recite to her upon her return to Mantua, his reading ability left something to be desired. The teacher suggested that Isabella exhort the boy to try harder to improve.[42] Another letter, written almost seven years later, suggests that Federico's study habits remained sporadic. The teacher explained that his pupil usually concentrated on his books for no more than an hour or so at a time. Nonetheless, sessions twice a day had facilitated progress. Federico was reading abbreviated versions of Livy, Ovid, and other ancient authors in their original language and studying one of Cicero's letters daily, in order to acquire a fine Latin prose style. Although Vigilio conceded that the youth preferred to read the stories of Orlando in the vernacular, he concluded reassuringly that even if Federico's age incited him to the occasional lascivious lapse, on the whole he promised well.[43]

---

[39] Federico Gonzaga's letters from Goito and Marmirolo are in ASMn, AG, 2116.

[40] Eleonora and Federico Gonzaga to Francesco Gonzaga, 31 May 1506, from Goito, ASMn, AG, 2116, c. 302.

[41] See Bourne, *The Soldier-Prince*, 455–7.

[42] Francesco Vigilio to Isabella d'Este, 8 July 1508, from Mantua, published in Alessandro Luzio, 'Federico Gonzaga ostaggio alla corte di Giulio II', *Archivio della Società Romana di Storia Patria* 9 (1886): 509–82 (567).

[43] Francesco Vigilio to Isabella d'Este, 5 February 1515, from Mantua, published in Luzio, 'Federico Gonzaga ostaggio', 567–8.

By insisting on the employment of Vigilio as Federico's tutor, Isabella made sure that her eldest son received a sound humanist education. But she conceded that Francesco's concern that the boy be well trained in the military arts was also right. The heir to the marquisate had to be physically fit, an excellent rider and swordsman, and not too squeamish about killing, if he was to be a soldier-prince in the tradition of his male forebears.[44] It was already apparent that the wars which had plagued the peninsula for more than a decade were unlikely to cease, given the belligerent competitiveness between the pope and the emperor and the monarchs of France and Spain. Thus, the couple remained in agreement about an issue that had caused some initial friction. However, a rapidly deteriorating diplomatic climate began to create conflict between them within a year of their second son's birth in November 1505.

Marital Discord

In early October 1506, Francesco sent an angry reprimand to his wife:

> We very much regret that Your Ladyship continues of your own accord to want to change our son's rightful name of Alvise, to whom we gave that name out of reverence for the king of France and which we wish absolutely he retains. So, Your Ladyship, cease to call him otherwise, if you do not want us to think that you are searching for new ways to annoy us.[45]

The couple had initially referred to the new baby generically as 'el peteghino', a fond diminutive inspired perhaps by the newborn's bird-like chirpings. Occasionally, they used the more standard northern Italian word, 'il puttino'. However, in three separate letters to Francesco of September 1506, Isabella referred to the infant as Ercole, convinced, perhaps, that it was high time for their son to be named.[46] In response to the marquis's bad-tempered reply of 1 October, Isabella sought to be placatory. She explained in a long letter, written in her own hand, there had been an unfortunate misunderstanding between them concerning the name: she had assumed Francesco was willing to call their second son

---

[44] On the preparation of aristocratic young boys for war through hunting, see Enrica Guerra, 'L'educazione militare del cardinale Ippolito I d'Este', in Formare alle professioni. La cultura militare tra passato e presente, ed. Monica Ferrari and Filippo Ledda (Milan: Franco Angeli, 2011), 101–15.

[45] 'Ni rincresce ben che la Signoria Vostra perseveri in volere al suo potere mutare il suo diricto nome a Loysi nostro figliol, a cui alegessimo quello nome per reverentia dil re di Franza, et a cui volemo per ogni modo el corri; perhò cessi, Vostra Signoria, di nominarlo altramenti, aciò ch'el non si pensassi che l'andassi cercando nove cause di noiarni.' Francesco Gonzaga to Isabella d'Este, 1 October 1506, from San Marino, ASMn, AG, 2914, libro 193, c. 23v.

[46] Isabella d'Este to Francesco Gonzaga, 12 September 1506, from Sacchetta; 21, 29 September, from Mantua, ASMn, AG, 2116, cc. 247, 250, 256.

Ercole since, when he had joined her at Sacchetta that summer, he had joked that the child strongly resembled her father. Isabella had therefore suggested naming the boy Ercole. She reminded Francesco that he had laughed, without commenting further and she had taken this as a sign that he agreed.[47] Ercole d'Este had died on 25 January 1505. It must have seemed reasonable to Isabella that his memory should be honoured, especially since their first son, Federico, carried his paternal grandfather's name. However, Francesco doubtless recalled the dangerously negative reaction of Louis XII, five years before, when the king had discovered that the principal godfather of the Gonzaga heir was Duke Albert of Bavaria. While a German relative may have seemed to Francesco entirely appropriate, given his maternal genetic heritage, the choice was regarded by the king as an insult and one that advertised the marquis's continuing diplomatic dalliance with enemies of France.[48]

As late as 21 August 1506, there is no sign of discord in the couple's letters. Francesco continued to write warmly to his wife, who was pregnant and confined to the Gonzaga residence at Sacchetta. When she fell seriously ill from fevers during that summer, Francesco was lovingly concerned, declaring, after receiving a handsome new bonnet from Isabella, that his devotion to her increased daily.[49] It seems, then, that an explanation for the marquis's reprimand to his wife was fear that the king of France would again take umbrage, if the diplomatic fiasco in relation to the choice of godfather for Federico was exacerbated by a tactless naming of their second son. The relationship with Louis XII could no longer be bolstered by the strenuous diplomatic efforts of his sister Clara, who had died in France in 1503. As widow of Gilbert de Bourbon, and a lady-in-waiting to the queen, Anne of Brittany, Clara had enjoyed enormous influence at the French court and it was she who was the decisive intermediary in preventing Mantua from being awarded to Venice by Louis XII in 1500, in retaliation for Francesco's unreliability as a French ally.[50] It is unlikely that Francesco was so naïve as to think that naming his second son Alvise, or Aloyse, would substantially redress his unpopularity in France, but Isabella's reference to the baby as Ercole likely rubbed salt into the marquis's wounded ego and exacerbated his worries about what he could do to restore friendly relations with the king.

Francesco's quick temper, never far below the surface, was also more prone to flare after the brutal murder of one of his most trusted courtiers. Antonio Maria di San Secondo Regazzi, known as 'Il Milanese', was assassinated, in November 1505, by agents of another well-favoured Mantuan courtier, Enea Furlano da

---

[47] Isabella d'Este to Francesco Gonzaga, 5 October 1506, from Mantua, ASMn, AG, 2116, cc. 262r–v. This letter is transcribed in Cockram, *Isabella and Francesco*, 213–14 and discussed at 161.

[48] Dupont-Pierrart, *Claire de Gonzague*, 242.

[49] Francesco Gonzaga to Isabella d'Este, 21, 22, 24 June 1506, from Viadana, ASMn, AG, 2913, libro 191, cc. 74v–75r; 76r and 21 August 1506, from Goito, ASMn, AG, 2913, libro 193, c. 94v.

[50] Dupont-Pierrart, *Claire de Gonzague*, 255–62.

Cavriano, who went by the nickname 'Il Cavaliere'. In the immediate aftermath of the crime, incredulous at Furlano's treachery, Francesco described to Angelo Tovaglia, his long-time representative in Florence, the utter and equal faith he had placed in the two men:

> They were exceptionally favoured by us. And as a sign of the love I bore them, one [Furlano], as well as being given a natural daughter of ours in marriage, was commissioned with the management and government of all our soldiers; the other [Regazzi] was given the management and government of the city and our whole state.[51]

Two days before the murder, however, Francesco had characterized Regazzi to another confident as someone in whom he had 'the highest degree of confidence and the liberty to make use of all we have in the world, such that there is nobody who knows our every thought more than he does'.[52] This confession suggests that the favours to the arch-rivals were not as equivalent as the marquis claimed. Certainly, the two had long seethed with resentment at the preferment each perceived the other as enjoying. The fact that Regazzi was in secret negotiations with Louis XII about a French military commission for the marquis probably became known to Furlano and fuelled his already well-ignited jealousy. The murder disrupted this covert diplomacy, to Francesco's intense frustration.[53] But Isabella seems to have been secretly glad to see the end of a man who had taken advantage of her husband's friendship to line his pockets and who represented a significant threat to her own role as her husband's deputy, as Francesco Secco had done in the early 1490s. She admitted to Francesco later that she had known of Furlano's murderous plans, but had not encouraged them.[54]

In the poisonous atmosphere of violence and court intrigue, it is unsurprising that the usual levels of trust between the marquis and his wife were difficult to maintain. Even comments that would normally be seen as innocuous, or benign, were now more likely to be greeted with suspicion, prompting a to-and-fro of barbed reproaches. So, for example, when Isabella lauded the structural works and pictorial embellishments being undertaken at this time within Francesco's palace of San Sebastiano, her husband expressed doubts about her sincerity. In a letter of 5 October 1506, written in her own hand, Isabella protested about

---

[51]   Quoted and translated in Cockram, *Isabella d'Este and Francesco Gonzaga*, 95.

[52]   Quoted and translated in Cockram, *Isabella d'Este and Francesco Gonzaga*, 95. For a discussion of the murder and Francesco's vendetta against Furlano, see 94–101.

[53]   On the motives for the murder and its repercussions, see Anna Maria Lorenzoni, 'Un omicidio alla corte mantovana profetizzato della Beata Osanna Andreasi', *Civiltà mantovana* 29 (1971): 317–25 (321). See also Clifford M. Brown and Anna Maria Lorenzoni, 'Il cinquecentesimo anniversario di un omicidio alla corte di Francesco II Gonzaga', *Civiltà mantovana* 120 (2005): 79–112.

[54]   See Cockram, *Isabella d'Este and Francesco Gonzaga*, 94–101.

Francesco's assumption that her praise of the palace, conveyed in an earlier dictated message, was mocking:

> A few days ago I was in Your Lordship's house and, as I wrote before, thought it most beautiful. You write that I am making fun of you, but this is not true, because if the rooms were not beautiful I would remain silent; but, as they seemed beautiful to me, I had this written to you, and again I tell you that they are beautiful, and even more so because Your Lordship has learned from the example of my room, although in truth you have improved upon it.[55]

Yet, the assurance that her husband had outshone what she had achieved in the *studiolo* fails to neutralize the force of the verb 'learned' and its implication that she possessed the superior conceptual power, which Francesco had merely built on. The combination of compliment and irony in the passage could hardly have disarmed the marquis.

It is not clear from the extant documentation what exactly Isabella saw at San Sebastiano. The Bolognese master, Lorenzo Costa, was already engaged on the *Coronation of a Woman Poet*, destined for the marchioness's *studiolo* before he was appointed court painter, following Mantegna's death in September 1506. He then assumed responsibility for some of the decorations in the palace of San Sebastiano, although his presence there is not definitively documented until April 1507.[56] The frescoes in Francesco's bedroom, the so-called *Camera del Costa*, described by Giorgio Vasari in his sixteenth-century account of the painter's life, were still not finished in 1510, so it is unlikely Isabella saw even early versions of these paintings by Costa, which were indeed to bear a notable similarity with works in her *studiolo*.[57] The ground-floor rooms, on the other hand, were almost complete when the marchioness made her visit and work had begun on the magnificent coffered ceiling of the large reception room on the first floor of the palace that would accommodate Mantegna's *Triumphs of Caesar*.[58] It is likely that Isabella could already see that Francesco intended to trump the decorative schemes of her apartments, which had increasingly become a drawcard for visiting dignitaries. Despite her denials of irony, Isabella's ambiguously phrased compliment in the letter of 5 October suggests she was none too pleased by her husband's competitiveness.[59]

[55] Isabella d'Este to Francesco Gonzaga, 5 October 1506, from Mantua, ASMn, AG, b. 2116, cc. 262r–v. Bourne, *The Soldier-Prince*, translation at 271, original letter transcribed at 445.

[56] Bourne, *The Soldier-Prince*, 444, n. 1.

[57] Clifford M. Brown and Anna Maria Lorenzoni, 'The Palazzo di San Sebastiano (1506–1512) and the Art Patronage of Francesco II Gonzaga, Fourth Marquis of Mantua', *Gazette des Beaux-Arts* 129 (1997): 131–80, 151–8, 174.

[58] Bourne, *The Soldier-Prince*, 196.

[59] On the various stages of the decoration of the palace of San Sebastiano, see Bourne, *The Soldier-Prince*, 183–222.

Although she apologized to her husband for the mix-up about the naming of Alvise/Ercole, Isabella stoutly defended herself from the suggestion that she was responsible for the marital tensions between them:

> Do not say, Your Lordship, that any person in the world has the power to make me stay at war with you, except you yourself, because when Your Lordship shows that you love me, others would not be at liberty to make me believe the contrary. It has needed few interpreters, however, to make it clear to me that Your Lordship has for some time loved me little, but since this subject is disagreeable, I will cut it short and say no more.[60]

Isabella's combative retort only seems to have further exasperated the marquis, prompting him to reflect in a letter of 13 October 1506 to Gian Francesco Tridapali, a Mantuan court secretary and bureaucrat who was about to marry, on the difficulties of wedlock:

> you are entering a new mode of life that will seem most strange in ways you cannot ever anticipate, and especially in your case, since it seems to us, that you are hardly equipped to satisfy a woman; and take it from us, who have already been in such a life nominally for twenty-five years, and seventeen in effect.[61]

In looking back to the year of his betrothal, Francesco here projects the mature Isabella onto the 6-year-old girl, wearily casting himself as a man who had dealt with a strong-willed and enigmatic female for two and a half decades.

The couple recovered quickly from their grievances with each other on this occasion, although it was Isabella who made the greater effort to be conciliatory. Francesco's grumpiness dissipated somewhat following his appointment as lieutenant-general of the papal troops, in place of Duke Guidobaldo Montefeltro of Urbino, who had succumbed to illness. After being denied reemployment as a mercenary captain by the republic of Florence, Francesco had, somewhat reluctantly, thrown in his lot with Pope Julius II, who was determined to reclaim the papal state of Bologna. The city's oligarchical regime, led by the Bentivoglio, had endured for more than half a century and both the marquis's brother, Giovanni, and Isabella's half-sister, Lucrezia d'Este, had married into the family, creating strong ties between Mantua and Bologna. Although uneasy about the prospect of

---

[60] Isabella d'Este to Francesco Gonzaga, 5 October 1506, from Mantua, ASMn, AG, 2116, cc. 262r–v. The original letter is transcribed in Cockram, *Isabella and Francesco*, 213–14.

[61] 'entri in uno novo modo di vivere, che tanto ti parerà strano in quanto non ti porresti mai imaginare e tanto più a te che ni pari pocho prosperoso a contentare una femina e credilo a noi che siamo in tal vita già xxv anni in titulo, e già dicesette in effecto.' Francesco Gonzaga to Gian Francesco Tridapali, 13 October 1506, from the papal military encampment at Castel San Pietro, near Bologna, ASMn, AG, 2914, libro 193, c. 37r.

destroying the political fortunes of his Bentivoglio relatives, the marquis was in urgent need of income and keen to preserve the momentum of his military career. While waiting idly for weeks with his troops near Bologna, as Julius II hammered out the terms of his reclaiming of the city following the flight into exile of Giovanni Bentivoglio and his family, the marquis's mind turned from battle to other ways of impressing his peers. He reflected on the impressive apparel he would wear during the pope's triumphal procession into Bologna.[62] He wrote to Isabella, ordering her to organize a new silk bonnet for him, declaring that as long as it was rich and gallant he would leave the style and ornamentation to her well-honed expertise in questions of fashion.[63] On 2 November, after finally receiving the finished product, which featured a large diamond and so many pearls that it had to be conveyed to him under armed guard, Francesco declared himself delighted with it.

> The hat in every respect demonstrates it has come from the hands of an ingenious and loving person and not only do we like it very much, but everyone who has seen it has tried it on, praised, and admired it; [thanks to] it, which we regard as your gift, we hope to be honoured beyond measure. Our thanks we will deliver personally.[64]

The magnificent piece of millinery could not entirely compensate for the unhappiness the marquis felt about his role in the fall from power of his Bolognese kin. He reflected grimly to Isabella on the fickleness of fortune.[65] His wife, on the other hand, took the view that there was no resisting the pope and the Bentivoglio had been unwise not to take Francesco's advice to 'convert necessity into a virtue'.[66] Still, the couple did their best to help the exiles, allowing the men to pass through Mantuan territory, and offering on-going refuge to the Bentivoglio women,

[62] On Julius II's entry into Bologna, see Maurizio Ricci, 'Giulio II e l'ideologia trionfale. Una lettera dell'ingresso a Bologna del 1506', in *Città in Guerra: Esperienze e riflessioni nel primo '500. Bologna nelle 'Guerre d'Italia'*, ed. Gian Mario Anselmo and Angela De Benedictis (Bologna: Minerva Soluzioni Editoriali, 2008), 249–68.

[63] 'Il capello che ni ha a fare la Signoria Vostra siamo contenti sia negro per il suo ragionevole rispecto, sol li ricordamo a farcelo richo e galante a modo suo, che al suo iudicio in tutto ni rimettemo e così anchor dil saglione.' Francesco Gonzaga to Isabella d'Este, 13 October 1506, from San Prospero, ASMn, AG, 2914, libro 193, cc. 38r–39v.

[64] 'Il capello che a tutte le sue parti dimostra uscir di mani de persona ingeniosa et amorevole, non sol a noi è summamente piaciuto, ma da ogniuno che l'ha visto è stato a prova, lodato et admirato. Di esso, che reputiamo dono vostro, speramo esser honorati ad ogni parenghone. Gli ringratiamenti faremo personalmente.' Francesco Gonzaga to Isabella d'Este, 2 November 1506, from Castel San Pietro, ASMn, AG, 2914, libro 193, cc. 82r–v.

[65] 'quanto sia varia e mutabile questa misera vita e quanto sia vaga e volubile la fortuna.' Francesco Gonzaga to Isabella d'Este, 2 November 1506, from Castel San Pietro, ASMn, AG, 2914, libro 193, cc. 82r–v.

[66] 'Son certa che a Vostra Excellentia rincresca la extirpatione de li Bentivolii per l'amicicia et coniunctione che hanno cum noi, ma non può né debe mancare del debito suo verso il summo pontifice et loro haveriano anche facto bene a seguire li amorevoli ricordi de Vostra Excellentia et convertire la necessità in virtù.' Isabella d'Este to Francesco Gonzaga, 26 October 1506, from Mantua, ASMn, AG, 2116, cc. 274r–v.

especially to Isabella's half-sister, Lucrezia d'Este, who was pregnant, and to the elderly Ginevra Sforza, the wife of the deposed leader of the regime. As a result of this succour, Mantua was placed under interdict by the pope, a situation that placed enormous political pressure on Isabella, as she battled to keep the population calm in the face of a papal ban on liturgical services, including funerals.[67] Given the threat of instability in the city as a result of the interdict, despite an advancing pregnancy, Isabella remained in Mantua, continuing to act as regent until she gave birth to Ferrante, the couple's third son, on 28 January 1507. This time, she endured a life-threatening labour and it was only the skill of the midwives that saved her. Although sobered by the danger his wife had faced, Francesco could visit Mantua only briefly, since he was summoned by Louis XII in the prelude to the king's military campaign to conquer Genoa.

As domestic political problems continued to accumulate, Isabella wrote worriedly to her husband in late April 1507 about the dangers he faced. Penned in her own hand and in a great hurry, the letter is affectionate, but there is also a hint of the frustration that she had expressed seven months before about the impulsiveness that remained such a fundamental part of her husband's character:

> I conclude it would be better to be the wife of a coward or, indeed, of a doctor, who returns home in the evening and remains there comfortably to eat in front of the fire, than a brave man who, with so much anguish, achieves so many honours. But although I say this to joke with Your Lordship, I wouldn't wish for a coward, nor change Your Lordship in this respect, even if in other respects I would willingly change him. . . . It remains for you to take more account of dangers and not be so desirous of always being in the front line, and to do more than is necessary and more than others do.[68]

The plea to Francesco not to place himself in physical danger reiterates the appeals that Isabella had expressed, to little avail, in 1503. The marchioness was painfully aware of the disaster that her husband's death in battle would pose when their son was still so little. But, as she well knew, Francesco was likely to forget about the need for prudence, once the lure of soldierly renown beckoned. Risk-taking was intrinsic to his conception of masculinity, as it was to many of his peers. A cool reckoning of what was required to acquit himself with honour, without putting his life in jeopardy, seems to have been beyond a man whose passions were easily aroused. It may have been in recognition of this reality that Isabella couched her

---

[67] 'Li preti del domo me hanno facto intendere che la città de Mantua è interdicta da li divini officii, tanto che alcuno de questi Bentivolij et soi seguazi vi stanno et tri giorni doppo se non sono absoluti, cosa che, perseverando, daria grande disturbo et per lo udire de le misse et per il sepelire de' morti.' Isabella d'Este to Francesco Gonzaga, 6 November 1506, from Mantua, ASMn, AG, 2116, c. 282.

[68] Isabella d'Este to Francesco Gonzaga, 26 April 1507, from Mantua, ASMn, AG, 2117, c. 86. The letter is transcribed in Alessandro Luzio, 'Isabella d'Este nelle tragedie della sua casa (1505-1506)', *Atti e memorie della R. Accademia Virgiliana di Mantova* 5 (1912) 55–122 (document at 119–20).

warning as a loving and uncharacteristically incoherent joke, one that was likely to remain in Francesco's mind, without annoying him. He could take a patronizing view of its (perhaps cunningly deployed) womanly sentiments.

In passages such as this Isabella continued to acknowledge conjugal love, while attempting to manipulate her spouse to behave more circumspectly. Despite episodes of conflict, the pair could still be reconciled by pride in their offspring and the perennial worries of parenthood. In late July 1508, for example, a heavily pregnant Isabella received news from Francesco of an accident that had befallen Federico, as the 8-year-old was riding his horse too intrepidly in the grassy environs of the Te island, on the outskirts of Mantua. Her reply expressed not only anger about the negligence of the child's attendants, but solicitude for Francesco, who had borne the brunt of the worry about whether the boy had been seriously hurt.

> Although Your Excellency writes to me calmly about Federico's accident and assures me that the danger was worse than any injury and the same thing was confirmed by the doctor, nevertheless I am all agitated, and my heart races thinking about the danger and the distress Your Excellency must have felt, being present, nor will I relax until I learn what happened.[69]

Similarly, the marquis made sure to reassure his wife about the incident, so she would not be too distressed in her delicate state of health.[70] Here we see the relationship at its best. The pleasurable distractions of family life provided relief from the worrisome political quandaries the pair faced and, as Isabella endured one pregnancy after another, Francesco could be in no doubt about her commitment to their shared dynastic enterprise. However, the departure from Mantua of the two eldest children—Eleonora in 1509 to marry and Federico in 1510 to act as guarantor of his father's loyalty to Pope Julius II by residing at the papal court—coincided roughly with the end of the second decade of the couple's marriage, a time which, despite several dramatic fallings out, was indubitably the golden years of their relationship. By the time Livia Osanna was born in August 1508, Francesco was seriously ill and his military career heading for the rocks. In the last decade of the couple's marriage, it proved far harder to resolve conflict. Thus, we witness in retrospect how important the children were in providing an emotional bridge between individuals whose temperaments and approaches to the political challenges that assailed them were not always well aligned.

---

[69] 'Anchora che la Excellentia Vostra mi scriva modestamente el caso de Federico, et mi assicuri essere stato magiore el periculo cha il male, et che questo medesmo me sii confirmato dal medico, non di meno tutta mi son comossa, et ho baticore pensando al periculo, et allo affanno nel quale si doveva ritrovare Vostra Excellentia, essendoli presente, né mi starà ben l'animo finché non intendi il successo.' Isabella d'Este to Francesco Gonzaga, 26 July 1508, from Cavriana, ASMn, AG, 2117, c. 202.

[70] Francesco's letters of 16 and 27 July reporting on the accident are in ASMn, AG, 2117, cc. 151 and 152.

7

Years of Crisis

Lent 1508 marked a tragic turning point in the lives of Francesco and Isabella. It was then rumours that something was seriously amiss with the marquis's health began to proliferate. Having suddenly retreated to Gonzaga to secure greater privacy, Francesco wrote from there to his wife, reassuring her in a letter of 27 March that while it was true he had been suffering from tremendous fevers and was so weak from vomiting and lack of sleep as to be barely alive, his doctors had concluded that the illness was ultimately 'neither grave, nor dangerous'.[1] Four days later, he reported that he was still a little feverish, but expected to recover completely with the new lunar phase. Nonetheless, to be on the safe side, he ordered that funds be released from the treasury, so that masses could be sung on his behalf in the main churches of the city, and asked Isabella to ensure that the nuns of every convent in the state prayed for him.[2] The marchioness replied at once, confirming that she had done as requested and that the masses would begin the next morning. She too purported to believe Francesco's symptoms were unlikely to endure, given their probable association with the recent conjunction of the moon.[3] But the activation of the entire religious community of Mantua suggests that they were both actually very worried about the nature of Francesco's illness. Their anxiety proved to be well founded. When he returned to Mantua at the beginning of Easter, Francesco had not recovered in the least.

News of the marquis's ill health quickly spread to Ferrara. The southern-born humanist scholar and courtier, Mario Equicola (c.1470–1525) had transferred from the Este to the Gonzaga court at the beginning of 1508, after being invited by Isabella to become her Latin tutor. At the end of April, he wrote to Cardinal Ippolito d'Este about what he had managed to glean about Francesco's situation:

---

[1] 'Come credemo haverà per voce inteso la Signoria Vostra, heri ne l'hora del disnare ni assali la febre cum gran forza et cum accidenti di vomito de molte collere e tutto il giorno ci crucio cum uno lamentovole tedio e diffidentia grande di poter più vivere....Se la Signoria Vostra haverà presso qualche sconforto alla prima voce dil male nostro, hor pigli conforto inteso ch'el non è né grave né periculoso.' Francesco Gonzaga to Isabella d'Este, 27 March 1508, from Gonzaga, ASMn, AG, 2915, libro 200, c. 3r.

[2] Francesco Gonzaga to Isabella d'Este, 31 March 1508, from Gonzaga, ASMn, AG, 2117, c. 139.

[3] 'spero che, come Lei scrive, non passarà più oltra, cognoscendosi la causa essere procedeta da la coniunctione de la luna, et essendo Vostra Excellentia evacuata, non poterà durarli el male adosso.' Isabella d'Este to Francesco Gonzaga, 31 March 1508, from Mantua, ASMn, AG, 2117, c. 184.

A Renaissance Marriage: The Political and Personal Alliance of Isabella d'Este and Francesco Gonzaga, 1490–1519.
Carolyn James, Oxford University Press (2020). © Carolyn James.
DOI: 10.1093/oso/9780199681211.001.0001

On Easter Monday, his Lordship the Marquis moved completely to stay day and night in San Sebastiano, and will not return to the Castello. He has commanded that nobody bearing the rank of *cameriere* or lower come to see or visit him there, unless specifically summoned. Truly, he does not feel very well. I do not know precisely what his ailment is, although I recall that in the beginning of March his genital member caused him great pain, and that later, in Gonzaga, he suffered from fevers. I am not sure what is afflicting him at present.[4]

Equicola carefully avoided identifying the disease, but the cardinal would have recognized the symptoms, since his brothers, Alfonso, Ferrante, and Sigismondo d'Este, were already suffering from what Italians dubbed the *mal francese*, later to become known as the Great Pox. Ippolito may himself have been infected by 1498.[5] It was widely believed the illness had been brought to Italy by Charles VIII's army in 1494. Although the first indications varied, suppurating ulcers, often beginning on the genitals, and intense pains in the limbs, were commonly experienced by victims.[6]

The Great Pox

The Ferrarese chronicler, Bernardino Zambotti, noted the appearance of the *mal francese* in northern Italy towards the end of 1496. Even in this early phase of its spread, he expressed the fear that the disease would resist every known treatment:

The French Disease began to be discovered in many people in this region, and also elsewhere in Italy: this disease [*male*] seems to be incurable, since it is the disease of St Job [*male di Santo Job*]; and it springs from men who do it with women in their vulva [*mona*]. As a result of it most of these men die; they suffer from pains in bones and nerves, and very big pustules [*brozole*] all over the body.[7]

Twelve months later, Zambotti recorded its impact on the duke of Ferrara's own family: Alfonso d'Este was apparently so covered with the pustules associated

---

[4] Mario Equicola to Ippolito d'Este, 28 April 1508, from Mantua, ASMo, Cancelleria Ducale, Ambasciatori, Mantova, 1, c. 64. This letter is partially transcribed in Bourne, *The Soldier-Prince*, 469–70. I quote from her translation at 186.

[5] Jon Arrizabalaga, Roger Kenneth French, and John Henderson, *The Great Pox: The French Disease in Renaissance Europe* (New Haven; London: Yale University Press, 1997), 49. News that Alfonso, Ferrante, and Sigismondo d'Este were infected with the *mal francese* was recorded by an anonymous Ferrarese diarist in a number of entries of 1499. See *Diario ferrarese*, 219, 224, 240.

[6] Jon Arrizabalaga et al., *The Great Pox*, 25–6, 46–9.

[7] Zambotti, *Diario ferrarese*, 267. Quoted and translated in Arrizabalaga et al., *The Great Pox*, 44.

with the disease that he was unable to appear in public to attend the funeral of his wife, Anna Sforza, who had just died in childbirth.[8] It was probably worry about his heir that prompted Duke Ercole d'Este to convene a series of meetings of court physicians and professors from the medical faculty of the University of Ferrara in the early spring of 1497. The experts represented a wide spectrum of medical thinking, ranging from the late medieval Avicennan-Galenic tradition to the newer Latin humanist camp inspired by the writings of Cornelius Celsus. Their task was to debate the nature of the disease that now afflicted so many, to determine its causes, to decide whether it was known to ancient authorities and to weigh up the merits of the therapeutic measures that had been deployed to combat its effects. The discussions about what they called the *morbus gallicus* prompted a spate of learned treatises, several of which were published by the end of 1497.[9]

Thus, the symptoms of the disease and possible cures would have been entirely familiar to Francesco when he became ill in 1508, especially since there were victims at the court of Mantua in 1496. At the end of July, Isabella had reported to Francesco that their court jester, the dwarf Diodato, had contracted a malady that was being referred to in Mantua as 'the French disease'. She added that Diodato had been banned from court until he recovered, since doctors feared that, even without direct physical contact, the disease could easily spread to others.[10]

It has been suggested by several scholars that, like his Ferrarese brothers-in-law, Francesco was an early victim of the *mal francese*. The fevers and flux that he suffered from in the summer of 1496, as the Neapolitan campaign concluded, may have marked its onset, a possibility that is supported by the fact that in October of that year, after his return home to Mantua, Ercole d'Este sent Francesco a salve made from turpentine, cloves, and storax to reduce the pain he was experiencing in his jaw. Bernardino Zambotti's cousin, Zaccharia, probably delivered the remedy, since the doctor reported on its effects to the duke, writing from Mantua that the potion had worked well.[11] Francesco certainly came back from southern Italy in an enfeebled state, sleep deprivation, the marshy terrain, and contaminated

[8]   Zambotti, *Diario ferrarese*, entry dated 3 December 1497, 276–7. The diarist was informed by his cousin, Zaccharia Zambotti, who was still a doctor at the Este court.

[9]   For the extant treatises, see Alfonso Corradi, 'Nuovi documenti per la storia delle malattie veneree in Italia dalla fine del Quattrocento alla metà del Cinquecento', *Annali universali di medicina e chirurgia* 269 (1884): 289–386. On the debate and its participants, see Arrizabalaga et al., *The Great Pox*, 56–87; and Darrel W. Amundsen, *Medicine, Society, and Faith in the Ancient and Medieval Worlds* (Baltimore: Johns Hopkins University Press, 1996), 310–71.

[10]   'Diodato è gionto e non è stato da me da la prima volta in qua, perché, havendo la rogna, che qua se chiama franzosa, Maestro Mattheo Cremascho non ha voluto ch'el ritorni, dicendo che etiam che la persona non se tochi, è male che se atacha solamente a vederlo. Attenderà a liberarse et poi venire a darmi qualche recretione.' Isabella d'Este to Francesco Gonzaga, 26 July 1496, from Mantua, ASMn, AG, 2992, libro 7, cc. 78r–v.

[11]   Arrizabalaga et al., *The Great Pox*, 46–9. See also Alessandro Luzio, 'Contributo alla storia del malfrancese ne' costumi e nella letteratura italiana del sec. xvi', *Giornale storico della letteratura italiana* 5 (1885): 408–32.

water having taken their toll on his health, but whether the medicine from Ferrara was to treat the *mal francese*, or a lingering battlefield ailment, is impossible to establish on the basis of the extant evidence.

Francesco himself seems to have been in little doubt in early 1508 that his malaise was newly acquired, although it is possible the disease had gone into remission and then reappeared with other symptoms. By the time he retreated to Gonzaga, he knew he was suffering from the *mal francese* and had likely contracted the disease through sexual contact, a conviction that he probably arrived at not by listening to current medical theories about how the disease was transmitted, but, rather, intuitively, by observing his own body. Less than two weeks after his evasive letter to Isabella of 27 March 1508, he wrote to Alberto Pio, instructing his representative at the French court to inform Louis XII of his illness and to tell the king that it was probably caused by 'love'.[12] Given his wife's frequent pregnancies in the years between 1500 and 1508, Francesco's libidinous activities had likely been more than usually extramarital in these years. So, while he was understandably reluctant to admit to Isabella that he was suffering from a sexually transmitted disease, he was frank with the king, no doubt hoping that his predicament would elicit Louis XII's sympathy, given past discussions between the pair about their mutual dedication to the goddess of love. The French king's empathy proved to be both shallow and unenduring, especially after he came to suspect Francesco of malingering to keep his diplomatic options open.

Following his move from the San Giorgio castle to the San Sebastiano palace in April 1508, Francesco spent the rest of the year subjecting himself to the purges, cauterization of pustules, and application of pain-relieving salves that had become standard medical responses to the *morbus gallicus*, at least for elite sufferers, in the decade after its appearance.[13] A new bathroom with a sophisticated heating apparatus was installed in the palace to facilitate the frequent baths and sweating sessions that the doctors recommended to expel the humours that prevented recovery. Some of the courtiers who kept Francesco company were also victims of the disease; even the painter, Francesco Costa, who was working on frescoes for the marquis's new chambers at San Sebastiano, had been stricken.[14] Those free of the disease were co-opted into a sodality of sufferers. In early autumn, having

---

[12] 'Vostra Signoria haverà possuto intendere come de la indispositione in la quale siamo stati questi dì passati, al presente ni ritrovamo in assai bon termine, benché anchor dil tutto non siamo revaluti. Causa ni è stato, a nostro iudicio, amore. Il che, parendovi, potreti far intendere alla Maestà Christianessima, alla qual desideramo ni teniati continuamente raccomandandati.' Francesco Gonzaga to Alberto Pio, 11 April 1508, from Gonzaga, ASMn, AG, 2915, libro 200, c. 18.

[13] Arrizabalaga et al., *The Great Pox*, 28–32.

[14] See Costa's letter of 2 August 1508 to Francesco Gonzaga, in Bourne, *The Soldier-Prince*, 472–3. On Francesco's fellow sufferers at court, see Sally Hickson, 'Syphilis, Suffering and Sodality: Friendship and Contagion in Renaissance Mantua', in *Friendship and Sociability in Premodern Europe: Contexts, Concepts and Expressions*, ed. Amyrose McCue Gill and Sarah Rolfe (Toronto: Iter Press, 2014), 153–70.

been transported back to Gonzaga to take advantage of the health-giving country air, Francesco confided to Isabella that he was in such excruciating pain that it was impossible to sleep. He had therefore ordered his courtiers to keep a vigil with him for the entire night, so he might be distracted from his utter misery.[15]

As this chapter will show, Francesco's illness had a calamitous effect on his military career. The marquis's physical decline contributed to his capture in humiliating circumstances by Venetian forces in 1509 and rendered the subsequent imprisonment in Venice a time of great physical suffering and mental anguish. Isabella was obliged to face the political challenges that Francesco's status as a helpless Venetian prisoner provoked. The evident success with which she kept the population of Mantua calm during their prince's imprisonment and achieved her husband's release, without succumbing to attempts by both Louis XII and the Holy Roman Emperor to take the 10-year-old Federico hostage in exchange, changed the subsequent marital dynamic forever. Following Francesco's return to Mantua in late 1510, Isabella sought to build on the experience she had gained and expected to be rewarded with a greater degree of political responsibility and autonomy. The marquis resisted. Indeed, he attempted to impose greater oversight of Isabella's activities to compensate for an increasing physical frailty that compromised the vision of masculinity that he had always assiduously cultivated. This mismatch of views fuelled conflict between the pair.

Hope and Despair

The Treaty of Cambrai, finalized in December 1508, represented a ray of brightness for the ill and politically embattled Francesco. The pact reconciled his competing allegiances and military obligations, while holding out the possibility of a solution to the troublesome incursions on Mantua's borders, which had followed Emperor Maximilian I's declaration of war on Venice in February of that year. Driven by the desire to reclaim cities such as Verona and Vicenza, theoretically part of the Holy Roman Empire, as well as areas in the Dolomites that he regarded as his rightful possessions as duke of Austria, the emperor-elect had moved troops close to Mantuan territory, forcing the marquis to upgrade the fortifications in towns such as Goito and Castiglione Mantovano, near the border with Venice. Maximilian's peremptory demands for funds and military support, on the grounds that Francesco was an imperial vassal, had constituted another pressing problem, since Louis XII, too, regarded the marquis as obliged to help him to

---

[15] 'Expectando noi heri la nocte passata asperissima, per posserla meglio tolerare, havemo facto vigilar cum noi quasi tutta la nostra corte, per il passatempo de la quale e per la imaginatione più crudeli dil conveniente che ci ne havemo facta la c'è parsa alquanto tolerabile, non già perhò che gli dolori non ci habbino tormentato e facto star in continua vigilia.' Francesco Gonzaga to Isabella d'Este, 30 September 1508, from Gonzaga, ASMn, AG, 2117, c. 161.

reconquer former Milanese land that the Venetians had captured in the 1490s. To deny either ally was perilous; to serve one risked retribution from the other.

The eventual agreement of Maximilian I and Louis XII to put aside their mutual antipathy and join forces was facilitated in no small measure by the brilliant diplomacy of Niccolò Frisio, a Gonzaga agent of German origins, who plied indefatigably throughout 1508 between Innsbruck, Lichtenstein, Milan, Bourges, Lyon, Malines, and finally Cambrai, following the peregrinations of the French and imperial courts, or setting off to resolve the disputes over Navarre, Guelders, and Flanders that prevented a French-imperial accord.[16] Pope Julius II also eventually joined the League, as did Ferdinand of Spain, who wished to recover sea ports on the Apulian Coast that Venice had captured in 1495. Mantua and Ferrara were junior partners in the Cambrai alliance. However, the rulers of these small states were similarly motivated by a desire to regain territory that had fallen under Venetian control. Alfonso d'Este wanted the Polesine di Rovigo, lost to Venice in the early 1480s, during the War of Ferrara, while Francesco Gonzaga aspired to regain towns on and near Lake Garda, such as Asola, Lonato, and especially Peschiera, renowned for its beauty, that had been part of the Mantuan state in the previous century. Thus, the coalition of large and small powers was united by the desire to strip Venice of the mainland territory that the republic had accumulated over the course of the fifteenth century.

With the return of King Louis XII to northern Italy in late April 1509, the Venetian republic realized that its involvement in a war against an alliance of the pope, the emperor-elect, and two of Europe's most powerful kings was inevitable. Despite the chequered relationship with their one-time captain general, Venetian authorities had endeavoured to persuade Francesco Gonzaga to change sides, sending Carlo Valerio, a friend of the marquis, to offer him the position of captain and lieutenant general of the republic's forces, a status that would have given him authority over Bartolomeo Alviano and Niccolò Orsini, count of Pitigliano, Venice's most prominent and able military figures.[17] Such an appointment could not fail to boost Francesco's reputation and honour. Valerio had also held out the prospect of a Venetian salary of 60,000 ducats and, when this did not entice the marquis, even as much as 100,000 ducats.[18] Although neither the members of the League of Cambrai, nor the republic's officials, considered Francesco a brilliant soldier, each side wished to have him as an ally, since he controlled territory that

[16] Alessandro Luzio, 'I preliminari della Lega di Cambrai concordati a Milano ed a Mantova', *Archivio storico lombardo* 38 (1911): 245–310. For Frisio's diplomatic updates from all these places, see his letters at 299–310.

[17] Giuseppe Coniglio, 'Francesco Gonzaga e la Lega di Cambrai', *Archivio storico italiano* 120 (1962): 3–31 (20).

[18] For Francesco Gonzaga's account of the meeting with Carlo Valerio, see his letter of 23 March to the Mantuan ambassador in Milan, Iacopo Suardo, in Luzio, 'La reggenza d'Isabella d'Este', 6–7.

would be strategically crucial in the coming war. Francesco was convinced the French would win the day and threw in his lot with Louis XII.

In mid-April 1509, after experiencing a reprieve from the fevers and pain that had confined him to bed, Francesco set off for the valley of Sabbioneta to prepare his infantry for battle. Alarmed by news of this impulsive act, Isabella sent a flurry of worried letters in her husband's wake, pointing out that in his enthusiasm to put the months of sickness and immobility behind him, he had neglected to take account of the crisis looming on his own borders at Governolo, Ostiglia, and Pontemolino, where there were now insufficient soldiers to guard towns threatened with Venetian attack. She urged the need to pay attention to defensive, as well as offensive, military strategy, given that Mantua itself could be in danger. On 16 April, she wrote of the panic in the city: 'We all had a bad night because of frequent letters and messengers and the flares that indicated the [enemy] encampment was threateningly near.'[19] Apart from lacking troop reinforcements and supplies to send to the Venetian-Mantuan border, the marquis's manipulation of the waterways to flood areas that would impede the Venetian advance had submerged the mills. As Isabella pointed out to her husband, it was now impossible to grind sufficient grain to supply bread to the city and to the thinly stretched defenders of outpost towns.[20]

Buoyed by an initial minor victory at Casalmaggiore, Francesco travelled to Ostiglia to address the problems described by Isabella. He may have returned briefly to Mantua, but, by 24 April, he had set off again, intending to pay homage to the king in Milan. He only got as far as Canneto, on the Oglio River, some one hundred kilometres south-east of the Lombard capital, before collapsing. On 2 May, he reported dolefully to Isabella:

> But the miserable and restless night we have had because of the tremendous catarrh that molested us made us delay leaving today; and we risked a recurrence of fever and so, because of this, we intend to stay here two or three more days to see what transpires, even if we have in mind to go if nothing worse develops and we hear naught to the contrary from Milan.[21]

The provenance of Francesco's letters to Isabella indicates he remained at Canneto until 5 May. Orders then came from the king for the League's army to assemble

---

[19] 'Tutti havemo havuti una pessima nocte per rispecto de le frequentissime lettere et messi et lumere che indicavano venire il campo a damni nostri.' Isabella d'Este to Francesco Gonzaga, 16 April 1509, from Mantua, ASMn, AG, 2118bis, c. 123.

[20] Isabella explained this situation in letters to Francesco of 18 and 28 April 1509: ASMn, AG, 2118bis, cc. 142 and 158.

[21] 'Ma la trista et inquieta nocte che havemo havuto per il gran catharo che ni ha molestato, ni ha facto restare di partir hoggi e quasi ni è venuto uno pocho di febre, e per questo designamo anchor restar dui o tre giorni per vedere quel che la farà, pur siamo in penser di andar, non succedendo peggio, né venendo a nui altro in contrario da Milano.' Francesco Gonzaga to Isabella d'Este, 2 May 1509, from Canneto, ASMn, AG, 2118, c. 30.

near Lodi, on the River Adda, to the south of Milan, in readiness for an assault on Venetian territory.[22] Having recovered somewhat, Francesco gathered his meagre strength and rode off to encounter Louis XII and his army, which included six thousand Swiss mercenaries, at Cassano d'Adda. On 8 May, he reported to Isabella that he had been welcomed warmly by the king and pleasingly honoured by the League's generals.[23] He crossed to the Venetian side of the Adda River with the French forces on 9 May, the opposing camps now only a short distance apart.

Two days later, the marquis was again too ill to fight. The king dispatched three of his own doctors to tend Francesco, while the French and Italian captains also sent their personal physicians, the result of which was likely to have been heated debate about how best to treat the patient by experts from different intellectual and cultural backgrounds. As usual, Francesco sought to deny the seriousness of his plight by explaining his collapse in terms of the arduous days of travel on horseback, fully armed, that he had endured to reach the League's encampment. He assured Isabella that a few days of rest would restore him.[24] But the onset of excruciating pains in the thighs wiped out that optimism and Francesco agreed to be transferred from the League's camp to within the walls of the town of Cassano d'Adda. There, he was bled by a doctor whom he descibed to Isabella as excellent, being both 'very diligent' and 'loving'.[25] Perhaps sceptical about the worth of this unfamiliar physician, Isabella sent an herbalist from Mantua, so her husband could be 'discreetly and faithfully served' by one of his own subjects.[26]

While the marquis struggled with sleeplessness and submitted to regular bloodletting that led to the 'great weakness and weariness' he reported feeling after the treatment, the Battle of Agnadello was fought and won without him on 14 May 1509.[27] Due to a breakdown in communications between the Venetian generals, the republic's infantry found itself outflanked and suffered heavy losses. Much of its artillery was captured and the hitherto brilliant military strategist, Bartolomeo d'Alviano, was injured and captured by the French.[28] The king's gloating communication to Francesco of 16 May had a malevolent undertone, since he insinuated, only half-jokingly, that the marquis had revealed himself to

[22] Coniglio, 'Francesco Gonzaga e la Lega di Cambrai', 26–7.

[23] Francesco Gonzaga to Isabella d'Este, 8 May 1509, from Cassano d'Adda, ASMn, AG, 2118, cc. 39r–40r.

[24] Francesco Gonzaga to Isabella d'Este, 11 May 1509, from Cassano d'Adda, ASMn, AG, 2118, cc. 41r–v.

[25] 'Veneri sera ni facessimo portar in Cassano per star commodamente e farni curare e cum nui havemo il medico del Signor Zoanne Iacomo, qual è excellente et a nui molto diligente et amorevole.' Francesco Gonzaga to Isabella d'Este, 13 May 1509, from Cassano d'Adda, ASMn, AG, 2118, cc. 44v–46r.

[26] 'Per satisfare al debito et assicurare meglio l'animo mio et provedere che la sii ben servita, mando il Grossino a visitarla in mio nome et Francisco speciale, perché la sii più discretamente et fidelmente servita.' Isabella d'Este to Francesco Gonzaga, 15 May 1509, from Mantua, ASMn, AG, 2118bis, c.189.

[27] 'possemo quasi dir di non haver altro male che gran debeleza e straccheza.' Francesco Gonzaga to Isabella d'Este, 17 May 1509, from Cassano d'Adda, ASMn, AG, 2118, cc. 52r–53r.

[28] Mallett and Shaw, The Italian Wars, 1494–1559, 89–90.

be 'a coward'.[29] This scepticism about the severity of Francesco's illness was a foretaste of Louis XII's increasingly dismissive attitude towards his unreliable ally.

Isabella sympathetically acknowledged her husband's frustration at missing the battle and attempted to relieve the sting of the king's insults with a description of the celebrations she had ordered in Mantua to mark the Venetian defeat:

> At the hour of the bonfire, the whole piazza and all the windows were full of nobles and commonfolk. The children from the various neighbourhoods of the city built it and on top some erected a boat with a Venetian inside, others a man made out of rags bearing a sign that said: 'I am Bartolomeo d'Alviano', and thus amid the wild enthusiasm of the children they were set alight.[30]

Francesco replied immediately, expressing appreciation for Isabella's efforts to rally both the city and his spirits and agreeing 'that the main source of anguish was not the pain in his thigh, but not being with the king during this exploit'.[31] The next day, he insisted the fever had gone and that he would be able to return to the camp before the army was scheduled to move towards Brescia.[32]

On 28 May, he wrote buoyantly, informing Isabella that, having joined his military colleagues, he was able to participate in the taking of Lonato and had entered the town's walls in triumph, amid great cries of 'Turco' and 'Gonzaga'. Bursts of celebratory artillery had accompanied the journey to his lodgings and many women had surrounded him, touching his hands lovingly in homage, apparently in acknowledgement that Lonato would be now ruled once more by the Gonzaga. Francesco made the same assumption and concluded the letter with the news that he had heard that the king also intended to give him the towns of Peschiera del Garda and Sirmione, much admired for their situation overlooking Lake Garda, a reward that he knew Isabella would savour. However, this rumour proved to be entirely false. Not only did Louis XII command Francesco formally to renounce any claim to Peschiera, he insisted on French oversight of the fortresses of Asola, Lonato, and of other conquered towns near Brescia that Francesco had captured.[33]

---

[29] Louis XII's letter to Francesco Gonzaga from Caravaggio, in which he referred to the marquis as 'ung poultron', is published in Luzio, 'La reggenza d'Isabella d'Este', 9.

[30] 'A l'hora dil fallò, tutta la piaza et finestre erano piene di nobilità et populo. Li putti per le contrate ni hanno facti, sopra li quali alcuni haveano una barcha cum un Venetiano dentro, altri un homo di straze, cum un breve che diceva: "Io son Bartholomeo de la Viola", et cossì a furore de' putti, sono sta' brusati.' Isabella d'Este to Francesco Gonzaga, 17 May 1509, from Mantua, ASMn, 2118bis, c. 191.

[31] 'La Signoria Vostra dice ben la verità che magior dolore ni è stato non esserni ritrovato col Re in questo facto, che non è stato il male de la costa.' Francesco Gonzaga to Isabella d'Este, 17 May 1509, from Cassano d'Adda, ASMn, AG, 2118, cc. 52r–53r.

[32] Francesco Gonzaga to Isabella d'Este, 18 May 1509, from Cassano d'Adda, ASMn, AG, 2118, c. 55.

[33] Francesco Gonzaga to Isabella d'Este, 6 June 1509, from Peschiera, ASMn, AG, 2118, c. 76; Coniglio, 'Francesco Gonzaga e la Lega di Cambrai', 28. The document renouncing any claims to

As he took stock of this unwelcome and insulting turn of events, the marquis learned that Isabella intended to take a few days recreation at Cavriana. He assumed she wished to see the new Gonzaga possessions at Lake Garda, not having yet learned the bad news. Fearing that Cavriana's proximity to the French camp would encourage Louis XII to summon the marchioness and the Gonzaga children to a royal audience, Francesco sternly forbade his wife from leaving Mantua.[34] He harboured suspicions that the king might use such an occasion to take members of his family hostage, as part of a bid to gain control of the marquisate. Isabella replied defensively that her husband had seriously underestimated her:

> I did not wish to come to Cavriana to remain there, nor to visit the camp, because I also now hate the French too much, nor would I in the least have considered taking the children, because Your Excellency knows well how unwilling I take them with me, unless given explicit permission by you, and if the king had said he wished to see them, I would have had enough courage to deny him.[35]

Isabella constructed herself as defiant in the face of French treachery, but, in subsequent letters, perhaps worried that Francesco would be encouraged by her virile words to reveal his anger to the king, she advocated a guarded approach, knowing that her husband's courage often expressed itself in impetuous behaviour. To defuse the ill temper that might prompt him to act rashly, Isabella joked in a letter written in her own hand that she had hoped the hot weather would help her to lose weight, but, since that had not happened, she wanted now to relieve him of some of his chagrin about the 'cowardly' French: righteous anger about those she dubbed 'the most ungrateful people in the world' would surely make her thinner.[36] At thirty-five, and after multiple pregnancies between 1501 and 1508, Isabella was indeed beginning to grow stout, a situation she so failed to reverse that eventually she had trouble ascending the stairs to her apartments on the first floor of the San Giorgio castle. The self-deprecatory humour in Isabella's letter of 22 June

Peschiera that Francesco was obliged to sign is published in Pélissier, 'Les relations de François de Gonzague', 93–5.

[34] Francesco Gonzaga to Isabella d'Este, 10 June 1509, from Peschiera, ASMn, AG, 2118, c. 80.
[35] 'Io non voria venire a Capriana per firmarmi, né per venire in campo, perché pur troppo ho in odio adesso Francesi, né haveria a modo alcuno condutti figlioli, perché Vostra Excellentia scia bene che malvolunteri li conduco se expressamente Lei non mi lo commanda, et s'el Re havesse dicto de volerli vedere, mi seria bastato l'animo de negargelo.' Isabella d'Este to Francesco Gonzaga, 10 June 1509, from Mantua, ASMn, AG, 2118bis, c. 219.
[36] 'spero che questo caldo me aiutarà a smagrare da bon senno, ma se io havesse havuto de le fantasie et affanni che ha havuto Vostra Signoria da questi poltroni de francesi, forsi che non seria cossì grassa, ma ad ogni modo non se po' negare che non siano la più ingrata gente del mondo. Dio ge mandi secondo che desidero.' Isabella d'Este to Francesco Gonzaga, 22 June 1509, from Mantua, ASMn, AG, 2118bis, c. 229.

was perhaps designed to remind Francesco of her loyalty and to neutralize his anger by presenting the king's behaviour as beneath contempt. Although the marquis continued to nurse a fierce resentment about Louis XII's treachery, he seems to have managed to hide those emotions adequately when he was obliged to follow the king to Milan in July 1509.

Louis XII fell ill soon after his triumphant entry into Milan and, in early August, returned to France, leaving the emperor to continue the war against Venice. Francesco proceeded to Verona, to make sure the city remained under the League's control. There, he had the consolation of being greeted with acclaim by the local population, whose representatives invited him to preside over the city's government, perhaps on the grounds that at least he was a familiar figure, being in effect a neighbouring lord. However, imperial orders arrived, commanding Francesco to leave Verona and to occupy Legnano, some twenty kilometres to the south of Milan. After meeting with the bishop of Trent and his fellow captain, Lodovico della Mirandola, to plan the expedition, the two leaders set off with their troops on 7 August, stopping for the night at Isola della Scala, after completing the first leg of their journey.[37]

Francesco's Capture and Imprisonment

Although Francesco had assumed from the friendly reception accorded him in Verona that he had nothing to fear from its inhabitants, spies loyal to Venice had secretly tailed him, gleaning intelligence about his next movements. Having learned that he and Lodovico della Mirandola were to head to Legnano, the spies reported this intelligence to Venetian authorities, who decided to attempt to capture the marquis before he and his men reached their destination. Venetian infantry and light horsemen, led by the Bolognese captain Lucio Malvezzi, were already in the vicinity of Isola della Scala, so the plan was easily implemented. Under cover of night, the Venetian contingent approached the building where Francesco was lodging and quickly overcame the guards. Disturbed from sleep by the noise of battle below, the marquis managed to escape through a window and fled into a field of millet, where, perhaps somewhat injured, he was discovered at first light and captured by peasants loyal to Venice. Handed over to Malvezzi, Francesco was taken to Legnano under armed guard. Fifty of his most valuable horses, as well as precious silver vessels, armour and weapons, jewels, and cash, together representing a loss of some 20,000 ducats, fell into the hands of his captors. This catastrophe was a severe blow to the marquis's soldierly pride, but it also left a

---

[37] Roberto Cessi, 'La cattura del marchese Francesco Gonzaga di Mantova e le prime trattative per la sua liberazione', *Nuovo archivio veneto* 25 (1913): 144–76 (144).

great hole in his treasury.[38] After being taken first to Padua, Francesco made the humiliating journey to Venice in chains. The hero of Fornovo was promptly jailed in the doge's palace and thereafter treated harshly as a Venetian prisoner of war.[39] For a man who was used to the best medical care available to treat the painful symptoms of the *mal francese*, incarceration represented a terrible disaster.

After a string of losses that saw Venice's mainland territory almost entirely eliminated, the capture of Francesco Gonzaga helped to restore the republic's fortunes and morale, already modestly on the ascendant with the recovery of Padua in mid-July 1509. Venetian resolve was strengthened by the possession of the considerable bargaining chip represented by their hostage, whose precarious health made his release from imprisonment a matter of urgency for Isabella, if, it seemed at first, for no one else. Having learned of her husband's predicament on 8 August, the marchioness immediately took steps to secure her control of the state. She wrote to the officials in charge of towns and villages throughout the marquisate, urging them to keep the borders under strict surveillance and reassuring them that she had things in hand. Isabella also summoned home her brother-in-law, Sigismondo Gonzaga, then serving as papal legate in Macerata, so he could bolster her authority, now more likely to be challenged without the direct backing of her husband. While Francesco was locked up in Venice, she took care to have Sigismondo counter-sign edicts and important diplomatic communications.

On 9 August, Isabella informed Pope Julius II of Francesco's imprisonment and appealed for help. Because of her efforts to help the Bentivoglio women in the years following the papal reclaiming of Bologna in 1506, Julius had hitherto regarded the marchioness with disfavour. However, he replied amiably enough a week and a half later, promising to do what he could to secure the marquis's release.[40] Louis XII, however, entertained scarce sympathy for his Mantuan ally, claiming Francesco had ignored his advice and had reaped the consequences. Indeed, the king's barely concealed readiness to profit from Francesco's plight was made plain by his immediate offer to instal a French presence in Mantua, purportedly to secure Isabella's authority, but opening the way for the possibility of adding Gonzaga territory to his northern Italian conquests. The marchioness replied politely, but resolutely, assuring the king that she remained his utterly loyal ally, but had no need of protection.[41] Maximilian then pressed her to accept an imperial advisor. Isabella resisted this suggestion as well, calling on her

---

[38] As Francesco admitted in a letter of 28 August 1509 to Lodovico Brognolo, his ambassador in Rome. See Luzio, 'La reggenza d'Isabella d'Este', 12.

[39] For contemporary accounts of Francesco's capture, see Cessi, 'La cattura del marchese Francesco Gonzaga'.

[40] Luzio, 'La reggenza d'Isabella d'Este', 15–16.

[41] Isabella d'Este to Louis XII, 12 August 1509, from Mantua, in Luzio, 'La reggenza d'Isabella d'Este', 18.

brother-in-law, Giovanni Gonzaga, stationed in Verona as an imperial captain, to make sure the emperor-elect did not attempt to implement such a plan.[42]

Although Isabella managed to evade the threat of imperial interference in the government of the marquisate, the emperor made other difficulties, by demanding financial help and provisions to continue the war against Venice. Squeezing more taxes out of the population already impoverished by the disruptions of war risked an upsurge of discontent from her subjects. Isabella therefore sent only minimal assistance, adroitly placating Maximilian through empty promises. But there were also serious border tensions, caused by the unruly, and sometimes criminal, behaviour of soldiers under French command, who treated Mantuan subjects as if they were enemies, rather than allies. Isabella admitted to her brother Alfonso that the problems engulfing her from all sides were so dire that she was often quite beside herself: 'my brain is rarely at home', as she colourfully put it.[43]

The unlikelihood of Louis XII assisting to bring about Francesco's release from imprisonment was borne in on Isabella by the news that he had received coldly the suggestion, approved by the pope, that the most important French prisoner of war, Bartolomeo d'Alviano, whom the Venetians were keen to get back, could be freed in exchange. The French envoy delivered a message from the king which asserted that d'Alviano's worth as a general far outweighed that of the marquis and the proposed swap was not equal enough.[44] Isabella therefore turned her attention more earnestly to Julius II. She decided to hasten the marriage of her daughter Eleonora to the pope's nephew, Francesco Maria della Rovere, hoping that the wedding would please the pontiff and provide an occasion for the young couple to lobby him to expedite Francesco's freedom.[45]

Around the same time, the Venetians attempted to turn the tide of the war by sending a fleet of ships to Polesine della Rovere, which the duke of Ferrara had occupied, hoping to regain this valuable area. On learning that seventeen Venetian war galleys and many other vessels were making their way down the Po, Isabella sent infantry and light horse to guard Mantuan settlements near the river and urged Count Iacopo Probo d'Atri, the Gonzaga ambassador in France, to persuade Louis XII to send help. Given earlier signs of the king's indifference to the fate of the marquisate, Isabella suggested to the envoy that he try to convince the king that he ought to ensure that Mantua remained safe, in order to protect Ferrara, his ally, since 'the ruin of one state would provoke that of the other'.

[42] Luzio, 'La reggenza d'Isabella d'Este', 18–19, 26.

[43] Isabella d'Este to Alfonso d'Este, 23 November 1509, from Mantua, in Luzio, 'La reggenza d'Isabella d'Este', 27.

[44] Luzio, 'La reggenza d'Isabella d'Este', 28.

[45] Isabella described her daughter's departure from Mantua in a letter to Lodovico Brognolo of 10 December. Published in Luzio and Renier, Mantova e Urbino, 191–2.

However, she warned d'Atri to put the case carefully, 'so that they do not decide to place troops here, because, as we have said, we hope there will be no need for that'.[46]

The almost complete rout of the powerful Venetian fleet by Ferrarese forces came as a great surprise to contemporaries. The victory was engineered by clever military strategy on the part of Isabella's brother, Cardinal Ippolito d'Este, who, under cover of darkness, positioned artillery at Polesella, where the Venetian fleet had withdrawn, after being forced back from Ferrara by artillery fire. The cardinal's forces attacked, as dawn was breaking, taking the stationary Venetian ships unawares and rendering them helpless in the first crucial part of the battle. Six galleys were destroyed and nine captured, the shocking defeat again causing utter despair in Venice.[47] A delighted Isabella impulsively sent the news of the Ferrarese victory to her brother-in-law, Giovanni Gonzaga, who was still stationed in Verona. Unfortunately, the letter fell into Venetian hands and helped further to inflame opinion against the marchioness, who was already viewed suspiciously by the Venetian regime because of her Ferrarese origins. Moreover, republican attitudes did not sit well with a woman exerting such significant political authority.

Thus, when Isabella dispatched the prior of the sanctuary of Santa Maria delle Grazie to Venice in mid-January 1510, to intercede for the conditions under which Francesco was being held to be improved, she received no satisfaction. As she complained by letter to the Mantuan ambassadors at the French court, her envoy Fra Anselmo was denied permission to visit the marquis and the authorities had sent him away with a message that the marchioness was regarded as an enemy of the Venetian state on the grounds that not only had she sought to help the duke of Ferrara, she had permitted the League's troops to traverse Mantuan territory and sent provisions to Verona at the request of the emperor. Isabella's gloating letter about the Venetian loss on the Po was the final straw. The republican authorities accused Isabella of being 'entirely Francophile' and of taking far too little account of the vulnerable situation of her imprisoned and seriously ill spouse.[48]

Isabella was reassured to learn from other sources that Francesco's health was stable. He had been visited by his stable master, whose humble social rank perhaps persuaded the Venetian authorities that he posed no danger and the two men had conversed at length about the marquis's beloved horses. The composer and singer, Marchetto Cara, and the lute player, Giovan Angelo Testagrossa, who had both been in Francesco's employ before he was captured, were also allowed to

---

[46] 'possiati ricordare che la ruina di uno stato tira drieto l'altro; ma adverteti parlare per modo che non si pensassi metterni gente in casa perché, come havemo dicto, speramo non bisognarà.' Isabella d'Este to Jacopo d'Atri, 4 December 1509, from Mantua, in Luzio, 'La reggenza d'Isabella d'Este', 32.

[47] Mallett and Shaw, *The Italian Wars*, 95.

[48] Isabella d'Este to Iacopo Suardo and Iacopo Probo d'Atri, 17 January 1510, ASMn, AG, 2192, unnumbered. This letter is partially transcribed in Cockram, *Isabella d'Este and Francesco Gonzaga*, 216–17.

visit from time to time, and it was perhaps via these means that husband and wife passed the occasional surreptitious message.[49] But Francesco was unable to communicate directly with Isabella by letter. Between 20 August 1509 and 29 September 1510, he was largely incommunicado. The stilted last letter of August 1509, sent from Venice immediately after his capture, is unusual for its use of singular personal pronouns, rather than the plural 'we' and 'our' that denoted Francesco's superior status. The communication reassured Isabella that he was well, entrusted 'his state, children, servants, and horses' to her, asked for money, sent greetings to his brother, Cardinal Sigismondo, and requested that prayers be said for him by the nuns of Corpus Christi.[50] The anxious and beaten tone of the message must have made it entirely clear to Isabella how entirely at the mercy of his captors her husband now was. This was the most testing political challenge she had yet faced.

Resolution of the Impasse

In early 1510, upset by the scale of the Venetian defeats which he considered would only facilitate the expansion of the Ottoman Empire, Julius II decided to reconcile with Venice and lift the papal interdict on the republic. The pope was intent on a crusade against the Turks and wanted Venetian help. He had also become alarmed at the prospect of the king of France controlling so much of northern Italy.[51] During early discussions between the papal and Venetian envoys, it was suggested that Francesco Gonzaga could be released, if he agreed to become captain-general of the Venetian forces and renounced his agreements with Louis XII and Maximilian I. Rumours of this possibility soon reached the ears of the emperor and the French king, who reacted furiously, each in turn insisting that the 10-year-old Federico Gonzaga be handed over as a hostage to prevent such an outcome. Maximilian's demand arrived in mid-March, while Louis sent his representative, Galeazzo Visconti, to Mantua in early May, with the message that Federico should be dispatched at once to Paris to guarantee that his father did not change sides.[52]

---

[49] 'Dal Buseto, qual andò col Folenghino a Venetia, ritornato, intendemo ch'el signore sta bene de la persona et che admisero Zoanfrancisco, maestro de stalla, et lui a visitarlo, pigliando sua excellentia grande spasso a parlare cum Zoanfrancisco di soi cavalli; et che gli admettono qualche volta Marchetto et Testa Grossa a recrearlo cum soni et canti. Queste cose ni portiamo qualche conforto, quando di cuore fussoro facte.' Isabella d'Este to Iacopo Suardo and Iacopo Probo d'Atri, 17 January 1510, from Mantua, ASMn, AG, 2192, unnumbered.

[50] 'io son sana et desidero il simile de voi, si stati de bona voglia et spero in la benignità et umanità di questa signoria presto la mi consolarà voi e mi; vi ricomando il stato, li figlioli, li mei servitori e li mei cavalli, mandatime denari et aricomandatime al cardinal se l'è venuto, et a voi, moier mia cara, mi ricomando faci pregare Dio per mi a le mie sore dil Corpo de Christo.' Francesco Gonzaga to Isabella d'Este, 20 August 1509, from Venice, ASMn, AG, 2118, c. 107.

[51] Mallett and Shaw, *The Italian Wars*, 97.

[52] Luzio, 'La reggenza d'Isabella d'Este', 46–7, 50–1.

Isabella refused to countenance either demand, although Alfonso d'Este put great pressure on his sister to capitulate to the French, on the grounds that it was too risky to resist such a powerful king. But the astute diplomacy of the marchioness and her envoys deflected disaster, even if Louis XII presented his agreement not to insist that Isabella send her son to Paris immediately as a temporary concession. On 8 June, she wrote gratefully to the king, thanking him for allowing her to keep Federico with her, while he was still so young. On the same day, Isabella also thanked the queen, Anne of Brittany, for permitting the postponement of Ippolita Gonzaga's departure for France to serve as a royal lady-in-waiting, until the girl reached the age of twelve or thirteen.[53] The prospect of two of her children being so far away, and in the hands of a great foreign power, was thoroughly unpalatable to Isabella. Ippolita, in fact, never left Mantua. In October 1511, when she was ten, her parents reluctantly agreed to allow her to profess her vows at the Dominican convent of San Vincenzo, where she eventually became prioress.[54]

The fate of Federico, however, continued to be an issue, since Venice now held out the possibility of releasing the marquis, if he agreed to allow his eldest son to replace him as a hostage. After ten months of incarceration, Francesco seemed to be open to this solution and apparently wrote to Isabella advocating the exchange. That letter does not survive, but Isabella refers to its contents in a response of 14 May 1510, in which she set out her many objections to the plan:

> Your Lordship must be certain that I want nothing in the world more than [to free you], but it pains and torments me to say I cannot do it, since I see clearly herein the danger—in fact the certainty—of ruin for our state, our children, and your own person, for I recognize that even if Federico were to go to Venice, we would still not be sure of your freedom. On the contrary, there would be motive to keep you longer in prison, as they would have both you and your son there, which would be a double worry for you and for me.... Though Your Excellency for this reason may disdain me and deny me your love and your grace, I will be more content to abide with you in this state of disobedience while preserving your state for you than I would be to reside in your grace and see you, together with your children, be deprived of it. I hope that in time, given your prudence and goodness, you will see that I have been more loving toward you than you have been toward yourself.[55]

The extent to which Francesco really wanted his young son to replace him as a Venetian hostage cannot be ascertained, given that information about his state of

---

[53] Isabella d'Este to Louis XII, 8 June 1510, from Mantua, in Isabella d'Este, *Selected Letters*, 327 and n. 47.

[54] Isabella d'Este to Lucrezia d'Este Bentivoglio, 3 and 5 October 1511, from Mantua, in Isabella d'Este, *Selected Letters*, 350–1.

[55] Isabella d'Este to Francesco Gonzaga, 14 May 1510, from Mantua, in Isabella d'Este, *Selected Letters*, 325–7.

mind comes almost entirely from Venetian sources. The chronicler, Marino Sanudo, for example, portrays the marquis as mentally fragile and resentful towards Isabella for preferring to help the Este cause, rather than that of her husband and children. According to Sanudo's account, upon receiving Isabella's letter, Francesco shouted: 'That whore, my wife, is to blame.' [56] Even if this version of the marquis's reception of his wife's letter is accurate, it is likely that Francesco staged his outrage for Venetian consumption. However, Isabella had no way of establishing her husband's attitude and worried that the rumours of his furious reaction to her letter meant that he bitterly disapproved of her refusal to send Federico to Venice to secure his release.

Eventually an agreement with Venice was worked out, thanks to the intervention of the pope. Although Julius II purported to resent Isabella's intransigent refusal to send Federico to Venice, he eventually brokered a deal in which Francesco would be freed, not on condition that he became captain-general of the Venetian forces, but rather standard-bearer, or gonfalonier, of the Church. Similarly, Federico would be sent as a hostage to the papal court, instead of to Venice. Francesco was set free on 14 July 1510 and travelled immediately to Rimini to thank the pope for securing his release. Having discovered that Julius II was actually in Bologna, he made his way there and was briefly reunited with his son, Federico, who had joined the papal entourage. Francesco was formally appointed as gonfalonier of the Church, a position that Julius II had taken away from Alfonso d'Este in retaliation for the duke of Ferrara's refusal to renounce his alliance with Louis XII and to restore the much-prized wetlands of the Polesine di Rovigo to Venice. Although Francesco was not able to return to Mantua for some time, Isabella's fears that her husband was angry with her were put to rest by the courtier, Federico Cattaneo, who had intercepted the marquis and reported he was well and in good spirits. In her reply, Isabella instructed Cattaneo to thank Francesco for the bracelet he had sent her, along with the gift of the town of Asola and all its income, as recompense for her diligence on his behalf.[57]

Francesco's satisfaction with his wife continued. Once Isabella could communicate again with her husband via messengers and letters, she was careful to defer to his authority, so as not to give the impression that the period in almost sole charge of the marquisate had changed the way she operated politically. After she apologized for opening a letter addressed to him from the Mantuan ambassador to France, Francesco replied warmly to Isabella, insisting he had complete faith in her:

Your Ladyship has done well to open the letter from Iacopo d'Atri, nor was it necessary to apologize to me. On the contrary, we want you henceforth to

---

[56] Luzio, 'La reggenza d'Isabella d'Este', 57.
[57] Isabella d'Este to Federico Cattaneo, 18 July 1510, from Mantua, in Isabella d'Este, *Selected Letters*, 330–1.

open everything, and then send only the most important, or a summary [of incoming mail].[58]

This reassuring letter in fact post-dated an incident which, Isabella admitted, had constituted an error of judgement on her part. With her husband and brothers on opposite sides of Julius's military campaign to reclaim Ferrara as a papal possession, Isabella had been working surreptitiously to impede the pope's plans by passing on intelligence to Alfonso and Ippolito d'Este. As she explained to Alfonso in a letter of 9 October, she had intended to meet secretly with Cardinal Ippolito at Brescello, travelling first to Viadana so that she might spend the night there and discretely cross the border early the next day to meet her brother. However, false rumours had spread within Mantua that Francesco Gonzaga was about to become captain-general of the Venetian forces and it was feared by some at court, including Giovanni Gonzaga, that if the marchioness left the state, the population might assume she would not return, preferring to support her natal family, rather than her husband and children.[59] Isabella was advised by her brother-in-law and senior bureaucrats that she should on no account leave Mantua. Although annoyed that she might be suspected of such absurd and treasonous behaviour, Isabella reluctantly stayed put and sent Mario Equicola and Benedetto Capilupi to explain the situation to Francesco. She also wrote a letter in her own hand, confessing to her mistake and begging forgiveness.[60]

Francesco does not seem to have doubted his wife's good intentions. Indeed, he too wished to aid the Este and to curry favour with Louis XII by doing so, since he was acutely aware of the dangers to Mantua that the French army's presence in northern Italy represented. The marquis approved Isabella's policy of tacitly allowing the king's infantry to pass through Mantuan territory and endorsed her measures to minimize pillaging and lawlessness by the soldiers. In late October 1510, when French soldiers sacked the area between Verona and Marmirolo, Francesco urged Isabella to organize the rounding up of livestock, so they could be brought to more secure areas.[61] He used the French incursions on his borders

---

[58] 'Vostra Signoria ha facto bene in aprire la lettera de Jacomo d'Hatria, né era necessario che la ni facessi scusa cum nuy. Anci, volemo che da mo in anti tutte si aprino per Lei, facendoni poi mandare lo exemplo o summario.' Francesco Gonzaga to Isabella d'Este, 30 October 1510, from Sermide, ASMn, AG, 2119, c. 22.

[59] Isabella d'Este to Alfonso d'Este, 9 October 1510, from Mantua, in Isabella d'Este, *Selected Letters*, 334–5.

[60] 'Confesso haver errato in volere uscire de Mantoa senza licentia de Vostra Signoria, cosa che mai più feci et spero non havendo più comisso tale errore se non adesso, spero che Vostra Signoria serà tanto più facile a perdonarmelo.' Isabella d'Este to Francesco Gonzaga, 21 October, 1510, from Mantua, ASMn, AG, 2119, c. 75.

[61] Isabella d'Este to Francesco Gonzaga, 31 October 1510, from Mantua, ASMN, AG, 2119, cc. 91 and 93r–92r; and Francesco Gonzaga to Isabella d'Este, 1 November 1510, from the papal encampment, ASMn, AG, 2119, c. 27.

as an excuse to seek permission from the pope to return to Mantua, hoping that Julius II, who had fallen gravely ill, would soon die.

Having secured a reluctant permission from the pope to return home, by 9 November, Francesco had moved to his palace at Goito, a well-fortified outpost on the road towards Brescia. He claimed to have had a relapse of *mal francese* and to be undergoing a cure. When Julius II unexpectedly recovered at the end of November and took up arms once more, the marquis refused to budge, citing chronic ill health to explain his inability to lead the papal armies. Not believing this excuse, the reinvigorated pope fulminated against Francesco, accusing him of being shamefully dominated by his Ferrarese-born wife, whose Francophile sympathies were entirely driving Gonzaga policy.

This criticism upset Ludovico (Vigo) Camposampiero, an intimate companion and agent of the marquis, who harboured a deep grudge against Isabella after she had punished him in 1504 for lewd behaviour towards Giovanna Boschetta, one of her ladies-in-waiting, and thereafter treated him with distain, aware that her husband's crony was also, occasionally, his pimp.[62] Camposampiero assured Francesco in a letter of 22 March 2011, sent from the papal encampment at Ravenna, that he had informed Julius II that his master was most keen to return to the battlefield and was certainly not ruled by his wife:

> I replied to His Holiness that... Your Excellency was one of those men who little allow themselves to be governed by women...and that you wore the trousers and that you treated the illustrious marchesa well, and better than any queen or duchess that was in Italy a long time hitherto, but that otherwise you left her to her trifling affairs and in matters of state you knew well how to act for yourself without female counsel, at which His Holiness was most pleased with my speech.[63]

Francesco thanked his defender, but in bland terms, since he had no intention of resuming his duties as standard-bearer of the Church and could hardly have failed to recognize that he himself had made sure that Isabella had never confined herself to trifling female tasks.[64]

Moreover, if the marquis's excuse, in late 1510, that he was too sick to fight was a fabrication, by the autumn of 1511 it was not. Writing from Goito, Francesco informed Isabella on 22 September that: 'since arriving here, we have felt not the

---

[62] On the mutual antipathy between Vigo Camposampiero and Isabella, see Cockram, *Isabella d'Este and Francesco Gonzaga*, 109–10. On this figure more generally, see Roberto Zappieri, 'Ludovico Camposampiero', in *Dizionario Biografico Italiano*, 17, 1974, http://www.treccani.it/enciclopedia/ludovico-camposampiero_%28Dizionario-Biografico%29.

[63] Lodovico Camposampiero to Francesco Gonzaga, 22 March 1511, from Ravenna, ASMn, AG, 859, cc. 483r–487r. Quoted and translated in Cockram, *Isabella d'Este and Francesco Gonzaga*, 176.

[64] See Cockram, *Isabella d'Este and Francesco Gonzaga*, 176–7, n. 79.

least bit better and we continue thus, passing the time, and among other things we have such a poor appetite, that we can't taste anything we eat.'[65] On 27 November, still at Goito, he reported to his wife in similarly melancholic terms: 'We are much the same, passing the time, without being able throw off the illness completely; when it is pleasing to the divine goodness we will recover.'[66]

With the belligerent Julius II still determined to wrest Ferrara from the Este, a new Holy League between Spain, the papacy, and Venice proclaimed in October 1511, the emperor demanding funds to promulgate his war against the Venetian republic, and soldiers of every stripe ravaging the Mantuan countryside, Francesco's poor health was a useful diplomatic excuse, since the only ways in which the Gonzaga regime could be preserved in the face of all these challenges was through subterfuge and systematic temporizing to see which way the political winds would ultimately blow. Although obliged to serve as standard-bearer of the Church until July 1512, the marquis continued to avoid his military obligations on the grounds of illness. Similarly, when the emperor demanded in March 1512 that the marquis represent him as governor of Verona, Francesco agreed, but continued to postpone taking up the position, arguing he was still too unwell.[67] To the king of France he was just as evasive, declaring that he could not be seen as overtly Francophile, because of Julius II's control over the fate of his eldest son, Federico. On 18 April 1512, Francesco even instructed Iacopo Probo d'Atri, the Mantuan ambassador to France, to explain to Louis XII that he could not promise any support in writing, because his illness had made his fingers so swollen that he could not wield a pen, even to sign his name.[68]

This letter was dispatched to the French court a week after the Battle of Ravenna, an epic encounter between Louis XII's army, led by the intrepid young commander, Gaston de Foix, and the papal-Spanish forces of the Holy League. Fought on Easter Sunday, the battle had resulted in the death of between ten and twenty thousand men, a figure that staggered contemporaries, still unused to the lethal consequences of more powerful artillery that had begun to be deployed around this time. The large canons of Isabella's brother, Alfonso d'Este, contributed significantly to the French victory. Nonetheless, while the League's losses were three times those of the French, Gaston de Foix and a disproportionate number of other French commanders were killed, news of which likely influenced Francesco's non-committal excuses to Louis XII. He perhaps suspected that the

---

[65] 'Dopo la venuta nostra qui, non ci sentimo melioramento alcuno, et andemo purre cusì passando il tempo, et tra le altre cose havemo tanto tristo appetito, che non gustamo cosa che manziamo.' Francesco Gonzaga to Isabella d'Este, 22 September 1511, from Goito, ASMn, AG, 2119, c. 197.

[66] 'Noi andammo purre cussì passando tempo, né possemo però levarci il male in tutto da dosso; quando piacerà alla divina bontà ci revaleremo.' Francesco Gonzaga to Isabella d'Este, 27 November 1511, from Goito, ASMn, AG, 2119, c. 207.

[67] Luzio, 'Isabella d'Este di fronte a Giulio II', 72–3.

[68] Francesco Gonzaga to Iacomo d'Atri, 18 April 1512, in Luzio, 'Isabella d'Este di fronte a Giulio II', 72.

decimation of the French leadership would ultimately cripple the king's military campaign, as indeed occurred. The main army was forced to retreat before a reinvigorated League attack in the late spring of 1512, leaving just a few French strongholds in northern Italy within fortified castles and bastions.[69]

The Congress of Mantua

The rapid collapse of French power on the Italian peninsula left the Holy League unprepared as to how the spoils of the war should be divided. Much to Julius II's fury, Cardinal Matthäus Lang von Wellenburg, bishop of Gurk and Maximilian I's representative, took the initiative, deciding that rather than proceeding to Rome, he should convene a conference of the victors in northern Italy, which would both decide the fate of Lombard cities no longer under French control and exact retribution from the Italian states, such as Florence and Ferrara, that had thrown in their lot with Louis XII. As an imperial feudatory, Mantua seemed to him a suitable place for that meeting.[70]

Scheduled for mid-August 1512, the Congress of Mantua provided Isabella with an opportunity to lobby the delegates not to support the eviction of the Este from Ferrara, or at least to delay obeying the pope's order that the League should launch an immediate military campaign against her brothers. Isabella had already ingratiated herself with Cardinal Lang months before, during the imperial campaign against Venice, by allowing his soldiers secretly to traverse Mantuan territory and cross the Po River near her isolated villa at Sacchetta. In the immediate prelude to the Congress, she also made contact with the other major attendee: Ramón Folc de Cardona-Anglesola, the Spanish viceroy of Naples and captain general of the League's army. She wrote to him on 25 July, a little over two weeks before his arrival in Mantua, thanking him for his benign attitude to her brother Alfonso and declaring herself at his service.[71] Although the duke of Ferrara was technically an enemy of Spain, like Isabella herself, he was connected to the Spanish royal house through maternal Aragonese descent, a relationship that served to mitigate his French allegiance.

Matthäus Lang arrived in Mantua at the end of July. He was welcomed by a reception in the San Giorgio castle and then with a banquet held the following day outside Francesco's palace of San Sebastiano, which had recently been extended and was still undergoing some final decoration.[72] These events are documented in letters from Amico Maria della Torre, a court secretary, to Federico Gonzaga

---

[69] Mallett and Shaw, *The Italian Wars*, 106–9.   [70] Mallett and Shaw, *The Italian Wars*, 117.
[71] Luzio, 'Isabella d'Este di fronte a Giulio II', 111–12.
[72] See Molly Bourne, *The Soldier-Prince*, 188–210.

in Rome.[73] Having learned of Cardinal Lang's susceptibility to female charm, Isabella organized what della Torre describes as 'an army of the principal noble-women of the land' to attend both occasions.[74] The other crucial attendee, Ramón de Cardona, was welcomed to Mantua on August 12. His first encounter with the marchioness is vividly narrated in another of Amico della Torre's letters to Federico:

> Milady came to meet him in the main room of the castle, where he greeted her with great courtesy, and those beautiful manners that she knows how to deploy so well stupefied the entire entourage of the viceroy. The pair vied for a good while to cede precedence and to place each other on the right, until Milady was forced by the viceroy to remain on the more honourable side, and thus everyone went into the painted room [Andrea Mantegna's *Camera degli sposi*] and, after remaining there talking for some time, the gentlemen of the viceroy went to see all the rooms of Milady, which they praised to the skies, the company claiming that they had never seen such refined spaces, not witnessed such refined decorations.[75]

As standard-bearer of the Church, the pope expected Francesco to lobby the Congress delegates for an attack on Ferrara at the earliest opportunity. However, after attending the first session of the Diet, held on 13 August, Francesco instructed his ambassador in Rome to inform Julius II that he had returned home 'so tired, destroyed, and in such a bad way' that he doubted he would be able to return. He claimed that he had advised the attendees that they should abandon Mantua and reconvene in Rome, something he knew the pope fervently wished for.[76] Isabella continued to be far more active. Through lavish hospitality offered against a backdrop of impressive architecture and art works, and with the help of the seductive charms of her female entourage, Isabella successfully influenced the outcome of the Congress without actually attending its sessions.

By 18 August, the marchioness could assure her brother, Cardinal Ippolito d'Este, that despite the pope's insistence that the League turn its immediate atten-tion to an attack on Ferrara, the conference attendees had decided to defer this campaign until other aims, such as returning the Medici to Florence and resolv-ing who would govern Milan, had been finalized.[77] After negotiations between

---

[73] Extracts from Amico Maria della Torre's letters to Federico Gonzaga are published in Luzio, 'Isabella d'Este di fronte a Giulio II', 112–15.

[74] Amico Maria della Torre to Federico Gonzaga, 4 August 1512, from Mantua, in Luzio, 'Isabella d'Este di fronte a Giulio II', 113.

[75] Amico Maria della Torre to Federico Gonzaga, 13 August 1512, from Mantua, in Luzio, 'Isabella d'Este di fronte a Giulio II', 114.

[76] Francesco Gonzaga to Folenghino, 14 August 1512, from Mantua, in Luzio, 'Isabella d'Este di fronte a Giulio II', 115–16.

[77] Luzio, 'Isabella d'Este di fronte a Giulio II', 117.

the Swiss and imperial representatives, it was agreed that Massimiliano Sforza, the 19-year-old son of Lodovico il Moro—who had been raised in exile by the emperor's niece, Margaret of Austria—should become the new duke of Milan. Although it was the presence at the conference of Cardinal Giovanni de' Medici that facilitated the decision to support the return of his family to Florence, Isabella welcomed this resolution as well, knowing that it would tie up the League's army in Tuscany and delay an attack on Ferrara.[78]

Following the conclusion of the Congress, a farewell party was held at Francesco's villa of Poggio Reale, situated on the other side of the lake from the San Giorgio castle and offering spectacular views across the water to the city. Inspired by the Florentine residence of the Gonzaga agent in Florence, Angelo Tovaglia, and probably influenced, too, by both Lorenzo de' Medici's villa of Poggio a Caiano and Alfonso II d'Aragona's palace of Poggio Reale in Naples, the Mantuan version of these all'antica buildings was largely complete by the end of 1508.[79] Isabella hosted the lavish occasion, again deploying Mantua's female elite to enchant the visitors. According to another of Federico's correspondents, the city was so impressively full during the imperial Diet that it seemed 'like another Rome'.[80]

While the pope did not resent the League's installation of Massimiliano as duke of Milan, on the grounds that at least the state was to be ruled by an Italian, rather than a foreigner, or even the reestablishment of Medici rule in Florence, he was outraged by the decision to postpone the military campaign against Ferrara. He blamed Francesco for failing to defend the papal agenda, instead remaining passively idle, while the outcome of the Diet was manipulated by Isabella from the sidelines. The marquis exculpated himself, citing his utter powerlessness to prevent his wife's secret manoeuvrings to help her relatives:

> It may well be, as we have written other times, that our lady consort, who is after all Don Alfonso's sister, and tender to that blood from which she is born and who is a woman of her own opinion, keeps some intelligence of letters and envoys with that court, but hidden from us, as she knows very well the displeasure we would have and the protest we would make if we knew.[81]

Francesco's disclaimer was patently a lie. Yet the papal barbs directed at his failure to control his wife may not have entirely glanced off. The perception that he was ruled by a woman, who had shown she could govern Mantua on her own and had now successfully swayed the outcomes of the Congress, must have been

---

[78] Mallett and Shaw, The Italian Wars, 117–18.   [79] Bourne, The Soldier-Prince, 165–79.

[80] Amico Maria della Torre to Federico Gonzaga, 20 August 1513, from Mantua, in Bourne, The Soldier-Prince, 500–1.

[81] Francesco Gonzaga to Alessandro Gabbioneta, 22 December 1512, from Mantua. Quoted and translated in Cockram, Isabella d'Este and Francesco Gonzaga, 181.

humiliating for a man who had always insisted on having ultimate oversight of Isabella's diplomacy.

The couple wrote rarely to each other in 1511 and 1512, since they were both in Mantua, or its environs, during these years. There are no indications of marital tensions in their few letters, which mainly discuss Francesco's poor state of health. But there is some indirect evidence that Francesco was concerned about Isabella's high political profile and determined to rein in her influence. He made sure, for example, that the palace of San Sebastiano was now the main centre of diplomatic engagement, not the San Giorgio castle. As the visit to her rooms by the Spanish viceroy and his entourage during the Congress attested, Isabella's *studio* and *grotta* had become a site of diplomatic pilgrimage. The marquis seems to have attempted to outshine Isabella's achievement in the magnificent later additions to his palace of San Sebastiano.

Giorgio Vasari describes a room in this urban palace, in which the painter, Lorenzo Costa, executed four allegorical works, in a combination of oil and tempera. According to his account: 'In one, there is a portrait of the marchioness Isabella with many ladies, who, accompanied by various instruments, sing with sweet harmony.'[82] The second work apparently depicted the story of Latona turning peasants into frogs, the third showed Francesco guided by the god Hercules along the path of virtue to the Mountain of Eternity, while the fourth portrayed the marquis standing on a pedestal holding the large silver baton he had received from the republic of Venice when he was appointed governor general of the League's forces in 1495, 'surrounded by many lords and his own servants holding banners, and all very joyful and full of jubilation at his greatness: among them were many life-like portraits'.[83] No trace of any of these paintings survives, so we are entirely reliant on Vasari's rather minimalist description of them.

According to archival evidence transcribed by Carlo d'Arco in the nineteenth century, but now lost, the painter, Matteo da Bologna, later completed a painting for another room, the *Camera Superiore del Sole*, which depicted the 'nine muses singing and Apollo playing, with Our Illustrious Lord listening'.[84] The thematic similarities between this lost painting by Matteo da Bologna and Mantegna's *Mars and Venus*, between Costa's *Coronation of a Woman Poet* and his later painting for San Sebastiano depicting Isabella surrounded by her singing attendants, and between Mantegna's *Minevra Expelling the Vices* and Costa's *Francesco Guided by the God Hercules along the Path of Virtue* have been seen by scholars as constituting a tribute by the marquis to his wife.[85] Other elements of the San Sebastiano

---

[82] Giorgio Vasari, *Le vite de' più eccellenti pittori scultori ed architettori: scritte da Giorgio Vasari, pittore aretino*, ed. Gaetano Milanesi, vol. 3 (Florence: G. Sansoni, 1906), 134.

[83] Milanesi, ed., *Le vite de' più eccellenti pittori*, 134.

[84] Brown and Lorenzoni, 'The Palazzo di San Sebastiano', 151–8, 174.

[85] Bourne, *The Soldier-Prince*, 280–2; Brown and Lorenzoni, 'The Palazzo di San Sebastiano', 144–5; Campbell, *The Cabinet of Eros*, 95.

palace decorations, such as the blue and gold Este colour scheme of the *Camera dei Brevi*, named after the painted scrolls that featured on the ceiling and recalling Isabella's lottery ticket devices from her San Giorgio apartment, have been similarly interpreted.[86]

Yet, by referencing Isabella's *imprese* and introducing recognizable portraits into allegories that reminded viewers of the *studiolo* paintings, it could also be argued that the marquis aimed to claim ultimate ownership of his wife's conception and subtly to dictate how the works she had commissioned for her apartments were to be interpreted. Translating the esoteric mysteries of Isabella's cycle of paintings into a more literal form of dynastic propaganda redirected their originality and prestige to his own artistic patronage and overarching authority. Thus, he attempted to take control of his wife's political self-fashioning at a time she wished to extend her diplomatic role, instead of stepping back into the shadows, as Francesco wished. The Congress of Mantua was the last time the couple presented themselves publicly as a united diplomatic force. The devastating effects of the *mal francese* increasingly confined Francesco to the palace of San Sebastiano and so cut off the regular face-to-face interactions with Isabella that had facilitated understanding in happier times. The conflict that had emerged briefly in 1506 now reappeared more often and resisted the reconciliations that the pleasure of parenthood and time shared together had facilitated.

---

[86] Bourne, *The Soldier-Prince*, 204.

8

A Mind of Her Own

When Massimiliano Sforza arrived in Mantua from Innsbruck in November 1512, following the Congress of Mantua's endorsement of him as the new duke of Milan, Isabella promised to visit his court in the new year. By doing so, she hoped to have unfettered access to the imperial, Spanish, and Swiss leaders of the Holy League, who intended to remain in the Lombard capital during the first crucial months of the transition from French rule to a reinstated Sforza regime. The marchioness aimed to help her politically inexperienced nephew, but also to lobby the League's representatives on behalf of her brothers, who were still in danger of being driven into exile by the pope. Isabella was also motivated to go to Milan by other factors. The redirection of much chancery business to the palace of San Sebastiano had facilitated the rise to an overweening influence of Tolomeo Spagnoli, the marquis's secretary. It was he who now presided over much of the everyday administration that Isabella had formerly overseen.

With the marquis and his wife residing at the two extremities of the city, the routine communication that had been possible when they were both in residence in the San Giorgio castle, with its interconnected spousal apartments, became far more difficult. Moreover, it is almost certainly the case that, in the years following Livia Osanna's birth in August 1508, Isabella and Francesco never again shared a bed, the *mal francese* having made its presence horrifyingly obvious shortly after this last child's conception. The reduced direct contact between the pair encouraged misunderstandings, a situation that was exacerbated by the fact that rival camps seem to have emerged within a court now split in two. Malevolent rumours, spread by courtiers who were intent on widening the emotional gulf between the couple in the hope of securing their own advancement, also had an insidious impact on marital relations.

Upset by her displacement in local affairs, Isabella was determined to exercise her well-honed political skills on a larger stage. From 1513, she spent as little time as possible in Mantua, preferring to travel to more important diplomatic hubs and to see parts of Europe that administrative duties had precluded her from exploring in earlier times. As she experienced the stimulus of a wider world and Francesco's horizons closed in, the stark contrast in the degree of mobility available to each of them became all too apparent. Conflict erupted spectacularly in March 1513, while Isabella was in Milan, and continued to bubble beneath the surface in the following years. The grievances are documented both in the couple's letters to each other, and in Capilupi's correspondence with the marchioness.

A Renaissance Marriage: The Political and Personal Alliance of Isabella d'Este and Francesco Gonzaga, 1490–1519.
Carolyn James, Oxford University Press (2020). © Carolyn James.
DOI: 10.1093/oso/9780199681211.001.0001

The aged secretary did not accompany Isabella to the Milanese court in early 1513, because he had fallen ill in the weeks before she left. He also remained in Mantua during her later sojourns in Milan and Rome, becoming a crucial link between husband and wife, as he had been in the early 1490s. Although Francesco and Isabella occasionally reflected on happier times and still sometimes expressed solidarity with each other in their correspondence, the divergence of Este and Gonzaga diplomatic policies, combined with the effects of the *mal francese* on Francesco's mind and body, proved to be powerful impediments to marital harmony in the last six years of their relationship.

Isabella at Large

Isabella arrived at the gates of Milan on 13 January 1513, after a five-day journey in abysmal winter weather, during which two of her ladies-in-waiting were almost killed when their horses slipped on a muddy bridge and fell into a canal. She reported the incident in detail to Francesco.[1] Despite Isabella having learned of rumours that her husband was unhappy about her departure and intended to recall her, the marquis replied in cordial terms in a letter dictated to his secretary. He commiserated about the discomfort Isabella and her entourage had endured and reported that he had been feeling much better since her departure, since he had been successfully purged of the humours that were making him so sick. Francesco insisted only that Isabella ensure that his favourite singer, Marchetto Cara, whom he had allowed to go to Milan to entertain the duke and his court during Carnival, was sent back to Mantua immediately. The solace of music would relieve the boredom of his confinement to bed.[2] Capilupi's letters reveal a grimmer reality. Although the secretary reassured Isabella that the gossip she had heard in Milan was almost certainly unfounded, he informed her that contacts at the San Sebastiano palace had told him that Francesco was actually extremely unwell and so afflicted by painful ulcers in the mouth that he was hardly able to speak.[3]

In contrast to her beleaguered and isolated husband, as soon as Isabella was established in her Milanese lodgings, she began a frenetic round of encounters

---

[1] Isabella d'Este to Francesco Gonzaga, 13 January 1513, from Milan, ASMn, AG, 2120, cc. 53r–54r. Isabella's dictated letters from Milan are preserved in duplicate, one set likely the drafts, since occasionally there are crossings out and revisions to the text. None of the letters from Milan appear in her copy books. It seems that Isabella left the relevant volume in Mantua with Capilupi. I cite only the first set of these duplicate letters. Isabella's secretary in Milan was Giovanni Francesco Tridapali, who took on this role permanently after the death of Capilupi's successor, Mario Equicola.

[2] Francesco Gonzaga to Isabella d'Este, 14 January 1513, ASMn, AG, 2120, c. 5. Francesco continued to insist he was almost totally cured in letters of 17, 20, 26, 29 January, all from Mantua: ASMn, AG, 2120, cc. 9, 10, 15, 19r–v.

[3] 'Il signore anchora non è uscito di camera, et poco di lecto, per non poter parlare liberamente, per esserli venuto tardi il male in bocha, ma dicesi ch'el spera la liberazione.' Benedetto Capilupi to Isabella d'Este, 19 January 1513, from Mantua, ASMn, AG, 2487, cc. 52 and 52bis.

with visiting dignitaries, including the viceroy of Naples, Ramón Folc de Cardona-Anglesola, and Cardinal Schinner, papal legate to the Swiss cantons, whose troops had been decisive in driving the French from the north.[4] The Spanish and Swiss leaders were soon joined in Milan by the imperial representative, Cardinal Lang. After meeting with Julius II in November 1512, Lang had come to an agreement with the pope, promising the emperor's adherence to the Lateran Council and his repudiation of the schismatic Council of Pisa. In return, the pope decided to support Maximilian I in his feud with Venice by excluding the republic from the Holy League, a move that, within months, prompted the Venetians to seek an alliance with the king of France.[5]

Isabella was prompt in describing her first diplomatic initiatives to Francesco. She reported that after paying a visit to Cardinal Schinner, she and her ladies-in-waiting had gone to see Cardinal Lang, at whose residence they also found Ramón Folc de Cardona-Anglesola. She recounted the galvanizing effect of Eleonora Compagni, known as La Brognina, on the two men. Remarkably beautiful, Eleonora was the daughter of Beatrice Brogna de' Lardis (nicknamed La Brognolla), who had left Ferrara with Isabella in 1490 to serve the marchioness as a lady-in-waiting. She had married Ercole Compagni in 1491. The couple's daughter had become a member of Isabella's female entourage once she reached adolescence. Both the cardinal and the viceroy had met Brognina during the Congress of Mantua and it was certainly no accident she was chosen by Isabella to be among the small group of attendants who accompanied her to Milan. The marchioness's critical view of Lang, who had become the butt of jokes at the Milanese court because of his maladroit attempts to speak Italian, emerges candidly from her description to Francesco of the cleric's unseemly behaviour during the visit to his lodgings.

> We chatted together about various pleasant things, with Brognina, whom I had sit next to me to please Monseigneur Gurgense (Lang), attracting very great favour. Not content with this, Monseigneur threw himself on the ground to be closer to her, forgetting in that moment the dignity and status of his position, and courted her for so long that night came upon us.[6]

In his reply, Francesco expressed no objection to Isabella's strategic use of her most comely lady-in-waiting to persuade the cardinal to be sympathetic to the political plight of her Este relatives. He merely requested that she use her

---

[4] Isabella d'Este to Francesco Gonzaga, 15 January 1513, from Milan, ASMn, AG, 2120, cc. 60r–v.
[5] Mallett and Shaw, *The Italian Wars*, 119–20.
[6] 'Stessimo in varii et piacevoli ragionamenti cum grandissimo favore di la Brognina, quale, havendo fatto venire presso me ad complacentia di Monsignor Gurgense, non contento esso Monsignore di questo, si gettò in terra per esserli più propinquo, non ricordandosi ad quella volta di la dignità et grado suo, et cum ley feci l'amore quanto gli parsi sino che la nocte ni sopragionsi.' Isabella d'Este to Francesco Gonzaga, 25 January 1513, from Milan, ASMn, AG, 2120, cc. 71r–v.

meetings with Lang to convince the cardinal to ensure that the town of Peschiera, on Lake Garda, finally became part of the Mantuan state, as had been promised in 1508, during the negotiations to establish the League of Cambrai. The marquis added that if she achieved nothing else in Milan, obtaining Peschiera would more than justify her stay.[7]

Reassured, Isabella kept her husband informed about the comedic rivalry between Lang and Cardona for Brognina's favour, writing, on 1 February, that during the staging of a play that dramatized the crushing of the French by the Holy League, the viceroy had publically trumped the cardinal by leaping forward as Brognina passed by and stealing a kiss. Later, he had sent her a very expensive gift of velvet cloth.[8] Francesco merely stipulated that Isabella should make sure that the young woman did not become too full of herself as a result of all the attention.[9] But, to his own courtiers, the marquis may have been far more critical, for new rumours reached Milan that Francesco deeply resented Isabella's departure while he was so sick and disapproved of the use of Brognina as sexual bait.

When Marchetto Cara returned to Mantua in late January, the singer conveyed the message that Isabella was very upset by the whispers circulating in Milan that Francesco was angry with her. However, Capilupi insisted in a letter of 2 February that the malicious gossip had no basis. He explained to Isabella that he had met the marquis and a group of courtiers at vespers on the previous evening, Francesco's state of health having improved enough for him to leave the palace of San Sebastiano and make the journey to the cathedral in the centre of town. According to Capilupi's account of the meeting, the men fell into conversation. They all agreed that husbands and wives should try to live in peace and that purveyors of gossip not be heeded, especially since, in the case of the marquis and his wife, there could be no doubt about their mutual devotion. As Capilupo then explained:

> His Lordship concurred and said that nothing was lacking in him, but you were too proud and too credulous, indicating with certain words that he wished you would change your ways and reconcile with him.

Some sexually suggestive banter ensued between the men and the marquis declared that he considered himself cured of the *mal francese*:

> Showing me his healed sores and the vigour which increases in him daily, he gave me to understand that he would willingly consummate matrimony with

---

[7] Francesco Gonzaga to Isabella d'Este, 29 January 1513, from Mantua, ASMn, AG, 2120, c. 19.

[8] Isabella d'Este to Francesco Gonzaga, 1 February 1513, from Milan, ASMn, AG, 2120, cc. 88r–v. On the long pursuit of Brognina by Ramón Folc de Cardona-Anglesola and Isabella's orchestration of the girl's final capitulation to her ardent lover in 1514, see Rita Castagna, *Un vicerè per Eleonora Brognina alla corte di Isabella d'Este Gonzaga* (Florence: Moretti, 1982). For several letters to the viceroy on the subject of Brognina, see Isabella d'Este, *Selected Letters*, 367–70.

[9] Francesco Gonzaga to Isabella d'Este, 5 February 1513, from Mantua, ASMn, AG, 2120, cc. 21r–v.

Your Ladyship, considering that which, in effect, must be true: that you are still like a fresh young girl.[10]

Capilupi advised Isabella to resign herself to making up for lost time in the marital bed and warned that she should come back to Mantua as soon as Carnival was over, since Francesco had interrogated him insistently about when she intended to return, but had looked satisfied when her secretary assured him that the marchioness would leave Milan, without fail, before the beginning of Lent. Capilupi concluded his letter on an encouraging note, assuring Isabella that her husband's feelings towards her were benign.

The worrying news regarding her sexual duties likely discouraged Isabella from returning promptly to Mantua, but political developments also prevented her from heeding her fretful secretary. Bernardo Dovizi da Bibbiena, Cardinal of Santa Maria in Portico and Julius II's envoy, had arrived in Milan to put pressure on Ramón Folc de Cardona-Anglesola to lead his troops immediately towards Ferrara.[11] The marchioness was on good terms with the cardinal and probably learned of his mission at once, since, on 5 February, Capilupi acknowledged receipt of a letter in cipher from Isabella directed to her brothers, that he forwarded with all haste to Ferrara.[12] Having warned Alfonso d'Este of the imminent danger of an attack on the city, Isabella set about delaying the Spanish viceroy's departure from Milan by dangling the prospect of his infatuation with Brognina having a satisfactory denouement.

Disappointed that he had been so evidently outdone in the contest for the beautiful Brognina's favour by the Spanish viceroy, Lang left Milan on 3 February, his extravagant promises, made only the night before, to arrange the transfer of Peschiera to Gonzaga jurisdiction left up in the air and unlikely ever to be fulfilled, as Isabella resignedly informed her husband on that same day.[13] The failure of Isabella's efforts to secure Peschiera, and the urgency with which his doctors advised him to convalesce in the country to ensure a complete recovery, prompted the marquis to summon his wife home at once 'to govern his affairs', as he put it,

---

[10] 'El signore confirmò et disse che da lui non mancava, ma che eravati troppo superba et troppo credula, dicendolo cum uno certo modo di volere che vi assettasti et componesti ben cum seco. Il Signor Zoanfrancesco fece officio di bon tabachino, né al signore dispiaque; anzi, mostrandomi le piage sue salde et la galiardeza ch'el va ogni giorno repigliando, compresi che volunteri consumaria matrimonio cum Vostra Signoria, stimando quel che in effecto debe essere, che siati como doncella et una bruscha robba.' Benedetto Capilupi to Isabella d'Este, 2 February 1513, from Mantua, ASMn, AG, 2487, cc. 56r–v.

[11] Luzio, 'Isabella d'Este di fronte a Giulio II', 404–5.

[12] Benedetto Capilupi to Isabella d'Este, 5 February 1513, from Mantua, ASMn, AG, 2487, c. 57r.

[13] 'Di la risposta sua fatta circa la causa di Pischera, il Suardino ni scrive diffusamente alla Signoria Vostra risposta non già correspondente alle sue large promisse che la sera inanti mi havea fatto.' Isabella d'Este to Francesco Gonzaga, 3 February 1513, from Milan, ASMn, AG, 2120, cc. 91r–v.

something she had not done for quite some time, but which Francesco may have proffered as an inducement to return.[14]

Capilupi anticipated that Isabella would not respond to this order as quickly as her husband expected and warned of the dire repercussions if she did not obey. Not only would Francesco be angry, he wrote, she would not be permitted to step foot out of Mantua ever again. He added: 'I know what I am saying.' Capilupi pressed the point home by explaining that Francesco had put on a production of the *Andrians* in the loggia of his palace of San Sebastiano to celebrate the end of Carnival and had ordered that the sets be left *in situ*, so the play could be performed again on Isabella's return. He added that three large boats would set off from Mantua the following day to collect her party for the river leg of the journey. Thus, he sugar-coated his warnings about the consequences of a failure to pack her bags immediately with an assurance of a warm welcome if she did.[15] On 13 February, the secretary wrote again, reiterating to Isabella that she should leave Milan forthwith, since her husband spoke of nothing else but her return. He reminded her about the stage sets waiting for the encore performance of the *Andrians*, planned especially in her honour.[16]

Political developments again intervened. With the death of Pope Julius II on 20 February, the immediate threat to the Este regime evaporated, but new imperatives kept Isabella in Milan. She dispatched a rider to Mantua to explain to Francesco why she needed to defer her departure, sending only an accompanying brief written message that she was well.[17] Perhaps interpreting the lack of response from Francesco as ominous, Isabella wrote a long letter to him in her own hand on 9 March, misdating the letter by a month. This error suggests a distracted frame of mind, as she sat down to justify her behaviour. The opening sentence, too, indicates a certain trepidation about how the explanation would be received: 'Perhaps Your Lordship is unhappy with me because of the long delay in my return, but once you understand why, I hope you will recognize that it was not

---

[14] 'Hora ch'el Carnevale serrà passato et che a noi conviene andar fori ad exercitarci, per consiglio de' medici per confirmarci ne la sanità ove, Dio gratia, semo redutti, serrà necessaria la Vostra Signoria a Mantua al governo de le cose nostre.' Francesco Gonzaga to Isabella d'Este, 9 February 1513, from Mantua, ASMn, AG, 2120, c. 26.

[15] 'Sì che, patrona mia, vi supplico che non vogliati differire, perché el Signore se turbaria e faresti che mai più non haveresti licencia di andare in loco alcuno.... Fati che [le barche] non siano venute in vano, ch'el Signore haveria per male, ch' io so quel che dico.' Benedetto Capilupi to Isabella d'Este, 9 February 1513, from Mantua, ASMn, AG, 2487, cc. 59r–v. The play, by the ancient Roman playwright Terence, was the second production recited in the Loggia. The first, by Niccolò da Correggio, or perhaps Publio Filippo Mantovano, was performed during Carnival 1512. See Bourne, *The Soldier-Prince*, 215–16; a transcription of the letter is at 512–13.

[16] 'Sua Excellentia non parla adesso di altro se non quando partirà [e] quando serrà qui la Vostra [Signoria]. Ha facto stare apparata la logia di Santo Sebastiano per fare di novo al conspecto vostro representare Andria.' Benedetto Capilupi to Isabella d'Este, 13 February 1513, from Mantua, ASMn, AG, 2487, cc. 60r–v.

[17] Isabella d'Este to Francesco Gonzaga, 22 February 1513, from Milan, ASMn, AG, 2120, c. 109.

without good reason that I remained here.'[18] But Isabella was no longer even in Milan. She wrote from Piacenza, where she had gone with the Spanish viceroy and the duke of Milan, who were intent on using the opportunity presented by the pope's death to reclaim Milanese territory seized by Julius II in mid-1512, when the French withdrew from northern Italy. Isabella's presence in Piacenza advertised her complicity in the attempt to retake the city at a time when no one knew how a new pope would view his predecessor's campaigns to reclaim papal territory.

In an attempt to downplay the controversial political implications of her presence in Piacenza, Isabella presented it to Francesco as an unforeseen detour on her journey home. She explained that having left Milan on 2 March, intending only to accompany her Sforza nephew and the Spanish viceroy to Parma, before continuing on to Mantua, she had been persuaded by the latter, who was keen to continue his pursuit of Brognina, to travel on to Lodi. The party had stopped for lunch and then found the road so poor that they arrived late and were obliged to stay overnight. Ambassadors then arrived at Lodi from Piacenza and persuaded the duke and the viceroy to go there immediately to claim the city, before a new pope was elected. Then, another envoy had arrived to discuss the fate of Reggio, formerly a Ferrarese possession, that had also been seized by Julius II in mid-1512. Isabella admitted she could not resist the opportunity to lobby the viceroy on her brother's behalf, so decided to accompany Cardona to Piacenza. Having assured Francesco at the beginning of the letter that loyalty to him outweighed that to everyone else in the world combined, she ended with a loving signature: 'desirous of seeing Your Lordship, the marchioness of Mantua, written in her own hand.'[19]

Francesco declared in a dictated reply that he had not even bothered to read Isabella's concocted excuses and was insulted by the final declaration that she was eager to see him, 'since if that were true... nothing should have stopped you from doing so'. He demanded she remember her duty and demonstrate the truth of the claim that nothing could compromise her utter loyalty to him, by returning home immediately, adding that their son, Federico, was on his way home from Rome and that if maternal love did not serve to hurry her departure, she should consider the harm to her reputation that the failure to come home was causing (Fig. 1).[20]

Francesco's disdainful letter provoked an equally angry response from Isabella, again written in her own hand.

[18] Isabella d'Este to Francesco Gonzaga, 9 March 1513, from Piacenza, ASMn, AG, 2120, cc. 98r–99, published in Luzio, 'Isabella d'Este di fronte a Giulio II', 419–20.

[19] Isabella d'Este to Francesco Gonzaga, 9 March 1513, from Piacenza, ASMn, AG, 2120, cc. 98r–99, published in Luzio, 'Isabella d'Este di fronte a Giulio II', 419–20.

[20] Francesco Gonzaga to Isabella d'Este, 11 March 1513, from Mantua, ASMn, AG, 2120, c. 36, published in Luzio, 'Isabella d'Este di fronte a Giulio II', 421; and in Cockram, *Isabella d'Este and Francesco Gonzaga*, 220–1 (translated on 186).

I don't believe that on this trip to Milan I have misbehaved or done anything to incite people's gossip. I know well that I have gained a thousand friends for Your Lordship and myself, by doing what I must do and what is my custom to do because, thanks to God and to myself, I have never required supervision or advice on how to govern my person. Though indeed I may be of no account in other matters, God had given me this gift, for which Your Lordship is as obliged to me as any husband ever was to a wife. And do not think that even if you loved me as much as any person has ever loved another you could ever repay my loyalty. That is why Your Highness sometimes says that I am haughty, because knowing how much you owe me for this, and seeing how badly I am repaid, I sometimes change complexion and seem in effect what I am not.[21]

The pride and combative self-righteousness that Francesco had bemoaned to his courtiers in Capilupi's presence at vespers, ten days before, is here on full display, but Isabella's demand that she be accorded greater respect is powerfully put. The marquis chose not to write back, his epistolary silence perhaps an admission that his wife had a good deal of right on her side. Yet, it was Isabella who made explicit efforts to be conciliatory, even if she did not obey Francesco by leaving immediately for Mantua. We see in her letters of 13 and 14 March the effect of a few days of pondering the wisdom of the impetuous rebuke to her husband, as well as the restraining influence of dictating to a secretary, especially one who was not her usual scribe. She explained that although she desired nothing more ardently than to set off for home, her nephew had insisted she accompany him to Parma, so she could witness him claiming that city as well. She begged for a few more days, so that she could take leave of Massimiliano, 'without losing in a moment that which had been acquired in many days with [His Excellency]' (Fig. 2).[22] The next day she admitted that their party could not enter Parma, since the city was occupied by five thousand Spanish soldiers, who had not been paid. The viceroy dared not show himself for fear of the demands for money that would inevitably be made by the desperate troops, who were running amok, stealing what they could from the city's sorely tried population.[23] Thus, Isabella's excursion to Milan ended on a rather flat note, although she contributed significantly to the survival of the Este regime by persuading the League's leaders to remain at the Milanese court much

[21] Isabella d'Este to Francesco Gonzaga, 12 March 1513, from Piacenza, ASMn, 2120, cc. 114r–115r, Isabella d'Este, *Selected Letters*, 361-1. The original letter is published in Alessandro Luzio, 'Isabella d'Este e la Corte Sforzesca', *Archivio storico lombardo* 15 (1901): 145–76.

[22] 'Vostra Signoria non haverà sdegno che per tri dì ch' io habbi anchor a dimorare qua. Lassi Sua Excellentia satisfatta compitamente di me et non perdi in uno puncto quello si è acquistato in tanti dì cum Ley.' Isabella d'Este to Francesco Gonzaga, 13 March 1513, from Piacenza, ASMn, AG, 2120, cc. 116r–v.

[23] Isabella d'Este to Francesco Gonzaga, 14 March 1513, from Piacenza, ASMn, AG, 2120, cc. 119r–v.

longer than they had intended. She arrived back in Mantua in late March, six weeks after the first attempts by her husband and secretary to secure her return.

The marital discord of February and March 1513 seems to have lingered for some time. Just before Christmas that year, Francesco expelled from court Alda Boiardo, one of Isabella's long-time ladies-in-waiting, on the grounds that she had stirred up such discord her presence in Mantua had become intolerable to him.[24] The marquis ignored his wife's protests about losing the company of a much-loved person. Exactly what Alda was guilty of remains unclear, but she perhaps unwisely and too stridently advertised the factional tensions between Isabella's household, based at the San Giorgio palace, and Francesco's attendants at San Sebastiano. By sending Alda back to Ferrara, Francesco exacted retribution from Isabella for her behaviour in Milan, while reminding the court of his absolute power over its members, including those who might have considered themselves under the marchioness's protection. It is little wonder that Francesco's temper was so short at the end of 1513. He had spent almost the entire year bed-ridden and, by autumn, his feet had become so swollen he could not walk at all.[25]

Yet even after the dramatic flaring of open conflict, there was a measure of rapprochement in the new year. In mid-March 1514, Isabella spent several weeks at Lake Garda to recuperate from a period of illness. She wrote almost every day to her husband. After receiving the first letter from Goito, Francesco expressed appreciation for her communications: 'We would be grateful if Your Ladyship visits us often with her letters because our situation being what it is, it will give us pleasure and consolation.'[26] Isabella was an accomplished raconteur and, as her own spirits lifted in response to the beauty of her surroundings, she attempted to improve those of her sick husband, by narrating her adventures and reflecting on her experiences in letters that resemble the travel journals that were beginning to emerge in this period as a new literary genre.[27]

From Lonato, then still a Gonzaga possession, Isabella wrote enthusiastically about the health-restoring properties of the fresh air, not only for herself, but for her secretary, who had accompanied the marchioness on this trip, after also being unwell: 'In the opinion of all my entourage, the air here is most perfect, and Capilupi in particular says his head, eyes, and ears—which have been causing him

---

[24] Francesco explained his decision in a letter to Alda's sister, who was a nun in Ferrara. Francesco Gonzaga to Suora Laura Boiardo, 25 December 1513, ASMn, AG, 2931, libro 231, cc. 51v–52r.

[25] See, for example, Francesco's letter of 1 October 1513, dictated from bed, to his ambassador, Gian Stefano Rozone: ASMn, AG, 2921, libro 231, cc. 22r–24r; and those to Isabella of 25 September and 15 October 1513, the first of which mentions that his feet were so enormous he had to stay in bed: ASMn, AG, 2120, cc. 43 and 46.

[26] 'Haveremo ben grato che la Signoria Vostra spesso ci visiti con sue lettere, perché, ritrovandoci nel termine ove semo, ni saranno di gran piacere e consolatione.' Francesco Gonzaga to Isabella d'Este, 17 March 1514, from Mantua, ASMn, AG, 2120, cc. 172r–v.

[27] Carolyn James, 'The Travels of Isabella d'Este, Marchioness of Mantua', *Studies in Travel Writing* 13 (2009): 99–109.

heaviness—all feel lighter than they have in some time.' She described the warm reception accorded her by the inhabitants, and ended that letter with an account of the miraculous escape from injury of a stable master's son, when a gun went off accidently and passed through all his clothing, leaving him completely unscathed.[28] This was the first of many anecdotes of miracles and accidents that her party witnessed, or experienced, with which she attempted to entertain Francesco.

In describing her visit to the fortress at Sirmione, from where she hoped to gain a panoramic view of Lake Garda, Isabella joked that she had taken possession of the place corporeally, by slipping over on the wet stairs, after being distracted by the chivalrous chatter of her host.[29] From Peschiera, she wrote in a similarly jocular style, although this time with a bitter edge she knew her husband would appreciate. She explained that having discovered that the fortress there was guarded by only a dozen or so Spanish infantrymen, of very small stature, she considered mobilizing her party to take them captive and proclaim herself mistress of the place. Thus, she would redress the treachery of the French king and the emperor in reneging on the promises made in 1508, as part of the treaty of Cambrai, that the town would become part of the Mantuan state:

> Lonato's setting is lovely; that of Sirmione is even more beautiful, but most beautiful of all is that of Peschiera, so we must do all we can to get it back. I confess to Your Excellency that during my return to Sirmione I was most disquiet, and the feeling remains with me still. When I think of the great wrong that is done us for something of little importance to those who have taken it, but that for us would be very useful and pleasing.... Well enough of this, I don't want to talk about it anymore.[30]

Isabella's indignation on her husband's behalf and the reminder of their mutual efforts to expand the borders of their tiny state rallied Francesco's spirits and resolve in the way she seems to have intended. He vowed in his reply that he would do all in his power to regain Peschiera, so they could, one day, enjoy its delights together, as they had always so fervently wished.[31] In these exchanges, we see the effectiveness of letters in preserving some of the camaraderie and sense of shared endeavour of earlier days.

Isabella returned to Mantua at the end of March, but Francesco left for Marmirolo soon afterwards, after being advised by his doctors that the lack of

---

[28] Isabella d'Este to Francesco Gonzaga, 17 March 1514, from Lonato, in Isabella d'Este, *Selected Letters*, 373–4.

[29] Isabella d'Este to Francesco Gonzaga, 19 March 1514, from Lonato, ASMn, AG, 2996, libro 30a, cc. 90r–91r.

[30] Isabella d'Este to Francesco Gonzaga, 21 March 1514, from Sirmione, in Isabella d'Este, *Selected Letters*, 374–5.

[31] Francesco Gonzaga to Isabella d'Este, 23 March 1514, from Mantua, ASMn, AG, 2120, c. 181r.

improvement to his health was due to the worries of government. He needed peace and a change of air. However, as usual, it was not Isabella who acted as deputy, but Tolomeo Spagnoli. Francesco's outgoing letters from this period, preserved in the chancery copy books, document the increasing responsibilities given to his secretary, a situation that soon prompted Isabella to leave Mantua again in disgust.

'We Were Too Embarrassed to Remain So Abject in Mantua'

In early June 1514, perhaps as a conciliatory gesture, Francesco gave Isabella permission to accept Massimiliano Sforza's invitation to join him in Cremona, on the condition that she returned quickly.[32] The couple corresponded cordially throughout June, and there is no hint in Francesco's letters that he was annoyed by Isabella's absence, as rumours that reached her at the Sforza court implied. This time it was Spagnoli who reassured the marchioness, writing in a letter of 24 June that the gossip was false.[33] Two weeks later, Francesco reported that he was feeling somewhat better and hoped to send good news soon.[34]

A series of letters, sent in July and August to a physician, referred to as Ioanne Francesco, document the basis of that optimism.[35] The doctor was experimenting on patients afflicted with the *mal francese* and Francesco had authorized payment for their treatment with drinkable gold. He demanded daily reports about the effects of the medicine, especially on a certain Balduzzo, who was extremely ill. The marquis sought information about the patient's appetite, fevers, the effects of the potion on his ulcers and whether, or not, he could sleep. Once the doctor had concluded his investigation, Francesco hoped to take the preparation himself. What happened to Balduzzo, after the administration of several doses of the expensive potable gold, does not emerge, but Francesco's sudden change of mood on 12 August suggests his hopes may have been dashed. That day he wrote to Spagnoli bemoaning the behaviour of his wife:

We believe that you will recall that before the illustrious lady, our consort, left she had you tell us that she wasn't a child who needed to be summoned home

---

[32] Francesco Gonzaga to Isabella d'Este, 2 June 1514, from Borgoforte, ASMn, AG, 2921, libro 234, c. 29.

[33] Tolomeo Spagnoli to Isabella d'Este, 24 June 1514, from Mantua, ASMn, AG, 2489, unnumbered folio.

[34] Francesco Gonzaga to Isabella d'Este, 11 July 1514, from Mantua, ASMn, AG, 2120, cc. 196r–v. On the same day, Tolomeo Spagnoli wrote to Isabella, informing her that Francesco was being treated by a Genoese healer, 'cum certa bevanda e certa acqua da bagnare l'ochi offesi'. Tolomeo Spagnoli to Isabella d'Este, 11 July 1514, from Mantua, ASMn, AG, 2489, unnumbered folio.

[35] Francesco Gonzaga to Giovan Francesco, physician, 29 July, 2 August, 4 August, 23 August, from Cavriana, ASMn, AG, 2921, libro 234, cc. 52r–v, 53v–54r, 56, 58.

every time she went away; we say this because now she has made it necessary for us to send for her.[36]

The marquis wrote in a similar vein to Benedetto Capilupi on the same day, expecting the secretary to alert Isabella to his growing impatience about her failure to return home.[37] Capilupi had not accompanied Isabella to Milan, probably because of the recurrent attacks of stones that plagued him until they were removed in a surprisingly successful, if excruciatingly painful and life-threatening, operation in May 1517.[38] His letters to Isabella reveal renewed intermittent tensions between the spouses in a period when Francesco's frame of mind see-sawed between optimism that he had, at last, found a cure for his illness, and misery, when the treatments produced no improvement.[39]

By early September, the marquis was in the hands of a doctor from Ferrara, who treated his ulcerated sores with a potion, probably containing mercury, the effects of which proved to be agonizing. Capilupi referred in a letter to Isabella to the intense burning that the treatment caused, while Spagnoli wrote disapprovingly to a colleague in Rome about the terrible suffering imposed on his master, to no avail. The complete failure of the latest cure cast Francesco into despondency.[40] After being informed by Capilupi that her husband's condition had once again deteriorated, Isabella wrote to Francesco from Milan offering her commiserations.[41] However, on the same day, she informed Capilupi that the date of her departure from Milan was now uncertain, despite having assured him on 22 July, and as late as 29 August, that she would return home very soon.[42]

Isabella did leave the Milanese court in mid-September, but, instead of returning to Mantua, she travelled to Genoa and then to Pisa, from where she wrote to Capilupi of her intentions to proceed to Rome. That letter, in which she set out the arguments for her decision, has not survived. However, the secretary's long reply of 10 October does. It is headed: 'This one will not annoy you; read it

---

[36] Francesco Gonzaga to Tolomeo Spagnoli, 12 August 1514, from Cavriana, ASMn, AG, 2921, libro 234, c. 58r.

[37] Francesco Gonzaga to Benedetto Capilupi, 12 August 1514, from Cavriana, ASMn, AG, 2921, libro 234, c. 58v.

[38] Benedetto Capilupi's nephew described the operation in gory detail in a long letter to Isabella. Giovanni Maria Capilupi to Isabella d'Este, 14 May 1517, from Mantua, ASMn, AG, 2496, cc. 253r–254r.

[39] Francesco Gonzaga to Tolomeo Spagnoli, 13 August 1514, from Cavriana, ASMn, AG, 2921, libro 234, c. 58v. However, the marquis authorized continuing experiments with potable gold with other patients.

[40] Benedetto Capilupi to Isabella d'Este, 3 September 1513, from Mantua; Tolomeo Spagnoli to Stazio Gadio, 10, 11, and 13 September 1514, from Mantua, ASMn, AG, 2489, unnumbered folios.

[41] Isabella d'Este to Francesco Gonzaga, 4 September 1514, from Milan, ASMn, AG, 2996, libro 31, cc. 39r–v.

[42] Isabella d'Este to Benedetto Capilupi, 22 July, 29 August and 4 September, from Milan, ASMn, 2996, libro 31, cc. 31v–32r, 38r, and 39v–40.

willingly.'[43] Capilupi was referring to a reproachful letter he had sent a few days earlier, which, as Isabella confessed, had angered her to the point that she had thrown it in the fire.[44] Capilupi informed Isabella that her requests for heavier clothing from her wardrobe in Mantua had stirred up a storm of speculation and controversy at court. Having heard rumours from the marchioness's household of her intention to go to Rome, he admitted that he too had initially concluded that she was motivated entirely by her own desires.[45] The secretary apologized, conceding that he had been unjust. However, he reproached Isabella for not confiding in him, while she was in Genoa, on the grounds that if she had spelled out the reasons for going to Rome then, as she had now done in the letter from Pisa, he would have had the ammunition to forestall the complaints of her husband and to stop the damaging comments of her enemies at court. Most importantly, it would have prevented the perception that he himself had colluded to keep Francesco in the dark. Since he had repeatedly and confidently stated in public that Isabella would on no account go to Rome, or to Naples, as the gossipers from the marchioness's household claimed she intended to do, he now appeared to be a liar.

Capilupi explained in the same letter that upon receiving Isabella's explanation, he had gone immediately to the palace of San Sebastiano and sought an audience with the marquis, whom he found closeted, as usual, with his doctors. Once the medical team departed he was admitted to Francesco's presence. After a speech about the dangers of jumping to negative conclusions about a person who had always proved to be loving and prudent, Capilupi had convinced the marquis to listen to Isabella's letter from Pisa. The timing of a letter from Francesco to Isabella of 8 October, granting his wife permission to go to Rome, appears to confirm the effective mediation of Capilupi.

Although we cannot know how Isabella justified the need to go immediately to the papal court, it is likely that her lost letter explained she wanted to consult Leo X about the prospect of a marriage between her nephew, Duke Massimiliano Sforza, and Queen Giovanna, the young widow of Ferrandino d'Aragona, a match that would unite her Milanese and Neapolitan relatives and provide Spanish support for her nephew's vulnerable regime. In response to Isabella's explanation of the need to go to Rome, Francesco purported to believe that it might actually be useful to have his wife at the papal court, if she could convince the pope to lend his support to Asola and Lonato remaining Gonzaga possessions, rather than

---

[43] 'Questa non vi porter dispiacere. Legetili voluntieri.' Benedetto Capilupi to Isabella d'Este, 10 October 1514, from Mantua, ASMn, AG, 2489, unnumbered folios.

[44] Isabella d'Este to Benedetto Capilupi, 15 October 1514, from Montefiascone, ASMn, AG, 2996, libro 31, cc. 43r–45r.

[45] 'La diffidentia che Vostra Signoria dimonstrava per il scrivere suo de non volere ritornare a Mantua, se non era chiara de non havere scorno, et la fede che poco prestava alle mie lettere, non mi lassavano pensare che altro che lo appetito l'havesse transportata.' Benedetto Capilupi to Isabella d'Este, 10 October 1514, from Mantua, ASMn, AG, 2489, unnumbered folios.

reverting to Venetian control, as the marquis feared would soon happen, an anxiety that proved to be well founded.[46]

Having given a reluctant permission to his wife to visit the papal court, Francesco remained anxious about what she might do there. He ordered the Mantuan ambassador to Rome, Alessandro Gabbioneta, to intercept the marchioness at Montefiascone and to travel with her party for the remaining part of the journey. He was then to keep her under close surveillance. Once Isabella arrived in Rome, the ambassador obediently sent long accounts of her activities to Francesco every few days. On 26 October, for example, he reported that after seeing Saint Peter's Basilica and the papal apartments, the marchioness had spent a whole afternoon admiring the antiquities that had been assembled in the Belvedere by Julius II and, then, on the following day, had toured the Coliseum.[47] Francesco responded agreeably to this news, perhaps comforted that his wife was confining herself to tourism:

> It pleases us that her ladyship has found appropriate food for her mind in contemplating those antiquities, something that has always greatly delighted her. Keep her happy as much as possible and make sure you conduct her home soon.[48]

As this same letter reveals, the marquis was again full of optimism about the possibility of a cure, which likely accounts for his friendly response to news of Isabella's enjoyment of Rome. He expressed the fervent hope that his wife's return would see him completely free of disease, since, in only three days of treatment, a Franciscan friar had wrought such an improvement to his health, that his usual doctors were astounded.

Capilupi's letters to Isabella confirm the extent of the miracle. On 7 November, the secretary sent news that Francesco had been able to get out of bed and make several excursions on horseback before returning to San Sebastiano to eat and rest. Afterwards he had attended vespers at the church of San Francesco, sung by the friar who was treating him and the chapel choir.[49] Although Francesco's letters do not mention this outing, perhaps because it overtaxed him and set the improvement back somewhat, on 17 November, he assured Isabella that he intended to leave his bed the next day and not return there, except to sleep, as healthy people did. He admitted that although he had hoped she would return

---

[46] 'Havemo pensato che l'andata di Vostra Signori a Roma viene a certo nostro proposito e per ciò la c'è gratissima.' Francesco Gonzaga to Isabella d'Este, 8 October 1514, ASMn, AG, 2921, libro 234, c. 73r.

[47] Alessandro Gabbioneta to Francesco Gonzaga, 26 October 1415, from Rome, published in Alessandro Luzio, 'Isabella d'Este ne' primordi del papato di Leone X e il suo viaggio a Roma nel 1514–1515', Archivio storico lombardo 33 (1906): 454–89 (468).

[48] 'Piaceni che Sua Signoria habbi ritrovato pasto conveniente al ingegno suo in contemplare quelle antiquità, cosa di che sempre la s'è delettata molto. Voi tenetila allegra più che sia possibile et procurati di ricondurla presto a casa.' Francesco Gonzaga to Alessandro Gabbioneta, 3 November 1514, from Mantua, ASMn, AG, 2921, libro 234, cc. 87r–89v.

[49] Benedetto Capilupi to Isabella d'Este, 7 November 1514, ASMn, AG, 2489, unnumbered folio.

home soon to witness the dramatic extent of his recovery, he was willing to grant her permission to visit Naples:

> since we wish always to indulge you in all your desires, we say to you that given you have a great yearning to see Naples, while you are so near, not only do we consent and freely give you licence, we beg that you go, since it seems to us it would be bad to have on our conscience to have impeded such a praiseworthy and honest wish.[50]

Five days later, the news from Francesco about his state of health was more circumscribed. He reported that he was managing to walk twice a day and no longer had his arms completely wrapped with bandages, but still wore gloves to protect his ulcerated hands and moving about caused him some pain. It seems these remaining problems were minor in comparison with earlier sufferings and Francesco assured Isabella he was content with his progress and looked forward to the future. He requested that she petition the pope to grant a bishopric to Serafino Ostuni da Puglia, the friar who had cured him.[51] Isabella promised to do her best to persuade the pope to agree. Her letters from Naples extrapolate on her own sources of satisfaction, especially the day trips, such as the one to Pozzolo, where she toured what she describes as 'infinite antiquities'.[52]

The desire to secure a papal reward for the Franciscan who had set him on the road to recovery, as well as the strongly worded requests of the pope to allow Isabella and her party to remain in Rome for Christmas and Carnival, prompted Francesco again to acquiesce to Isabella's requests for an extension to her trip. However, the frequent fretful reminders to Gabbioneta, and to Isabella herself, that no more delays could be contemplated, suggest that Francesco was keen to have his wife back in Mantua, although whether to recover some of their former companionship after so many months of separation, or to stop the rumours and speculation in Mantua about her long absence does not emerge from his letters.

On 19 January, the marquis wrote at length to Isabella, expressing gratitude for the news of the sudden death of King Louis XII, which he had already learned from other sources, but appreciated having confirmation of from Rome.[53] But he also emphasized his disappointment that she would not see the performances of

---

[50] 'e come quel che volemo esserle sempre indulgente in tutti gli soi desyderii, le significamo che se pur l'havesse gran piacere de vedere Napoli poi che l'è tanto oltra, non solamente ge lo consentemo, e ge ne damo bona licentia, ma la pregamo vi vadi, che grave ce pareria patir nota de haverle impedito così laudabile et honesta voluntà sua.' Francesco Gonzaga to Isabella d'Este, 17 November 1514, from Mantua, ASMn, AG, 2120, c. 219.

[51] Francesco Gonzaga to Isabella d'Este, 21 and 22 November 1514, from Mantua, ASMn, AG, 2120, cc. 220 and 221r–v.

[52] Isabella d'Este to Francesco Gonzaga, 16 December 1514, from Pozzolo, ASMn, AG, 2120, cc. 298r–299v.

[53] Isabella d'Este to Francesco Gonzaga, 10 January 1515, from Rome, ASMn, AG, 2120, c. 103.

the comedies that he had commissioned for Carnival. To persuade his wife not to break her promise to return promptly to Mantua at the beginning of Lent, Francesco assured her that he awaited her homecoming 'with the greatest desire in the world'. However, he also slyly attempted to activate her competitiveness and desire always to be in the right:

> We cannot however believe that Your Ladyship would seek an excuse for any extension [to your stay] because we know that you also desire to see us, as one who, even if she doesn't usually win, always tries to outdo us in love. Besides the desire to see us so well restored to health after our long illness, there is the prospect of seeing Federico and our other children, who are all well and eagerly await the return of Your Ladyship, to whom we heartily recommend ourselves.[54]

Francesco was no doubt remembering Isabella's combative retorts during their epistolary wrangles of 1506 and 1513, when she had indeed claimed to be the more loving and dutiful marital partner.

While this letter was still in transit, Isabella wrote reassuringly that she was making preparations to leave Rome, armed with a written undertaking from Leo X that he would award the next available benefice to Serafino Ostuni.[55] She had also persuaded the pope to give Osanna Andreasi—the Mantuan tertiary who had died in 1505 and whose tomb had become a prominent devotional site for pilgrims—the status of 'beata', the first step to a possible canonization.[56] These achievements were a modest recompense for her extraordinarily long stay away and Isabella feared a cold reception from Francesco. However, he received Isabella as cordially as his letters suggested he would.

Nonetheless, after the stimulating experience of being in Milan and Rome, Mantua seemed more than ever a backwater and the prominent role of Spagnoli as her husband's primary political collaborator was none the less galling. Isabella's copy books record dozens of letters she sent, in the weeks after her return, to the cardinals and other well-connected people she had met in Rome. That barrage of

---

[54] 'A Vostra Signoria dicemo che ne contentamo per reverentia di Nostro Signore che la resti alla obedientia di Sua Beatitudine per tutto Carnevale prossimo, con questo, che passato il ditto tempo, subito la se metti in via per ritornare più presto che la può a noi, che l'aspettamo col magiore desiderio del mondo.... Non possemo però credere che Vostra Signoria cerchi causa alcuna Lei di più longo indugio, perché sapemo che anch' ella desidera di vedere noi, come quella che sole sempre, se non vincerne, almeno contenderne di vincerne in amore, oltra che al desiderio di revedere noi così ben revagliuti del nostro longo male, se ve aggiunge quello di vedere Federico et gli altri nostri figlioli, che tutti sono sani et stanno in aspettatione del ritorno di essa Vostra Signoria, alla quale di core ne raccomandiamo.' Francesco Gonzaga to Isabella d'Este, 19 January 1515, from Mantua, ASMn, AG, 2921, libro 235, cc. 32r–v. Francesco wrote in similar vein on 6 and 24 February 1515, ASMn, AG, 2121, cc. 4–5.

[55] Isabella d'Este to Francesco Gonzaga, 17 February 1515, from Rome, ASMn, AG, 2996, libro 31, c. 72r.

[56] Alessandro Gabbioneta to Francesco Gonzaga, 30 December 1515, from Rome, published in Luzio, 'Isabella d'Este ne' primordi del papato di Leone X', 475–6. On the Mantuan cult of Osanna Andreasi, see Bourne, *The Soldier-Prince*, 253–70.

correspondence testifies to a determination to preserve the social networks she had cultivated at the papal court during her stay on Rome, so that she could continue to tap into the main currents of European political intercourse at a time when many of the ambassadorial reports that came into the chancery bypassed her.

Looking back from the perspective of widowhood on the motives for prolonging her absence from Mantua in 1514 and early 1515, it was not the excitement of being at two major diplomatic hubs that Isabella remembered, but, rather, the ignominy of her political eclipse in Mantua itself. In a letter of 21 July 1519 to Baldassare Castiglione, who was then the Mantuan envoy in Rome, she put the blame entirely on Tolomeo Spagnoli.

> He kept us so low that, whereas in our younger years we had some authority in this state, now we were entirely stripped of it, as is known to you and to the entire city. His Holiness knows that, as a consequence, we spent nine months away from home, four of them in Rome, because we were too embarrassed to remain so abject in Mantua.[57]

Although Isabella exacted swift retribution on her enemy following Francesco's death in March 1519, she could do little to dent Spagnoli's influence in the four years before that, when the secretary's propinquity to his master at the palace of San Sebastiano made him the marquis's right-hand man. Moreover, once illness prevented Francesco from engaging in hunting and the other vigorous sporting activities he had always so enjoyed, he sought vicarious pleasures by surrounding himself with courtiers whose carousing reminded him of the pleasures of his youth. For Isabella, the atmosphere at Francesco's palace was alienating and she made her disdain clear by removing herself from Mantua.

In the autumn of 1515, the political kaleidoscope of northern Italy was again transformed by the arrival of a foreign army. Francesco had briefly hoped that the new king of France would not follow his predecessors' attempts to win glory and territory by promulgating war on Italian soil. His hopes were immediately dashed, since the young François I began at once to make preparations to reclaim Milan. The French victory over the Swiss contingents of the Holy League's army, at Marignano, near Milan, on 14 September 1515, spelled the end of Massimiliano Sforza's days as duke of Milan. On 4 October, Isabella's nephew agreed to renounce his claim to the duchy in return for a generous pension and a comfortable exile in France. François I waited in Pavia until the last forces in the fortified Castello capitulated and then rode triumphantly into Milan on 11 October, proclaiming the city once more a French possession.

---

[57] Quoted in Alessandro Luzio, 'Isabella d'Este e Leone X dal Congresso di Bologna alla presa di Milano (1515–1521)', *Archivio storico italiano* 44 (1909): 72–128 (77).

Spanish and papal troops did nothing to help Massimiliano Sforza defend his territory, Cardona obeying King Ferdinand of Spain's orders to focus on defending any challenge to Spanish conquests further south, while Leo X was intent on persuading François I not to attack Parma and Piacenza, which he hoped to retain as part of his nepotistic ambitions for Medici relatives. In the end, however, the pope decided to abandon the Holy League for a French alliance. At a meeting with the king in Bologna, Leo X agreed to recognize French jurisdiction over Milan and to cede Parma and Piacenza, so the cities were once more part of the Milanese state. The pope even desisted, eventually and very reluctantly, from his efforts to claim the duchy of Ferrara, since the Este had remained staunchly Francophile and had the king's fulsome support.[58]

Once the papal-French alliance was in place, the marquis scrambled to ingratiate himself with François I, fearing that his own state might be the target of the king's expansionist designs. He did so by dispatching his 15-year-old heir to Milan to pledge Gonzaga allegiance to the French crown. On 22 October 1515, Federico Gonzaga sent the first of the many letters he wrote to one or other of his parents during an absence from Mantua that was to last until the spring of 1517.[59] Although it was not initially envisaged that the youth would remain in Milan for so long and then leave Italy when the king returned to France, Federico's success in establishing excellent relations with François, and the invaluable information that came from his Mantuan retinue, which included the experienced envoy, Stazio Gadio, convinced his parents of the merit of their son following the court to France when it left Milan at the beginning of 1516.

In early November 1515, a Venetian delegation visited the marquis in the palace of San Sebastiano. Their task was to negotiate the restitution of the towns of Asola and Lonato, former Venetian possessions that Francesco had managed to hold on to, after claiming them on behalf of the Holy League in 1509, shortly before his capture and imprisonment. Whether Isabella had tried to lobby the pope to prevent this restitution, as Francesco asked her to do, does not emerge from their exchanges. It is likely she assumed her husband's request was unlikely to succeed. However, the prospect of losing these much-prized towns was a heavy blow for both of them. Isabella had been given Asola by Francesco as a reward for her stewardship of the Gonzaga regime during his imprisonment in Venice, while the marquis had intended to build a lodging within the fortress at Lonato to take advantage of what Isabella described, after a visit to the town's citadel, as its beautiful setting and most perfect air.[60]

[58]   Mallett and Shaw, *The Italian Wars*, 130–1.

[59]   Raffaele Tamalio, ed, *Federico Gonzaga alla corte di Francesco I di Francia nel carteggio privato con Mantova (1515–1517)* (Paris: Honoré Champion Éditeur, 1994).

[60]   Isabella d'Este to Federico Cattaneo, 18 July 1510, from Mantua, in Isabella d'Este, *Selected Letters*, 330–1; Isabella d'Este to Francesco Gonzaga, 17 March 1514, from Lonato, ASMn, AG, 2120, cc. 230r–231r.

Faced with another political humiliation, Francesco rallied defiantly, mounting an elaborately theatrical reception of the delegation, which included Antonio Grimani, Domenico Trevisan, Giorgio Cornaro, and Andrea Gritti, all from prominent Venetian families. After they were ushered into the San Sebastiano palace, the envoys were led past Andrea Mantegna's *Triumphs of Caesar*, the nine canvasses displayed to spectacular advantage in the great hall of the first floor, before being led into a smaller audience chamber, where the marquis awaited in carefully curated splendour. The encounter is described in a letter of Piero Soranzo, a member of the Venetian party:

> He was seated next to the fireplace, with three fans that aired him without losing the merest feather, surrounded by three fierce greyhounds and an infinite number of falcons and gyrfalcons held on the fists [of his attendants], and set above the wainscoting were painted representations of his beautiful horses and beautiful dogs and there was a dwarf dressed in gold.[61]

Enthroned amidst his hunting dogs and birds of prey, and against a painted backdrop of portraits of his favourite hounds and horses, Francesco proclaimed the princely identity that he had always cultivated. This diplomatic performance did nothing to prevent the loss of Asola and Lonato, which passed back into Venetian control shortly afterwards. However, it salvaged a measure of honour and proclaimed to the representatives of a hostile neighbour that Francesco still maintained a firm hold over his state, despite his physical frailty. Although the official envoys retired to their lodgings after the visit to San Sebastiano, Soranzo and several other men visited Isabella's *grotta*, within her apartments in the San Giorgio castle. There they saw 'an infinity of beautiful things'. However, Soranzo mentions the *grotta* amid a list of other sights which impressed him, including the ladies-in-waiting, the marquis's military accoutrements, and the many fine horses in the palace stables. It appears from his account that the Venetians were not particularly interested in the marchioness, or her cultural patronage, an attitude that was in keeping with their sternly republican attitudes to the female sex.

Sidelined on state occasions such as this, and with her eldest son increasingly taking over aspects of the diplomatic role she had previously performed in Milan and elsewhere, Isabella took up residence in the fortified Gonzaga residence at Borgoforte in mid-1516. Her usual summer retreat of Porto had no defences and was therefore too dangerous, given the proximity of the on-going war. French troops under the command of Odet de Foix, viscomte de Lautrec, were encamped

---

[61] Piero Soranzo to Marco Contarini, 6 November 1515, from Chiari near Brescia, published in Bourne, *The Soldier-Prince*, 529–30. Amico Maria della Torre also described the Venetian delegation's visit to Mantua in a letter to Federico II Gonzaga of 3 November 1515, ASMn, AG, 2491, cc. 18r–19v. Published in Bourne, *The Soldier-Prince*, 528–9.

in Mantuan territory, within striking distance of Verona, where several thousand German, Swiss, and Spanish troops were garrisoned and in effect besieged, in the aftermath of the emperor's failed attempt, in March 1516, to challenge French control of Milan.[62]

Capilupi wrote twice to Isabella on 17 June, urgently begging her to return to Mantua, even for a few days, on the grounds that her presence at Borgoforte, so near to territory that was being contested by rival armies, was provoking great controversy in the city and especially at court.[63] He received an immediate and stinging refusal. Yet, despite the rebuke and his subsequent grovelling apology, Capilupi wrote again on 18 June, explaining his doggedness in terms of a deep concern for Isabella's reputation. The secretary informed her that he had learned from contacts at the palace of San Sebastiano that the marquis had complained to some of his courtiers about his wife's presence at Borgoforte. This limited and relatively private lament had become far more public the following day. Although Capilupi was not among the much larger group of people at the palace that day either, he assured Isabella he had heard several reliable accounts of what had transpired. Francesco had bemoaned to those gathered at his palace that while even the peasants from the surrounding countryside had sought the protection of the city, the marchioness inexplicably refused to return home. Although the marquis conceded that the fortress at Borgoforte offered secure protection from the war, the presence there of his wife and her ladies-in-waiting had been noted by the soldiers in the vicinity and had become the butt of their jokes, impugning Isabella's honour, but also his. After Francesco invited explanations from members of the court for Isabella's intransigence, complete silence had ensued until Tolomeo Spagnoli suggested that the marquis ought simply to order his wife to return. According to Capilupi: 'He [the marquis] replied "she has a mind of her own. If she has no desire to come, she won't come on my orders and her failure to obey me will give me a bigger problem."'[64]

Capilupi urged the marchioness to consider the seriousness of the crisis, now that Francesco had now so publically aired his displeasure. He insisted her presence in Mantua was required to put an end to the gossip that her stubbornness was fuelling at court and warned that the patience of her husband was again being tested beyond what he was prepared to tolerate. The letter ends with a candid reflection on Isabella's character.

---

[62] Mallett and Shaw, *The Italian Wars*, 133.

[63] 'Segnora mia, disponetive a volere satisfare a tutto il mondo et al honore vostro di venire a stare qualche pochi giorni a Mantoa, perché il murmuro publico, ma più il privato, è grandissimo dil vostro stare fori in tempo che li private citadini non li stanno et fassine diversi commenti.' Benedetto Capilupi to Isabella d'Este, 17 June 1516, from Mantua, ASMn, AG, 2494, c. 132. The second letter of 17 June is c. 133.

[64] 'Rispose "ha uno cervello a modo suo. Se la non havesse volia de venire, non veneria per mio dire, et me seria maior carico che la non me obedesse."' Benedetto Capilupi to Isabella d'Este, 18 June 1516, from Mantua, ASMn, AG, 2494, cc. 134r–136r.

Pardon me Your Ladyship if I write too freely, because duty compels me, as does Your Ladyship's reputation for being too wilful and exposing yourself too recklessly to dangers and giving far too many opportunities to those who wish to criticize you by saying that you place your own comfort above the welfare of your children and of the state.[65]

None of Capilupi's trenchant appeals worked. However, five days later, he was able to inform Isabella that, as a result of his astute manipulations and many lies, he had convinced the marquis to approve her remaining in Borgoforte.[66] Isabella did not return to Mantua until the end of July.

The marchioness worked out a very effective way of protesting against her political marginalization in the years after her husband's release from imprisonment, at first by finding excuses to prolong her sojourns in Milan and Rome, but, eventually, by refusing to budge from her various retreats in the Mantuan countryside. As Francesco conceded, commanding his wife, only to have her refuse to obey, risked a greater blow to his husbandly honour than her absences did. The marquis therefore let Isabella know of his displeasure through secretarial intermediaries and the occasional ironic comment in letters. Sometimes, he recalled happier days in an attempt to rekindle his wife's affection, so she would cede to his wishes.

In the spring of 1517, the marchioness travelled to Casale Monferrato to meet Maria Paleologo, the 8-year-old daughter of the marquis, Guglielmo IX of Monferrato, and his wife, Anne of Alençon, whose betrothal to the adolescent Federico Gonzaga had recently been finalized. This task provided an excuse for a much longer journey that saw Isabella travel over the Alps into Provence, where she toured various holy sites and visited cities such as Marseilles and Arles. Francesco had given his wife an excellent mule to convey her safely over the rough terrain that would inevitably await her in the foothills and then the Alps themselves. When Isabella reported that the animal had, on one occasion, lost its footing and in a panic thrown her to the ground, Francesco responded with concern about the accident, worrying about the fact that she had hit her head hard.[67] Five days later, he was more explicitly affectionate, declaring his health had

---

[65] 'Perdonami Vostra Signoria se troppo liberamente scrivo, perché la servitù mi stringe et lo nome che ha Vostra Signoria di essere troppo di sua testa et di exponersi troppo facilmente a' pericoli et che troppo grande campo dati a chi vole calumniarvi cum dire che non extimati figlioli ni stato per uno vostro commodo.' Benedetto Capilupi to Isabella d'Este, 18 June 1516, from Mantua, ASMn, AG, 2494, cc. 134r–136r.

[66] 'Il signore resta troppo contento che restiati a Burgoforte, merce de le astutie et bosie mie, che sono però verità in effecto.' Benedetto Capilupi to Isabella d'Este, 23 June 1516, from Mantua, ASMn, AG, 2494, c. 143r.

[67] Isabella d'Este to Francesco Gonzaga, 28 April 1517, from Casale, in Isabella d'Este, *Selected Letters*, 419–20. Francesco Gonzaga to Isabella d'Este, 5 May 1517, ASMn, AG, 2123, cc. 42r–43r. Isabella d'Este to Francesco Gonzaga, 10 May 1517, from Tallard, France, ASMn, AG, 2123, cc. 111r–v.

improved since her departure and he very much regretted her absence.[68] In return, Isabella described her travels, the stimulation of new sights and experiences glossing over her unhappiness about developments in Mantua and prompting her to write to her husband amicably.

However, when she returned to Mantua in June 1517, Isabella retired almost immediately to Porto for the summer, as she did the following year. In October 1518, she returned to Casale to pay her respects to the family into which Federico was to marry, following the death of Maria Paleologo's father, after his leg became infected and had to be amputated.[69] During these years, Francesco was sometimes well enough to travel by carriage to Revere and to Marmirolo. These movements occasioned the small number of letters exchanged by the couple in the final years of their marriage. They sent seasonal produce when they were close enough for this to be practical, kept each other informed about their offspring, and exchanged news about political developments in Italy and elsewhere, gleaned from their respective epistolary networks. The tone of these last letters is cordial, occasionally even affectionate, but as duty became the primary reason for their correspondence, as it had in the first phase of their marriage, their communications became briefer and more formal, reflecting their parallel existences, physically far apart and emotionally with far less to share.

At the heart of the resentments which simmered between the pair from early 1513, and occasionally flared into open eruptions of conflict in the following three years, was a failure to agree about the give and take of their long, and remarkably successful, political collaboration. Francesco took the view that while urgent circumstances had sometimes required his wife to take the initiative politically, as in 1509 and 1510, there was to be no building on such experience. Ultimately, she was always to return to his control. Isabella disagreed. After years of diplomatic experience, she felt there was less need to await instructions before she acted and a reduced requirement to provide a detailed account of her every movement and decision. Francesco's appeals to the assembled court to explain his wife's refusal to leave Borgoforte suggests he was sure he had the weight of convention and public opinion on his side. But in the face of Isabella's resistance to his commands, he had to concede defeat and resign himself to a truce. Thus, the last years witnessed a peaceful, if more distant, epistolary rapport.

Isabella's last extant letter to her husband, written from Genoa on 4 November 1518, is typical of many others she wrote to him during her travels. It provides a lively account of an excursion to a fair at Asti, where she had admired the sumptuous fabrics for sale, and of a carriage ride to see the mountain scenery. It also

---

[68] 'la procuri di conservarse sana et di ritornare presto a casa, sí per evitare il caldo che cominciarà a molestare, sí perché a noi pareria strano a stare molto a vederla.' Francesco Gonzaga to Isabella d'Este, 10 May 1517, from Marmirolo, ASMn, AG, 2123, cc. 44r–v.

[69] Isabella d'Este to Francesco Gonzaga, 22, 27, and 29 October, from Casale Monferrato, ASMn, AG, 2123, cc. 323–5.

describes the violent bouts of sea sickness experienced by members of her entourage when they had sailed in rough seas to the port of Genoa. Along with her letter, Isabella sent a local culinary delicacy that she hoped would stimulate Francesco's poor appetite, her thoughtfulness signalling a continuing concern for his suffering and melancholy.[70] The marquis's final letter to Isabella bears the same date. It too contains a hint of the affection that still bound them: 'We are in the usual state, with the hope of improving. Federico and our other children are well, thanks be to God. Your Ladyship, too, keep well and return soon, because we desire to see you.'[71] The deeper currents of their feelings are not revealed in these polite exchanges, but, as Francesco's illness worsened inexorably, the pair likely knew they would soon be parted permanently and wrote to each other with kindness.

Francesco died in the San Sebastiano palace on 29 March 1519, surrounded by his family and the courtiers who had served him during his years as an invalid. He was fifty-three. According to Mario Equicola, who would shortly become Isabella's secretary—the faithful Capilupi having died towards the end of 1518— the marquis rallied enough in his final hours to farewell those gathered around his bed. Turning to his wife, he praised her prudence and integrity and declared 'he had always been aware of her marvellous intelligence and judged her to be capable of every endeavour'.[72] Francesco's final words to Isabella may well have been an acknowledgement of his enduring affection and admiration for a woman who, despite their quarrels, had served him faithfully. Yet the praise reported by Equicola was also, and more crucially, a public endorsement of the person who would support their son Federico, still a little short of nineteen years old, as he began to take on the weighty responsibilities of ruling the marquisate. We learn nothing of Isabella's feelings about the death of her husband from the formulaic acknowledgements she sent in response to the many letters of condolence which flooded into the chancery.

Francesco's will, drawn up during his last hours of life, stipulated that his brothers, Sigismondo and Giovanni, together with Isabella, would act as regents until Federico reached his majority at the age of twenty-two. The young man's uncles were named as caretaker rulers to avoid the perception that a woman would be head of state, but, in effect, it was Isabella who did most of the work.

---

[70] Isabella d'Este to Francesco Gonzaga, 4 November 1518, from Genoa, ASMn, AG, 2123, cc. 326r–327v.

[71] 'noi stemo pur nel termino solito con speranza di meglio. Federico et gli altri nostri figlioli stanno sani, gratia di Dio. Vostra Signoria anche lei se conserve sana et sia di presto ritorno, perché desideramo vederla.' Francesco Gonzaga to Isabella d'Este, 4 November 1518, from Mantua, ASMn, AG, 2123, c. 287.

[72] 'Voltossi ultimamente alla consorte, Signora Donna Isabella da Este, riferendo molte sue lodi di prudenza, et integrità. Disse haverla sempre conosciuta di maraviglioso ingegno, et giudicatala sufficientissima ad ogn'altra impresa, però gli raccomandava i communi figliuoli.' Equicola, Dell'istoria di Mantova, 269.

She resumed the political role she had performed in the two decades after her marriage and again had full access to the diplomatic and administrative organs of government. Tolomeo Spagnoli was stripped of his position and sent into exile. Thus, for a few precious years, Isabella recovered and reasserted the honour which her political eclipse after 1513 had so fatally destroyed, in her own estimation, if not in that of others.

Once Federico attained his majority and wished to assert his princely maturity, Isabella was again politically sidelined. A long infatuation with his lover, Isabella Boschetti, one of the marchioness's former ladies-in-waiting, had prompted Federico to refuse to honour the marriage his mother had arranged with Maria Paleologo and which he himself had impetuously confirmed by exchanging rings with her in 1517. When he became marquis, Federico repented that action and persuaded the pope to annul the betrothal. He hoped to make a more politically advantageous match. Annoyed by Federico's behaviour and disgusted by the influence which her son's mistress enjoyed at court, in 1525, Isabella left Mantua for an extended period, as she had ten years before. This time, she remained in Rome for two years, witnessing the tragic sack of the city by the army of Charles V in 1527.[73]

Eventually, Federico embraced his marital duty. In 1531, he wed Margherita Paleologo, the sister of Maria, who had died suddenly the year before. Margherita's only brother had met an accidental death around the same time, after falling from his horse. Thus, Margherita inherited the duchy of Monferrato, and became a far more enticing marital prospect for Federico.[74] However, like his father, Federico died prematurely, in his case at only forty years old, leaving Margherita Paleologo and his brother Ercole to rule Mantua as regents. Margherita governed Monferrato with the help of her mother, Anne of Alençon, who remained in Casale and oversaw the everyday administration of the duchy.

The careers of the other sons of Isabella and Francesco produced useful new diplomatic connections for the Gonzaga regime, as the Italian Wars continued to create political and social chaos in the peninsula's city states. The status of Ferrante Gonzaga as a leading general in Charles V's army saved his mother's life, and those of the hundreds of aristocratic refugees that Isabella allowed to seek refuge with her in the Colonna palace, during the 1527 sack of Rome by imperial and Spanish mercenaries.[75] Ercole Gonzaga, the son over whose name his parents had squabbled in 1506, became a cardinal, thanks largely to Isabella's assiduous diplomatic efforts. Ercole played an important role as papal legate during the Council

---

[73] Alessandro Luzio, *Isabella d'Este e il Sacco di Roma* (Milan: L. F. Cogliati, 1908).

[74] On Federico Gonzaga's marital manoeuverings, see Deanna Shemek, 'Aretino's *Marescalco*: Marriage Woes and the Duke of Mantua', *Renaissance Studies* 16.3 (2002): 366–80.

[75] Luzio, *Isabella d'Este e il Sacco di Roma*.

of Trent.[76] Although only Eleonora married, the dedication of the other daughters, Ippolita and Livia Osanna, to a life of prayer as nuns contributed to the perception that the Gonzaga regime was a pious one and the family deserving of its privileges and power. Thus, the children of Francesco and Isabella fulfilled their dynastic duty, just as their parents had done. Isabella died in February 1539, after twenty years of widowhood, at the age of sixty-four. She was buried, not in Francesco's tomb, but in the Clarissan convent of Santa Paola, where her daughter, Livia Osanna, who became Suor Paola, was cloistered and would eventually become prioress.

[76] Giampiero Brunelli, 'Ercole Gonzaga', in *Dizionario Biografico Italiano*, 57 (2001) http://www.treccani.it/enciclopedia/ercole-gonzaga_%28Dizionario-Biografico%29.

Conclusion

The richly nuanced epistolary sources on which this study is based have revealed the extent to which the normative rules of premodernity regarding how a man and his wife ought to relate to each other might be observed, ignored, contested, and modified by an elite couple as a result of urgent political pressures, or the evolution of the relationship over time. Ultimately, marital relationships were negotiated by the individuals who inhabited them. Isabella outgrew the docile role of subordinate. As a mature woman, she sought a modest loosening of traditional marital strictures. In his more generous moments, Francesco conceded that Isabella was both trustworthy and politically prudent. During the first two decades of marriage, he often gave ground to his wife by accommodating her desire for a degree of physical mobility and a measure of diplomatic autonomy. However, as illness undermined his strongly physical interpretation of masculinity, Francesco's conviction in his status as the dominant partner found expression in a greater desire to be seen to command a wife whose reputation as strong willed and overly independent had become public, albeit with his own collusion, when that perception had proved politically expedient. Thus, in the last years, following a period which had witnessed Isabella ably negotiate her husband's release from a year-long Venetian imprisonment and even govern Mantua alone, the couple failed to see eye-to-eye over how their relationship was to work in its mature phase.

Inevitably, the conventional template of marital relations was subjected to intense pressure by the fact that Francesco and Isabella were near equals in terms of social status, intelligence, and education. Indeed, Isabella outranked her husband by virtue of her royal blood. Her lineage and sophisticated mind gave her a natural confidence that she should be recognized as no ordinary woman. Yet deeply entrenched notions that the gender hierarchy could not legitimately be challenged and strong prejudices against a woman exercising significant political authority, even if it were delegated by a male relative, proved powerful forces. We have seen that in the summer of 1495, Antonio Donato refused to obey Isabella's order to send grain to the guards patrolling the Mantuan border at Ostiglia and, less than a year later, the local hospital board ignored her instructions regarding the appointment of a new rector. When war came dangerously close to Mantua in April 1509, there were mutinous murmurings in the city about whether the marchioness's loyalty to her adopted city could be relied upon, while Francesco

A Renaissance Marriage: The Political and Personal Alliance of Isabella d'Este and Francesco Gonzaga, 1490–1519.
Carolyn James, Oxford University Press (2020). © Carolyn James.
DOI: 10.1093/oso/9780199681211.001.0001

was far away on the battlefield and could not supervise his wife's decisions about the city's defences.

These incidents were indicative of the negative attitudes associated with a woman, and a foreign one to boot, being left in charge of state affairs. Isabella prevailed over her enemies for much of the time, but, when her husband's imprimatur was erratic, or not forthcoming at all, she was exposed to the sting of social disapproval. The malevolent gossip within the court and the city stirred up by Isabella's long absences from home between 1513 and 1515 show the backlash that was directed at a woman who so blatantly demonstrated an unsanctioned level of autonomy. Francesco too risked censure for his failures to maintain full patriarchal control over his wife. However, as he admitted, he did not actually possess the power to force Isabella to do his bidding, without risking ignominy if the attempt to impose his will on her failed. Thus, the marquis preferred to negotiate with his wife and to exert emotional blackmail by letter, just as Isabella used all the force of her epistolary eloquence to persuade Francesco to cede to her desires.

Indeed, amid the intrigues and chattering tongues of the court, letter-writing provided a crucial means through which this couple negotiated the changing dynamics of their personal rapport and political alliance. Although hardly a private forum, given the routine mediation of a secretary in producing most of the letters, written communication provided a space for dialogue and emotional release. It allowed Isabella and Francesco to bridge the unfamiliarity and awkwardness of the early days of their union, then to nurture the intimacy that blossomed amid the joys and worries of parenthood, and, finally, to express the mutual grievances that emerged as their relations grew frostier.

We have seen that the stilted formulaic phrases of the early letters largely disappeared after the mid-1490s, to be replaced by an amiable epistolary conversation between a man happy to delegate some of the routine aspects of government to an eager apprentice and a woman keen to rise to the challenges of that circumscribed authority. Even when Isabella's ambitions to play a larger role in diplomacy first unsettled Francesco's understanding of how the division of political work with his wife ought to function, his own burgeoning role as a military captain convinced the marquis that Isabella's stewardship of his regime posed no risk to his husbandly authority. Combined with the parental joy they took in their children, especially after the birth of Federico, the couple's well-oiled political collaboration prompted a relaxation of epistolary formality. Their regular letter exchanges encouraged jokes, affectionate anecdotes, and a sense of camaraderie. Occasionally they even attempted to capture in writing the cadences of their children's babble, so the absent spouse could experience the enjoyable sounds and routines of family life. But, in the last years of marriage, long periods of separation and the inevitable misunderstandings that the lack of face-to-face contact created saw more frequent recriminations between the two, before the pair reached an emotionally cool reconciliation, in the prelude to Francesco's premature death. Their letters returned to the formal style of the immediate aftermath of their marriage, when they sought to fulfil their marital obligations by keeping in touch during periods of physical separation. Thus, their approach to letter-writing came full circle, mirroring the path of their personal rapport.

Although the correspondence between this aristocratic couple is certainly unusual, it is not unique. The letters exchanged by Francesco's grandparents, Lodovico Gonzaga and Barbara of Brandenburg, share much in common with those of Francesco and Isabella, both in terms of their excellent state of preservation and even the size of the collection. Although the letters remain understudied, because they too are widely dispensed in many files within the Gonzaga archive, a systematic analysis of this earlier marital correspondence would no doubt reveal a relationship as complex and idiosyncratic as that of their grandson Francesco and his wife Isabella. Such a study would also permit a comparison of how the political scene of the mid-fifteenth century shaped the way that Lodovico Gonzaga and Barbara of Brandenburg collaborated diplomatically and administratively. The thousand or so letters between Isabella's parents, Ercole d'Este and Eleonora d'Aragona, which survive within the Este archive, also have the potential to throw a fascinating light on how the duchess's royal blood and political clout as daughter of the king of Naples influenced the mostly cordial, but occasionally stormy, relationship with her husband.

Many more examples of spousal correspondence are being discovered in other Italian and European archives. These epistolary sources will enrich our understanding of how early modern marital unions were experienced and negotiated by individuals from aristocratic and mercantile backgrounds and how the emotional dynamic of a range of relationships changed over time in different social and political contexts, as children were born and died, illnesses undermined youthful hopes, and external events impacted on family life. The tensions between static gendered orthodoxies and the dynamic individual interpretations of appropriate behaviour that we have seen in the relationship between Francesco and Isabella are likely to be writ similarly large.

Bibliography

Archival Sources

Mantua
Archivio di Stato
Archivio Gonzaga
Autografi Volta, busta 1
Carteggio degli inviati e diversi, Ferrara, buste 1229, 1231, 1232, 1234
Carteggio degli inviati e diversi, Milano, busta 1630
Carteggio degli inviati e diversi, Napoli e Sicilia, busta 807
Carteggio degli inviati e diversi, Roma, buste 852, 859
Copialettere ordinari misti, buste 2904, 2906, 2911, 2913, 2914, 2915, 2921, 2931
Copialettere particolari d'Isabella d'Este, buste 2992, 2996, 2997
Copialettere riservati, busta 2961
Corrispondenza colla Marchesa Isabella d'Este, busta 1894
Lettere degli Estensi ai Signori di Mantova, buste 1184, 1185
Lettere ai Gonzaga da Mantova e paesi dello stato, buste 2433, 2438, 2447, 2449, 2450, 2487, 2489, 2491, 2494, 2496
Lettere originali dei Gonzaga, buste 2104, 2106, 2107, 2108, 2108bis, 2109, 2110, 2110bis, 2111, 2112, 2113, 2114, 2114bis, 2115, 2115bis, 2116, 2117, 2118, 2118bis, 2119, 2120, 2121, 2122, 2123, 2123bis
Minute della cancelleria, busta 2192

Modena
Archivio di Stato
Casa e stato
Carteggio ambasciatori, Mantova, busta 1
Carteggio ambasciatori, Milano, busta 6
Carteggio principi esteri, minute di lettere ducali a principi esteri, Milano, busta 1507
Carteggio tra principi Estensi, buste 67, 132, 133

Printed Primary Sources

Arienti, Giovanni Sabadino degli. *Gynevera de le clare donne*. Edited by Corrado Ricci and Alberto Bacchi della Lega. Bologna: Presso Romagnoli-dall' Acqua, 1888.
Arienti, Giovanni Sabadino degli. *The Letters of Giovanni Sabadino Degli Arienti (1481–1510)*. Edited and introduced by Carolyn James. Florence: L.S. Olschki; Perth: University of Western Australia, 2002.

Brown, Clifford M., and Anna Maria Lorenzoni, eds. *Isabella d'Este and Lorenzo da Pavia: Documents for the History of Art and Culture in Renaissance Mantua*. Geneva: Librairie Droz, 1982.

Brown, Clifford M., Anna Maria Lorenzoni, and Sally Hickson, eds. *'Per dare qualche splendore a la gloriosa città di Mantua': Documents for the Antiquarian Collection of Isabella d'Este*. Rome: Bulzoni, 2002.

Caleffini, Ugo. *Croniche: 1471–1494*. Ferrara: Deputazione provinciale ferrarese di storia patria, 2006.

Commynes, Philippe de. *The Memoirs of Philippe de Commynes*. Edited by Samuel Kinser. 2 vols. Columbia, S.C.: University of South Carolina Press, 1969.

Dolfo, Floriano. *Lettere ai Gonzaga*. Edited by Marzia Minutelli. Rome: Edizioni di Storia e Letteratura, 2002.

d'Este, Isabella. *Selected Letters*. Edited and translated by Deanna Shemek. Toronto: Iter Press, 2017.

Equicola, Mario. *Dell'istoria di Mantova libri cinque*. Edited by Benedetto Osanna. Mantua: Francesco Osanna stampatore, 1607, republished Bologna: Forni, 1968.

Equicola, Mario. *De mulieribus. Delle donne*. Edited by Giuseppe Lucchesini and Pina Totaro. Pisa, Rome: Istituti editoriali e poligrafici internazionali, 2004.

Ferrarini, Girolamo. *Memoriale estense: 1476–1489*. Edited by Primo Griguolo. Rovigo: Minelliana, 2006.

Ferrato, Pietro. *Il marchesato di Mantova e l'impero ottomano alla fine del secolo 15: documenti inediti tratti dall'archivio storico dei Gonzaga*. Mantua: Stabilimento tipografico Mondovi, 1876.

Giovio, Paolo. *Elogia virorum bellica virtute illustrium*. Basel: Pietro Perna (for Heinrich Petri), 1575.

Grati, Antonella, and Arturo Pacini, eds. *Carteggio degli oratori mantovani alla corte sforzesca (1450–1500)*. Vol. 15 (1495–1498) Rome: Ministero per i beni e le attività culturali, Direzione generale per gli archivi, 2003.

Medici, Lorenzo de'. *Lettere*. Vol. VII. Edited by Michael Mallett. Florence: Giunti-Barbèra, 1998.

Pélissier, Léon-Gabriel. 'La politique du marquis de Mantoue pendant la lutte de Louis XII et de Ludovic Sforza (1498–1500)'. *Annales de la Faculté des lettres de Bordeaux*. 1 (1892): 35–120.

Pius II. *Commentaries*. Edited by Margaret Meserve and Marcello Simonetta. 2 vols. Cambridge, Mass.: Harvard University Press, 2003.

Rucellai, Giovanni di Pagolo. *Zibaldone*. Edited by Gabriella Battista. Florence: Simel Edizioni del Galluzzo, 2013.

Sanudo, Marino. *La spedizione di Carlo VIII in Italia*. Edited by Rinaldo Fulin. Venice: Marco Visentini, 1883.

Simonetta, Marcello, ed. *Carteggio degli oratori mantovani alla corte sforzesca (1450–1500)*. Vol. 11 (1478–79). Rome: Ministero per i beni e le attività culturali, Direzione generale per gli archivi, 2001.

Tamalio, Raffaele, ed. *Federico Gonzaga alla corte di Francesco I di Francia nel carteggio privato con Mantova (1515–1517)*. Paris: Honoré Champion Éditeur, 1994.

Vasari, Giorgio. *Le vite de' più eccellenti pittori scultori ed architettori: scritte da Giorgio Vasari, pittore aretino*. Edited by Gaetano Milanesi. Vol. 3. Florence: G. Sansoni, 1906.

Visconti, Carlo, ed. 'Croniche del marchese di Mantova'. *Archivio storico lombardo* 6 (1879): 37–68, 333–56, 500–13.

Zambotti, Bernardino. *Diario ferrarese dall'anno 1476 sino al 1504*. Edited by Giuseppe Pardi. Vol. 7. *Rerum Italicarum Scriptores*, XXIV. Modena: Zanichelli, 1934.

Printed Secondary Sources

Adams, Tracy. 'Married Noblewomen as Diplomats: Affective Diplomacy'. In *Gender and Emotions in Medieval and Early Modern Europe: Destroying Order, Structuring Disorder*. Edited by Susan Broomhall, 51–65. Farnham: Ashgate, 2015.

Albala, Ken. *Eating Right in the Renaissance*. Berkeley, Calif.: University of California Press, 2010.

Allsen, Thomas T. *The Royal Hunt in Eurasian History*. Singapore: Institute of Southeast Asian Studies, 2013.

Ames-Lewis, Francis. *Isabella and Leonardo: The Artistic Relationship between Isabella d'Este and Leonardo da Vinci*. New Haven, Conn.; London: Yale University Press, 2012.

Amundsen, Darrel W. *Medicine, Society, and Faith in the Ancient and Medieval Worlds*. Baltimore: The Johns Hopkins University Press, 1996.

Antonovics, Atis. 'Hommes de guerre et gens de finance: The Inquest on the French Defeat in Naples 1503–4'. In *Italy and the European Powers. The Impact of War, 1500–1530*. Edited by Christine Shaw, 26–32. Leiden: Brill, 2006.

Arrizabalaga, Jon, Roger French, and John Henderson. *The Great Pox: The French Disease in Renaissance Europe*. New Haven, Conn.; London: Yale University Press, 1997.

Baernstein, P. Renée, and John Christopoulos. 'Interpreting the Body in Early Modern Italy: Pregnancy, Abortion and Adulthood'. *Past & Present* 223.1 (2014): 41–75.

Béguin, Sylvie et al. *Le studiolo d'Isabelle d'Este: Catalogue*. Paris: Editions des musées nationaux, 1975.

Biow, Douglas. 'The Beard in Sixteenth-Century Italy'. In *The Body in Early Modern Italy*. Edited by Julia Hairston and Walter Stephens, 176–94. Baltimore: The Johns Hopkins University Press, 2010.

Blanchard, Joël. 'Political and Cultural Implications of Secret Diplomacy: Commynes and Ferrara in the Light of Unpublished Documents'. In *The French Descent into Renaissance Italy*. Edited by David Abulafia, 231–47. Aldershot: Ashgate, 1995.

Bourne, Molly. 'Francesco II Gonzaga and Maps as Palace Decoration in Renaissance Mantua'. *Imago Mundi* 51 (1999): 51–82.

Bourne, Molly. *Francesco II Gonzaga: The Soldier-Prince as Patron*. Rome: Bulzoni Editore, 2008.

Bourne, Molly. 'Mail Humour and Male Sociability: Sexual Innuendo in the Epistolary Domain of Francesco II Gonzaga'. In *Erotic Cultures of Renaissance Italy*. Edited by Sara F. Matthews-Grieco, 199–221. Aldershot: Ashgate, 2010.

Bourne, Molly. 'The Turban'd Turk in Renaissance Mantua: Francesco II Gonzaga's Interest in Ottoman Fashion'. In *Mantova e il Rinascimento italiano. Studi in onore di David S. Chambers*. Edited by Philippa Jackson and Guido Rebecchini, 53–64. Mantua: Sometti, 2011.

Bowd, Stephen. *Renaissance Mass Murder: Civilians and Soldiers during the Italian Wars*. Oxford: Oxford University Press, 2018.

Broomhall, Susan. '"Women's Little Secrets": Defining the Boundaries of Reproductive Knowledge in Sixteenth-Century France'. *Social History of Medicine* 15.1 (2002): 1–15.

Broomhall, Susan. '"My Daughter, My Dear": The Correspondence of Catherine de Médicis and Elisabeth de Valois'. *Women's History Review* 24.4 (2015): 548–69.

Brown, Clifford M. *Isabella d'Este in the Ducal Palace in Mantua: An Overview of Her Rooms in the Castello di San Giorgio and the Corte Vecchia*. Rome: Bulzoni, 2005.

Brown, Clifford M., and Anna Maria Lorenzoni. 'The Palazzo di San Sebastiano (1506–1512) and the Art Patronage of Francesco II Gonzaga, Fourth Marquis of Mantua'. *Gazette des Beaux-Arts* 129 (1997): 131–80.

Brown, Clifford M., and Anna Maria Lorenzoni. 'Il cinquecentesimo anniversario di un omicidio alla corte di Francesco II Gonzaga'. *Civiltà mantovana* 120 (2005): 79–112.

Brown, Richard. 'The Politics of Magnificence in Ferrara 1450–1505: A Study in the Socio-Political Implications of Renaissance Spectacle'. Unpublished doctoral thesis, University of Edinburgh, 1982.

Brunelli, Giampiero. 'Ercole Gonzaga'. In *Dizionario Biografico Italiano*, 57, 2001 http://www.treccani.it/enciclopedia/ercole-gonzaga_%28Dizionario-Biografico%29.

Campbell, Stephen J. *The Cabinet of Eros: Renaissance Mythological Painting and the Studiolo of Isabella d'Este*. New Haven, Conn.; London: Yale University Press, 2006.

Cartwright, Julia. *Isabella d'Este, Marchioness of Mantua, 1474–1539. A Study of the Renaissance*. 2 vols. London: J. Murray, 1903.

Castagna, Rita. *Un viceré per Eleonora Brognina alla corte di Isabella d'Este Gonzaga*. Florence: Moretti, 1982.

Cessi, Roberto. 'La cattura del marchese Francesco Gonzaga di Mantova e le prime trattative per la sua liberazione'. *Nuovo archivio veneto* 25 (1913): 144–76.

Cevizli, Antonia Gatward. 'More Than a Messenger: Embodied Expertise in Mantuan Envoys to the Ottomans in the 1490s'. *Mediterranean Studies* 22.2 (2014): 166–89.

Cevizli, Antonia Gatward. 'Portraits, Turbans and Cuirasses: Material Culture between Mantua and the Ottomans in the 1490s'. In *Global Gifts: The Material Culture of Diplomacy in Early Modern Europe*. Edited by Zoltán Biedermann, Anne Gerritsen, and Giorgio Riello, 34–55. Cambridge: Cambridge University Press, 2017.

Cheles, Luciano. *The Studiolo of Urbino: An Iconographic Investigation*. Wiesbaden: Ludwig Reichert, 1986.

Chiappini, Luciano. *Eleonora d'Aragona: prima duchessa di Ferrara*. Rovigo: S.T.E.R., 1956.

Clough, Cecil H. 'Art as Power in the Decoration of the Study of an Italian Renaissance Prince: The Case of Federico da Montefeltro'. *Artibus et Historiae* 16.31 (1995): 19–50.

Clough, Cecil H. 'The Romagna Campaign of 1494: A Significant Military Encounter'. In *The French Descent into Renaissance Italy*. Edited by David Abulafia, 191–215. Aldershot: Ashgate, 1995.

Clubb, Louise George. 'Staging Ferrara: State Theatre from Borso to Alfonso II'. In *Phaethon's Children. The Este Court and Its Culture in Early Modern Ferrara*. Edited by Deanna Shemek and Dennis Looney, 345–62. Tempe, Ariz.: Arizona Centre for Medieval and Renaissance Studies, 2005.

Cockram, Sarah D. P. 'Epistolary Masks: Self-Presentation and Dissimulation in the Letters of Isabella d'Este'. *Italian Studies* 64.1 (2009): 20–37.

Cockram, Sarah D. P. *Isabella d'Este and Francesco Gonzaga: Power Sharing at the Italian Renaissance Court*. Farnham: Ashgate, 2013.

Cockram, Sarah D. P. 'Interspecies Understanding: Exotic Animals and their Handlers at the Italian Renaissance Court'. *Renaissance Studies* 31.2 (2017): 277–96.

Coniglio, Giuseppe. 'Francesco Gonzaga e la Lega di Cambrai'. *Archivio storico italiano* 120 (1962): 3–31.

Coniglio, Giuseppe. 'La politica di Francesco Gonzaga nell'opera di un immigrato meridionale: Iacopo Probo d'Atri'. *Archivio storico lombardo* 88 (1961): 131–67.

Corradi, Alfonso. 'Nuovi Documenti per la storia delle malattie veneree in Italia dalla fine del Quattrocento alla metà del Cinquecento'. *Annali universali di medicina e chirurgia* 269 (1884): 289–386.

Crawford, Patricia. *Blood, Bodies and Families in Early Modern England*. Harlow: Pearson/ Longman, 2004.

Crescenzo, Lisa di. ' "Leaving Hell and Arriving in Paradise": Between Victimhood and Agency in the Exilic Experience of Luisa Donati Strozzi (1434–1510)'. *Parergon* 34.2 (2017): 99–131.

Daybell, James. *The Material Letter in Early Modern England: Manuscript Letters and the Culture and Practices of Letter-Writing, 1512–1635*. Basingstoke: Palgrave Macmillan, 2012.

Daybell, James, and Andrew Gordon, eds. *Cultures of Correspondence in Early Modern Britain*. Philadelphia: University of Pennsylvania Press, 2016.

Daybell, James, and Peter Hinds, eds. *Material Readings of Early Modern Culture: Texts and Social Practices, 1580–1730*. Basingstoke: Palgrave Macmillan, 2010.

Dean, Trevor. 'Ferrarese Chroniclers and the Este State, 1490–1505'. In *Phaethon's Children. The Este Court and Its Culture in Early Modern Ferrara*. Edited by Deanna Shemek and Dennis Looney, 169–87. Tempe, Ariz.: Arizona Centre for Medieval and Renaissance Studies, 2005.

Dean, Trevor. 'Ferrara and Mantua'. In *The Italian Renaissance State*. Edited by Andrea Gamberini and Isabella Lazzarini, 112–31. Cambridge: Cambridge University Press, 2012.

Dean, Trevor, and Kate J. P. Lowe, eds. *Marriage in Italy, 1300–1650*. Cambridge: Cambridge University Press, 1998.

De Giorgio, Michela, Christiane Klapisch-Zuber, and Marina Beer, eds. *Storia del matrimonio*. Rome, Bari: Laterza, 1996.

Dupont-Pierrart, Nicole. *Claire de Gonzague Comtesse de Bourbon-Montpensier (1464–1503). Une princesse italienne à la cour de France*. Lille: Septentrion, 2017.

Ferrari, Monica. 'Lettere di principi bambini del Quattrocento lombardo'. *Mélanges de l'école française de Rome* 109.1 (1997): 339–54.

Ferrari, Monica. ' "Per non manchare in tuto del debito mio": L'educazione dei bambini Sforza nel Quattrocento'. In *I bambini di una volta. Problemi di metodo. Studi per Egle Becchi*. Vol. 3, 15–40. Storia dell'educazione. Milan: Franco Angeli, 2006.

Ferrari, Monica, Isabella Lazzarini, and Frederico Piseri. *Autografie dell'età minore. Lettere di tre dinastie italiane tra Quattrocento e Cinquecento*. Rome: Viella, 2016.

Ferraro, Joanne Marie. *Marriage Wars in Late Renaissance Venice*. Oxford: Oxford University Press, 2001.

Ferraro, Joanne Marie. 'Childhood in Medieval and Early Modern Times'. In *The Routledge History of Childhood in the Western World*. Edited by Paula S. Fass, 61–77. Abingdon: Routledge, 2013.

Folin, Marco. 'Gli Estensi e Ferrara nel quadro di un sistema politico composito, 1452–1598'. In *Storia di Ferrara*. Vol. 4, 22–76. Ferrara: Corbo, 2000.

Folin, Marco. 'Le cronache a Ferrara e negli stati estensi (Secoli XV–XVI)'. In *Storia di Ferrara*. Vol. 4, 460–92. Ferrara: Corbo, 2000.

Folin, Marco. 'La corte della duchessa: Eleonora d'Aragona a Ferrara'. In *Donne di potere nel Rinascimento*. Edited by Letizia Arcangeli and Susanna Peyronel, 481–512. Rome: Viella, 2008.

Franklin, Margaret Ann. *Boccaccio's Heroines: Power and Virtue in Renaissance Society*. Aldershot; Burlington, VT: Ashgate, 2006.

Frizzi, Antonio. *Memorie per la storia di Ferrara*. Vol. 4. Ferrara: Abram Servadio, 1848.

Gardner, Edmund Garratt. *Dukes and Poets in Ferrara*. New York: Haskell, 1904.

Guerra, Enrica. 'L'educazione militare del cardinale Ippolito I d'Este'. In *Formare alle professioni. La cultura militare tra passato e presente*. Edited by Monica Ferrari and Filippo Ledda, 101–15. Milan: Franco Angeli, 2011.

Guerra, Enrica, and Angela Giallongo. 'Eleonora d'Aragona e *I doveri del principe* di Diomede Carafa'. In *Donne di palazzo nelle corti Europee. Tracce e forme di potere dall'età moderna*, 113–19. Milan: Edizioni Unicopli, 2005.

Gundersheimer, Werner L. *Ferrara: The Style of a Renaissance Despotism*. Princeton, N.J.: Princeton University Press, 1973.

Harris, Barbara J. *English Aristocratic Women, 1450–1550: Marriage and Family, Property and Careers*. Oxford, New York: Oxford University Press, 2002.

Hickson, Sally. 'Syphilis, Suffering and Sodality: Friendship and Contagion in Renaissance Mantua'. In *Friendship and Sociability in Premodern Europe: Contexts, Concepts and Expressions*. Edited by Amyrose McCue Gill and Sarah Rolfe, 153–70. Toronto: Iter Press, 2014.

James, Carolyn. 'The Travels of Isabella d'Este, Marchioness of Mantua'. *Studies in Travel Writing* 13 (2009): 99–109.

James, Carolyn. 'Margherita Cantelmo and the Worth of Women in Renaissance Italy'. In *Mirrors of Princesses: Virtue Ethics for Women 1250–1550*. Edited by Karen Green and Constant Mews, 145–63. Dordrecht: Springer, 2011.

James, Carolyn. 'Marriage by Correspondence: Politics and Domesticity in the Letters of Isabella d'Este and Francesco Gonzaga, 1490–1519'. *Renaissance Quarterly* 65.2 (2012): 321–52.

James, Carolyn. 'Florence and Ferrara: Dynastic Marriage and Politics'. In *The Medici: Citizens and Masters*. Edited by Robert Black and John E. Law, 365–78. Florence: I Tatti Harvard Centre for Renaissance Studies, 2015.

James, Carolyn. 'What's Love Got to Do with It? Dynastic Politics and Motherhood in the Letters of Eleonora of Aragon and Her Daughters'. *Women's History Review* 24.4 (2015): 528–47.

James, Carolyn. 'In Praise of Women: Giovanni Sabadino Degli Arienti's *Gynevera de le clare donne*'. In *The Intellectual Dynamism of the High Middle Ages*. Edited by Clare Monagle. Amsterdam: Amsterdam University Press, 2020.

James, Carolyn, and Jessica O'Leary. 'Letter Writing and Emotions, 1100–1700'. In *The Routledge History Handbook to Emotions in Europe, 1100–1700*. Edited by Susan Broomhall and Andrew Lynch, 256–68. Abingdon: Routledge, 2019.

Kallins, Gail A. 'Mantegna's Minerva Overcoming the Vices Reconsidered'. *Athanor* 12 (1994): 35–43.

King, Margaret L. 'Concepts of Childhood: What We Know and Where We Might Go'. *Renaissance Quarterly* 60.2 (2007): 371–407.

Kirkham, Victoria. 'Creative Partners: The Marriage of Laura Battiferra and Bartolomeo Ammannati'. *Renaissance Quarterly* 55.2 (2002): 498–558.

Kissling, Hans-Joachim. 'Francesco II Gonzaga ed il Sultan Bàyezîd II'. *Archivio storico italiano* 125 (1967): 34–68.

Klapisch-Zuber, Christiane. 'Zacharias, or the Ousted Father: Nuptial Rites in Tuscany between Giotto and the Council of Trent'. In *Women, Family, and Ritual in Renaissance Italy*, translated by Lydia Cochrane, 178–212. Chicago, London: University of Chicago Press, 1985.

Kolsky, Stephen. *The Ghost of Boccaccio: Writings on Famous Women in Renaissance Italy.* Turnhout: Brepols, 2005.

Kuehn, Thomas. *Law, Family, and Women: Toward a Legal Anthropology of Renaissance Italy.* Chicago: University of Chicago Press, 1994.

Kuehn, Thomas. 'Marriage in the Archives: A Review Essay'. *The Sixteenth Century Journal* 39.3 (2008): 731–6.

Lazzarini, Isabella. 'I Gonzaga, la città, e territorio. Strutture dell'insediamento e potere signorile a Mantova fra Tre e Quattrocento'. In *Il paesaggio mantovano nelle tracce materiali, nelle lettere e nelle arti.* Vol. 3. Edited by Eugenio Camerlenghi, Viviana Rebonato, and Sara Tammaccaro, 511–32. Florence: L.S. Olschki, 2007.

Lazzarini, Isabella. 'Paola Gonzaga'. In *Dizionario Biografico Italiano*, 57, 2001. http://www.treccani.it/enciclopedia/paola-gonzaga_%28Dizionario-Biografico%29.

Lazzarini, Isabella. 'Écrire à l'autre. Contacts, réseaux et codes de communication entre les cours italiennes, Byzance et le monde musulman aux XIVe et XVe siècles'. In *La correspondance entre souverains, princes et cités états: Approches croisées entre l'Orient musulman, l'Occident latin et Byzance (XIIIe-début XVIe s.).* Edited by Denise Aigle and Stéphane Péquignot, 165–94. Turnhout: Brepols, 2013.

Lehmann, Phyllis W. 'The Sources and Meaning of Mantegna's Parnassus'. In *Samothracian Reflections: Aspects of the Revival of the Antique.* Edited by Phyllis W. Lehmann and Karl Lehmann, 57–178. Princeton, N.J.: Princeton University Press, 1973.

Lightbown, R. W. *Mantegna: With a Complete Catalogue of Paintings, Drawings, and Prints.* Berkeley: University of California Press, 1986.

Lorenzoni, Anna Maria. 'Un omicidio alla corte mantovana profetizzato della Beata Osanna Andreasi'. *Civiltà mantovana* 29 (1971): 317–25.

Luiten, Loek. 'Friends and Family, Fruit and Fish: The Gift in Quattrocento Farnese Cultural Politics'. *Renaissance Studies* 33.3 (2019): 342–57.

Luzio, Alessandro. 'Contributo alla storia del malfrancese ne' costumi e nella letteratura italiana del sec. XVI'. *Giornale storico della letteratura italiana* 5 (1885): 408–32.

Luzio, Alessandro. 'Federico Gonzaga ostaggio alla corte di Giulio II'. *Archivio della Società Romana di Storia Patria* 9 (1886): 509–82.

Luzio, Alessandro, ed. *I precettori di Isabella d'Este: appunti e documenti.* Ancona: Morelli, 1887.

Luzio, Alessandro. 'Isabella d'Este e la corte sforzesca'. *Archivio storico lombardo* 15 (1901): 145–76.

Luzio, Alessandro. 'Isabella d'Este ne' primordi del papato di Leone X e il suo viaggio a Roma nel 1514–1515'. *Archivio storico lombardo* 33 (1906): 454–89.

Luzio, Alessandro. *Isabella d'Este e Francesco Gonzaga promessi sposi.* Milan: L. F. Cogliati, 1908.

Luzio, Alessandro. *Isabella d'Este e il sacco di Roma.* Milan: L. F. Cogliati, 1908.

Luzio, Alessandro. 'Isabella d'Este e Leone X dal congresso di Bologna alla presa di Milano (1515–1521)'. *Archivio storico italiano* 44 (1909): 72–128.

Luzio, Alessandro. 'La reggenza d'Isabella d'Este durante la prigionia del marito (1509–1510)'. *Archivio storico lombardo* 14 (1910): 5–104.

Luzio, Alessandro. 'I preliminari della Lega di Cambray concordati a Milano ed a Mantova'. *Archivio storico lombardo* 38 (1911): 245–310.

Luzio, Alessandro. 'Isabella d'Este di fronte a Giulio II negli ultimi tre anni del suo pontificato'. *Archivio storico lombardo* 17 (1912): 245–334.

Luzio, Alessandro. 'Isabella d'Este nelle tragedie della sua casa (1505–1506)', *Atti e memorie della R. Accademia Virgiliana di Mantova* 5 (1912): 55–122.

Luzio, Alessandro. *Isabella d'Este e i Borgia*. Milan: L. F. Cogliati, 1915. Also in *Archivio storico lombardo* 41 (1914): 469–553, 673–753; 42 (1915): 115–67, 412–64.

Luzio, Alessandro, ed. *L'Archivio Gonzaga di Mantova. La corrispondenza familiare, amministrativa e diplomatica dei Gonzaga*. Vol. 2. Verona: Mondadori, 1922.

Luzio, Alessandro, and Rodolfo Renier. 'Delle relazioni di Isabella d'Este Gonzaga con Ludovico e Beatrice Sforza'. *Archivio storico lombardo* 17 (1890): 74–119, 346–99, 619–74.

Luzio, Alessandro, and Rodolfo Renier. *Mantova e Urbino (1471–1539): Isabella d'Este ed Elisabetta Gonzaga nelle relazioni famigliari e nelle vicende politiche: narrazione storica documentata*. Torino: Roux, 1893.

Luzio, Alessandro, and Rodolfo Renier. *Francesco Gonzaga alla battaglia di Fornovo (1495)*. Mantua: Adalberto Sartori, 1976.

Luzio, Alessandro, and Rodolfo Renier. *La coltura e le relazioni letterarie di Isabella d'Este Gonzaga*. Edited by Simone Albonico. Milan: Sylvestre Bonnard, 2005.

Malacarne, Giancarlo, and Costantino Cipolla, eds. *El più soave et dolce et dilectevole et gratioso bochone: amore e sesso al tempo dei Gonzaga*. Milan: Angeli, 2006.

Mallett, Michael. 'Horse-Racing and Politics in Lorenzo's Florence'. In *Lorenzo the Magnificent. Culture and Politics*. Edited by Michael Mallett and Nicholas Mann, 251–62. London: The Warburg Institute University of London, 1966.

Mallett, Michael. 'Personalities and Pressures: Italian Involvement in the French Invasion of 1494'. In *The French Descent into Renaissance Italy*. Edited by David Abulafia, 151–64. Aldershot: Ashgate, 1995.

Mallett, Michael, and Christine Shaw. *The Italian Wars, 1494–1559: War, State and Society in Early Modern Europe*. Harlow, New York: Pearson, 2012.

Manca, Joseph. *The Art of Ercole de' Roberti*. Cambridge: Cambridge University Press, 1992.

Margaroli, Paolo. '"Traitres Lombardi": The Expedition of Charles VIII in the Lombard Sources up to the Mid-Sixteenth Century'. In *The French Descent into Renaissance Italy*. Edited by David Abulafia, 371–89. Aldershot: Ashgate, 1995.

Mazzoldi, Leonardo. *Mantova: La storia, le lettere, le arti*. Vol. 2. Mantova: Istituto Carlo d'Arco per la storia di Mantova, 1961.

McClive, Cathy. 'The Hidden Truths of the Belly: The Uncertainties of Pregnancy in Early Modern Europe'. *Social History of Medicine* 15.2 (2002): 209–27.

McClive, Cathy. 'Blood and Expertise: The Trials of the Female Medical Expert in the Ancien-Régime Courtroom'. *Bulletin of the History of Medicine; Baltimore* 82.1 (2008): 86–108.

McCue Gill, Amyrose. 'Vera Amicizia: Conjugal Friendship in the Italian Renaissance'. Unpublished doctoral dissertation. Berkeley: University of California, 2008.

Molho, Anthony. *Marriage Alliance in Late Medieval Florence*. Cambridge, Mass.: Harvard University Press, 1994.

Nosari, Galeazzo. 'Una Leggenda Metropolitana: Francesco II a Fornovo'. *Civiltà mantovana* 101.3 (1995): 91–5.

O'Leary, Jessica. 'Politics, Pedagogy, and Praise: Three Literary Texts Dedicated to Eleonora d'Aragona, Duchess of Ferrara'. *I Tatti Studies in the Italian Renaissance* 19.2 (2016): 285–307.

Palvarini Gobio Casali, Mariarosa. 'Ceramic Tiles for the Gonzaga'. In *Splendours of the Gonzaga*. Edited by David Chambers and Justine Martineau, 44–5, 173. London: Victoria & Albert Museum, 1981.

Pélissier, Léon Gabriel. 'La politique du marquis de Mantoue pendant la lutte de Louis XII et de Ludovic Sforza (1498–1500)'. *Annales de la faculté des lettres de Bordeaux* 14 (1892): 35–120.

Pélissier, Léon Gabriel. *Louis XII et Lodovic Sforza (8 avril 1498–23 juillet 1500)*. Paris: Librairie Thorn et Fils, 1896.

Pizzagalli, Daniela. *La signora del Rinascimento. Vita e splendori di Isabella d'Este alla corte di Mantova*. Milan: Rizzoli, 2001.

Pope-Hennessy, John. *The Portrait in the Renaissance*. London: Phaidon, 1966.

Prizer, William F. 'Isabella d'Este and Lorenzo da Pavia, "Master Instrument-Maker"'. *Early Music History* 2 (1982): 87–127.

Rizzi, Maurizio. 'Giulio II e l'ideologia trionfale. Una lettura dell'ingresso a Bologna del 1506'. In *Città in Guerra: Esperienze e riflessioni nel primo '500. Bologna nelle 'Guerre d'Italia'*. Ed. Gian Mario Anselmo and Angela De Benedictis, 249–68. Bologna: Minerva Soluzioni Editoriali, 2008.

Rodella, Giovanni. 'L'ingegnere Giovanni da Padova e i principali interventi idraulici nel territorio gonzaghesco durante la seconda metà del Quattrocento'. In *Il paesaggio mantovano nelle tracce materiali, nelle lettere e nelle arti*. Vol. 3. Edited by Eugenio Camerlenghi, Viviana Rebonato, and Sara Tammaccaro, 159–72. Florence: L.S. Olschki, 2007.

Romani, Marina. *Una città in forma di palazzo: Potere signorile e forma urbana nella Mantova medievale e moderna*. Brescia: Ed. Centro di Ricerche Storiche e Sociali Federico Odorici, 1995.

Rublack, Ulinka. 'Pregnancy, Childbirth and the Female Body in Early Modern Germany'. *Past & Present* 150 (1996): 84–110.

San Juan, Rose Marie. 'The Court Lady's Dilemma: Isabella d'Este and Art Collecting in the Renaissance'. *The Oxford Art Journal* 14 (1991): 67–78.

Schiappoli, Irma. 'Isabella di Chiaromonte, regina di Napoli'. *Archivio storico italiano* 95 (1940): 109–24.

Schneider, Gary. *The Culture of Epistolarity: Vernacular Letters and Letter Writing in Early Modern England, 1500–1700*. Newark: University of Delaware Press, 2005.

Secco, Fermo d'Aragona. 'Francesco Secco, i Gonzaga e Paolo Erba. Un capitolo inedito di storia mantovana'. *Archivio storico lombardo* 6 (1956): 210–61.

Seidel Menchi, Silvana, ed. *Marriage in Europe, 1400–1800*. Toronto: University of Toronto Press, 2016.

Seidel Menchi, Silvana, and Diego Quaglioni, eds. *Coniugi nemici: la separazione in Italia dal XII al XVIII secolo*. Bologna: Il Mulino, 2000.

Seidel Menchi, Silvana, and Diego Quaglioni, eds. *Matrimoni in dubbio: unioni controverse e nozze clandestine in Italia dal XIV al XVIII secolo*. Bologna: Il Mulino, 2001.

Seidel Menchi, Silvana, and Diego Quaglioni, eds. *Trasgressioni: seduzione, concubinato, adulterio, bigamia (14–18. secolo)*. Bologna: Il Mulino, 2004.

Seidel Menchi, Silvana, and Diego Quaglioni. *I tribunali del matrimonio (secoli XV–XVIII)*. Bologna: Il Mulino, 2006.

Shaw, Christine. *Isabella d'Este. A Renaissance Princess*. London: Routledge, 2019.

Shemek, Deanna. *Ladies Errant: Wayward Women and Social Order in Early Modern Italy*. Durham, N.C.: Duke University Press, 1998.

Shemek, Deanna. 'Aretino's *Marescalco*: Marriage Woes and the Duke of Mantua'. *Renaissance Studies* 16.3 (2002): 366–80.

Shemek, Deanna. ' "Ci Ci" and "Pa Pa": Script, Mimicry, and Mediation in Isabella d'Este's Letters'. *Rinascimento* 43 (2003): 75–92.

Shemek, Deanna. 'Mendacious Missives: Isabella d'Este's Epistolary Theater'. In *Writing Relations: American Scholars in Italian Archives*. Edited by Deanna Shemek and Michael Wyatt, 71–86. Florence: L.S. Olschki, 2008.

Signorini, Rodolfo. 'Paesaggio mantovano urbano e del contado nella *Cronaca* di Andrea Stanziali/Vidali da Schivenoglia e non solo, fino al 1496'. In *Il paesaggio mantovano nelle tracce materiali, nelle lettere e nelle arti*. Vol. 3. Edited by Eugenio Camerlenghi, Viviana Rebonato, and Sara Tammaccaro, 287–382. Florence: L.S. Olschki, 2007.

Stone, Lawrence. *The Family, Sex and Marriage in England 1500–1800*. London: Weidenfeld and Nicolson, 1977.

Sullivan, Ruth Wilkins. 'Three Ferrarese Panels on the Theme of "Death Rather Than Dishonour" and the Neapolitan Connection'. *Zeitschrift Für Kunstgeschichte* 57.4 (1994): 610–25.

Swain, Elisabeth Ward. '"My Excellent and Most Singular Lord": Marriage in a Noble Family of Fifteenth-Century Italy'. *Journal of Medieval and Renaissance Studies* 16 (1986): 171–95.

Swain, Elisabeth Ward. 'Strategia matrimoniale in casa Gonzaga: Il caso di Barbara e Ludovico'. *Civiltà mantovana* 14 (1986): 1–14.

Syson, Luke. 'Reading Faces. Gian Cristofano Romano's Medal of Isabella d'Este'. In *La corte di Mantova nell'età di Andrea Mantegna: 1450–1550*. Edited by Cesare Mozzarelli, Roberto Oresko, and Roberto Venturi, 281–94. Rome: Bulzoni, 1997.

Syson, Luke, and Dora Thornton. *Objects of Virtue: Art in Renaissance Italy*. Los Angeles, Calif.: J. Paul Getty Museum, 2001.

Thornton, Dora. *The Scholar in His Study: Ownership and Experience in Renaissance Italy*. New Haven, Conn.: Yale University Press, 1997.

Tobey, Elizabeth. 'The Palio Horse in Renaissance and Early Modern Italy'. In *The Culture of the Horse*. Edited by Karen Raber and Treva Tucker, 63–90. Houndsmills, Basingstock, and New York: Palgrave Macmillan, 2005.

Torello-Hill, Giulia. 'The Revival of Classical Roman Comedy in Renaissance Ferrara: From the Scriptorium to the Stage'. In *Terence between Late Antiquity and the Age of Printing*. Edited by Giulia Torello-Hill and Andrew Turner, 219–35. Leiden, Boston: Brill, 2015.

Tuohy, Thomas. *Herculean Ferrara: Ercole d'Este, 1471–1505, and the Invention of a Ducal Capital*. Cambridge, New York: Cambridge University Press, 1996.

Vaini, Mario. *Dal comune alla signoria: Mantova dal 1200 al 1328*. Milano: Angeli, 1986.

Verheyen, Egon. *The Paintings in the Studiolo of Isabella d'Este at Mantua*. New York: New York University Press, 1971.

Zappieri, Roberto. 'Ludovico Camposampiero'. In *Dizionario Biografico Italiano*, 17, 1974. http://www.treccani.it/enciclopedia/ludovico-camposampiero_%28Dizionario-Biografico%29.

Zuccolin, Gabriella. 'Gravidanza e parto nel Quattrocento'. In *Beatrice d'Este, 1475–1497*. Edited by Luisa Giordano, 111–45. Pisa: ETS, 2008.

Index

For the benefit of digital users, indexed terms that span two pages(e.g., 52–53) may, on occasion, appear on only one of those pages.

Agnadello, battle of 141–2
Alberti, Leon Battista, architect, humanist 13
Albret, Charlotte d', wife of Cesare Borgia 104
Alexander the Great 67
Alexander VI (Rodrigo Borgia), pope 2–3, 105–8
Alviano, Bartolomeo, military
     captain 139–42, 146
Amboise, Charles II d', Grand Master
     of France 108–9
Andreasi, Osanna, Dominican tertiary 107–8,
     128–9, 174
Anne of Alençon, consort of Guglielmo IX of
     Monferrato 179–80, 182
Anne of Brittany, queen of France, consort of
     Charles VIII and Louis XII 127, 149
Anselmo, Fra, prior of the sanctuary of Santa
     Maria delle Grazie [Curtatone] 147
Antimaco, see Sachetti, Matteo
Aragona, Alfonso II d', duke of Calabria, king of
     Naples 19–20, 75, 156
Aragona, Beatrice d', queen of Hungary 27
Aragona, Eleonora d', consort of Ercole I d'Este,
     duchess of Ferrara 1–2, 15–19, 25–6,
     29–30, 32–5, 38–44, 46–50, 54–6, 58–9,
     62–4, 78–9, 187
Aragona, Ferrante d' (also called Ferdinardo),
     king of Naples 1–2, 55, 75
Aragona, Isabella d', consort of Gian Galeazzo
     Sforza 73
Arrivabene, Giampaolo, Mantuan envoy 22
Asola 139, 142, 150, 171–2, 176–7
Asti 106, 180–1
Aubigny, Stuart Bérault d', French envoy 75, 79

Balzo, Antonia del, consort of Gianfrancesco
     Gonzaga 120
Barbara of Brandenburg, see Hohenzollern,
     Barbara von
Barco, Este hunting park 15–18, 24
Bastard of Bourbon [Mathieu de Bourbon] 74
Bâyezîd II, Ottoman sultan 68–71
Beccaguto, Alessio, Gonzaga envoy and military
     engineer 69–70

Belfiore, Este villa 15–16
Bellini, Giovanni, painter 63
Bentivoglio, family 2–3, 31, 130–2, 145–6
     Annibale II, son of Giovanni
          Bentivoglio 11–12
     Giovanni II, lord of Bologna 25, 130–1
     Laura, consort of Giovanni Gonzaga 117–18
Bey, Casim, Ottoman ambassador 68, 70, 90
Boiardo, Alda, lady-in-waiting 167
Bonacolsi, family 12–13
Bonsignori, Francesco, painter 90
Borgia, Cesare ('Valentino'), duke of Valentinois
     and the Romagna 2–3, 65–6, 93, 104–7
Borgia, Lucrezia, consort of Alfonso
     I d'Este 105–6
Borgoforte, Gonzaga fortress at 177–80
Boschetta, Giovanna, lady-in-waiting 152
Boschetti, Isabella, mistress of Federico II
     Gonzaga 182
Bourne, Molly, art historian 6
Bracciolini, Poggio, humanist 32
Brognina, see Eleonora Compagni
Brognolla, see Brogna de' Lardis, Beatrice
Brognolo, Giorgio, Mantuan ambassador
     to Venice 64, 70, 86, 96
Brognolo, Lodovico, Mantuan ambassador
     to Rome 145–7
Buonarotti, Michelangelo 65–6, 107

Cairo 43, 67–8
Caleffini, Ugo, Ferrarese notary and
     chronicler 21–3, 26–9, 55
Cambrai, League of 139–40, 161–2
Cambrai, Treaty of (1508) 138–9, 168
Camposampiero, Ludovico di (Vigo), agent of
     Federico II Gonzaga 146–7, 152–3
Cantelmo, Sigismondo, Ferrarese courtier 23–4
Capilupi, Benedetto, secretary to Isabella
     d'Este 34–6, 46–9, 74, 76, 80–2, 97, 99,
     102, 104, 117–19, 124–5, 151, 159–60, 162–4,
     166–8, 170–3, 178–9, 181
Cara, Marchetto, composer and singer 147–8,
     160, 162

Carignano, Agostino da, friar and Mantuan
    secret agent 98
Carnival, celebration of 3, 17, 19, 23–4, 26, 70, 73,
    163–4, 173–4
Castelli, Giovanni Battista, canon lawyer 45–6
Castiglione, Baldassare, courtier and envoy 70–1,
    138–9, 175
Cattaneo, Federico, courtier 150, 176
Cattaneo, Gian Lucido, Gonzaga agent 66
Cavriana, Gonzaga castle at 143
Cem, Ottoman prince, half-brother of
    Bâyezîd II 69
Ceresara, Paride da, humanist 60–1
Charles IV, Holy Roman Emperor 3
Charles V, Holy Roman Emperor and King
    of Spain 182–3
Charles VIII, king of France 2, 51, 69–71, 73,
    75–7, 79–80, 84–6, 97–9, 101–2, 135
Coliseum 172
Collenuccio, Pandolfo, Gonzaga courtier
    and diplomat 31, 67–8
Collenuccio, Teofilo, son of Pandolfo 67
Collis, Antonio Maria de, courtier 74
Collona, governess of Isabella d'Este 34–6, 47
Colonna, Costanza, Roman noblewoman 45–6
Comacchio, coastal wetlands 12, 17–18, 38
Commynes, Philippe de', French
    chronicler 84–5
Compagni, Eleonora (La Brognina),
    lady-in-waiting to Isabella d'Este 161–5
Compagni, Ercole, husband of Beatrice Brogna
    de' Lardis 161–3
Constantinople 67–72, 90
Contrari, Beatrice de', lady-in-waiting to
    Isabella d'Este 34–5, 38–43, 46–9, 93–4,
    118–19
Contrari, Ippolita de', wife of Giulio Tassoni 25
Cornaro, Giorgio, Venetian envoy 177
Cornazzano, Antonio, humanist, literary
    figure 62–3
Corradi, Girolamo, painter 67–8
Correggio, Niccolò da, humanist and
    playwright 25, 62
Costa, Lorenzo, painter 60–2, 129, 157–8
Cumari, Diana di, lady-in-waiting to Eleonora
    d'Aragona 29–30, 36–7
Cusatro, Beltramino, lawyer and
    magistrate 11–12

Diodato, Gonzaga court jester 23, 136
doctors 38–9, 46–7, 49–50, 82, 116, 124, 132–4,
    136–8, 141, 163–4, 168–72
Dolfo, Floriano, Bolognese priest and teacher
    of canon law 31–2

Donato, Antonio, Gonzaga official 74, 185–6
Dovizi da Bibbiena, Bernardo, cardinal,
    envoy of Julius II 163

Equicola, Mario, courtier, humanist 8, 70–1,
    134–5, 151, 181
Este, Alfonso I d', third duke of Ferrara 15, 17,
    19–20, 23–4, 28–9, 39, 55, 105–6, 135–6,
    139, 150, 154
Este, Beatrice d', duchess of Bari and Milan
    marriage to Lodovico Sforza 32–3, 39, 78
    pregnancy and childbirth 41, 47–8, 73
    relationship with Isabella d'Este 29, 75–6
Este, Borso, marquis, first duke of
    Ferrara (1471) 12
Este, Ercole I d', second duke of Ferrara 1–2, 21,
    32–4, 105–6
    character of 22
    cultural patronage of 13–14, 24–5, 60, 66–7
    death of 93, 112
    marriage to Eleonora d'Aragona 54, 187
    princely magnificence of 20, 23–5
    relationship with Francesco II Gonzaga
        14–16, 22–5, 103–4
    relationship with Isabella d'Este 38–9, 47–8,
        57–8, 102
Este, Ferrante d', brother of Isabella 135–6
Este, Ippolito d', cardinal, brother of
    Isabella 134–5, 147, 151, 155–6
Este, Isabella d', marchioness of Mantua.
    art patronage of 8, 59–66, 157–8, 177
    character of 13–15, 22, 74, 93, 96
    diplomacy of 3, 70, 74, 76–80, 95–100, 102–5,
        149–50, 154–7, 160–5, 176
    early years of 11, 14–21, 53
    education of 53–4
    emblems and devices of 65, 158
    emotions of 15, 29–30, 165–6, 175
    government responsibilities of 3, 54, 56–9,
        87–91, 94–5, 98, 101, 106–9, 121, 140–1,
        145–9, 159–60, 175, 185–6
    historiography 5–6
    involvement in horse riding,
        horseracing 42–3
    letter-writing practices of 4–5, 8–10, 29,
        180–1, 186–7
    portraits of 11, 62–5, 157
    relationship with Alfonso d'Este 146, 149,
        151, 163
    relationship with Eleonora d'Aragona 38–41,
        43–4, 46, 49–50
    relationship with Eleonora Gonzaga 117–19
    relationship with Federico Gonzaga 119–25,
        149, 179–80, 182

relationship with Francesco Gonzaga 1–2, 4,
    35–8, 40–1, 80–2, 93–4, 110, 114–17,
    126–33, 142–3, 149–52, 161–7, 173–5,
    177–81, 185–6
sex, pregnancy and childbirth 16, 31–5,
    39–50, 93–4, 111, 113, 117–18, 122,
    162–3
travels of 3–4, 50–1, 167–73, 179–80, 182
visits to Ferrara of 35, 37–40, 46–50, 60, 70,
    74–5, 80–2, 93–4, 101, 115, 163
wedding of 26–7
widowhood of 175
Este, Lucrezia d', natural daughter of Ercole
    d'Este and consort of Annibale
    Bentivoglio 25, 130–2
Este, Sigismondo d', brother of Isabella 135

Ferrara
cityscape of 13–14
civic culture of 22–3, 25, 27, 105–6
ducal palace and Este castle in 20–2, 26,
    28–9, 35, 55
duchy of 1–2, 7–8
Herculean Addition 13–14
practice of medicine in 136–7, 170
university of 20–1, 135–6
War of 19–21, 24, 55, 139
Ferrarese chroniclers 14, 20–3, 27–9, 135–6
Ferrarini, Girolamo, Ferrarese lawyer
    and chronicler 21–3
Florence
city of 42, 60–2, 67–8, 127–8, 156
republic of 7–8, 80, 130–1, 154–6
Foix, Gaston de, duke of Nemours 153–4
Foix, Odet de, lord of Lautrec 177–8
Folenghino, envoy 148, 155–6
Fornovo, battle of 70–1, 83–6, 89–90, 93–4,
    98, 144–5
Francesco da Castello, doctor at Este
    court 38–9, 47
François I (Valois), king of France 2, 175–6
Fregoso, Fregosino, military captain 86
Frisio, Niccolò 139
Furlano, Enea(known as Il Cavaliere)
    courtier 127–8

Gabbionetta, Alessandro, Gonzaga envoy
    and archdeacon of the Cathedral of
    Mantua 172–3
Gadio, Stazio, envoy 176
Gallerani, Cecilia, mistress of Duke
    Lodovico Sforza 63
gambling 22, 121
Garda, Lake 38, 139, 142–3, 167–8

Genoa
city of 67–8, 75–6, 86, 170–1, 180–1
republic of 2, 31, 131–2
George (Giorgio), Saint, feast of 22–3, 115
Ghisolfo, Bernardino, master mason 33–4
Gifts and gift giving 11, 23, 38, 42–3, 49–50, 54,
    63, 65–6, 80, 85–6, 99, 114, 116–17, 121–2,
    124–5, 131, 162, 166, 180
Giovio, Paolo, humanist, writer 30
Goito, fortified Gonzaga castle 16–17, 32–3, 114,
    116–17, 138–9, 152–3, 167
Golfo della Pergola, Sigismondo, teacher to
    Eleonora Gonzaga 119
Gonzaga, county palace and estate 34, 37–8,
    56–7, 66–8, 90, 98, 100, 114, 123, 134–5,
    137–8
Gonzaga, Caterina, illegitimate daughter of
    Lodovico Gonzaga 53
Gonzaga, Clara, consort of Gilbert de
    Montpensier-Bourbon 74–6, 98, 103, 105
Gonzaga, Eleonora, eldest daughter of Isabella
    d'Este and Francesco Gonzaga, duchess
    of Urbino 50, 118–21, 124–5, 133, 146, 161
Gonzaga, Elisabetta, consort of Guidobaldo da
    Montefeltro 19, 30, 34, 42–3, 50, 60, 106
Gonzaga emblems and devices 59, 92
Gonzaga, Ercole (Alvise), second son of Isabella
    d'Este and Francesco Gonzaga 126–7,
    130, 182–3
Gonzaga, Federico I, third marquis of
    Mantua 11–12, 15, 18–20, 53, 59
Gonzaga, Federico II, eldest son of Isabella
    d'Este and Francesco Gonzaga, marquis
    and then duke of Mantua 124–5, 148,
    154–5, 176, 179–82
Gonzaga, Ferrante, third son of Isabella d'Este
    and Francesco Gonzaga 131–2, 182–3
Gonzaga, Francesco II, fourth marquis
    of Mantua 16–18
art patronage of 66–7, 92, 129, 157–8, 177
death of 181–2
diplomacy of 97–101, 104–5, 107–8, 112, 177–8
horse-breeding 17, 125
illnesses of 30, 98, 134–8, 140–2, 147–8, 152–3,
    158–9, 167, 169–70, 172–3
imprisonment of 144–5, 147–50
masculinity of 3, 6–7, 15–18, 26, 30–2, 66–72,
    90–2, 132–3, 177
military career of 25–6, 80–6, 89–94, 107–8,
    112, 132–3, 138, 141–2, 144, 152–4, 175,
    186–7
parenthood 113–14, 116–19, 122–4
princely qualities of 6–7, 23, 30, 177
relationship with Ercole d'Este 15–16, 20, 22–4

relationship with Isabella d'Este 1–2, 4, 15,
    17–18, 35–8, 40–1, 80–2, 93–4, 110–11,
    114–17, 126–33, 140–3, 149–52, 156–7, 159,
    161–7, 171–5, 177–81, 185–6
relationship with Ottoman empire 68–71, 90
relationship with the Sforza dukes 77–80, 86,
    102, 169
sexuality of 30–2, 93–4, 107–8, 117–18,
    137, 162–3
Gonzaga, Gianfrancesco, first marquis of
    Mantua 12–13, 52
Gonzaga, Gianfrancesco, lord of
    Bozzolo 53, 57–8
Gonzaga, Giovanni, brother of Francesco
    Gonzaga 18–19, 79–80, 99, 104–5, 117,
    130–1, 145–7
Gonzaga, Giovanni Maria, military
    captain 84–5
Gonzaga, Ippolita, daughter of Isabella d'Este
    Francesco Gonzaga, nun in the convent
    of Sant'Ippolita 46, 119–20, 149, 182–3
Gonzaga, Livia Giulia, daughter of Isabella d'Este
    and Francesco Gonzaga, died in
    childhood 119–20, 122
Gonzaga, Livia Osanna (Suor Paola), last-born
    child of Isabella d'Este and Francesco
    Gonzaga, nun in Clarissan convent of
    Santa Paola 133, 159, 182–3
Gonzaga, Lodovico, bishop of Mantua 53, 57–8
Gonzaga, Lodovico III, marquis of Mantua 1–2,
    12–13, 52–4, 59, 67, 71, 187
Gonzaga, Maddalena, consort of Giovanni
    Sforza of Pesaro 105–6
Gonzaga, Margherita, daughter of Isabella d'Este
    and Francesco II Gonzaga, died as a
    baby 118–19
Gonzaga, Margherita, illegitimate daughter of
    Francesco II Gonzaga 30
Gonzaga, Rodolfo, lord of Castiglione and
    Luzzara 53, 57–8, 76–7, 83–5
Gonzaga, Sigismondo, protonotary, cardinal
    (1505) 80, 97, 99, 145, 147–8, 181–2
Gorlino, Venetian military captain 97
Great Pox (mal francese) 7, 30, 134–8, 140–2,
    144–5, 147–8, 152–3, 158–9, 169–70, 173
Grimani, Antonio, Venetian envoy 177
Gritti, Andrea, Venetian envoy 177
Guarino, Battista, humanist, tutor to
    Isabella d'Este 19, 24

Hohenzollern, Barbara von (of Brandenburg),
    consort of Lodovico III Gonzaga 1–3,
    25–6, 52–4
Holy League 13, 153–4, 159–62, 166–7, 175–6

hunting 6–7, 15–20, 22–5, 29, 37–8, 56–7, 66–7,
    70, 74, 99, 124, 175, 177

Italian League 70–1, 80, 82–6, 88–9, 93–4, 97
Italian Wars 2–3, 51, 75–7, 82–6, 92, 104–11,
    138–56, 159, 164–7, 175–6

jewellery 27, 80, 82, 144–5
jousts 22–5, 27–9, 78–9
Julius II (Giuliano della Rovere), pope 2–3, 120,
    130–3, 139, 145–6, 148, 150–5, 160–1,
    163–5, 172

Lang von Wellenburg, Matthäus bishop of Gurk
    and imperial agent 154–5, 160–4
Lardis, Brogna de', Beatrice (Brognolla),
    lady-in-waiting to Isabella d'Este 161
Leo X (Giovanni de' Medici), pope 171–2, 174, 176
Leonardo da Vinci, artist and polymath 63–4
Letter-writing 8–10, 36–8, 118–19, 124–5
Liombeni, Gian Luca, painter 33–4
Livia, Roman empress 65
Lonato 139, 142, 167–8, 171–2, 176–7
Loredan, Leonardo, doge of Venice 144–5
Louis XII (Valois), king of France 2–3, 85, 101–11,
    114, 126–8, 131–2, 137–54, 173–4
Ludwig, Holy Roman Emperor 3
Luzio, Alessandro, archivist and scholar 5–6
Lyon, armistice of 111

mal francese, see Great Pox.
Malvezzi, Luzio, military captain 144–5
Manfredi, Astorre, lord of Faenza 105
Mantegna, Andrea, painter 13, 129
    Camera degli sposi 52, 58–9, 155, 177
    Madonna della Vittoria 90
    Mars and Venus (Parnassus) 61–2, 157–8
    Minerva Expelling the Vices (Pallas and
        the Vices) 61–2, 157–8
    Triumphs of Caesar 129, 177
Mantua,
    cityscape of 13, 25, 62, 156
    Congress of 154–61
    Castello San Giorgio 16–17
        Camera degli sposi 52, 58–9, 155
        grotta 58–9, 64–6, 102, 157, 177
        studiolo 58–62, 64–6, 70–1, 158
    Poggio Reale, Gonzaga urban villa 156
    San Sebastiano, urban palace of Francesco
        Gonzaga 3, 92, 128–9, 135, 137–8, 154–5,
        157–60, 164, 167, 171–3, 175–8, 181
    Santa Maria dei Voti [San Pietro
        Cathedral] 90
    Te Island 124–5, 133

Marignano, Battle of (1515) 175
Marmirolo, Gonzaga country palace and
    estate 33–4, 40, 59, 66–8, 70, 92, 98,
    118–19, 151–2, 168–9, 180
Marriage
    celebrations of 27–8
    descriptions of 28
    early modern attitudes to 7–8,
    historiography 5
Matteo da Bologna, painter 157–8
Maximilian I (Hapsburg), emperor 101–2, 138–9,
    145–6, 148, 154, 160–1
Maynier, Accurse, French ambassador 104
Medici, family. 19, 155–6, 176
Medici, Giovanni de', cardinal 155–6
Medici, Giuliano de', cardinal 155–6
Medici, Lorenzo de' 42, 58, 156
Messaglia, Bernardino, head of Mantuan
    armoury and Gonzaga envoy 69–70
midwives 131–2 see also Beatrice de' Contrari
Milan 2–3, 18–19, 39, 41, 73–83, 86, 90–1, 95, 98–9,
    101–9, 144, 155–6, 159–67, 170–1, 175–9
Mirandola, Lodovico della, military captain 144–5
Modena 12, 19
Montefeltro, Guidobaldo da, duke of Urbino 30,
    50, 60, 65–6, 93, 97, 106, 120, 130–1
Montpensier-Bourbon, Gilbert de, French
    count 17, 74–5, 77, 97, 127

Naples
    city of 55, 67, 77, 86, 97, 156, 170–3
    kingdom of 1–2, 27, 51, 54, 73–5, 80, 93–4,
    107–8
Niccoli, Niccolò, humanist 32
Novara 85–6, 105

Oglio, river 79–80, 140
Ostiglia [Mantua] 88, 140, 185–6
Orsini, Niccolò, count of Pitigliano 139–40
Ostuni, Serafino da Puglia, Franciscan friar 172–4

Paleologo, Guglielmo IX, marquis of
    Monferrato 179–80
Paleologo, Margherita, duchess of Mantua and
    marchioness of Monferrato 179–80, 182
Paleologo, Maria, sister of Margherita
    179–80, 182
Perugino, Pietro, painter 60–2
Peschiera del Garda 139, 142, 161–4, 168
Piacenza 164–5, 176
Picenardi, Alessandro, courtier 33
Pio, Alberto of Sabaudia, Gonzaga envoy
    to France 119, 136–7
Pintoricchio, Bernardino, painter 67

Pisa 160–1, 170–1
plague 19–20, 119–20, 126, 170
Plautus, plays of 24–5
Po, river 12, 15, 27, 95, 154
Poggio a Caiano [Prato], villa of Lorenzo
    de' Medici 156
Poggio Reale [Naples], villa of Alfonso II
    d'Aragona 156
Polidoro, painter 67–8
Porto, surburban villa of the marchionesses of
    Mantua 16–17, 44, 177–8, 180
Praxiteles of Athens 65–6
Preti, Donato de', Gonzaga agent and official 104
Preti, Violante de', Gonzaga governess and
    lady-in-waiting 118–19
Prisciani, Pellegrino, humanist 24
Probo d'Atri, Iacopo, count of Pianella,
    Gonzaga envoy 146–7, 153
Pusterla, Bernardino, Mantuan envoy 15

Ravenna, battle of 153–4
Redini, Fra Girolamo, Augustinian friar,
    Gonzaga envoy 99–100
Regazzi, Antonio Maria di San Secondo (known
    as il Milanese) courtier 127–8
Revere, Gonzaga country estate 114, 124, 180
Roberti, Ercole de', painter 27, 55–6
Romano, Gian Cristoforo, sculptor and
    medallist 62–3, 65, 70–1, 92
Rome 99–100, 105–6, 155, 170–9
Rovere, Francesco Maria della Rovere, nephew
    of Julius II, duke of Urbino 33, 120, 146
Rovere, Giuliano della, see Julius II, pope

Sacchetta, Gonzaga country villa 119–20,
    127–8, 154
Sacchetti, Matteo (Antimaco), secretary of
    Francesco Gonzaga 67–8, 70
Sanseverino, Galeazzo, military captain 101–2
Sanseverino, Giovanfrancesco, military
    captain 83
Sanseverino, Roberto, military captain 19–20
Santa Casa, Loreto, religious santuary and
    pilgrimage site 50
Sanudo, Marino, Venetian chronicler 83, 149–50
Schinner, Matthäus, cardinal 160–1
Secco d'Aragona, Francesco, Gonzaga envoy and
    political deputy 11, 25–6, 53, 57–9, 128
Sforza, Anna, consort of Alfonso I d'Este 39,
    44–6, 135–6
Sforza, Francesco, duke of Milan 45–6
Sforza, Gian Galeazzo, duke of Milan 88
Sforza, Giovanni, lord of Pesaro 105–6
Sforza, Ippolita Maria, duchess of Calabria 64

Sforza, Lodovico (il Moro), duke of Bari and
    Milan 29, 32–3, 39, 44–5, 73, 75–6, 78–80,
    86, 93, 95–6, 98–9, 101–5, 114, 155–6
Sforza, Massimiliano, duke of Milan 3, 155–6,
    159, 166–7, 169, 171–2, 175–6
Sigismund of Luxembourg, Holy Roman
    Emperor 12–13
Sirmione 142, 168
Spagnoli, Battista, Carmelite friar and poet 67–8
Spagnoli, Tolomeo, secretary to Francesco
    Gonzaga 3, 31, 116–17, 159, 168–70, 174–5,
    178, 181–2
Stanga, Gerolamo, Mantuan envoy 76–7
Stone, Lawrence, historian 19–20
Strozzi, Luisa, Florentine governess to
    Isabella d'Este 19
Strozzi, Palla, Florentine merchant 19

Tassoni, Giulio, Ferrarese courtier 23–5
Testagrossa, Giovan Angelo, lute player 147–8
theatrical productions 24–5, 98, 164, 173–4
Tondi, Tondo de', painter 33–4
Torre, Amico Maria della, Gonzaga
    secretary 154–5
Tovaglia, Angelo, Gonzaga agent in
    Florence 127–8, 156
transport, forms of
  barges 15–16, 27–8
  carriages 27, 180–1
  horseback 17–18, 27, 29, 35, 43, 49–50, 85, 103,
    124, 133, 141
  mules 179–80
Trevisan, Domenico, Venetian envoy 177
Tridapali, Gian Francesco, courtier, secretary 130
Trivulzio, Gian Giacomo, military captain 99

Trocio (Troche), Francisco of Avila, envoy of
    Cesare Borgia 106–7
Trotti, Giacomo, Ferrarese ambassador
    to Milan 32–3
Trotti, Giovanni Maria, Ferrarese courtier 41
Tura, Cosmè 11

Urbino, duchy of 2–3, 33, 50, 60, 65–6, 70, 93,
    106, 120

Valerio, Carlo, Venetian envoy 139–40
Varano, family 50
Vasari, Giorgio, artist and biographer 129, 157
Venice, republic of 12, 19–20, 31, 44, 55, 64, 76–80,
    86, 94, 97–8, 103, 138–40, 144–51, 176
Vercelli, Peace of 86
Viadana, Pietro Marcheselli da, grammarian and
    schoolmaster 123
Vigilio, Francesco, humanist schoolmaster 120,
    125–6

wedding celebrations 25–9, 32–3, 39, 78–9,
    87, 105–6
Wittelsbach (von), Margarete, consort of
    Federico I Gonzaga 16–17, 52–3
women
  as political deputies 1–2, 7–8, 25–6, 54–8,
    77–8, 94–5
  education of 7–8, 53–4
  philosophical defences of 8, 62–3

Zambotti, Bernardino, Ferrarese chronicler 20–3,
    25–9, 135–7
Zambotti, Zaccharia, doctor at Este court 20–1,
    23, 136–7